A TALE OF TWO BALCONIES

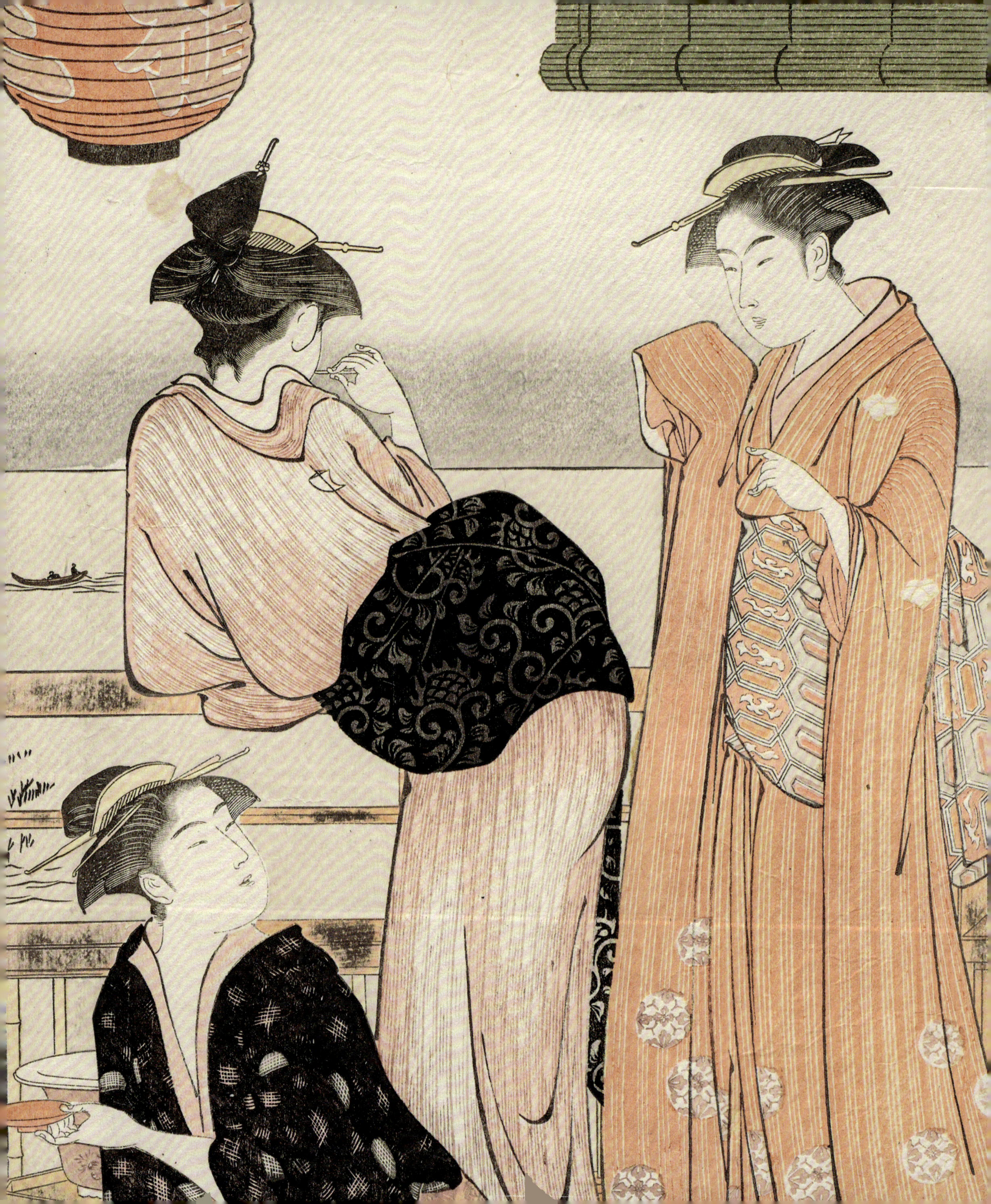

A TALE OF TWO BALCONIES

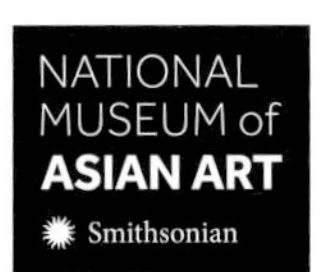

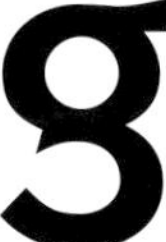

National Museum of Asian Art, Smithsonian Institution in association with D Giles Limited

National Museum of Asian Art,
Smithsonian Institution
1000 Jefferson Drive SW
Washington, DC, 20560

First published in 2024 by GILES
An imprint of D Giles Limited
66 High Street
Lewes, BN7 1XG, UK
gilesltd.com

Library of Congress Cataloging-in-Publication Data
LCCN: 2024016123

ISBN: 978-1-913875-82-4

Support for *A Tale of Two Balconies* is provided by the Anne van Biema Endowment Fund

For the National Museum of Asian Art:
Managing Editor, Judy Lee
Publication Assistant, Sophie Loring
Editor, Akiko Yamagata

For D Giles Limited:
Proofreader, Jenny Wilson
Designer, Alfonso Iacurci
Printed and bound in China

All measurements are in meters and centimeters.

Image credits

Front cover
Katsushika Hokusai / National Museum of Asian Art, Smithsonian Institution, Freer Collection, Gift of the family of Eugene and Agnes E. Meyer, F1974.63

Frontispiece
Museum of Fine Arts, Boston, William Sturgis Bigelow Collection, 11.13900

Pop-out model
National Museum of Asian Art, Smithsonian Institution: Photograph © Cory Grace

Museum of Fine Arts, Boston
2 (detail), **70**, William Sturgis Bigelow Collection, 11.13900
22 bottom, William S. and John T. Spaulding Collection 21.9777
26, William Sturgis Bigelow Collection 11.20162
27, William Sturgis Bigelow Collection 11.37810
29, William Sturgis Bigelow Collection 11.17876
33, **81**, William Sturgis Bigelow Collection 11.19640
34, Bequest of William Perkins Babcock, 00.829
61, William S. and John T. Spaulding Collection 21.9452

National Museum of Asian Art Archives
68, George C. Cox / Gift of the Estate of Charles Lang Freer, FSA A.01 12.03.07

National Museum of Asian Art, Smithsonian Institution
15, Ogata Gekkō / Robert O. Muller Collection, S2003.8.1656
44 (detail), **46**, Katsushika Hokusai / The Anne van Biema Collection, S2004.3.211

National Museum of Asian Art, Smithsonian Institution, Freer Collection
6 (detail), **8-9** (detail), **10**, **16** (detail), **45** (detail), **49** (detail), Katsushika Hokusai / Gift of the family of Eugene and Agnes E. Meyer, F1974.63
13, James McNeill Whistler / Gift of Charles Lang Freer, F1892.23a-b
28 (detail), **30**, Okumura Masanobu / Gift of Charles Lang Freer, F1902.250
42, Hashimoto Gahō / Gift of Charles Lang Freer, F1902.228
53, Katsushika Hokusai / Gift of the family of Eugene and Agnes E. Meyer, F1974.67
57, Okumura Masanobu / Gift of the family of Eugene and Agnes E. Meyer, F1974.81
59, Katsushika Hokuun / Gift of Charles Lang Freer, F1898.419

National Museum of Asian Art, Smithsonian Institution, Freer Study Collection
14, Utagawa Hiroshige / Gift of Alan, Donald, and David Winslow from the estate of William R. Castle, FSC-GR-61
18 (detail), **23**, FSC-R-438
50, Utagawa Hiroshige / Gift of Alan, Donald, and David Winslow from the estate of William R. Castle, FSC-GR-69

National Museum of Asian Art, Smithsonian Institution, Freer Study Collection, Purchase, The Gerhard Pulverer Collection — Charles Lang Freer Endowment, Friends of the National Museum of Asian Art and the Harold P. Stern Memorial Fund in appreciation of Jeffrey P. Cunard and his exemplary service to the Museum as chair of the Board of Trustees (2003-2007)
22 top (detail), **32**, Katsushika Hokusai / FSC-GR-780.233.1-14
25, Sekichūshi / FSC-GR-780.526.1-5
35, Katsushika Hokusai / FSC-GR-780.246.1-3
51, **52**, Katsushika Hokusai / FSC-GR-780.228.1-2
56 (detail), **60**, Kitagawa Utamaro / FSC-GR-780.327.1-2
58, Attributed to Keisai Eisen / FSC-GR-780.5.1-4
65, Katsushika Hokusai / FSC-GR-780.246.1-3

Other Collections
12, Japanese Maps of the Tokugawa Era, Rare Books and Special Collections, University of British Columbia Library, G7964 .E3 1689 I8
20-21, From the National Diet Library Digital Collections, NDL Digital Collections Database
24, Photo: Kobe City Museum / DNPartcom
31, Honolulu Museum of Art, Gift of James A. Michener, 1991 (21630)
36 (detail), **41**, Image copyright, © The Metropolitan Museum of Art. Image source: Art Resource, NY, 2013.718a-f
38-39 left, Seattle Asian Art Museum, Eugene Fuller Memorial Collection, 35.73, 35.74, 35.75
39 right, **40** (detail), Harvard Art Museums/ Arthur M. Sackler Museum, Asian Art Objects Fund, 1965.4
43, From the National Diet Library Digital Collections, NDL Digital Collections Database
47, © THE SUMIDA HOKUSAI MUSEUM / DNPartcom
48, Brooklyn Museum, Gift of Frederic B. Pratt, 42.91
54-55, © Taiko Chandler, photo by Scott Dressel-Martin
62-63, University of Manchester
64, © EDO-TOKYO-MUSEUM / DNPartcom
66 (detail), **72**, © Edward Luper
69, The Miriam and Ira D. Wallach Division of Art, Prints and Photographs: Print Collection, The New York Public Library. New York Public Library Digital Collections
71, Portland Art Museum, Portland, Oregon, Museum Purchase: Jean Y. Roth Memorial Fund, © 2024 Artists Rights Society (ARS), New York / ADAGP, Paris, 2012.104.1a,b
73, © Nishiyama Terumi
74, Collection of the Boise Art Museum, Purchased with donations to the Roger Shimomura Acquisitions Fund, Courtesy of the Boise Art Museum, Boise, Idaho

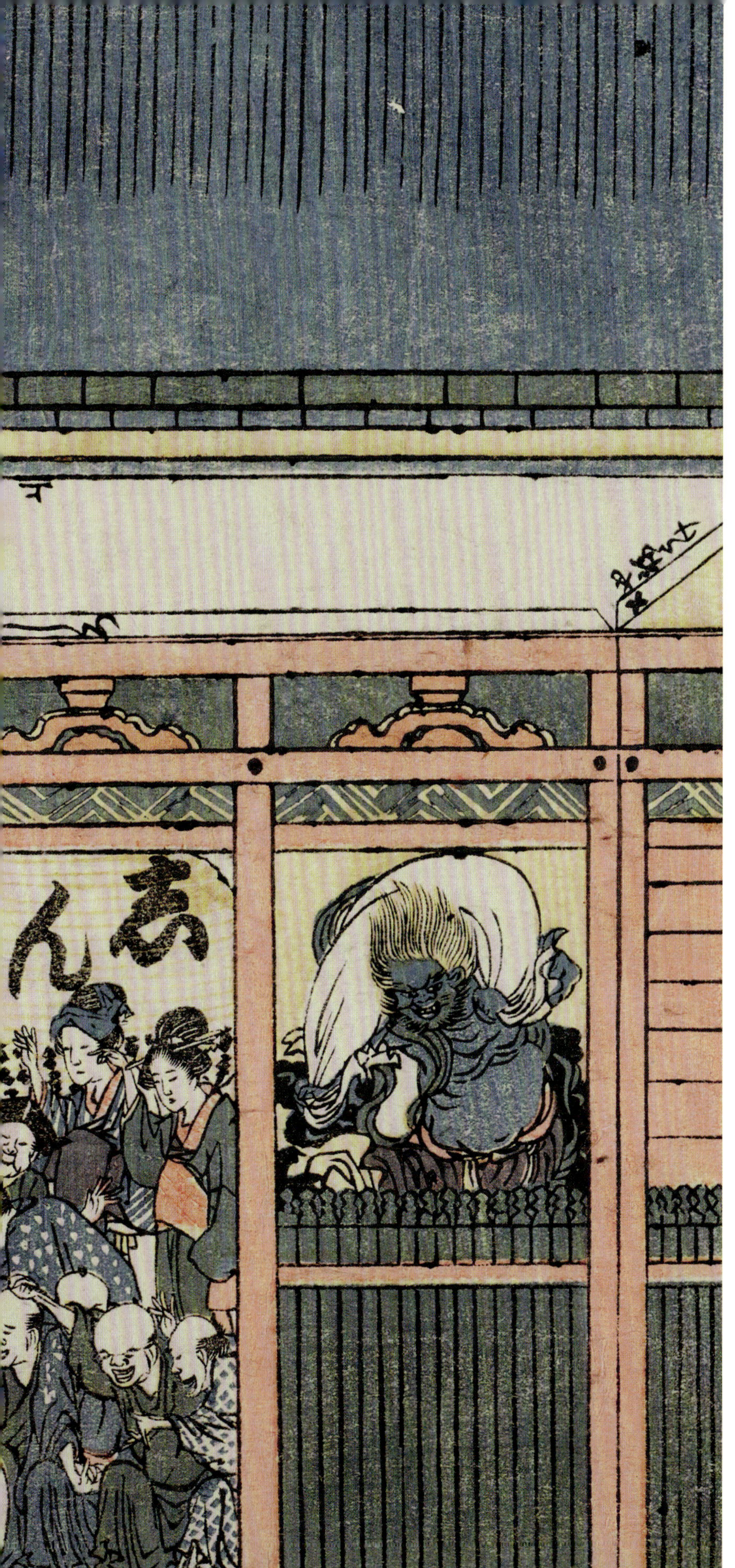

CONTENTS

HOKUSAI
KIT BROOKS

APPROACH

As you sketch out a view from a balcony—what do you see? How much is memory and how much is fantasy in that self-constructed reality? How do balconies define our relationship to our surroundings? Within an image, a balcony can present the viewer with a space that is, at once, private and public, and the geometry of its architecture creates a picture within a picture. It constructs a view, defined by the building and the location, that provides an opportunity to visualize and juxtapose different worlds. Railings, barriers, balustrades—these separate the intimate space of viewers from their environment but also present artists with the opportunity to bend reality and create the perspectives they want us to see.

This book examines two specific balcony views, Katsushika Hokusai's *The Sazaidō of Gohyakurakanji* and James McNeill Whistler's *Variations in Flesh Colour and Green—The Balcony* (fig. 1), with a center section providing prompts for readers to make their own balcony-inspired creations. It is an exercise in complementary analysis—although the two works have previously been linked by their compositional similarities, each work is examined here on its own terms using parallel analytical categories. The intent is not to compare them to each other, but to provide a comparable treatment of each separately. Utilizing a mirrored presentation that divides the book into two equal parts,

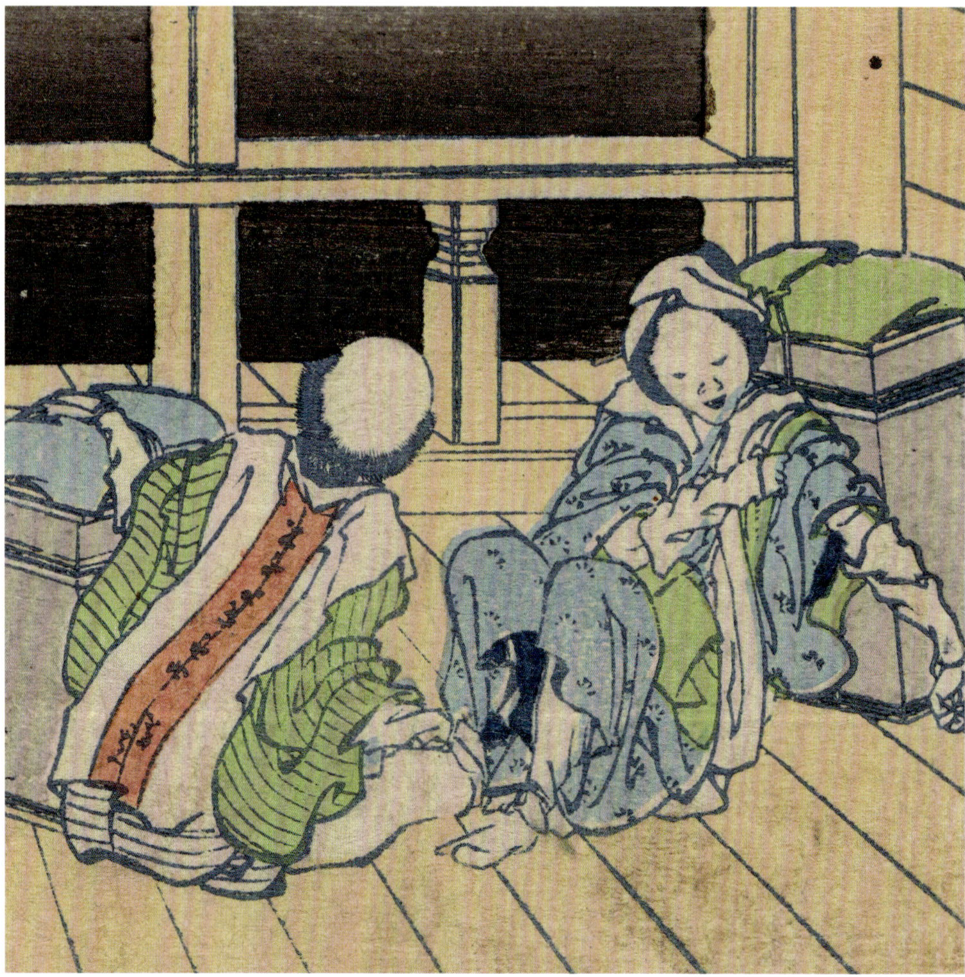

Katsushika Hokusai, *The Sazaidō of Gohyakurakanji*, from the series *Thirty-Six Views of Mount Fuji* (*Fugaku sanjūrokkei*) (detail). Japan, Edo period, ca. 1830–1831. Woodblock print; ink and color on paper; 24.5 × 37 cm.

by two different authors, this publication explores the individual history of each work and what makes it distinctive, with particular emphasis on the context of its reception and the particularity of the location it depicts. As images of balconies, the two works can be immersive for the viewer and offer a space for self-referential looking, as if we are tacitly included as part of the group of figures depicted within the scenes. The reader can start here, or at the opposite end.

Hokusai's *The Sazaidō of Gohyakurakanji* is often eclipsed by his *Under the Wave off Kanagawa*, another print within the same series of views of Mount Fuji. Whistler's work is often understood as an instance of Japonisme—a late nineteenth-century trend for Western artists to incorporate and appropriate aspects of Japanese art and design, which was newly available in this period. However, this book is *not* a book about Hokusai, or Whistler, or Japonisme. It is an attempt to move beyond reductive narratives of influence and propose a new model for comparative art historical explorations. Each artist made careful choices about what to include, discard, or adapt, based on a variety of possibilities, their artistic practices, and contemporary currents in their own artistic traditions. As much as a balcony is a physical structure, it is also a compositional and intellectual framework that can be applied to many artworks and contexts.

A Tale of Two Balconies is physically divided into two halves with a parallel organizational structure. Mirrored sections—**view**, **site**, **perspective**, **figure**, **pigment**, **restriction**, and **(freer) association**—examine the details of each work by taking the reader through the specificities of the geographical location depicted in the background, the pictorial devices, innovations, and pigments used, the visual strategies incorporated by each artist, and the significance of the balcony as a framing device for representing landscapes that combine the real and the imagined. Additionally, the sections address broader concerns that likely lay beyond the conscious attention of these artists, such as race and gender dynamics, tourism and urbanization, globalization, and the circulation of ideas and materials. These ideas may not be explicit in the image, but embedded clues can help reconstruct the assumptions of a contemporary viewer. The section headings are far from an exhaustive list of possible angles of interpretation but are, rather, generative prompts to trigger alternate perspectives. The headings are like balcony railings—guide rails, but not impassable. They are also flexible, as the authors have taken the same prompt in different directions for each of the works. Throughout, readers are encouraged to make their own expansive reflections regarding the compositions, culminating in the shared central section, **remix**, which contains several creative exercises to provoke construction of their own balcony scenes. Embarking on such a close consideration allows us to appreciate each work's own particular features as well as provide an arsenal of interpretive approaches to interrogate other images or create new ones.

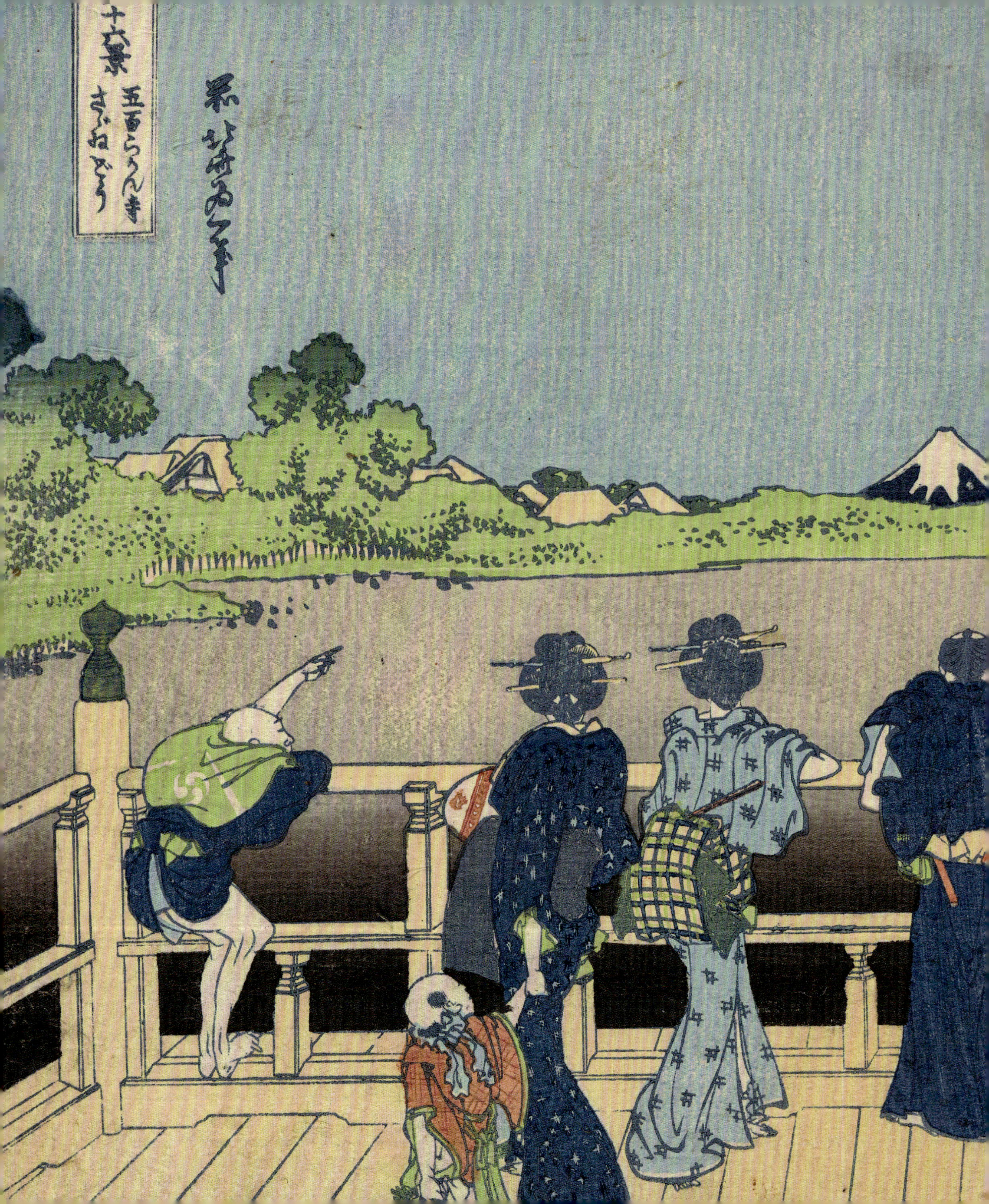
十六景
五百らかん寺
さゞゐどう

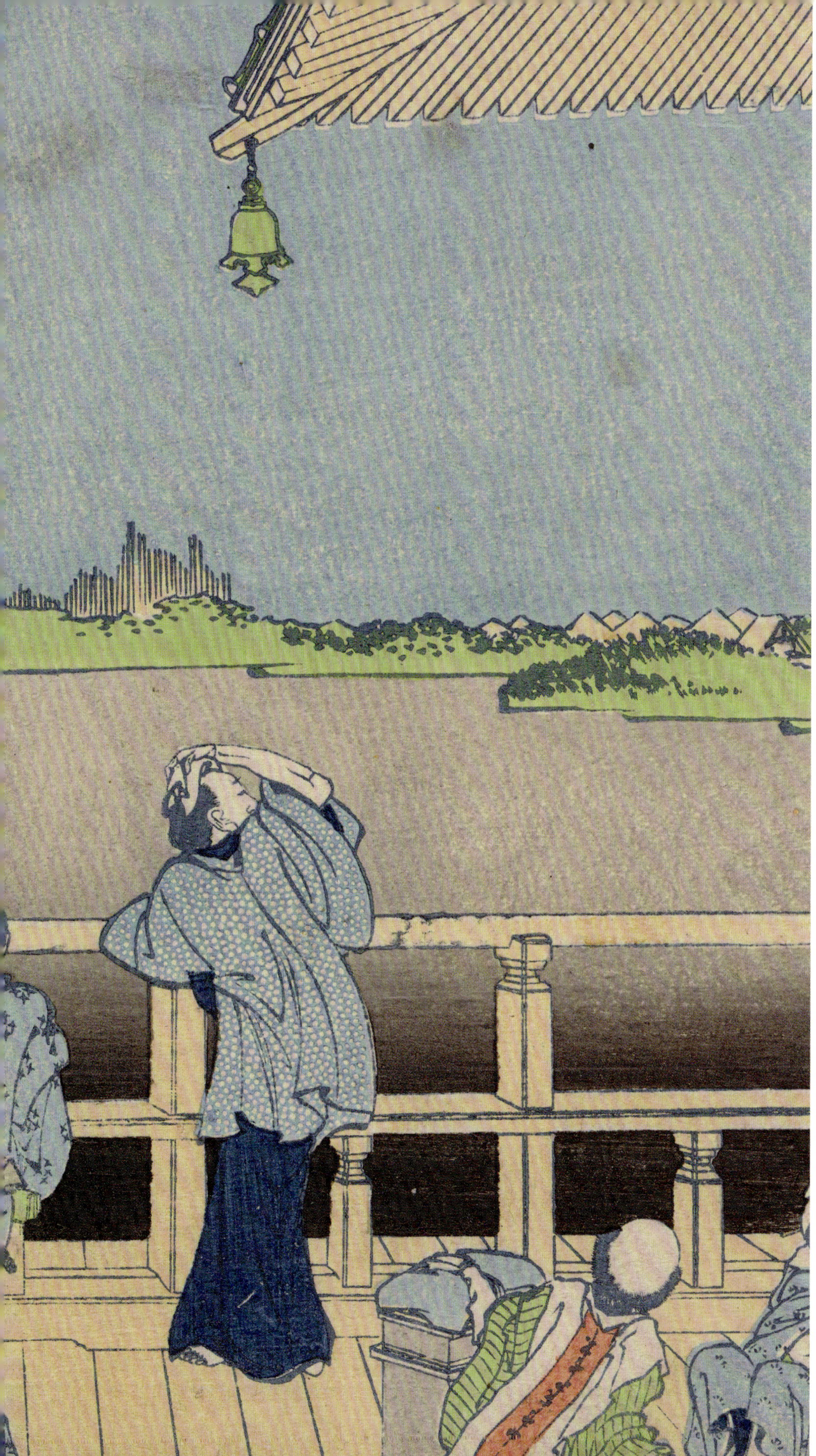

HOKUSAI

The Sazaidō of Gohyakurakanji

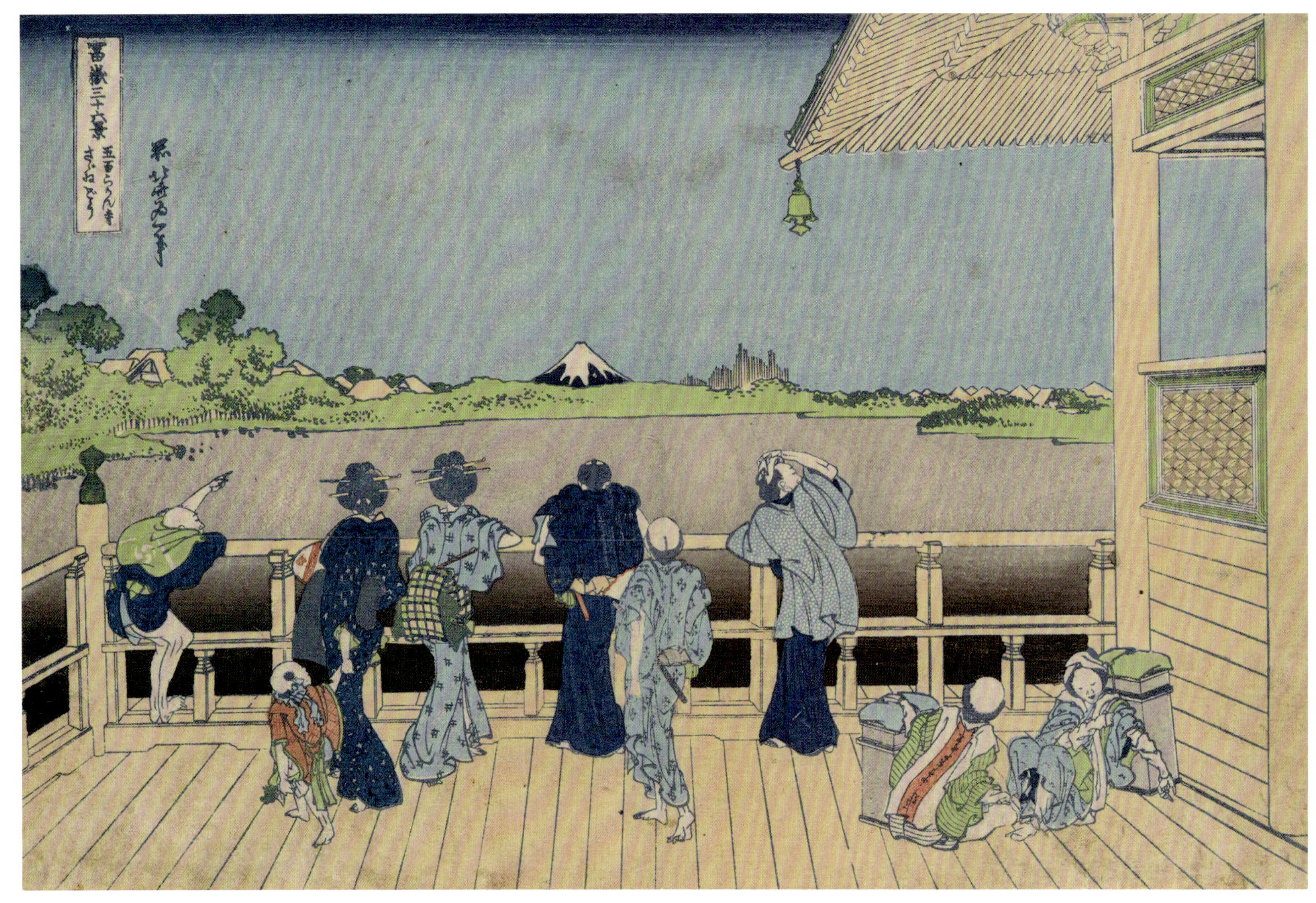

Fig. 1
Katsushika Hokusai, *The Sazaidō of Gohyakurakanji.*

VIEW

What are we looking at? Whether we gaze ahead as one of the depicted figures or a viewer of the print, our eyes are inexorably drawn to the conical peak of Mount Fuji. This is encouraged by the use of perspective, but also through the similar forms and colors throughout the image that echo that focal point. For example, the deep indigo robe of the central male figure is colorized with the same pigment as the slopes of the distant peak located directly above him, and seen from behind, the shape of his head and hunched shoulders repeats the volcano's triangular outline. The jagged contour of the Fukagawa lumberyards along the horizon to the right of Mount Fuji forms another peak, although man-made and imperfect; its closer proximity gives the illusion of comparable size. Although Fuji's symmetrical form is slightly to the left of the center line, it nonetheless acts as the central node of the image, drawing the perspectival lines of the composition toward it with an almost magnetic pull.[1] The artist of this print creatively skips over the dull farmland fields in the middle ground by covering them with a wash of gray. In a darker tone close to the edge of the balcony, this gray expanse becomes lighter the closer we get to Mount Fuji, drawing our eyes upward. The linear perspective is exaggerated by the directionality of the wooden boards and the pointed finger of the eager child beside the metal-capped railing post at the far left. As a viewer of the print, our vantage point just behind the sightseeing figures places us together on the balcony with this spellbound group, while the cool-hued blues and greens chosen by the printer offset the yellow wood of the architecture. Together the composition and the color scheme create a harmonious scene whereby the viewer feels a comparable sense of inclusion and absorption.

Even without the assistance provided by the blue inscription in the title cartouche at the upper left, viewers contemporary to the artist, Katsushika Hokusai 葛飾北斎 (1760–1849), would have immediately recognized the vista in *The Sazaidō of Gohyakurakanji* (*Gohyakurakanji Sazaidō* 五百らかん寺さざゐどう) (fig. 1) as a vantage from one very specific location. This wide, elevated platform, with its privileged view of iconic Mount Fuji in the far distance, was the viewing terrace of a three-story building within the truly extraordinary complex of Gohyakurakanji 五百羅漢寺, the Temple of the Five Hundred Arhats.[2] In the early 1830s when Hokusai's print was published, the temple was located in a relatively newly developed district, Honjo 本所, across a river to the east of the main metropolis of Edo (now Tokyo) (fig. 2).[3] Five thematic headings are discussed in the following sections as potential avenues for locating and decoding the visual languages in this print. Knowledge of the **site** depicted in the print affects a viewer's reading of the image, as does an awareness of the innovations of **perspective** and **pigment** that Hokusai brought to bear in his design. The public **figure** of Hokusai himself is a latent presence in the work, as are the social contexts of **restriction** that would have curtailed the freedoms of women viewers. Finally, **(freer) association** reviews some of the afterlives of this image and the connections that have been made with other works, as well as other comparable views, as an encouragement for the reader to form their own perspectives. Between the two halves of this book lies a liminal space for the reader to experiment, question, and **remix** their own creative ideas about balconies and the perspectives they offer, whether formal or methodological. The structure is not intended to be prescriptive, but just as we make space for readers to explore their creative impulses, we as authors challenged ourselves to find new ways of interacting with objects, history, and different regional disciplines.

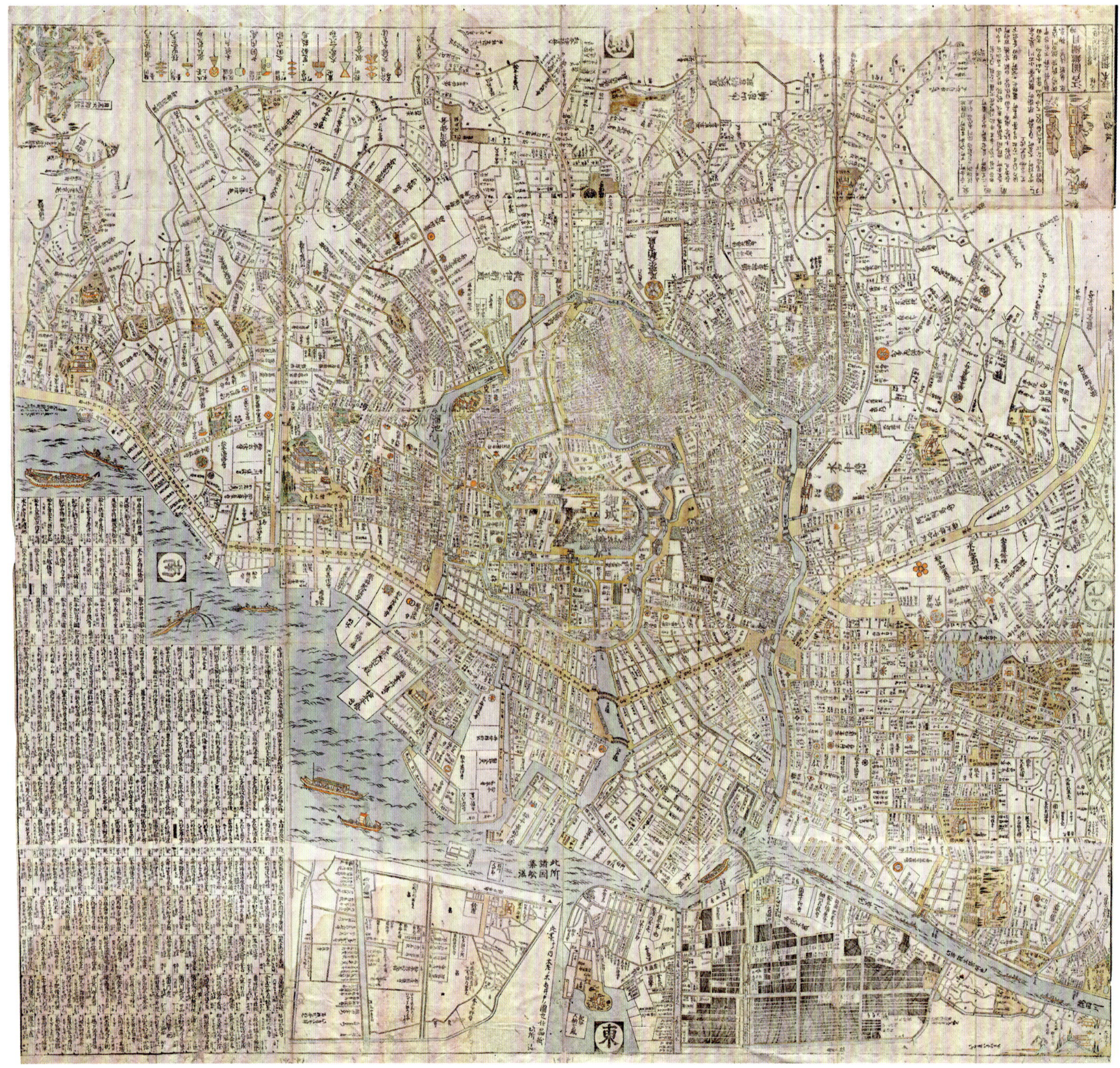

Fig. 2
Ishikawa Ryūsei, *Outline Map of Edo* (*Edo zukan kōmoku*). Japan, Edo period, 1696. Woodcut, manuscript, color; 126.8 × 135.3 cm.

Published one year after land was granted to establish Gohyakurakanji, the map shows the site to the far east of the city, across the Sumida River and amid swathes of blacked-out agricultural land in the lower right portion of the image.

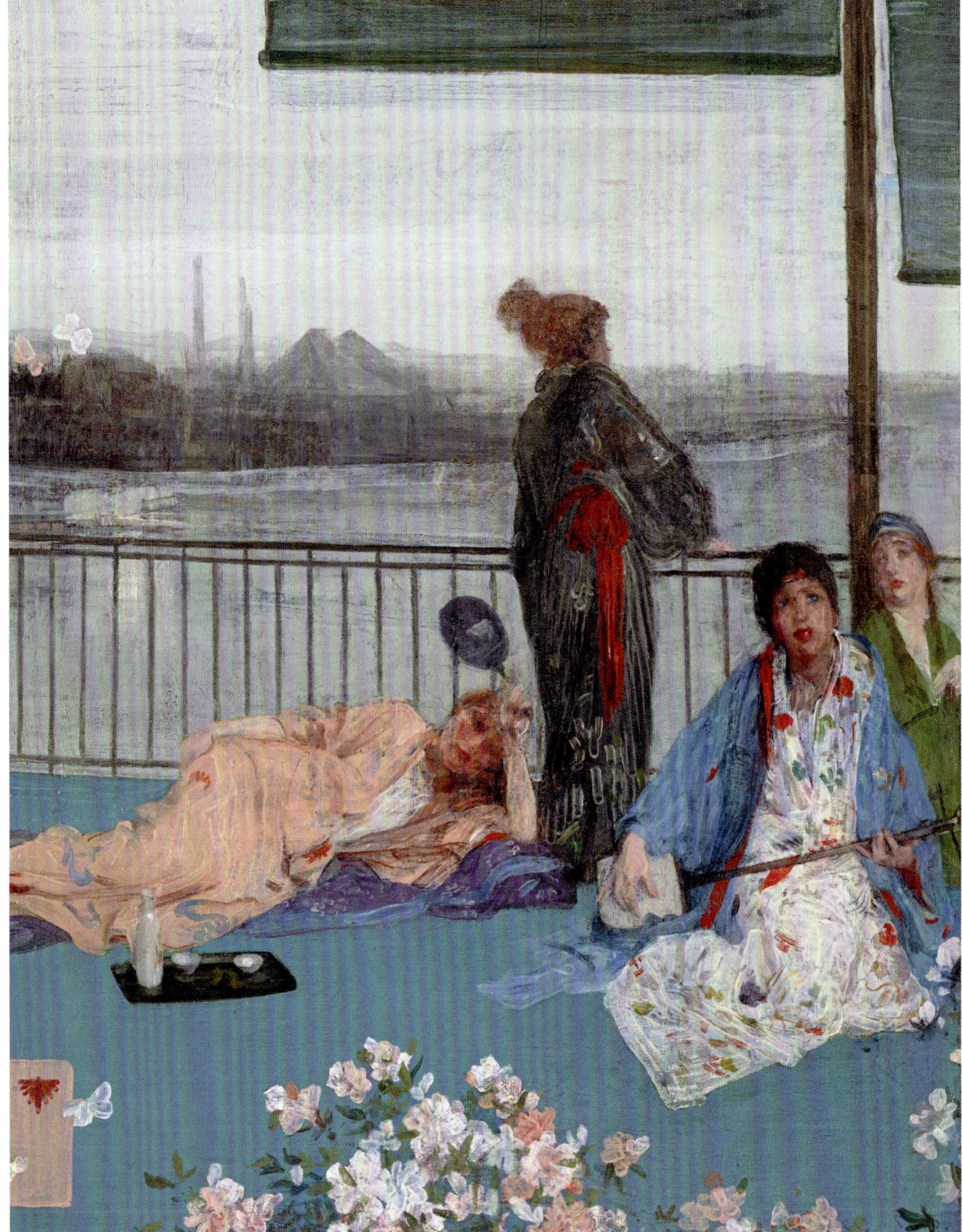

Fig. 3
James McNeill Whistler, *Variations in Flesh Colour and Green—The Balcony*. England, 1864–1870, additions 1870–1879. Oil on wood panel; 61.4 × 48.5 cm.

Hokusai's *The Sazaidō of Gohyakurakanji* has been cited as a direct influence on the compositions of artists within the broad genre of Japonisme and others influenced by Japanese art, such as James McNeill Whistler's (1834–1903) *Variations in Flesh Colour and Green—The Balcony* (fig. 3). In such analyses, *The Sazaidō of Gohyakurakanji* is usually offered as a representative example of a Japanese "landscape" print from the late Edo period (1603–1868). However, such characterizations misunderstand both the genre of *meisho-e* 名所絵 (literally "famous place picture") to which the print belongs and Hokusai's creative deviations from that genre's conventions. Reconsidering

Fig. 4
Utagawa Hiroshige, *The Sazaidō Hall at the Five Hundred Rakan Temple* (*Gohyaku Rakan Sazaidō*), from the series *One Hundred Famous Views of Edo* (*Meisho Edo hyakkei*). Japan, Edo period, 1857, 8th month. Woodblock print; ink and color on paper; 33.9 × 22.6 cm.

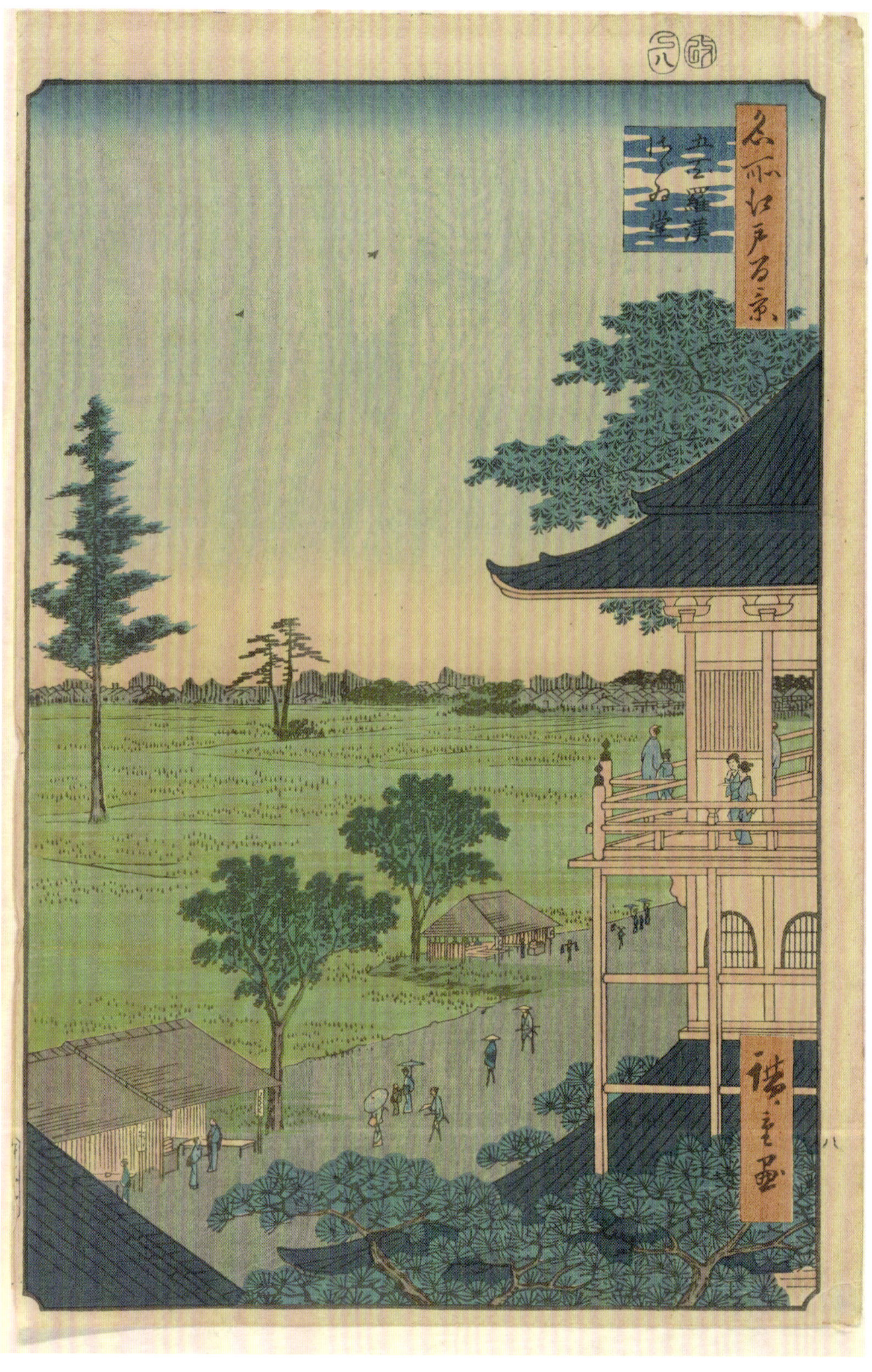

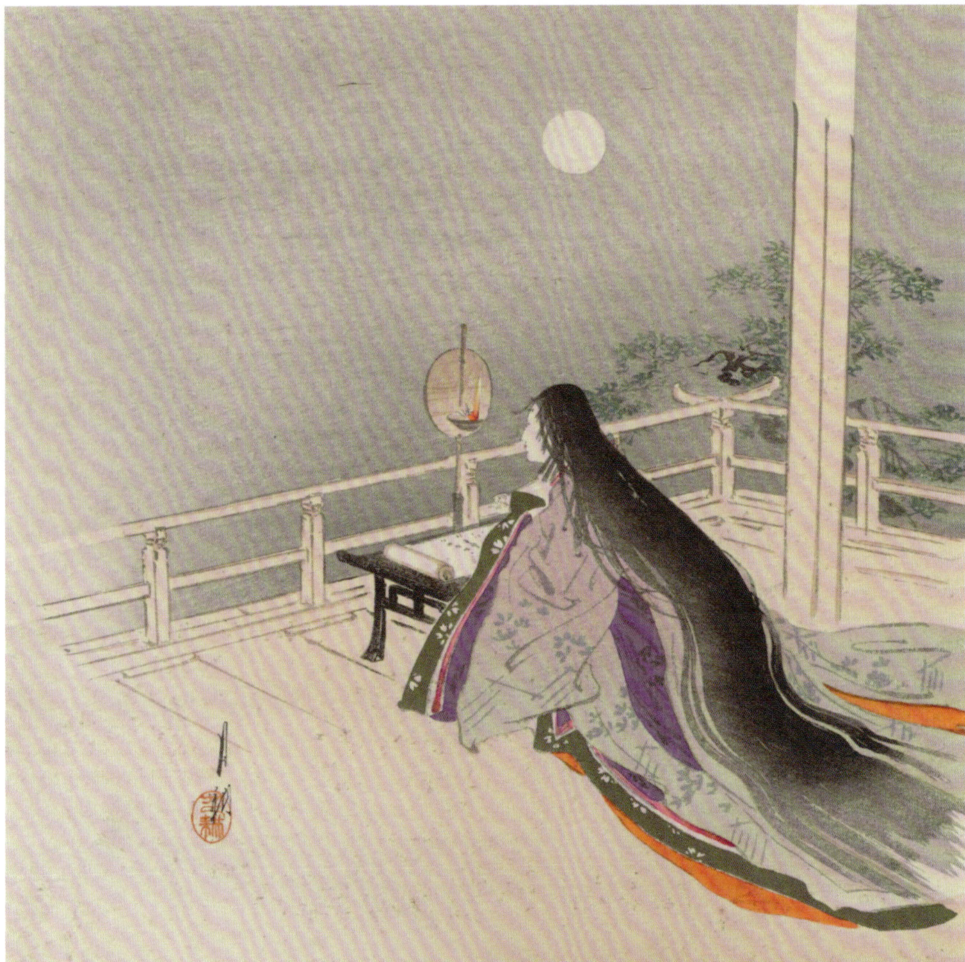

Fig. 5
Ogata Gekkō, *Lady Murasaki on Her Balcony Under a Full Moon Writing by Oil Lamp*. Japan, Meiji era, ca. 1900. Woodblock print; ink and color on paper; 23.2 × 23.7 cm.

on its own terms within its own cultural contexts is thus a worthwhile and rewarding exercise for thinking anew about images that have entered global public consciousness and been absorbed into oversimplifying narratives of "comparison." The following sections are not intended to be comprehensive. Each section can be considered independently, in the context of the others, or in combination or contrast with the parallel sections in the other half of the book by Katherine Roeder, which takes *The Balcony* as its object of study, interpreting the same section prompts in different ways.

Hokusai was not the first to present the precincts of Gohyakurakanji in the print medium, although his presentation was remarkable, including the viewer in a group of depicted figures looking out *from* the building, rather than a conventional presentation *of* the building and its surrounds (fig. 4). Despite his innovations, Hokusai's choice of location is still identifiable as it relies on visual signifiers that were understood by a literate audience acquainted with the easily accessible printed materials constituting the "library of public information" of his day.[4] Mount Fuji, the locus for this image as well as the entire series of which the print is a part, was a backdrop to the lives of the city's denizens, and perhaps even the country as a whole, given its status as a

Fig. 6
Katsushika Hokusai,
The Sazaidō of Gohyakurakanji (detail).

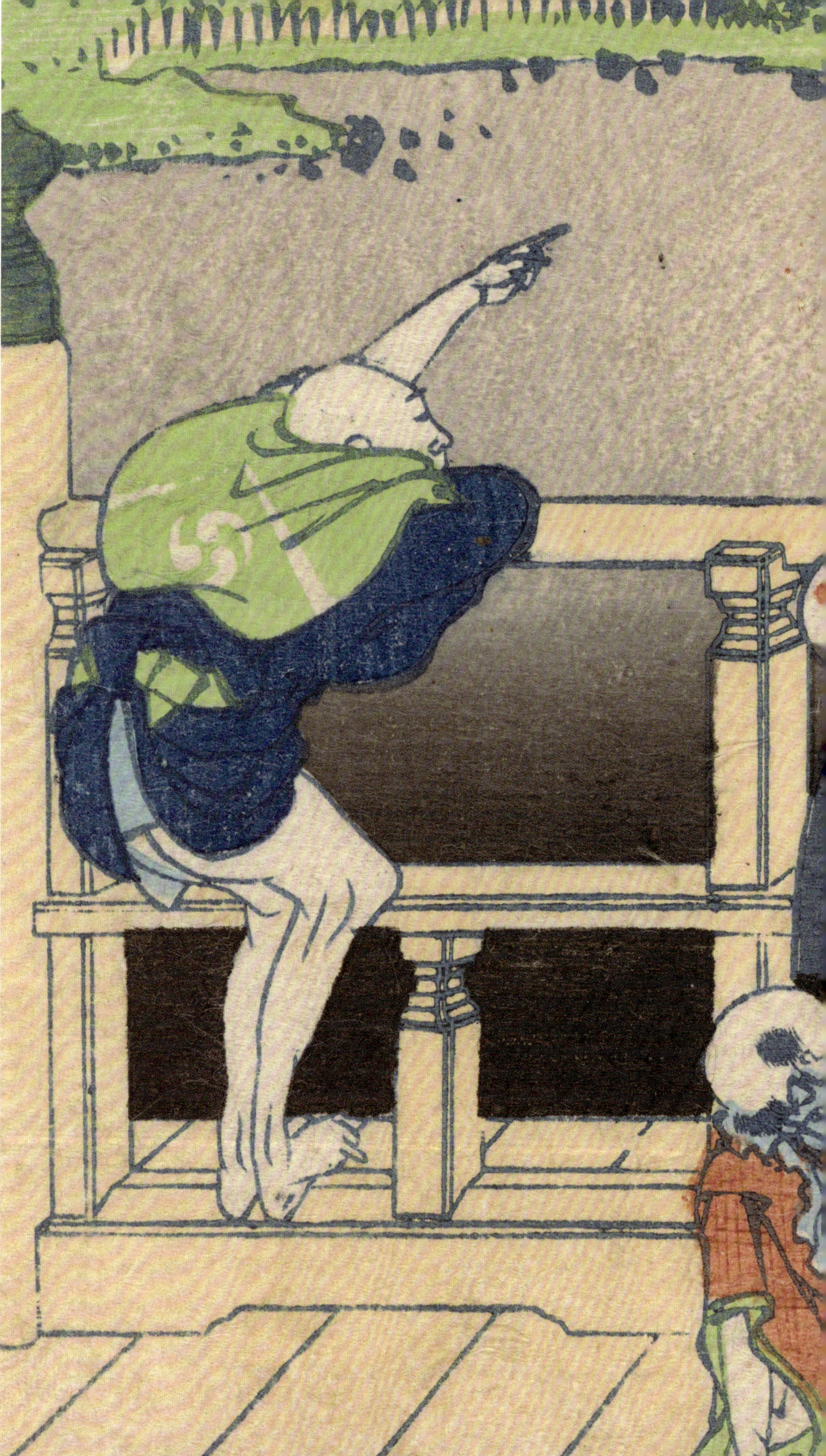

universally recognizable icon. Although its most recent eruption, in 1707, collapsed the mountain's southeastern side into a less than perfect configuration, Mount Fuji occupies an important position in Japan's cultural imagination as a stable and enduring symbol. Further, both domestically and internationally, Hokusai's own reputation is tied to the volcano. As he is regarded as an artist who is exemplary of Japanese taste, the pages of Japanese passports issued since February 2020 have been illustrated with twenty-four images from the same *Thirty-Six Views* series that includes *The Sazaidō of Gohyakurakanji* and other well-known designs, most notably the iconic *The Great Wave* (full title: *Under the Wave off Kanagawa* [*Kanagawa-oki nami-ura* 神奈川沖浪裏]).

While the balcony in *The Sazaidō of Gohyakurakanji* offers the onlookers an elevated and privileged view of Mount Fuji, we can also think of it as a heuristic device—a different type of platform from which we can survey the foundational structure of local knowledge possessed by contemporaneous viewers of the print. The special ability of balcony images to offer a space for self-reflection or self-insertion, which is encouraged by the essential function of a balcony as a place for seeing—but also for being seen—can be found elsewhere in Japanese art. For example, a lone, long-haired beauty in Heian-period (794–1185) attire at a desk on a balcony is a frequently encountered iconography (fig. 5). This wistful scene can immediately be identified as Murasaki Shikibu 紫式部 (d. ca. 1014) penning the epic early novel *The Tale of Genji* (*Genji monogatari* 源氏物語). The author's true personal name is unknown—she has historically been referred to as "Murasaki" as a pen name in reference to the main female character *within* her own novel. Here, she is shown gazing beyond the railings of a balcony at Ishiyamadera 石山寺, the temple near Kyoto where she wrote that famous work. As a viewer of this image, we are watching a woman contemplating herself—looking over a vista and imagining a fictional world that would come to define her existence over and beyond the reality of her own life. Although Hokusai himself does not appear within *The Sazaidō of Gohyakurakanji*, there is a different self-referential detail within the print; the figure of the boy at the far left has a green textile draped over his shoulders decorated with the symbol of three commas within a circle under a mountain—the mark of Eijudō 永寿堂 (fig. 6), the publisher of the print. In addition, the print viewer's position behind the depicted figures, but looking in the same direction, blurs the boundary between audience and subject by inviting us to stand both inside and outside the print, reconstructing the view for ourselves just as we might consider the circumstances of its production and the figures that brought about its creation.

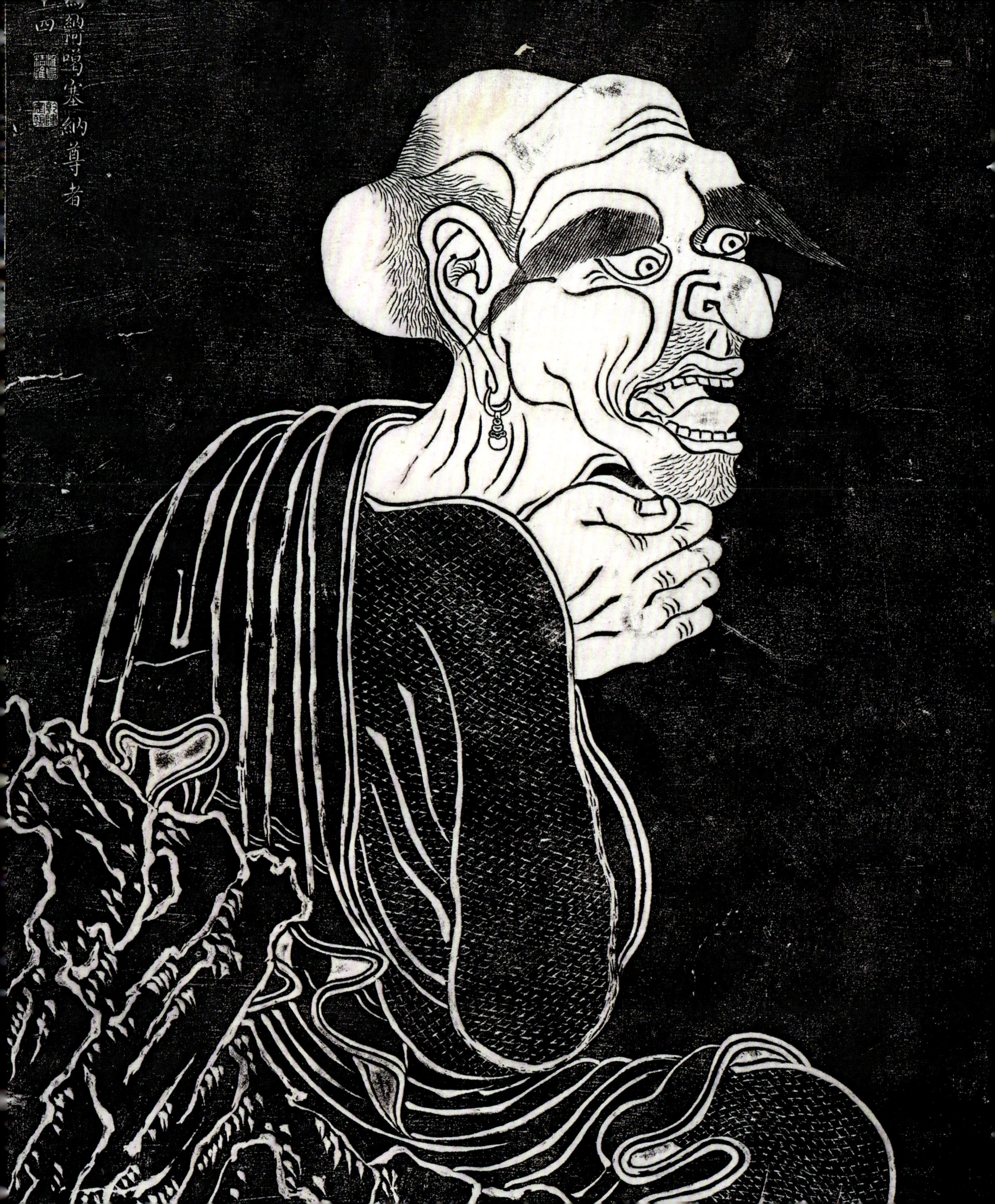
納噶塞納尊者
四

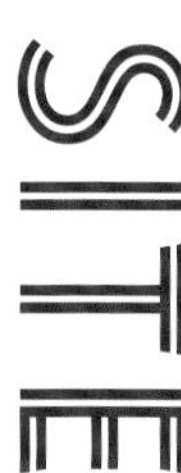

What was so remarkable about the real-life setting of Hokusai's print that viewers would have immediately recognized the location from the balcony view alone? Located on the eastern outskirts of Edo, the Gohyakurakanji temple complex had a reputation for being spectacularly exotic.[5] This notoriety was achieved through several means, such as the markedly continental aesthetics of the architectural style that visitors encountered on their approach to the temple. In addition, the sculptures within were arranged in an absorptive installation that was intended to evoke events from India. Further, the temple displayed imported European oil paintings that enacted a new type of artistic visuality. That the site's extraordinary attractions were well-known and much visited is evidenced, for example, by the lengthy inclusion of Gohyakurakanji in the 1836 travel guidebook *Illustrated Famous Places in Edo* (*Edo meisho zue* 江戸名所図会) (fig. 1). That volume devotes a total of forty-six pages to the temple, including fourteen illustrations—far exceeding the few pages given to any other site in the city.

The temple was of the Ōbaku Zen sect. "Zen" is the Japanese name given to the Chan sect of Chinese Buddhism, established when its patriarch, the Buddha's disciple Bodhidharma, left India for East Asia and settled in China. Zen was first transmitted to Japan in the thirteenth century but received a new impetus during the 1660s, as Chinese monks fled to Japan after the collapse of the Ming dynasty (1368–1644). An officially designated outpost in the Japanese city of Nagasaki had allowed Chinese monks to disseminate elements of Ming culture for several decades prior to the sect's formal founding in Japan. That milestone was officially marked in 1661 when the émigré monk Ingen Ryūki 隠元隆琦 (Ch. Yinyuan Longqi) (1592–1673) founded the Manpukuji 萬福寺 temple in Uji, a town near Kyoto. In his native Fujian Province in China, Ingen had established a training center on Mount Huangbo 黄檗—pronounced Ōbaku in Japanese—from which the sect takes its name. By the end of the nineteenth century, there were over four hundred Ōbaku temples throughout Japan. As befitting their origins, these temples conducted services in Chinese. Their architecture was also visibly distinct from other styles of Buddhist sects with longer histories in Japan. Such exotic features included tiled roofs, arched ceilings, and latticed balustrades. In addition, twin flagpoles mark the approach to Ōbaku temples, demarcating the site as a different realm from the everyday. These poles were sufficient to suggest the temple in the public imagination (fig. 2).

Gohyakurakanji was the life's work of the monk Shōun Genkei 松雲元慶 (1648–1710), made possible by the actions of the ruling shogunate family, the Tokugawa 徳川. Shōun began carving life-sized Buddhist sculptures in public, and the spectacle of these performances successfully generated income for the production of even more sculptures. In fact, the mother of the fifth Tokugawa shogun, Tsunayoshi 綱吉 (1646–1709), was so impressed by the in-progress carvings that Shōun had erected outside the Sensōji 浅草寺 temple in northeastern Edo that she sponsored ten more statues. Likely learning of Shōun and his activities through his mother, Tsunayoshi granted the monk a tract of land in 1695 to build his own temple. This generous but unusual gesture of shogunal support would contribute to the temple's liminal status, already suggested by its location on the city's outer reaches, surrounded by farmland.[6] A depiction by Hokusai's younger contemporary Utagawa Hiroshige 歌川広重 (1797–1858) hints at an uneasy positioning (fig. 3). With the distant Fuji at the far left, the

Detail of fig. 4

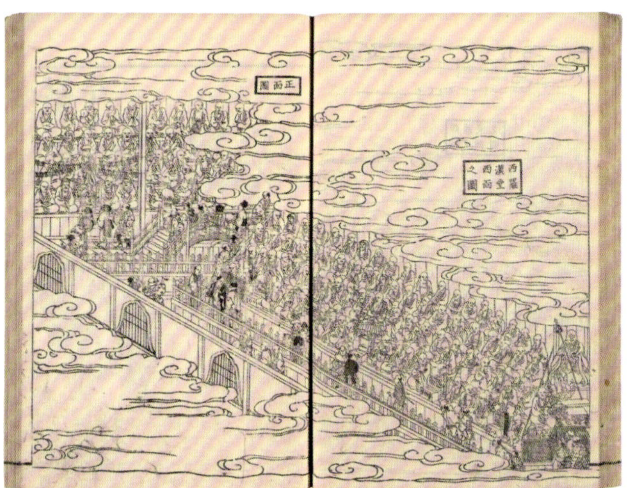
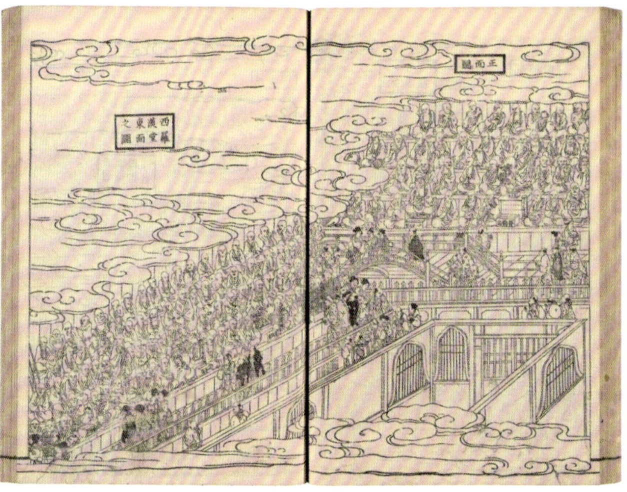
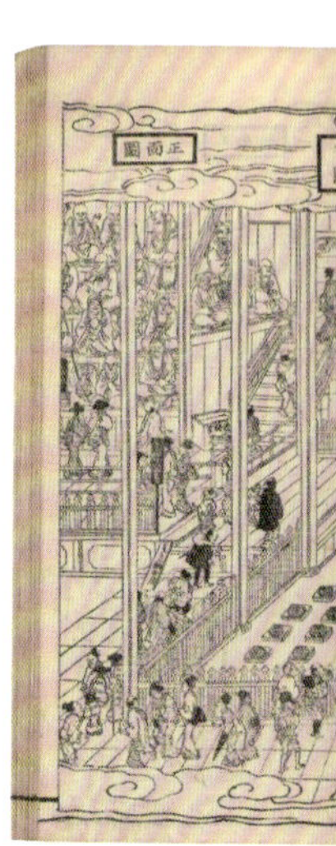

Fig. 1
Interior of the Hall of the Arhats (*Rakandō*) at Gohyakurakanji, from *Illustrated Famous Places in Edo*, vol. 18. Japan, Edo period, 1836. Woodblock-printed book (20 vols.); ink and color on paper; H: 26 cm (each, approx.).

composition is heavily weighted at the right by the solidity of the temple building, whose height exceeds the boundaries of the frame. In the Edo period, every family unit was required under ordinary circumstances to register at a local Buddhist temple, and the regular donations they were obliged to pay financed that temple's operations. When Gohyakurakanji was founded, it was located amid mostly uninhabited farmland and had no such registrants. Without a source of stable local income, it depended entirely on occasional government grants and visitor donations. It was likely this economic reality that led the temple to include many strange features to attract more visitors.

Gohyakurakanji's name alludes to an early and well-known chapter in the history of Buddhism. The historical Buddha, Shakyamuni, gave a transformative sermon to five hundred disciples on the mountain known as Vulture Peak, located in Rajgir, India. By listening to the Buddha's words, those attendees gained instantaneous enlightenment and achieved the status of arhat while retaining their earthly physical form. The Japanese word for "arhat" is *rakan* 羅漢, and the temple's name combines it with the word for "five hundred" (*gohyaku* 五百) plus the suffix for "temple" (*ji* 寺). In art, the arhats are typically represented as an idiosyncratic group devoid of the beatific physical perfection found in Buddhist divinities of higher tiers. Rather, arhats are characterized by their exaggeratedly grotesque appearance (fig. 4), which emphasizes their human and imperfect status and contrasts markedly with the flawless countenances of the buddhas and bodhisattvas.

Shōun sought to realize the vision of Vulture Peak in its most literal sense. He is usually credited with personally carving life-sized versions of all five hundred arhats displayed at the Rakandō 羅漢堂, the "Hall of the Arhats" (see **figure**). The arhats stand before a pedestal of sculpted rock surmounted by a monumental sculpture of Shakyamuni, measuring over four meters in height (the double life-size proportions believed to have been attained by the Buddha after death) and holding a lotus flower and preaching. Visitors followed a predetermined route through this carved congregation, hoping that after their death, their devotions would be repaid by rebirth in a similarly enlightened state. The grotesque features of the arhats are often understood as a means to make them more approachable to ordinary believers. Indeed, visitors to

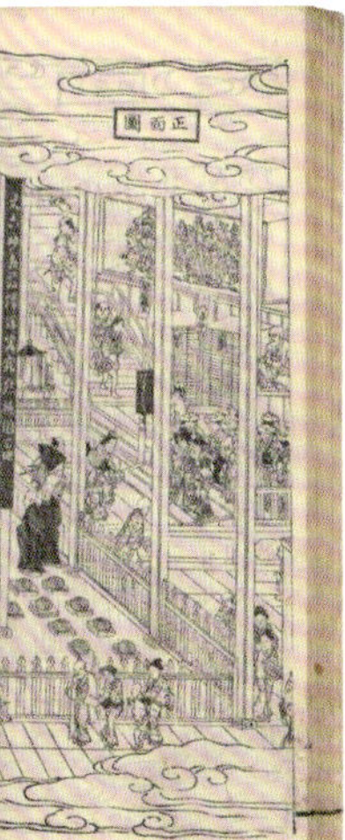
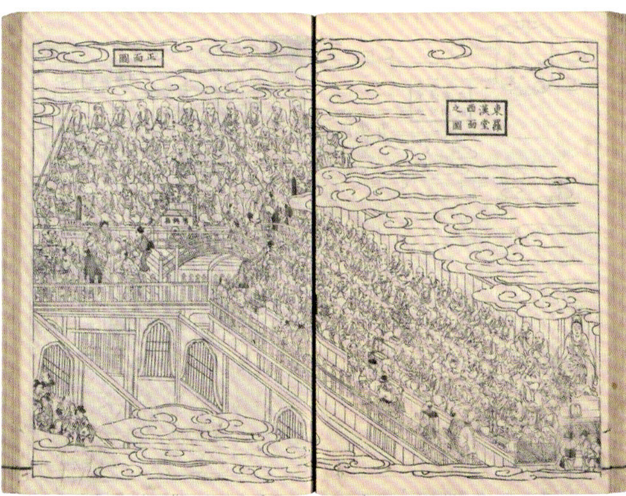
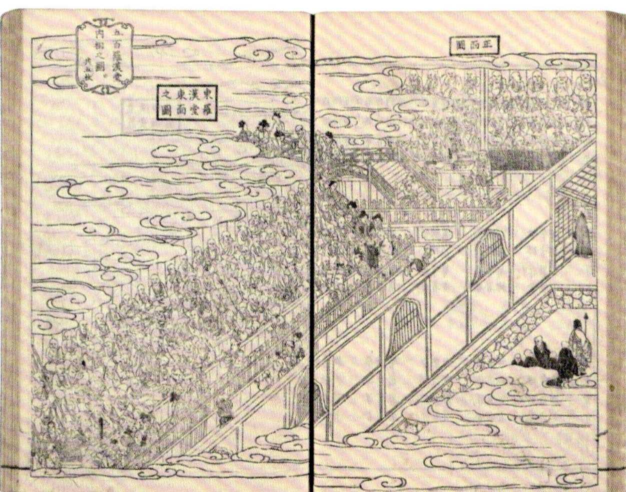

Gohyakurakanji seem to have felt moved in this way, as the production of over 70 percent of the sculptures was sponsored by direct donations from members of the merchant and townsman class, rather than by elite social groups like the Tokugawa shogunal family.[7] Donors would have hoped their pious generosity, even beyond a mere visit to the temple, would lead to reward in the next life—but in the earthly realm, it also offered a chance to contribute to the temple's spectacle.

This sense of spectacle was not limited to the Rakandō. The platform seen in Hokusai's print composition belongs to a different structure within the same complex that was no less astounding, the Sazaidō or Sazaedō 栄螺堂, the "Spiral Shell Hall." That building contained a spiral staircase allowing for continuous traffic between its three stories, with each floor containing a miniaturized version of one of the famous real-life pilgrimage circuits of Chichibu, Kantō, and Shikoku. Completing those circuits on foot is still a feat of endurance for pilgrims today. They can take weeks or months to complete, as the Kantō circuit alone is over 1,300 kilometers long. Each route connects thirty-three temples that house icons of Kannon 観音, the bodhisattva of compassion. The number thirty-three is important as it represents the thirty-three manifestations of the deity. In imitation of those full-scale pilgrimage routes, each of the three floors of the Sazaidō contained thirty-three corresponding life-sized icons. By visiting the Sazaidō, visitors could symbolically perform these pilgrimages, finally emerging on a balconied platform, over seventeen meters in height, that opened onto a view of Japan's iconic mountain.[8]

The delights of Gohyakurakanji referenced places even further westward, beyond China, which inspired the aesthetics, and India's Vulture Peak, recreated in sculptural form. In 1722, the eighth Tokugawa shogun, Yoshimune 吉宗 (1684–1751), requested five oil paintings by the Dutch painter Willem Hendrik van Royen (1672–1742), which were delivered via the Dutch East India Company in 1726. The Dutch East India Company had maintained a trading outpost in Nagasaki since 1609 and regularly imported art, scientific materials, chemicals, and many other goods that were deemed safely devoid of corrupting Christian content. Yoshimune appears to have quickly tired of the paintings, however. Likely because of the Tokugawa's long familial association with

Fig. 2
Katsushika Hokusai, *Rakan Temple* (*Rakanji*), from *Hokusai Manga*, vol. 8 (detail). Edo period, 1819. Woodblock-printed book (8 vols.); ink and color on paper; 22.9 × 15.9 × 1 cm (each).

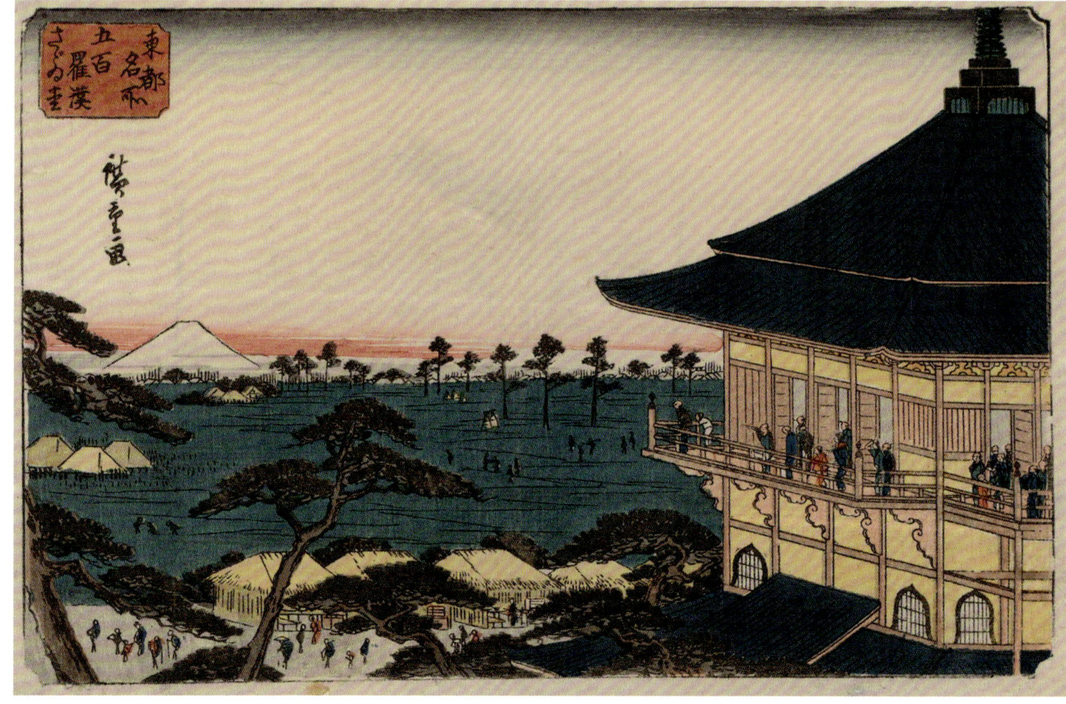

Fig. 3
Utagawa Hiroshige, *The Spiral Hall at the Temple of the Five Hundred Arhats* (*Gohyaku Rakan Sazaidō*), from the series *Famous Places in the Eastern Capital* (*Tōto meisho*). Edo period, ca. 1840–1842. Woodblock print; ink and color on paper; 23.8 × 35.7 cm.

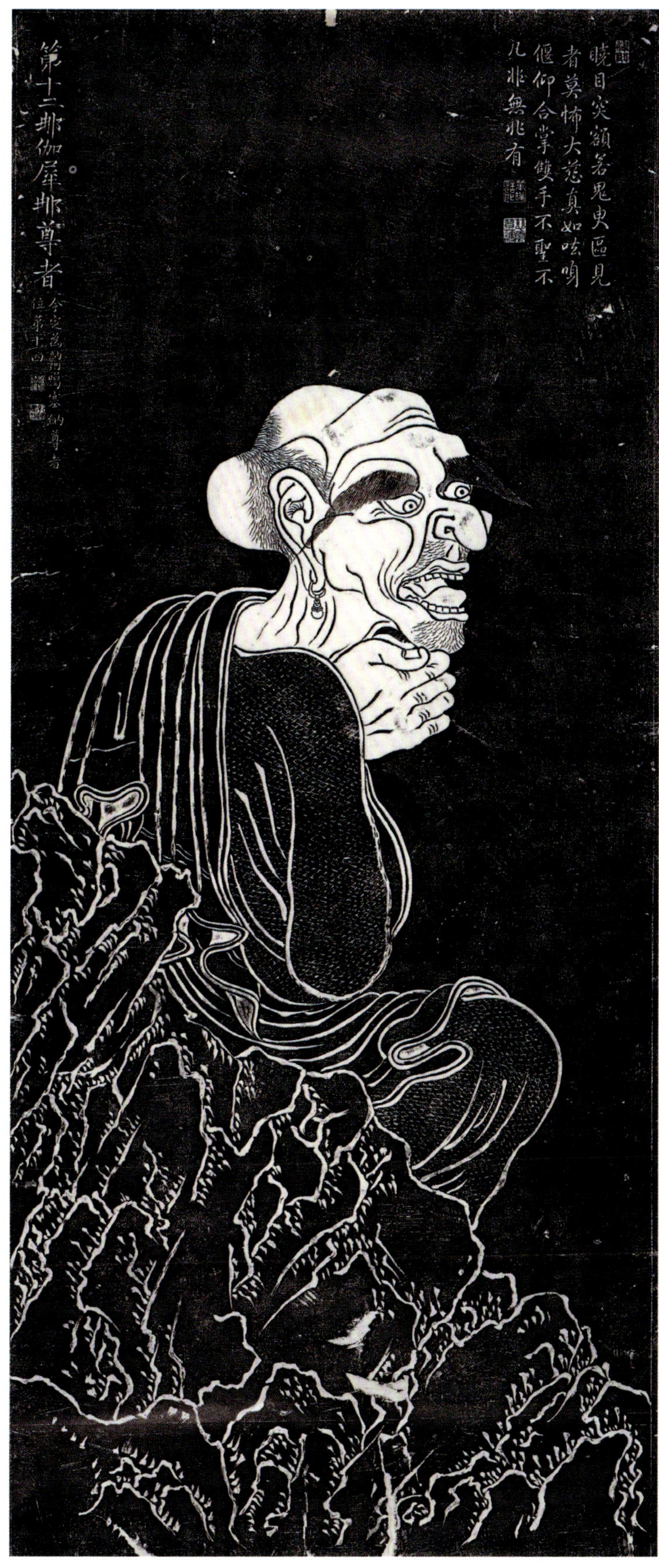

Fig. 4
Unknown artist, *Nagasena*, after a set attributed to Guanxiu. China, Qing dynasty, 18th or 19th century. Rubbing; ink on paper; 120.8 × 54 cm.

Fig. 5
Tani Bunchō, *Copy of Flowers and Birds by Willem Hendrik van Royen*. Japan, Edo period, early 19th century. Hanging scroll; color on paper; 231.8 × 96.5 cm.

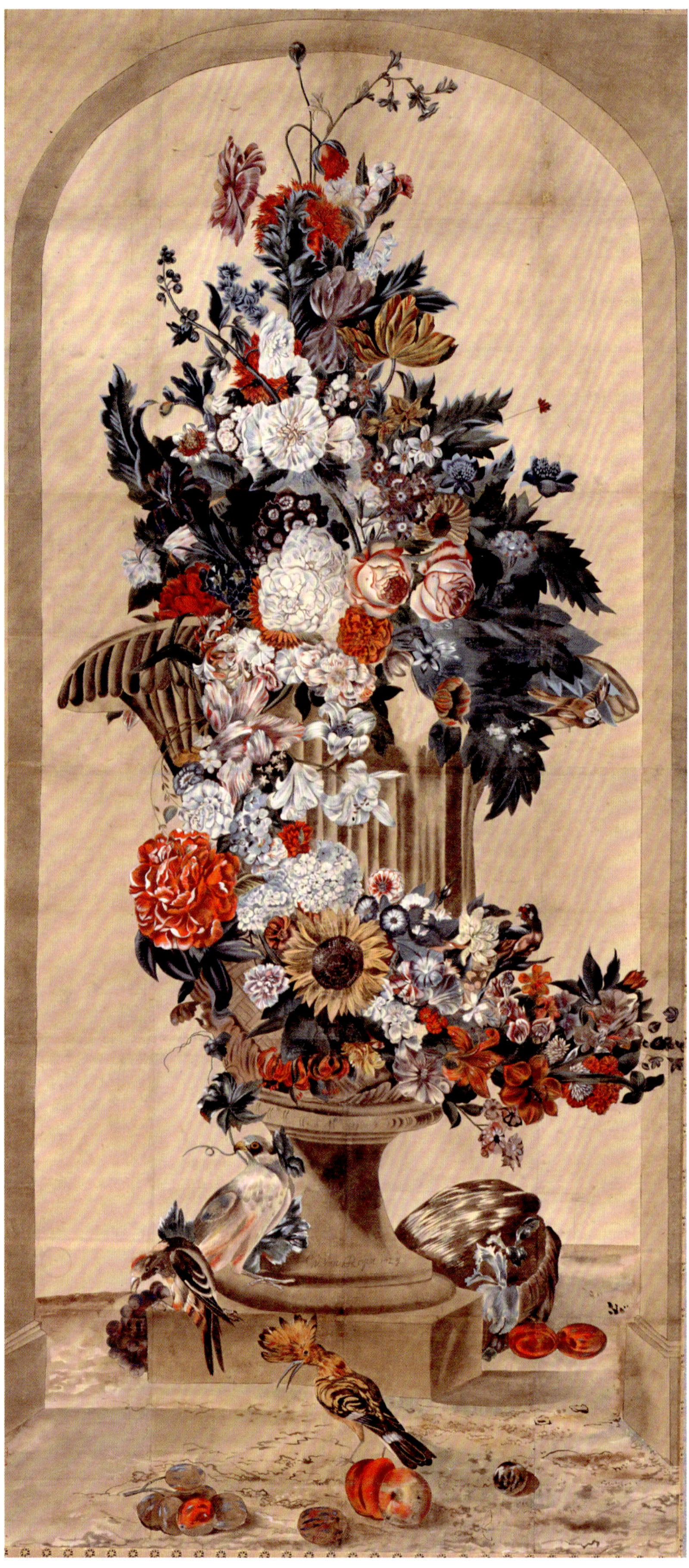

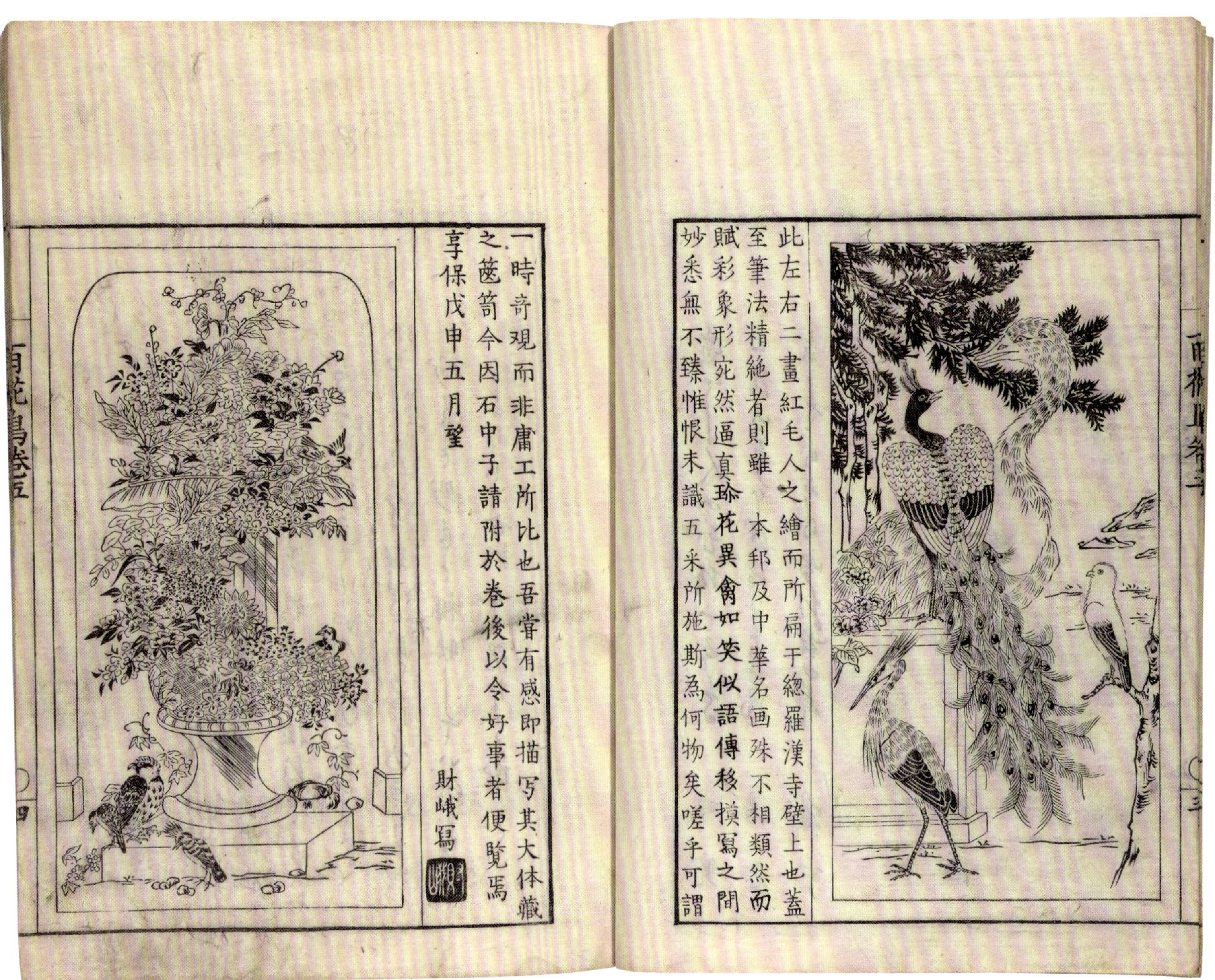

此左右二畫紅毛人之繪而所扁于總羅漢寺壁上也蓋
至筆法精絶者則雖 本邦及中華名画殊不相類然而
賦彩象形宛然逼真珎花異禽如笑似語傳移摸寫之間
妙悉無不臻惟恨未識五采所施斯為何物矣嗟乎可謂

一時奇観而非庸工所比也吾嘗有感即描写其大体藏
之篋笥今因石中子請附於巻後以令好事者便覧焉
享保戊申五月望
財峨寫

Fig. 6
Sekichūshi, copies of Willem Hendrik van Royen's paintings displayed at Gohyakurakanji, from *Illustrations of One Hundred Flowers and Birds* (*Gazu hyakkachō*), vol. 5. Japan, Edo period, 1729. Woodblock-printed book (5 vols.); ink on paper; 27.4 × 19.1 × 0.9 cm (each).

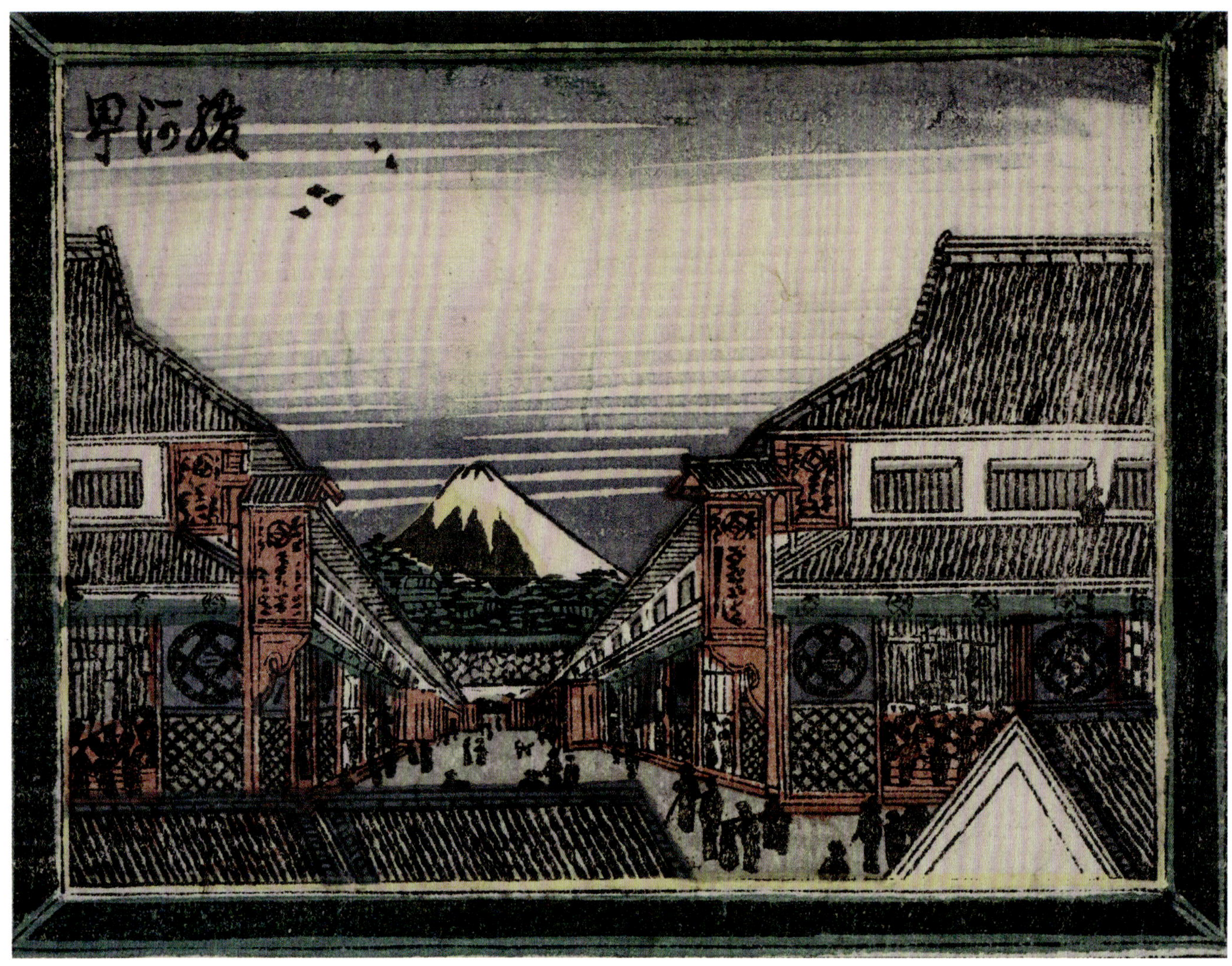

Fig. 7a
Katsushika Hokusai, *Suruga-chō*, from the series *The Dutch Picture Lens: Eight Views of Edo*. Edo period, ca. 1802. Woodblock print; ink and color on paper; 8.6 × 11.4 cm.

the temple, he donated them to Gohyakurakanji. As the only Western oil paintings on public display throughout the Edo period, they were a destination for Japanese artists studying Western representational styles, who studied them in the hopes of learning exotic methods of compositional framing and technique (fig. 5).[9] They also became a tourist attraction, and their compositions were disseminated widely through reproductions in printed books (fig. 6).[10]

Although we cannot be sure if Hokusai himself made a visit to see the paintings, he was undoubtedly a student of Western perspectival techniques. In 1802, Hokusai designed a set of eight diminutive prints showing major Edo landmarks, *The Dutch Picture Lens: Eight Views of Edo* (*Oranda gakyō Edo hakkei* 阿蘭陀画鏡江戸八景) (fig. 7a). Despite being executed in woodblock, the images emulate the aesthetic of the Dutch copperplate prints circulating in Japan at the time, imitating the straight carved lines characteristic of the copperplate technique. The first copperplates in Japan were made by Shiba Kōkan 司馬江漢 (1747–1818), an artist and scholar of Dutch learning who was known to Hokusai through their mutual publisher and acquaintance, Tsutaya

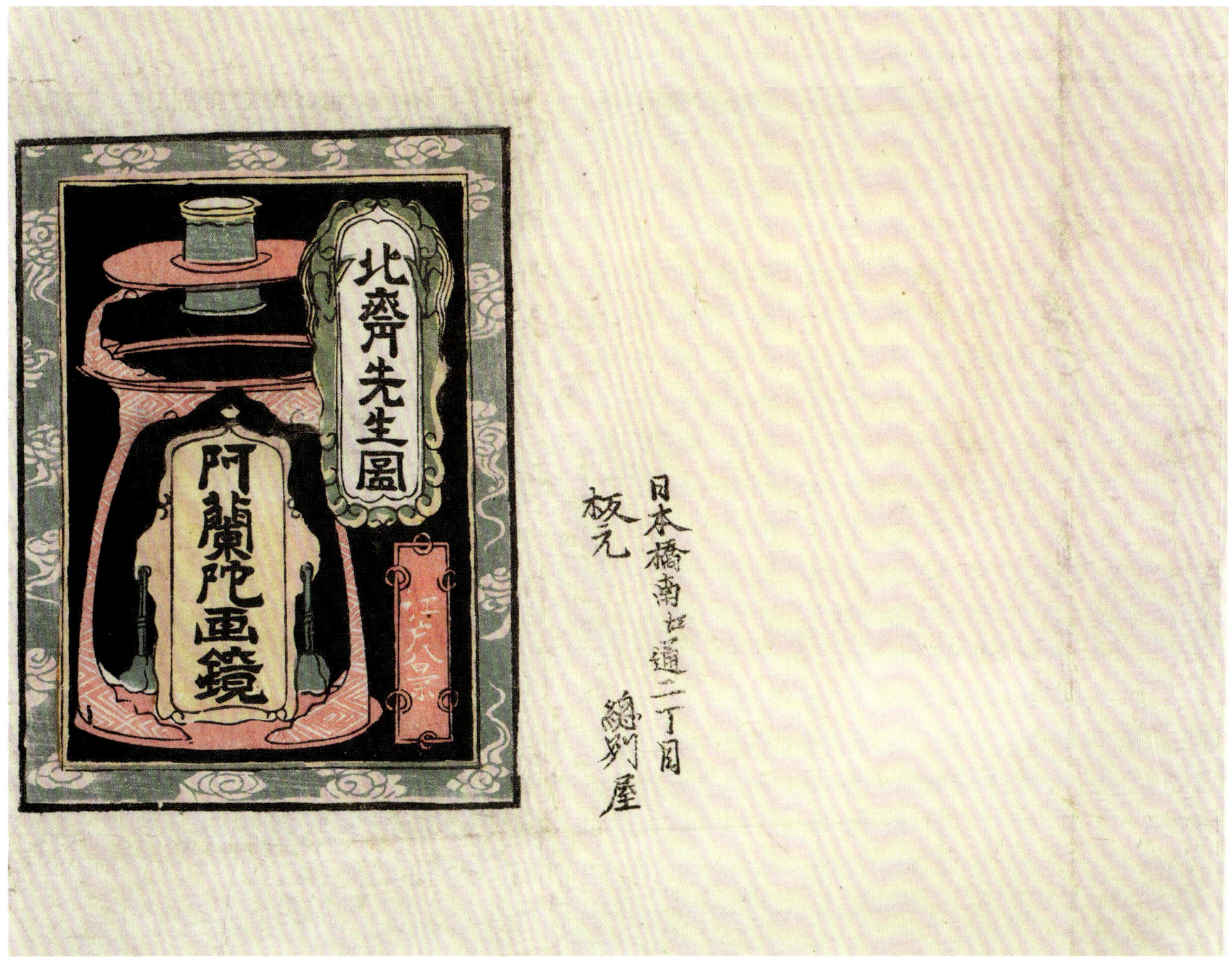

Jūzaburō 蔦屋重三郎 (1750–1797). Hokusai followed Kōkan in signing and titling some of his Dutch-style works by writing the characters horizontally so that they resembled Western alphabets. The wrapper for *The Dutch Picture Lens* set is illustrated with a Western microscope, indicating that its contents will evoke these foreign ways of seeing (fig. 7b). Thirty years later, these perspectival techniques were masterfully deployed in *The Sazaidō of Gohyakurakanji* (see **perspective**).

Fig. 7b
Katsushika Hokusai, wrapper for the series *The Dutch Picture Lens: Eight Views of Edo*. Edo period, ca. 1802. Woodblock print; ink and color on paper; 18.4 × 22.5 cm.

Although not evident at first glance, all these references are latent in Hokusai's print: the pronounced vanishing point perspective associated with Western representational methods, the far-off lands of India and ancient buddhas that lie underfoot, and the exotic and contorted features of the arhats that gave the famous temple its name and raison d'être. These resonances lurk beneath the printed surface of Hokusai's composition, but because of the temple's renown and associations, they would have been an essential embedded component of a contemporary viewer's experience of the print. Far from a "representative" example of a Japanese landscape view, the site specificity in *The Sazaidō of Gohyakurakanji* is multilayered, omnipresent, and unique.

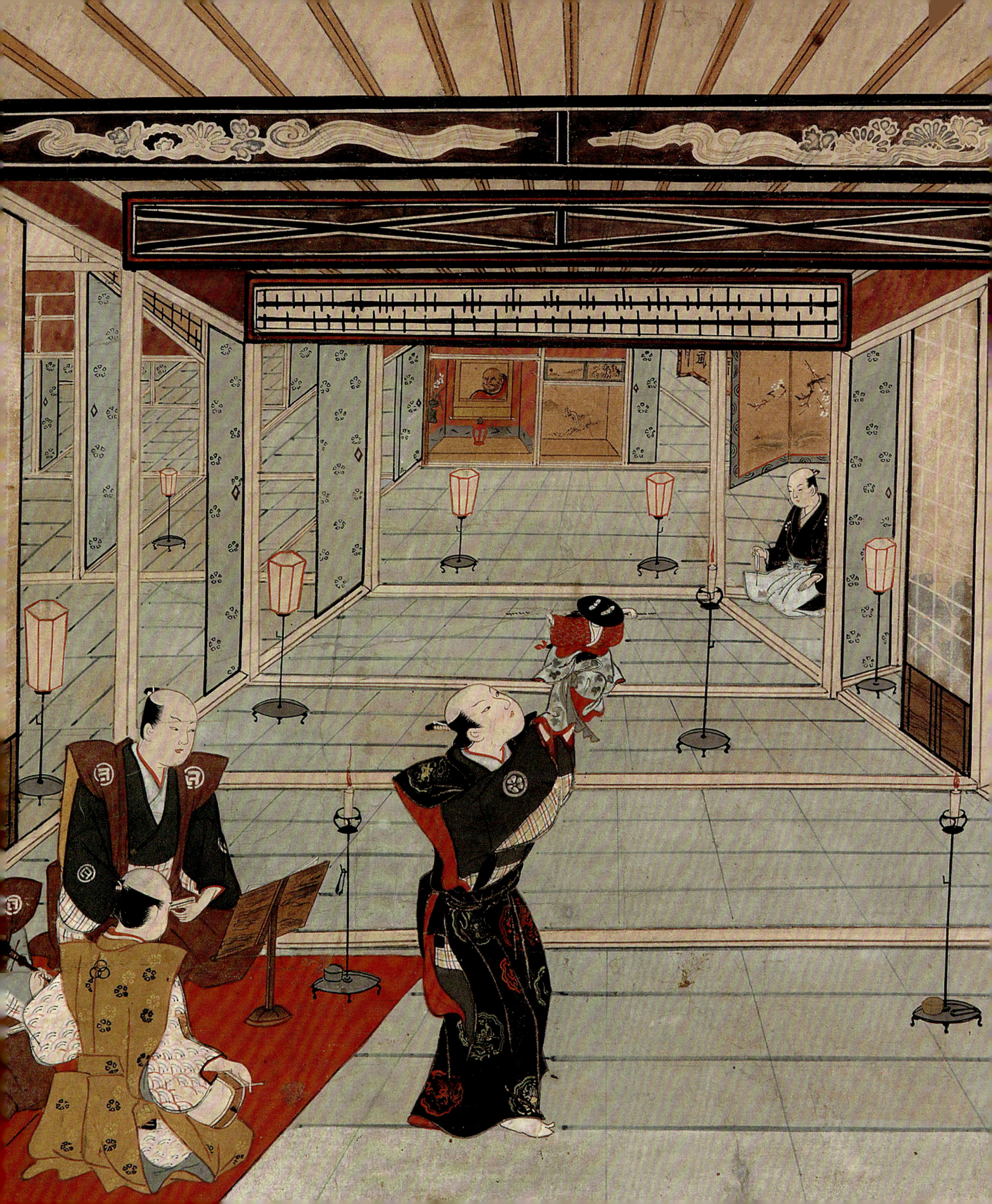

PERSPECTIVE

How effective is the use of perspective in Hokusai's print? Previous—and subsequent—depictions of Gohyakurakanji did not place the same subjective emphasis on the view *from* the temple as did Hokusai's unique composition in *The Sazaidō of Gohyakurakanji*. The "standard" depiction gives a more traditional view *of* the temple, with an overview of different buildings in the complex, crowds of worshipper-tourists, refreshment stands outside the gates, and rice fields beyond (fig. 1). Depicting the site provided artists with disparate compositional elements—height, distance, crowds, and a vacant expanse—with which they could experiment using various colors and perspectival arrangements to create different senses of mood and positionality. Hokusai was particularly talented at rendering landscape scenes in his print compositions, demonstrating a refined understanding of how to adapt the flat color fields of the ukiyo-e woodblock print style to provide a more convincing sense of perspective and spatial positioning than had been achieved in previous generations.

The sophisticated use of perspective in Hokusai's later work is attributable to decades of experimentation and adaptation by the ukiyo-e community. Okumura Masanobu 奥村政信 (1686–1764) was an early pioneer of landscape prints who claimed to be the inventor of the *uki-e* 浮絵, literally "floating pictures." Although terminologically similar to the broader genre of ukiyo-e 浮世絵 (literally "pictures of the floating world"), the designator *uki-e* captures a feeling—the unusual sensation experienced by the viewer when looking at this type of image, where the use of vanishing point perspective emphasizes the proportions of the scene to an uncomfortable degree (fig. 2). Intended to have a slightly bizarre or uncanny effect, these works create implausible spaces with an exaggerated sense of depth. The forced use of perspective is especially jarring when two distinct spaces are shown in a single view, such as semiprivate interiors juxtaposed with surrounding landscape elements (fig. 3). In depicting the background, which lacked the supporting guidelines provided by beams, floorboards, and tatami floor mats, Masanobu seems to have struggled to reconcile the more amorphous contours

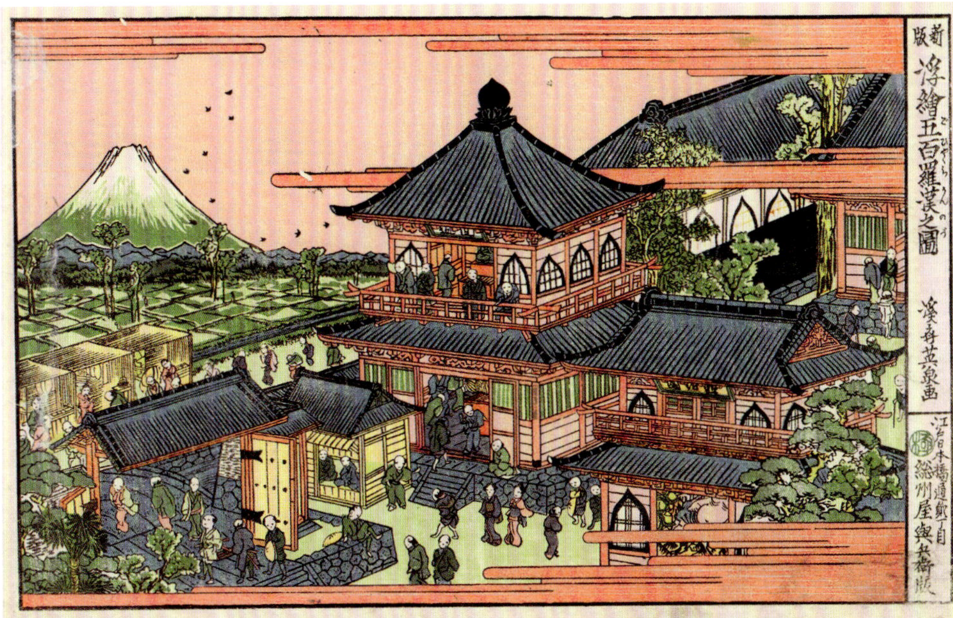

Fig. 1
Keisai Eisen, *Picture of the Temple of the Five Hundred Arhats* (*Gohyakurakan no zu*), from the series *New Edition of Perspective Pictures* (*Shinpan uki-e*). Japan, Edo period, ca. 1811. Woodblock print; ink and color on paper; 25.9 × 37.2 cm.

Detail of fig. 2

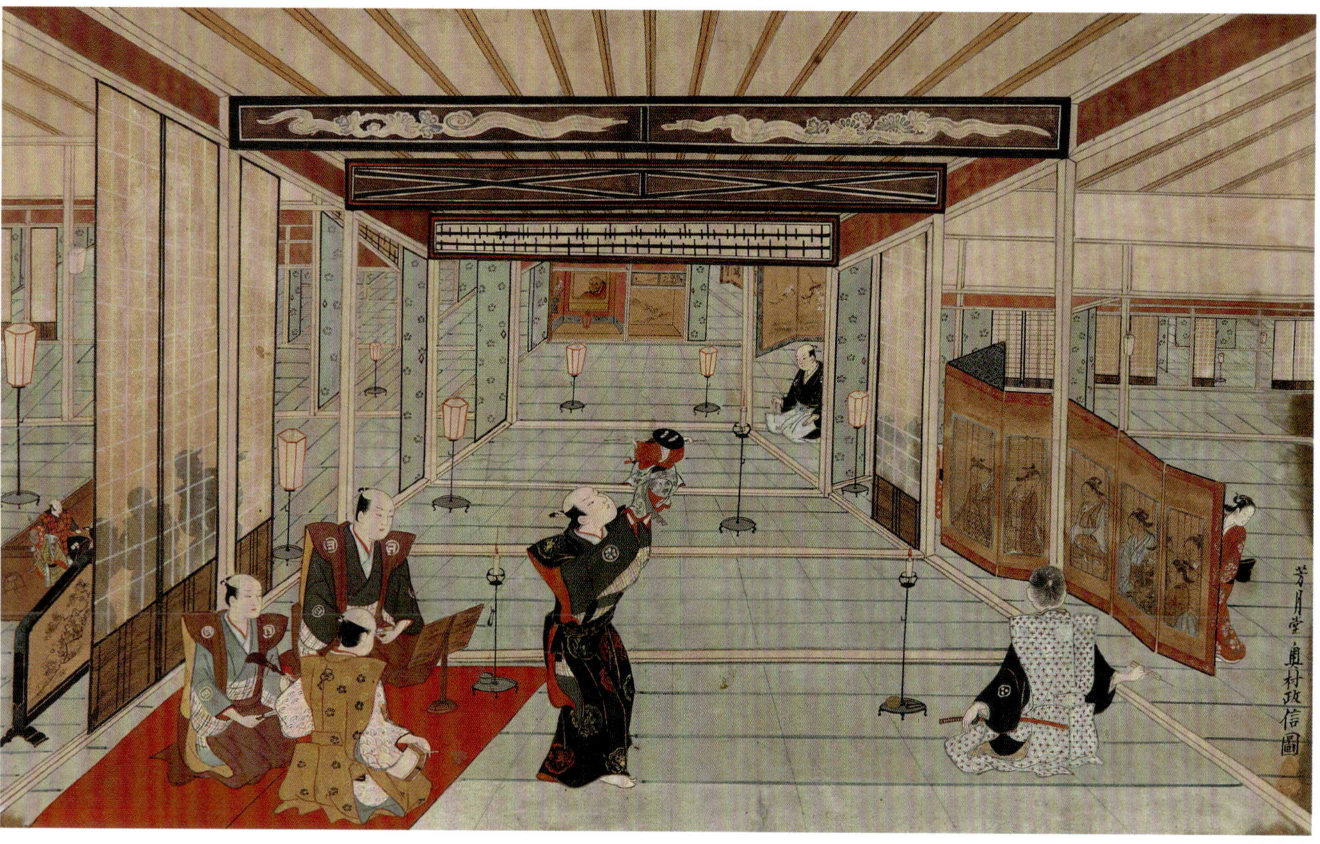

Fig. 2
Okumura Masanobu, *A Private Puppet Performance*. Japan, Edo period, 18th century. Color on paper; 54.5 × 92.8 cm.

of nature with the regimented architectural elements of the interior. Nonetheless, this disjunction serves a conceptual function: it reinforces the division between private and public in the image, established by the low railing and separating a more intimate group gathering from the bustling crowds in the city beyond.

Working almost a century after Masanobu, Hokusai would grow to be much more nuanced in his use of perspective. Some of Hokusai's earliest-known commercial prints, produced while he was using the name Shunrō 春朗 from the age of twenty to thirty-five, were *uki-e*.[11] He remained interested in systems of perspective; one of his associates, the popular fiction author Ryūtei Tanehiko 柳亭種彦 (1783–1842), mentions in an 1810 diary entry that Hokusai demonstrated to him the use of a "Dutch mathematical device."[12] It has been speculated that this device may have been a drafting instrument such as a square or a compass, or another kind of calculation apparatus in Hokusai's possession. While we cannot confirm the extent of his use of such a tool, in the context of Hokusai's numerous geometrical diagrams, the diary entry supports his awareness of, and interest in, perspectival mechanisms (fig. 4). Hokusai also sought to transmit this heightened understanding to other artists and the public, and he produced several works for such a purpose.[13] The *Hokusai Manga*, his fifteen-volume compendium of sketches that also partially served as an instructional guide, included diagrams that demonstrated the use of perspective. Also, his 1836 manual *Picture Book of New Patterns for Various Trades* (*Shoshoku ehon shin hinagata* 諸職絵本新鄙形) focused on techniques for drawing architecture according to proper scale.

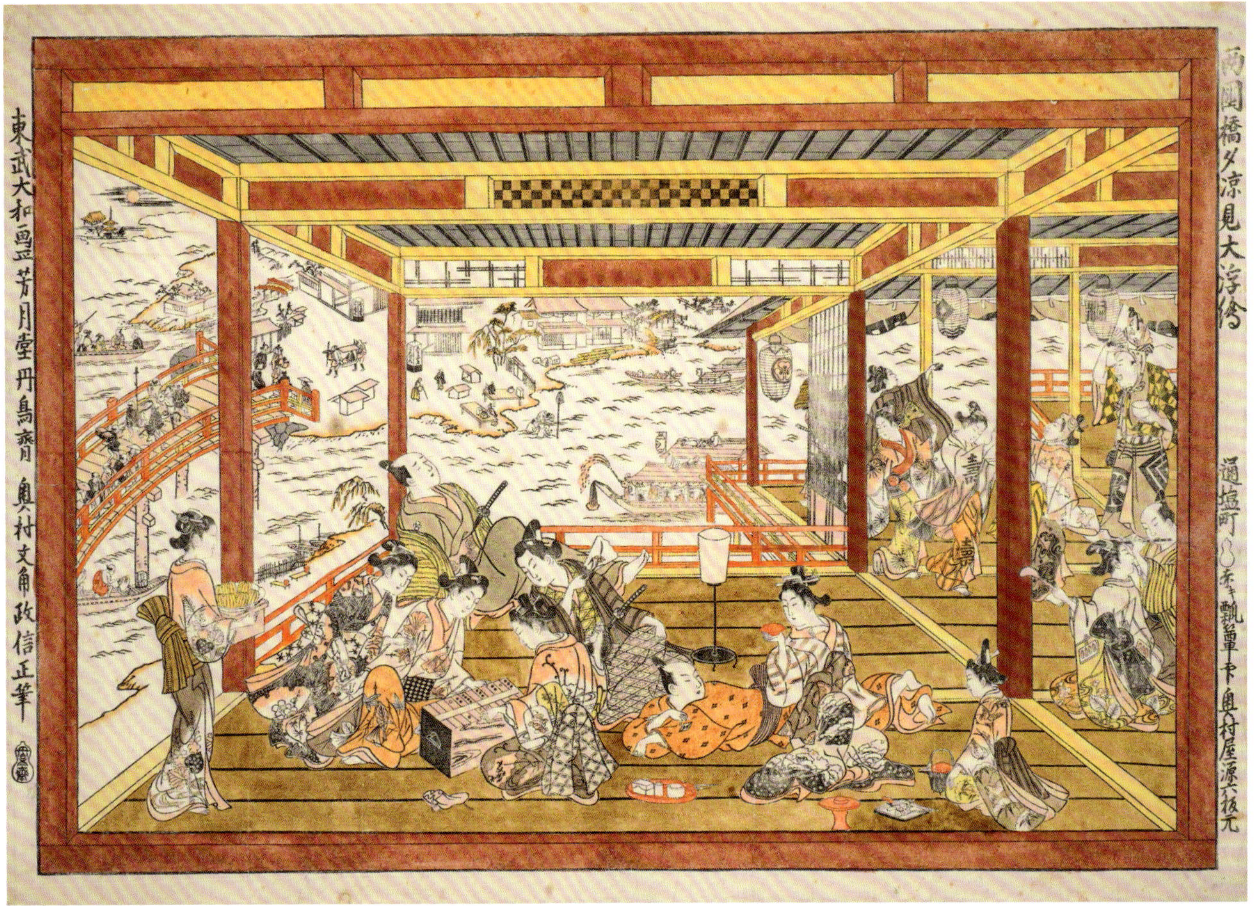

Fig. 3
Okumura Masanobu, *Large Perspective Picture of Evening Cool by Ryōgoku Bridge* (*Ryōgokubashi yūsuzumi ōuki-e*). Edo period, ca. 1748. Hand-colored woodblock print; 46.5 × 63.3 cm.

Conventions of perspective were available to art-consuming audiences in various forms. Whereas the drawings in the *Manga* taught novice artists how to make flat renderings appear three-dimensional, printed dioramas known as "construction prints" (*tatebanko* 立版古), which recreated kabuki plays, famous places, and historical episodes, illuminated the process in the opposite direction. Hokusai designed several *tatebanko* earlier in his career (fig. 5). Developed in the nineteenth century, these types of "do-it-yourself" dioramas are still popular papercraft items today.[14] *Tatebanko* were printed in sections, often across multiple sheets, to be cut out and assembled by the consumer. Printed on thin paper, they need to be pasted onto a thicker support before constructing the diorama. The final appearance of the scene is helpfully printed in miniature on one of the sheets as a vignette to guide the assembly (see **remix**).

The prevalence of consumer objects like *tatebanko*, *uki*-e, and Hokusai's best-selling instructional manuals demonstrates that the average Edo resident in the nineteenth century was more acclimated to perspectival systems than is commonly assumed by Western audiences, who often attribute the flat pattern fields of Japanese prints to ignorance rather than preference. The Japanese use of perspective was not always scientifically calculated but depended on the genre and function of the image. This is one of the ways that many Japanese prints do not align with Western conventions of a

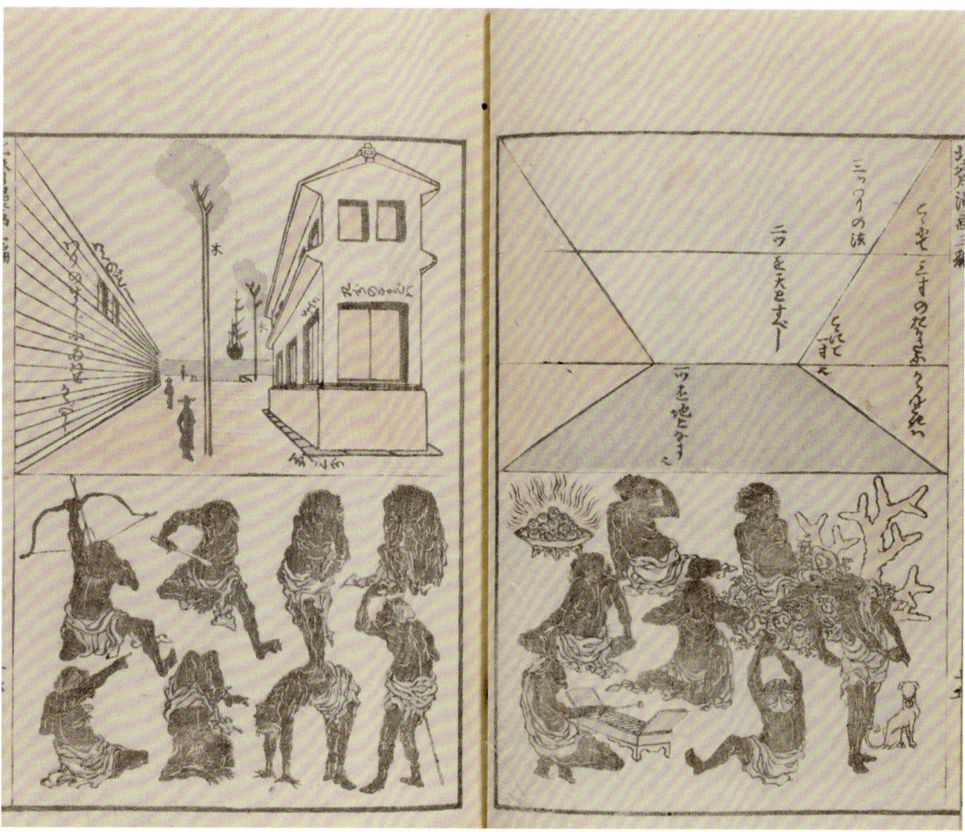

Fig. 4
Katsushika Hokusai, *Hokusai Manga*, vol. 3. Edo period, ca. 1850s. Woodblock-printed book (14 vols.); ink and color on paper; 22.9 × 15.9 × 1 cm.

"landscape" painting. The term often used in Japanese as an equivalent to "landscape picture" is *sansui-ga* 山水画. However, this term is conventionally applied to real and imagined topographies rendered as ink paintings, and not the scenes depicted in ukiyo-e prints. Instead, works like Hokusai's *The Sazaidō of Gohyakurakanji* were categorized as "famous place pictures," or *meisho-e*. "Famous places" (*meisho*) were locations where legendary events had occurred and classic poems had been composed; and depictions of these places were not conceived in a detached, naturalistic sense that emphasized the purely picturesque, but rather as a site of active, shared recollection.[15] Although ukiyo-e artists might have visited those sites in person, it is more common to find *meisho-e* compositions that are assemblages of images from well-known guidebooks or other preexisting visual media, rather than being based on plein-air sketches.

The different logic at work in *meisho-e* compared with Western landscapes went unrecognized from the very beginning of their appreciation in the West. For example, many *meisho* are included as a small inset picture, or *koma-e* こま絵, often designed by a student of the primary artist, that may appear to have only superficial connection to the subject of the main image (fig. 6). In the 1887 French novel *Madame Chrysanthème* by Pierre Loti, for example, *koma-e* are summarily dismissed as "incoherent and inappropriate."[16] It is easy to sympathize with this position: the inclusion of an elderly woman in a series of beauty prints may indeed seem incongruous for a viewer unaware of Gohyakurakanji, pictured in the inset, and its sculptures. However, the older woman here is a reference to the wizened forms of the arhats that reside *within*

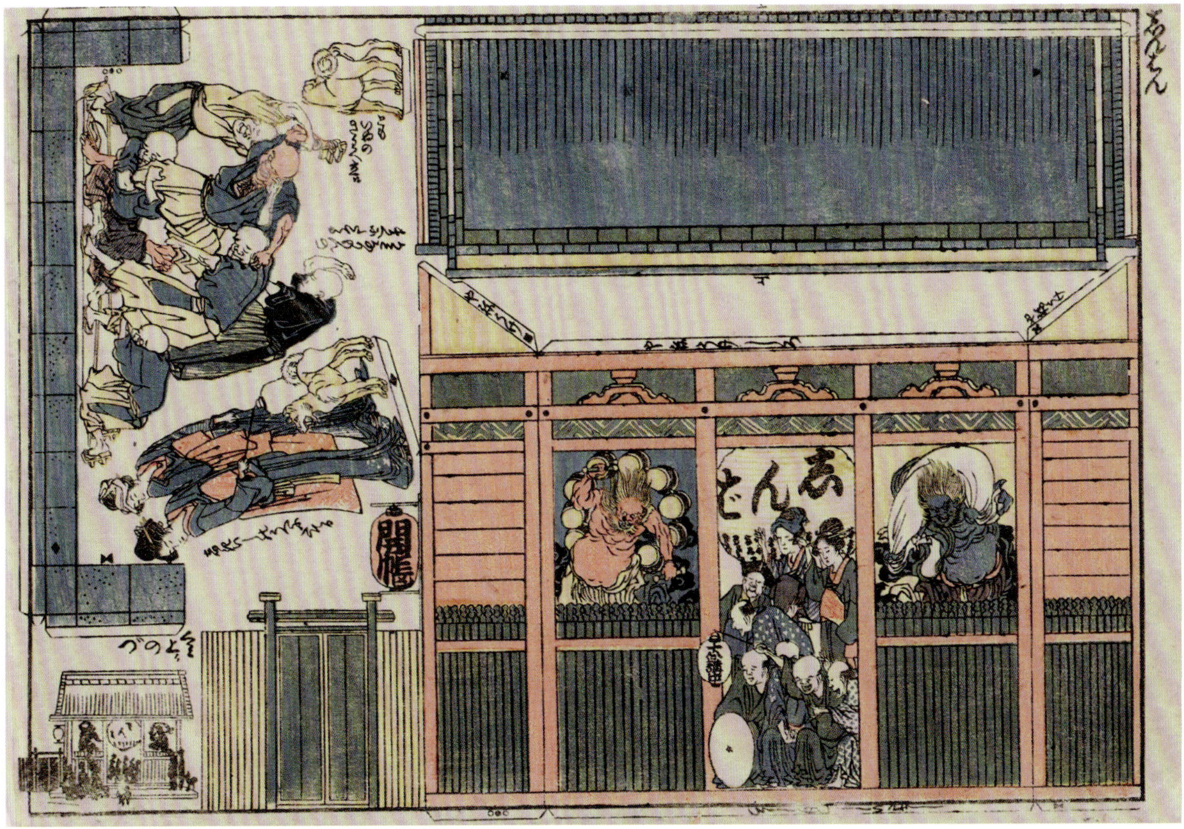

the temple, which would have been known to every Edo resident (see **site**, **figure**). While old age might await the statuesque beauty by her side, so, too, might rebirth in a paradisical afterlife. Although such insertions of miniature landscapes, famous food products, or other still life assemblages may seem disconsonant to viewers more familiar with the conventions of Western painting, they demonstrate the essence of *meisho-e* as opposed to a naturalistic landscape—targeting points of cultural interest rather than notions of the picturesque for their own sake. Instead, *meisho-e* locations all but vibrate with collective memory, a set of associations inherited and reinforced through generations of image making, poetry, and storytelling. Certain established ways of representing specific locations were more important for the audience's ability to recognize the subject-location than a strict adherence to the physical contours of the topography in a photorealistic sense.

Fig. 5
Katsushika Hokusai, single sheet from *The Kaminarimon at Asakusa Sensōji* (*Asakusa Sensōji no Kaminarimon*). Edo period, ca. 1808–1813. Woodblock print; ink and color on paper; 24.4 × 36.6 cm.

If *meisho* were repositories of social memory, the final form that a *meisho-e* took was shaped by the sensitivities, proclivities, and abilities of the particular artist responsible. Despite the disorienting effects sometimes produced by the use of perspective in some examples of ukiyo-e, *The Sazaidō of Gohyakurakanji* uses both perspective and *meisho-e* elements more subtly. The view from the balcony may be novel, yet the image is still embedded with the recognizable elements of the temple site. The elevated platform providing a view of distant Mount Fuji and the group of tourists is the most obvious marker, but the two seated figures in the lower right also allude to the experience of visiting the temple. Unburdening themselves of heavy

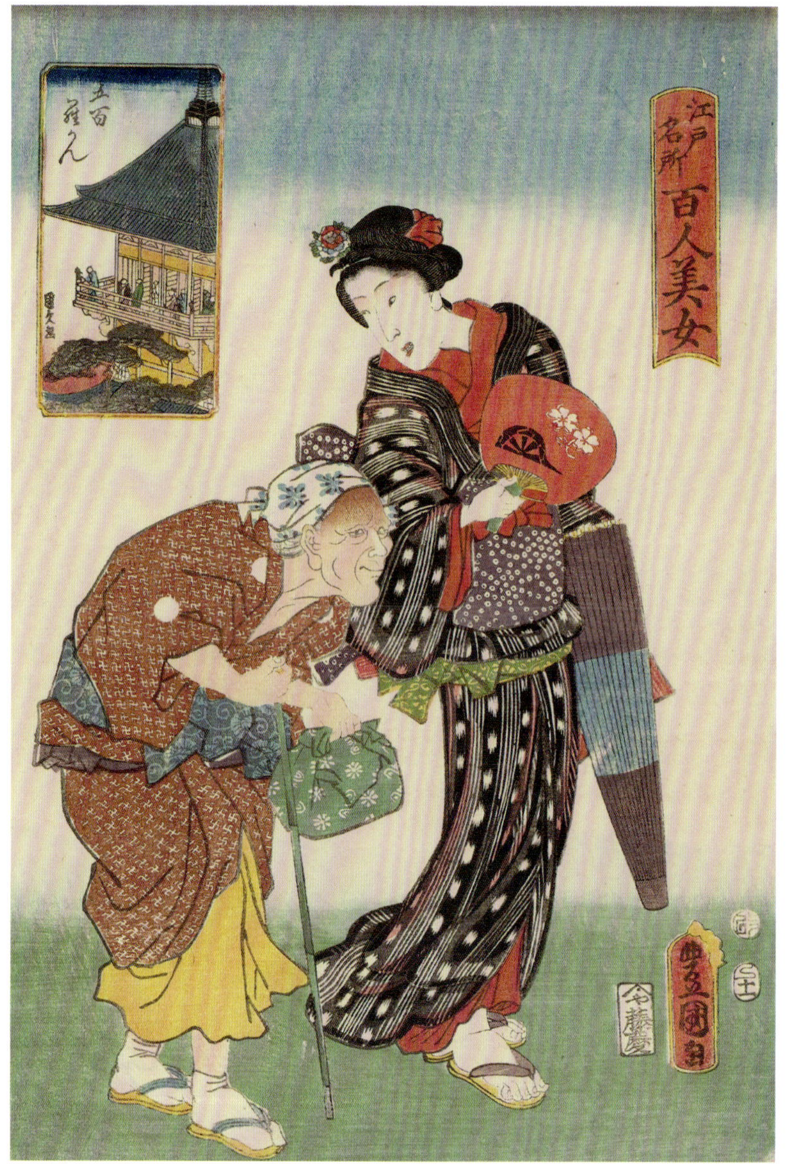

Fig. 6
Utagawa Kunisada, *The Temple of the Five Hundred Arhats* (*Gohyaku rakan*), from the series *One Hundred Beautiful Women at Famous Places in Edo* (*Edo meisho hyakunin bijo*). Japan, Edo period, 1857, 11th month. Woodblock print; ink and color on paper; 37.1 × 25.2 cm.

Fig. 7
Katsushika Hokusai, *Fuji from Rakanji* (*Rakanji no Fuji*), from *One Hundred Views of Mount Fuji* (*Fugaku hyakkei*), vol. 3. Edo period, ca. 1849. Woodblock-printed book (3 vols.); ink on paper; 22.9 × 15.8 × 0.8 cm.

backpacks, these figures are stand-ins for the pilgrims resting along the actual pilgrimage routes that the scaled dioramas inside the temple halls reproduced in miniature (see **restriction**). The shape of the small bronze bell that hangs from the rafters recalls the finial that adorned the top of the Sazaidō, a known feature that challenged the dizzying heights of Mount Fuji itself (fig. 7). Understanding the full context for *The Sazaidō of Gohyakurakanji* reveals not only the adoption of geometric perspectival systems, but also the personal perspectives and expectations of Hokusai himself and his audiences when viewing ukiyo-e "landscapes."

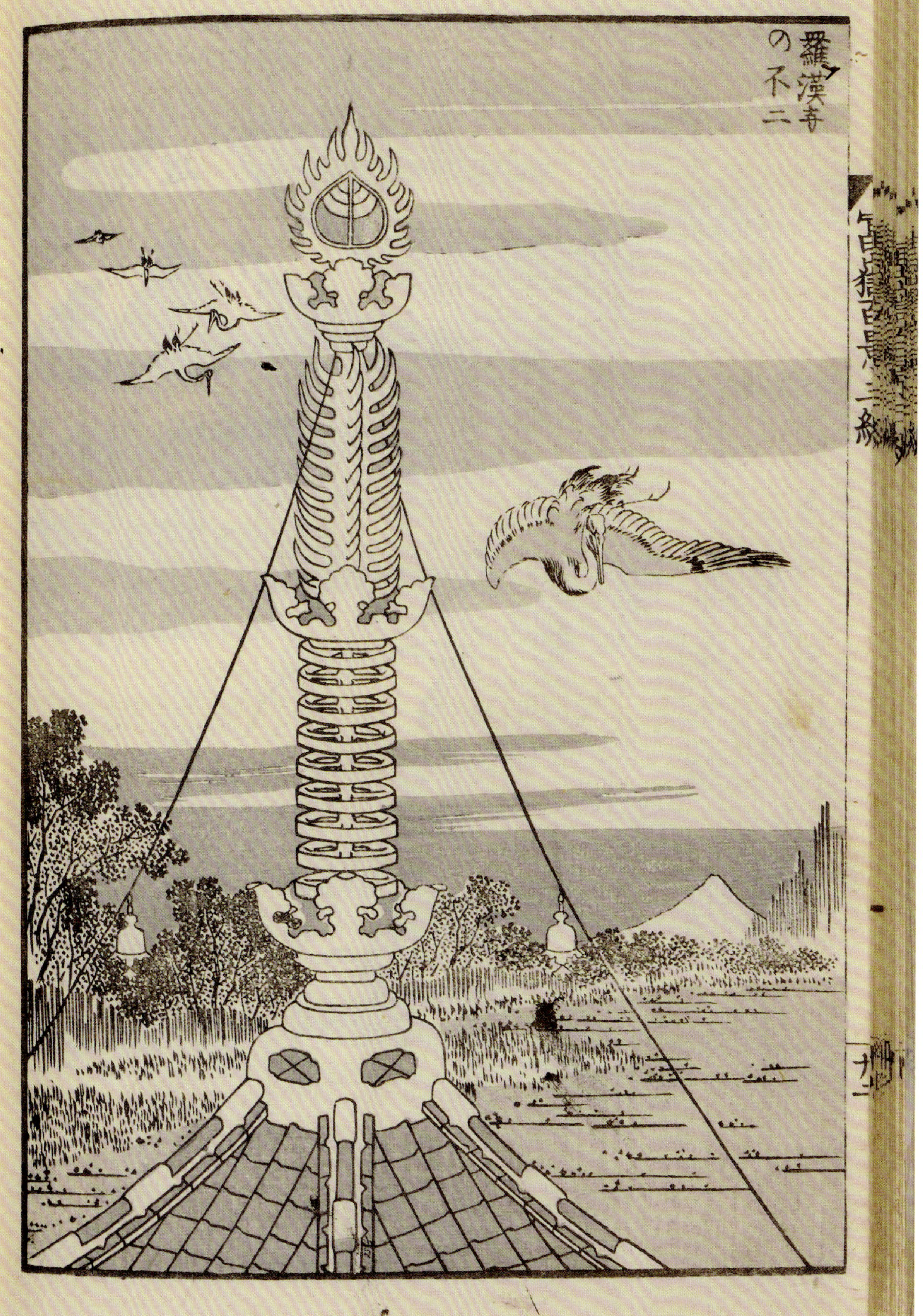
羅漢寺の不二

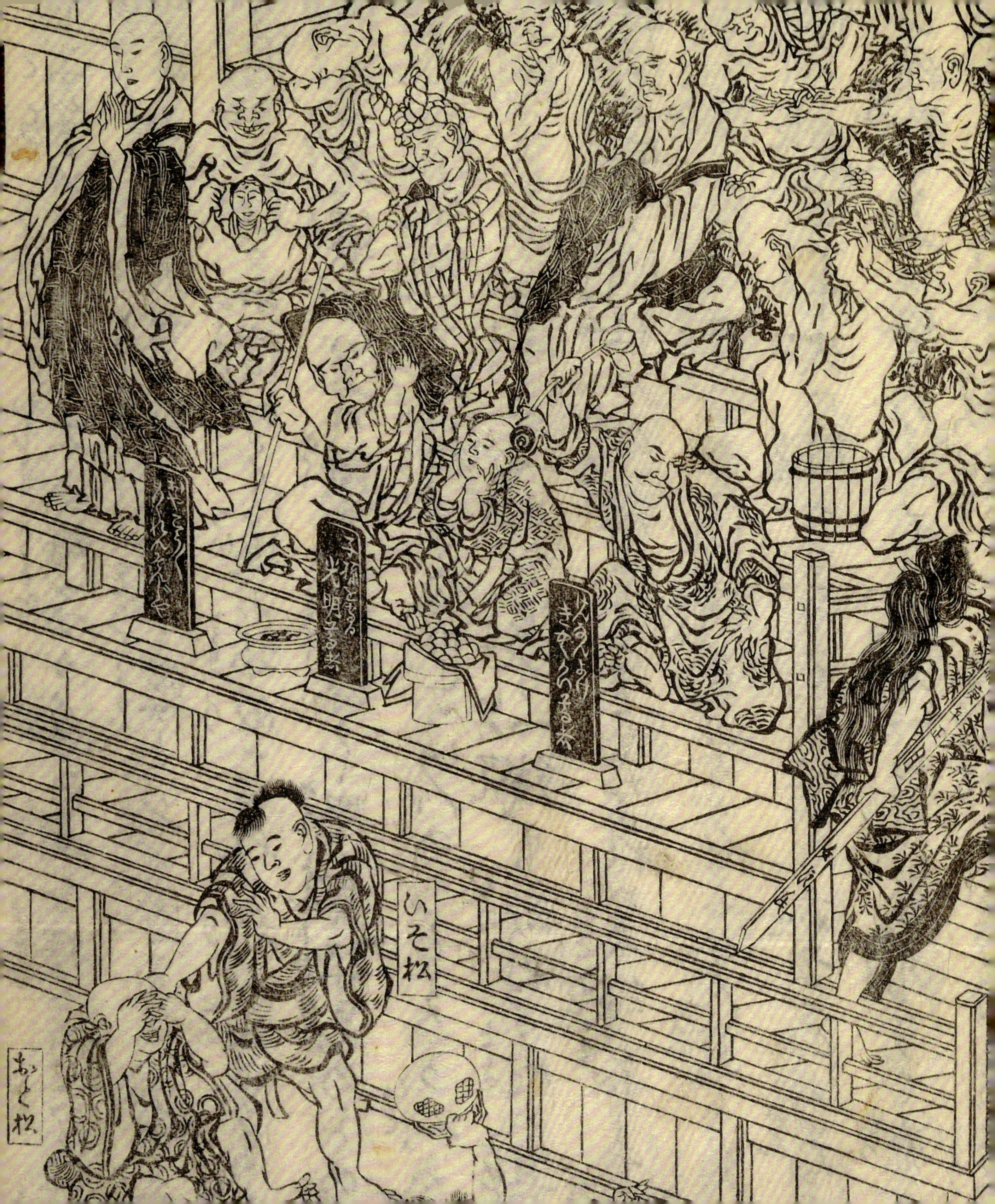
ひそ松
おとく松

FIGURE

How much does an artist's persona factor into our understanding of a work? In terms of the architecture represented in *The Sazaidō of Gohyakurakanji* and the style of its composition, the spectacle within the print is attributable to two very public figures: the monk Shōun Genkei, who was credited with realizing the temple and its sculptures, and Katsushika Hokusai, the print's designer. The temple and the extraordinary sculptures it contained were so famous that for any viewer in Hokusai's day, the print would have immediately called to mind the monumental tableau that lay beneath the balcony, even though it was not depicted (see **site**). Both Shōun and Hokusai were known for their outsized artistic accomplishments; those reputations may have created a notional link in the mind of a viewer of the *Gohyakurakanji* print, connecting the grandeur of the location with the ingenuity of Hokusai's artistry. In his own time, Hokusai's reputation was somewhat different than it is in the twenty-first century, and many viewers then would have also known him as a performance painter of enormous Buddhist artworks. Though no Buddhist images are explicitly shown in the image, their presence—and the presence of their creators—are latent in the composition.

It is unquestionable that the five hundred arhat sculptures that gave the Gohyakurakanji temple complex its name were the product of Shōun's singular vision. The popular narrative during the Edo period—and still today—was that Shōun's devotion and commitment enabled him to complete this feat by his hands alone, carving all five hundred life-sized arhat sculptures himself.[17] However, it is likely that they were constructed at least partially with the assistance of a workshop that operated under his supervision. Like his father, Shōun had trained as a Buddhist sculptor in the classic style associated with his birthplace, Kyoto, whose sculptures are characterized by perfectly balanced proportions, rounded limbs, and an aura of tranquility. After his conversion to the Ōbaku sect in his early twenties, Shōun incorporated some of the aesthetics and techniques introduced to Japan by Chinese émigré monk-sculptors from that tradition into his own practices; these would later be deployed in Edo for the construction of the Gohyakurakanji figures. Over three hundred of the sculptures remain: 305 examples are found at the modern-day incarnation of the original Gohyakurakanji (now located in Tokyo's Meguro district), with others in international collections. In keeping with the conventional manner of representing arhats, each figure has decidedly grotesque features, such as long fingernails and toenails, ragged clothing, and gaunt physiques with protruding ribs (fig. 1a–d). Despite their apparently individualized appearances, the sculptures' sheer number and scale were made possible by their manufacture in modular fashion: pre-carved arms, torsos, legs, and heads were connected using joined woodblock construction (*yosegi zukuri* 寄木作り), a technique of mass sculpture production practiced in Japan since the late tenth century.

The arhats would have appeared exotic to their audiences in Edo not only because of their "foreign" physical attributes but also as a result of an unusual surface technique of lacquer decoration, *qixiandiao* 漆線彫 (literally "lacquer wire sculpting"), which has recently been identified by the art historian Yan Yang as originating in the Fujian region of China.[18] Several of the 311 extant arhat sculptures display remnants of *qixiandiao*, as a stylized, high-relief patternation used on the figures' robes (fig. 2). For this technique, lacquer, powdered clay, and tung oil are kneaded to form a very firm dough. The mixture is then rolled into a thin tube and sculpted by coiling and molding

Detail of fig. 3

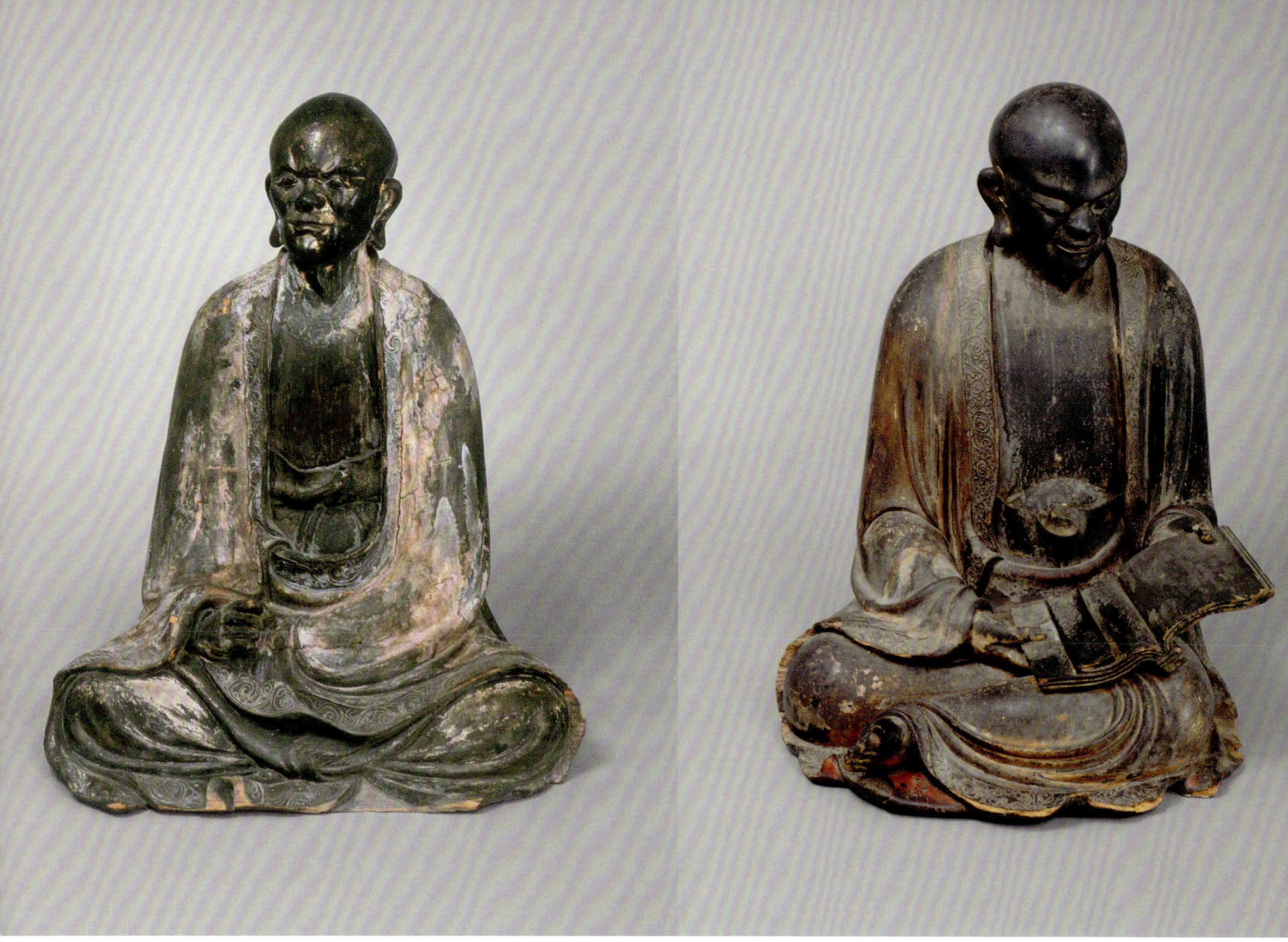

Fig. 1a–c
Arhats (Holy Men), three from the *Five Hundred Arhats*. Japan, Edo period, 1684–1695. Wood, dry lacquer, and gold, with colors (applied later); 81.3 × 61 × 58.4 cm (approx. each).

before being gilded. This rare technique, which was apparently so exotic that there was no Japanese terminological equivalent for it, would have emphasized the sense of the foreign and the strange, an effect that would have seemed almost overwhelming when a visitor stood before the five hundred sculptures, all contained within a single room on a tiered dais. For the figures depicted in *The Sazaidō of Gohyakurakanji*, a view of this diorama would have been their primary motivation for visiting the temple and the experience that contemporary viewers of the print would have immediately associated with the site depicted.

Prior to this design in the *Thirty-Six Views* series, Hokusai had depicted Gohyakurakanji several times, including both interior and exterior views. One particularly memorable interpretation that includes Shōun's sculptures is found in volume 5 of *The Mountains of Husband and Wife* (*On'yō imoseyama* 陈陜妹背山), a popular illustrated novel authored by Shinrotei 振鷺亭 (d. 1815) and published in 1810 (fig. 3). Originally written for the puppet theater but also performed as a kabuki play, this six-volume text tells the story of two lovers from rivaling families and the internecine, political, and even supernatural obstacles to their romance. Clearly showing the tiered

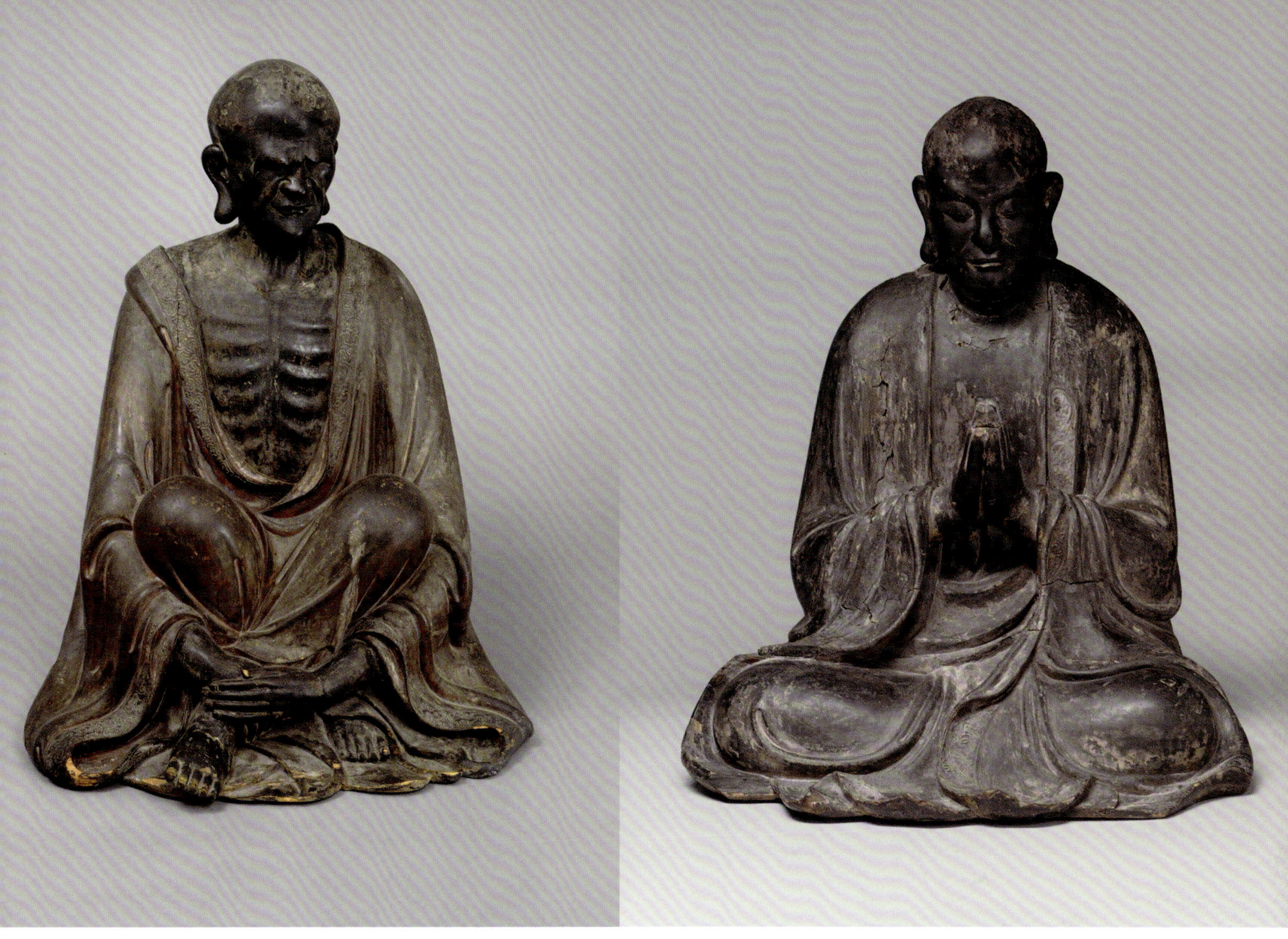

structure of the display platform in the Rakandō, the Hall of the Arhats, this scene shows the characters gathered at Gohyakurakanji, where the sculptures have come to life to join in the melee. To Edo readers of this story who had visited the temple, their memory of seeing the human-sized sculptures with their individualized features and the naturalistic folds of their delicately rendered clothing would have made the likelihood of the sculptures coming to life seem even more plausible. It is as though the sculptures were just waiting for a spark to animate them, given here by Hokusai as if he had the power to make them come alive.

Today, Hokusai is one of the best-known artists in the world, a reputation crystalized by another print from the *Thirty-Six Views* series, commonly known as *The Great Wave*. His international recognition began early, as his *Hokusai Manga* was known in Europe already in the mid-nineteenth century. His global renown was built upon his domestic reputation as a skilled artist who could capture facial expressions in only a few strokes. His flora and fauna studies were appropriated by many European craftspersons working within the idiom of Japonisme and were used as decorative motifs on dinnerware sets and other craft items. However, earlier in his career, Hokusai's

Fig. 1d
Shōun Genkei, *Seated Rakan (Arhat) from Ten'onzan Gohyaku Rakanji (Five Hundred Rakan Temple), Tokyo.* Japan, early Edo period, late 17th century. Wood, multiple-woodblock construction, with lacquer-applied gold leaf; 82.8 × 69 × 62.5 cm.

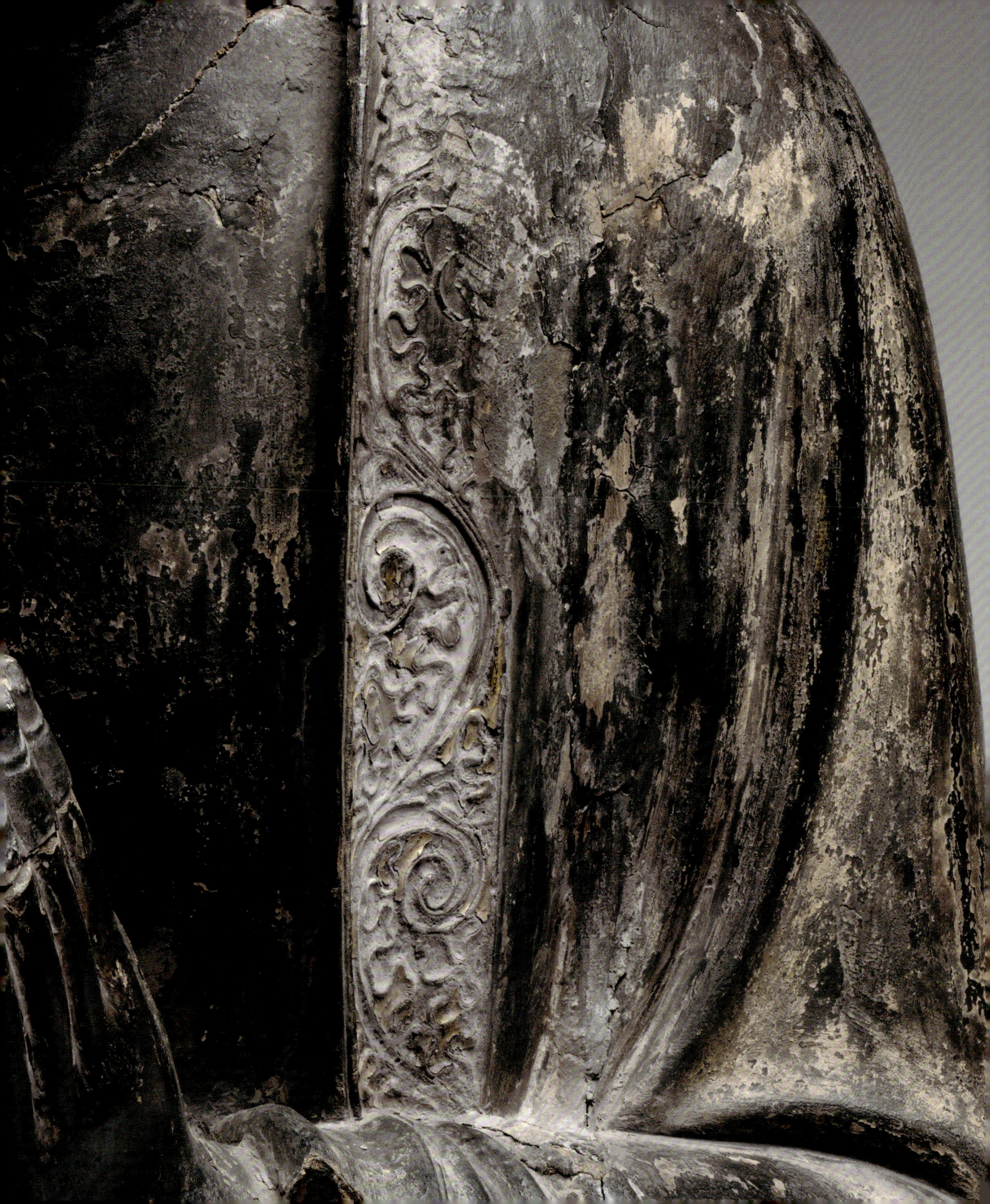

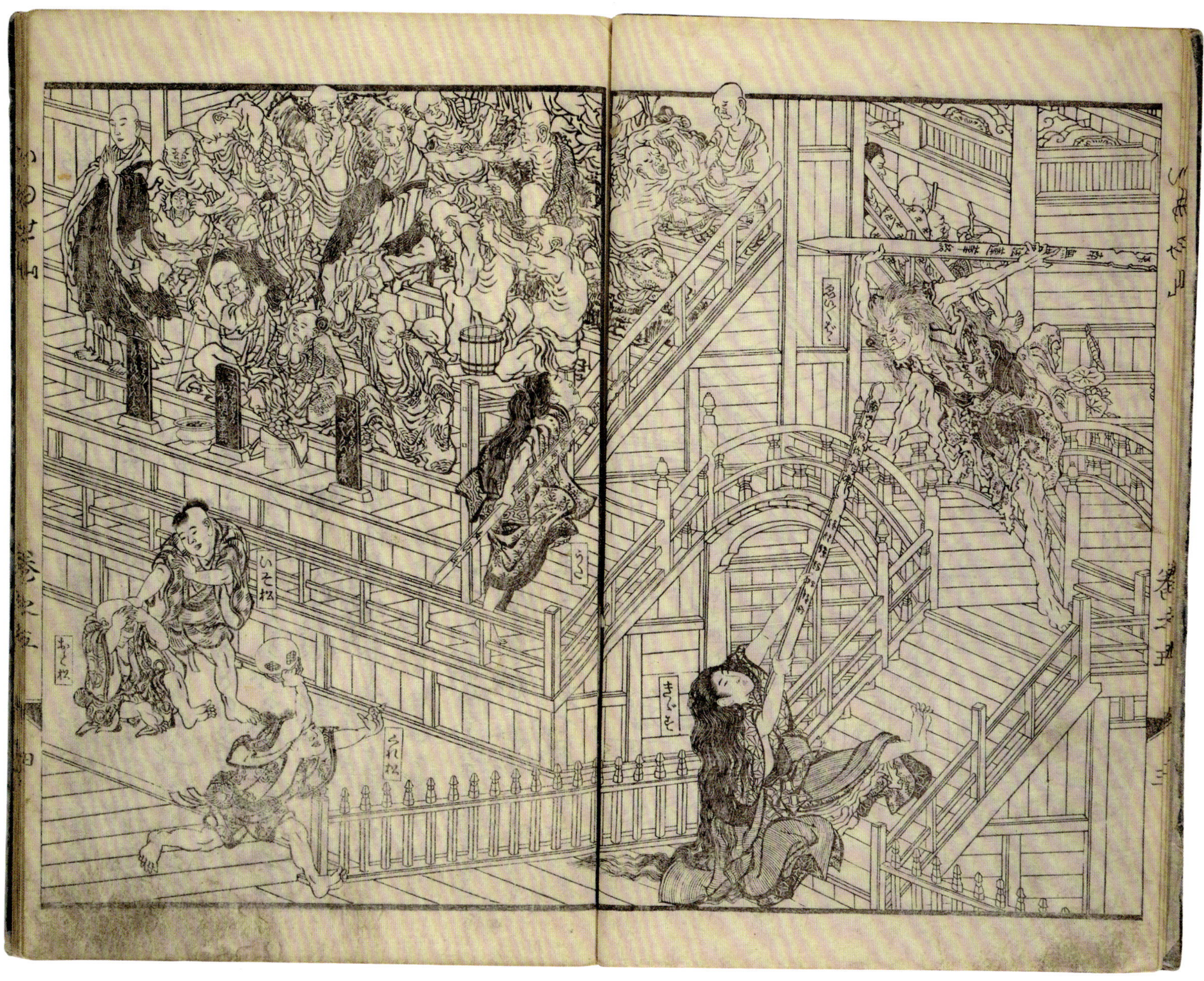

status in the Japanese public imagination was as an artist who, like Shōun, produced religious imagery on a grand scale. Though this phase of his life is less often recounted in modern biographies, which focus on his career as a print designer, during the early eighteenth century, Hokusai was famous for his oversized depictions of Bodhidharma, known as Daruma 達磨 in Japanese—the first Chinese patriarch of Zen Buddhism, the broader sect of which Ōbaku was one school. A semilegendary figure, Daruma is believed to have been born in Central Asia or the Indian subcontinent and is invariably depicted in Japanese art of this period with the thick body hair and bushy eyebrows that bodily identify him as of non-East Asian descent, and with voluminous bright red robes (fig. 4).

Also like Shōun, Hokusai had a larger-than-life public presence, and on two occasions—in 1804 at Gokokuji 護国寺 in Edo and in 1817 at Honganji 本願寺 in Nagoya—

Fig. 2
Shōun Genkei, *Seated Rakan* (detail).

Fig. 3
Katsushika Hokusai, *The Mountains of Husband and Wife*, vol. 5. Edo period, 1810. Woodblock-printed book (6 vols.); ink on paper; 22.8 × 15.8 cm.

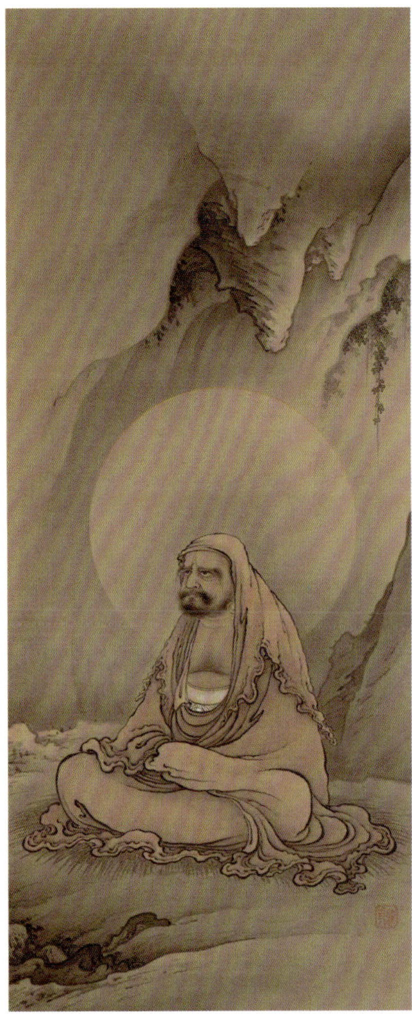

Fig. 4
Hashimoto Gahō, *Bodhidharma Seated in Meditation*. Japan, Meiji era, ca. 1885. Ink and tint on paper; 118.5 × 50.1 cm.

he painted enormous Daruma paintings before a large crowd as a type of performance art that built his reputation and renown. The 1817 event is better known as it was extensively recorded in Kōriki Enkōan's 高力猿猴庵 (1756–1831) manuscript *Detailed Illustrations of Hokusai's Large-Scale Sketches* (*Hokusai taiga sokusho saizu* 北斎大画即書細図) (1817), with some images reproduced in later printed volumes such as the *Famous Places in Owari Province* (*Owari meisho zue* 尾張名所図会) (fig. 5).[19] Hokusai's painting was performed on a paper surface measuring almost 200 square meters, and illustrated handbills promoting the event in advance boasted that each of Daruma's eyes would measure 180 centimeters wide, and that he would have a 270-centimeter-long nose, with a mouth of 210 centimeters across.[20] Hokusai used enormous brushes of bound straw to make the painting, and even an ink-soaked sack of rice dragged with a rope to give form to the monk's iconic robes. This later 1817 work was preserved until the destruction of Honganji during the bombing of Nagoya in World War II, when the work was lost.

Hokusai had an unconventional career path. He drew from an eclectic range of sources and styles, and ultimately established his own school—the Katsushika school. However, although Hokusai had several successful students, he did not build a multigenerational studio as did some other accomplished artists. Rather than achieving a manner of artistic immortality through a studio legacy, Hokusai was apparently more concerned with the process of self-actualization and the attainment of longevity through his own artistic practice (see **pigment**). It is known that he drew every day to hone his skills; but moreover, he believed such actions had an apotropaic function. For example, he regularly painted images of the demon-queller Shōki 鍾馗 in the belief that they would protect him against smallpox. He frequently gave himself new artistic sobriquets as he felt his abilities develop, constantly reflecting upon his level of artistic skill. A much-quoted passage taken from the colophon to the first volume of *One Hundred Views of Mount Fuji* (*Fugaku hyakkei* 富嶽百景) reads:

> From the age of six, I had a penchant for copying the form of things, and from about fifty, my pictures were frequently published; but until the age of seventy, nothing I drew was worthy of notice. At seventy-three years, I was somewhat able to fathom the growth of plants and trees, and the structure of birds, animals, insects, and fish.[21]

Passages like this show the persistent concern that plagued Hokusai over the course of a lifetime about his abilities. The specific age of seventy-three is, however, unusual enough that it seems significant. In premodern Japan, people were counted as one year old at the time of their birth, which means that Hokusai is referring to being seventy-two years of age by Western count. As Hokusai was born in 1760, he was seventy-two years of age in 1832—the same year that the *Thirty-Six Views of Mount Fuji* series was completed. We might then attribute particular significance to the work he accomplished at this time—like *The Sazaidō of Gohyakurakanji*—as marking a meaningful step in Hokusai's journey to self-creation and self-realization.

In his own lifetime, Hokusai's status as a public figure would have been a significant factor in viewers' appreciation of his artworks. As described above, by the mid-nineteenth century when *The Sazaidō of Gohyakurakanji* print was published, Hokusai had established a reputation for huge, dynamic performance paintings of the first Zen patriarch that earned him the nickname Daruma Master (Darusen 達先).[22] The Ōbaku Zen sect was associated with iconoclastic foreign figures on an equally colossal scale, epitomized by the life-sized sculptures at Gohyakurakanji. Both Shōun and Hokusai made and directed the production of public, eclectic, experiential, and immersive Buddhist art. These hulking presences are not explicitly depicted but are latent in the composition of the print—lurking behind the name Hokusai inscribed in the upper left and in the minds of the tourists gripping the wooden railing after a day of sightseeing Shōun's sculptures at the temple.

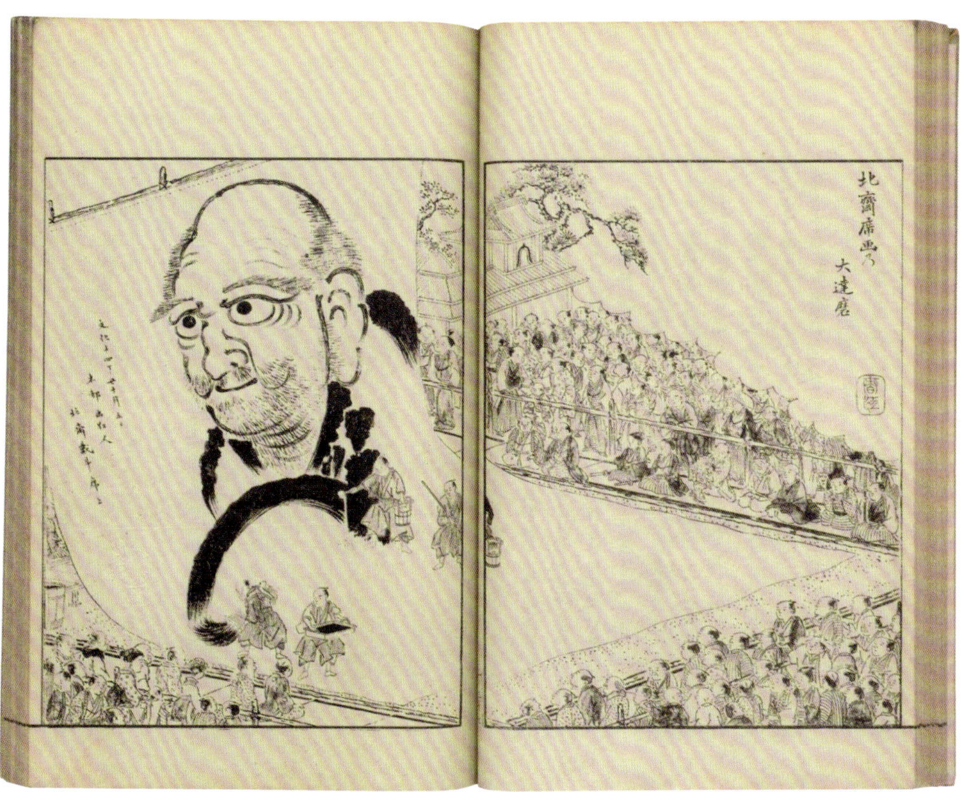

Fig. 5
Reproduction of one image from Kōriki Enkōan's *Detailed Illustrations of Hokusai's Large-Scale Sketches*, in Okada Kei, *Famous Places in Owari Province*. Japan, Edo period, 1868, 1930 edition. Woodblock-printed book (6 vols.); ink on paper; H: 28 cm (each).

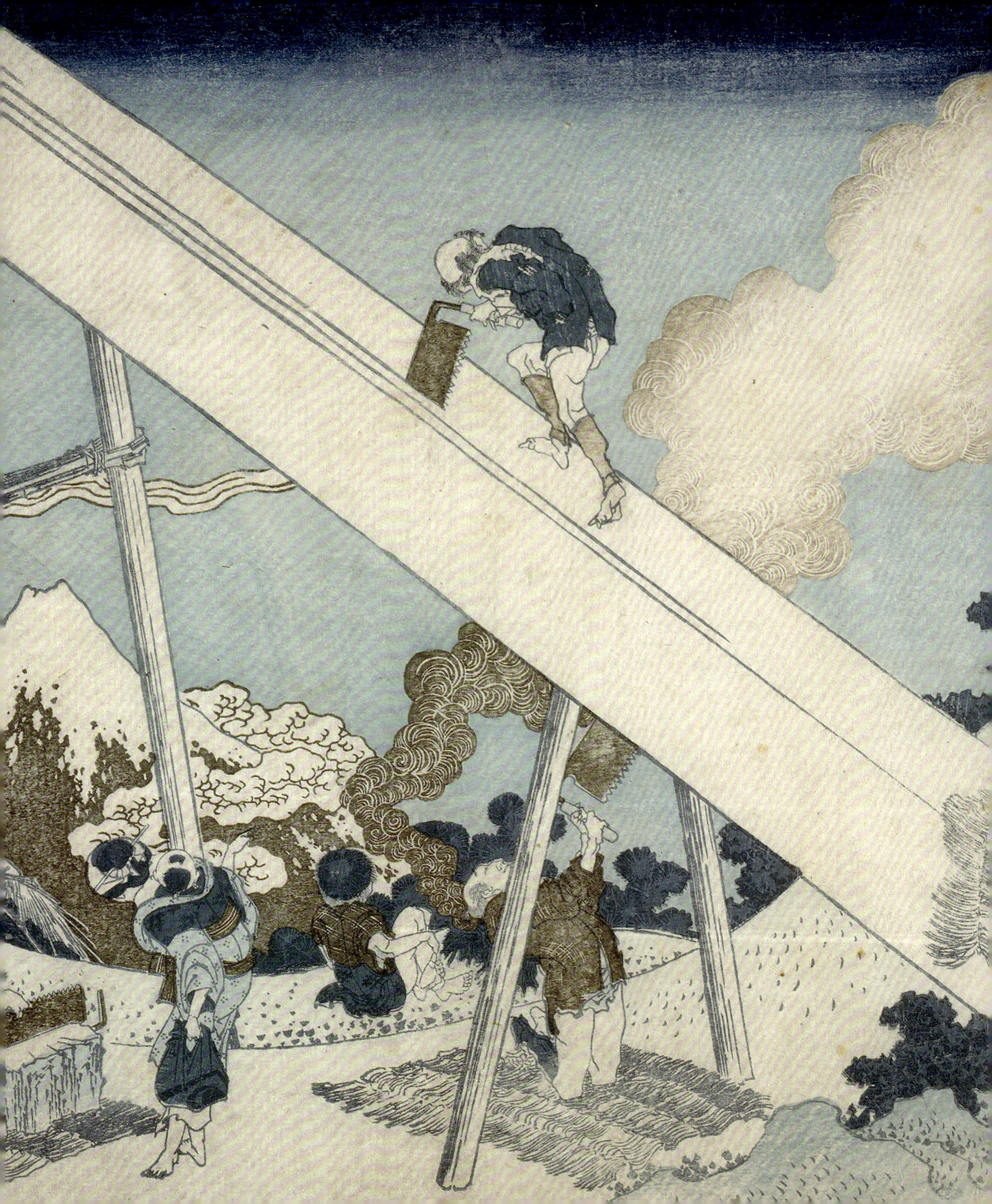

PIGMENT

Can a particular color in an artwork have a resonance that goes beyond mere surface effect? Viewers familiar with Japanese woodblock prints may notice that the outlines in *The Sazaidō of Gohyakurakanji* are printed in dark blue (fig. 1), unlike the black sumi ink that is most often used for printing keyblock outlines. The publisher of the *Thirty-Six Views* series, Nishimura Yohachi 西村屋与八 (dates unknown), certainly expected contemporary viewers to appreciate this difference. He promoted the heavy use of blue as the prints' primary selling point in an advertisement for the series, and it remains one of the most striking features of the designs today (fig. 2). The advertisement promised a series of single-sheet views of Mount Fuji that would be *aizuri* 藍刷, or "printed in blue."[23] However, it was not merely the presence of blue that was unusual but also the *type* of blue, as the *Thirty-Six Views* series marked the first commercial use on such a sustained scale of the imported chemical pigment Berlin blue (also known as Prussian blue). Aside from its graphic strength and compositional balance, the success of this series and its part in establishing Hokusai's world renown has been attributed to this use of blue, a color that has had an almost magical hold over the human imagination across many cultures and time periods. Although Hokusai might have hoped to gain longevity through other chemical elixirs, the blue used in the *Thirty-Six Views* series has undoubtedly contributed to his artistic immortality.

Berlin blue, known as *Bero-ai* ベロ藍 in Japanese, had been used sparingly in Japanese paintings for decades prior to the production of the *Thirty-Six Views* and occasionally in the deluxe, privately sponsored and circulated prints known as *surimono* 摺物 (fig. 3).[24] It likely debuted in commercial single-sheet printing in 1829 with the publication of a

Fig. 1
Katsushika Hokusai,
The Sazaidō of Gohyakurakanji (detail).

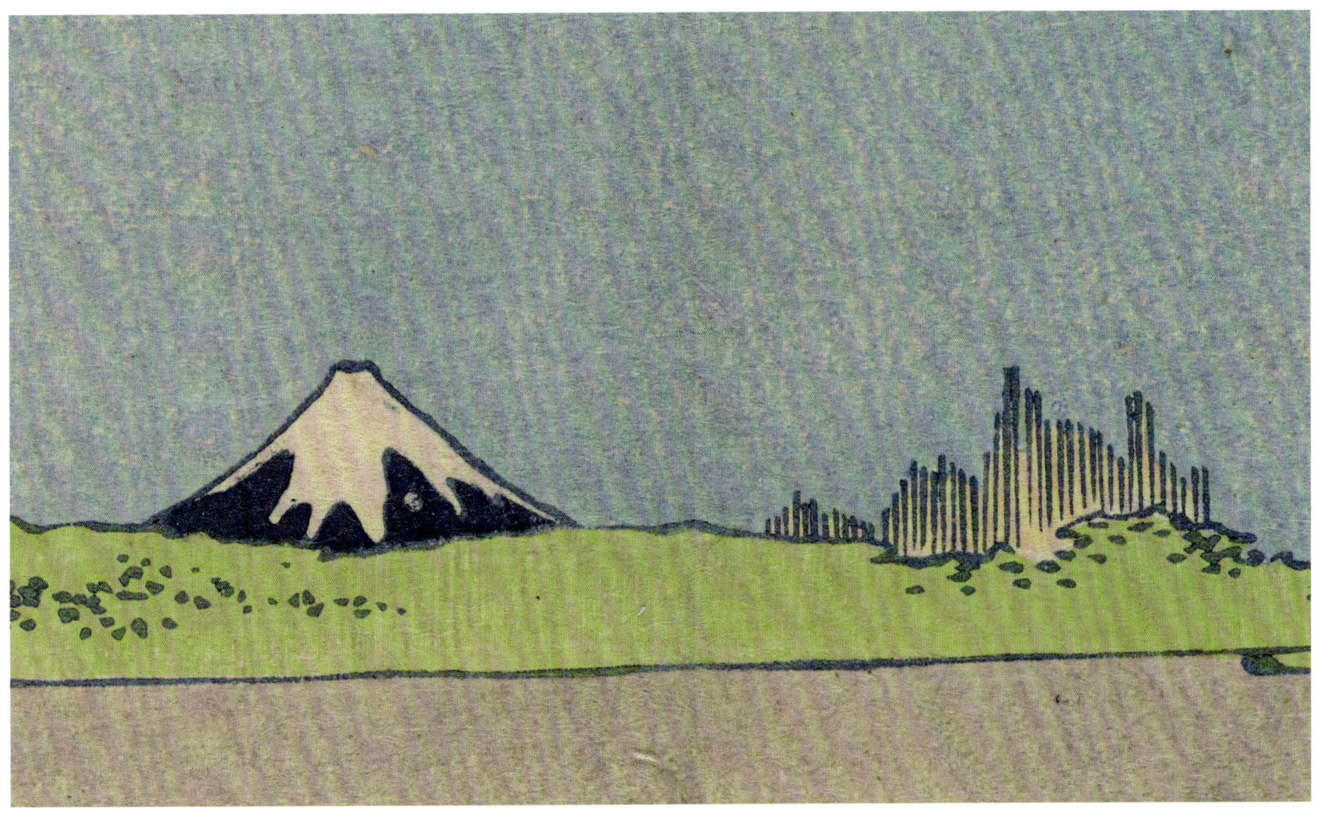

Detail of fig. 2

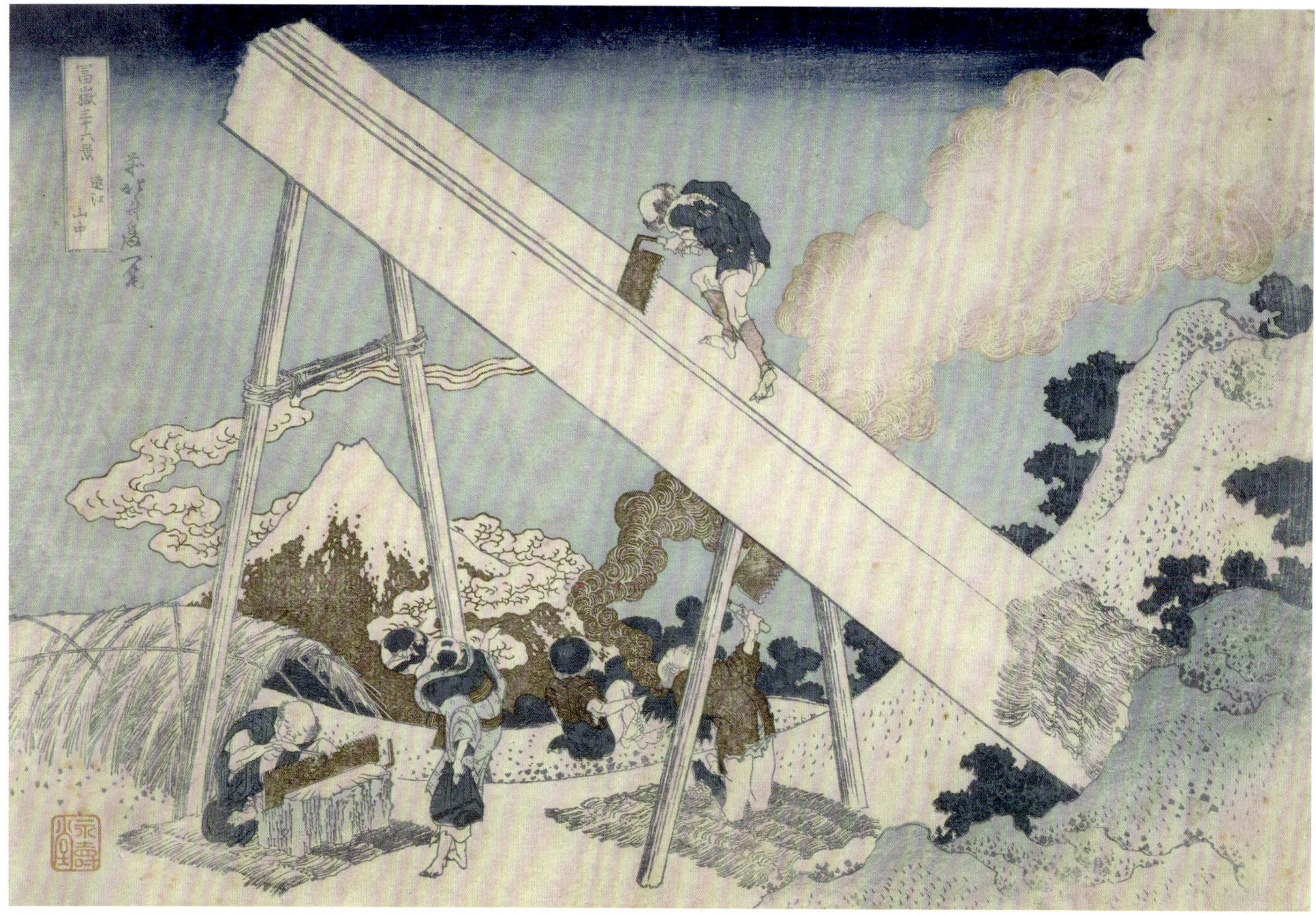

Fig. 2
Katsushika Hokusai, *In the Mountains of Tōtomi Province* (*Tōtomi sanchū*), from the series *Thirty-Six Views of Mount Fuji*. Edo period, ca. 1831. Woodblock print; color on paper; 25.6 × 38.5 cm.

Fig. 3
Katsushika Hokusai, *Sazaidō*, from the series *Thirty-Six Genroku Poem Shells* (*Genroku kasen kai-awase*). Edo period, 1821. *Surimono* print; ink and color on paper; 21 × 19 cm (approx.).

Chinese-style landscape by Keisai Eisen 渓斎英泉 (1790–1848) (fig. 4), just one year prior to the publication of the first prints in Hokusai's series.[25] The visual novelty of this pigment was apparently popular with audiences, and it was quickly adopted into landscape prints of this period, initiating what the art historian Henry D. Smith II has referred to as "the blue revolution" in Japanese woodblock prints.[26] A natural fit for depicting the skies and seas that permeate Japan's panoramic vistas, Berlin blue also spread to other genres as the imported pigment became cheaper in the mid-1830s. At the time of Hokusai's series, Berlin blue was still expensive, and recent scientific analysis has suggested that the dark blue outlines in the *Thirty-Six Views* series are actually a mixture of Berlin blue and indigo—likely a strategy to reduce costs.[27]

In the centuries prior to the importation of Berlin blue, Japanese artists had used a variety of other blue-colored pigments, such as azurite (*iwa gunjō* 岩群青), indigo (*ai* 藍), dayflower (*aigami* 藍紙), and smalt (*hana gunjō* 花群青). A natural and abundant vegetal dye, indigo could be used to achieve deep blue hues comparable to those of Berlin blue, though this required a large quantity of pigment and multiple applications. Among the urban populace of the time, deep, dark blue would have been associated also with textiles, as indigo was used to dye summer robes in stylish blue-and-white

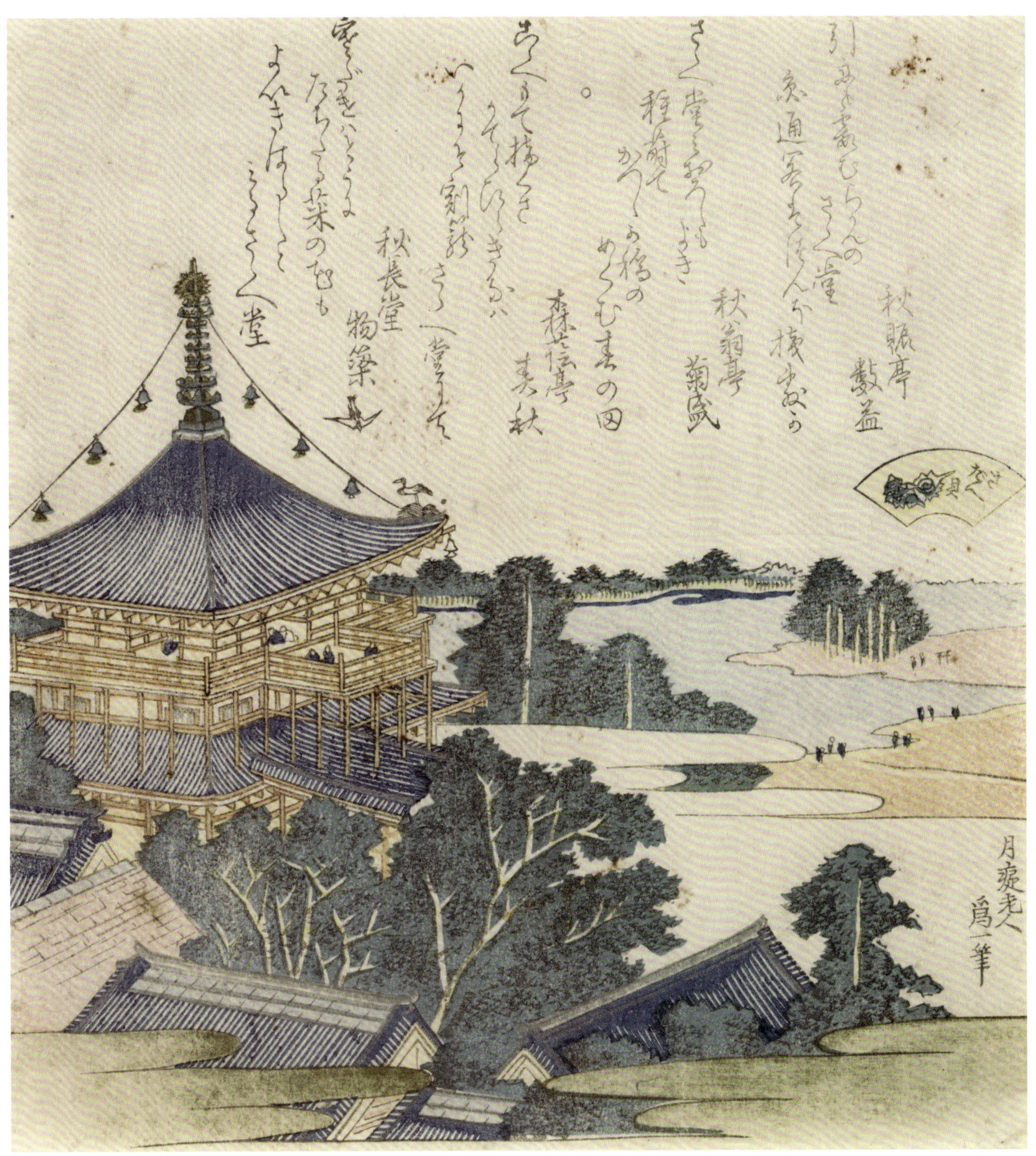

patterns. This trend can be seen in the garments of several of the figures within the *Gohyakurakanji* print itself (fig. 5). Such garments would have been dyed in the Kanda district of Edo, the location of many facilities for dyeing with indigo (fig. 6). The rich color of Berlin blue is achieved by the oxidation of ferrous ferrocyanide salts, which were first synthesized by a Swiss painter in early eighteenth-century Berlin and imported to Japan through Chinese, and later Dutch, trading ships. It first appeared in woodblock printing in the early nineteenth century, in theatrical prints sponsored by actor fan clubs operating in the Osaka kabuki community. Like *surimono*, these actor prints were sponsored by fee-paying fans, and so their producers could use more expensive techniques without worrying about losing money if the print failed to sell. Further, Osaka's closer proximity to the international trading port of Nagasaki may explain the relative ease with which artists and printmakers in that city acquired this rare pigment.

The precise date for the first use of Berlin blue in commercial printing has long been debated, although Hokusai has been considered a prime candidate given his well-known interests in new and unusual pigments.[28] For example, he authored and illustrated a two-volume text, *Picture Book on the Use of Coloring* (*Ehon saishikitsū*

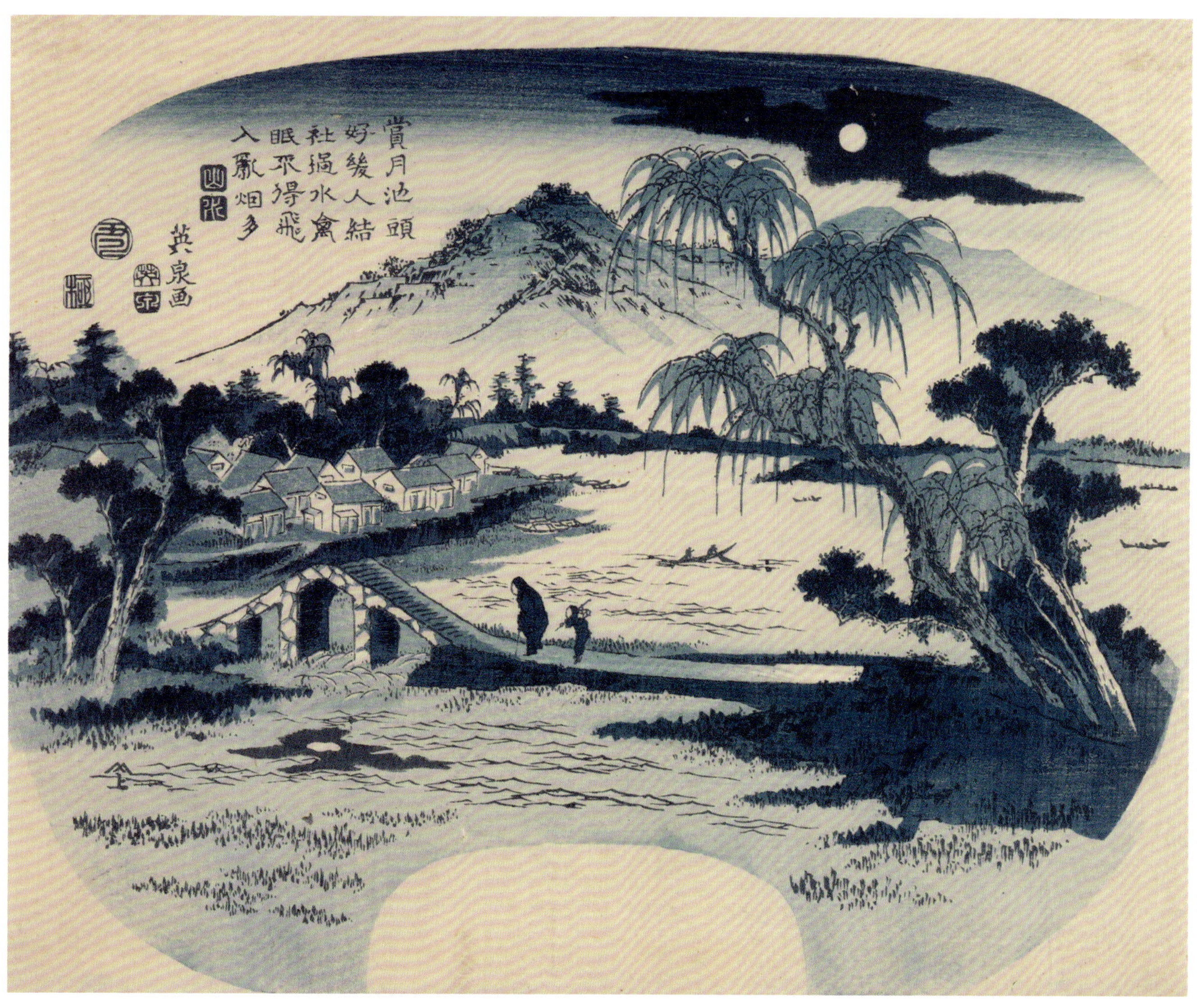

Fig. 4
Keisai Eisen, *View of Shōgetsu Pond*. Edo period, 1829. Woodblock print; color on paper; 24.1 × 30.2 cm.

Fig. 5
Katsushika Hokusai, *The Sazaidō of Gohyakurakanji* (detail).

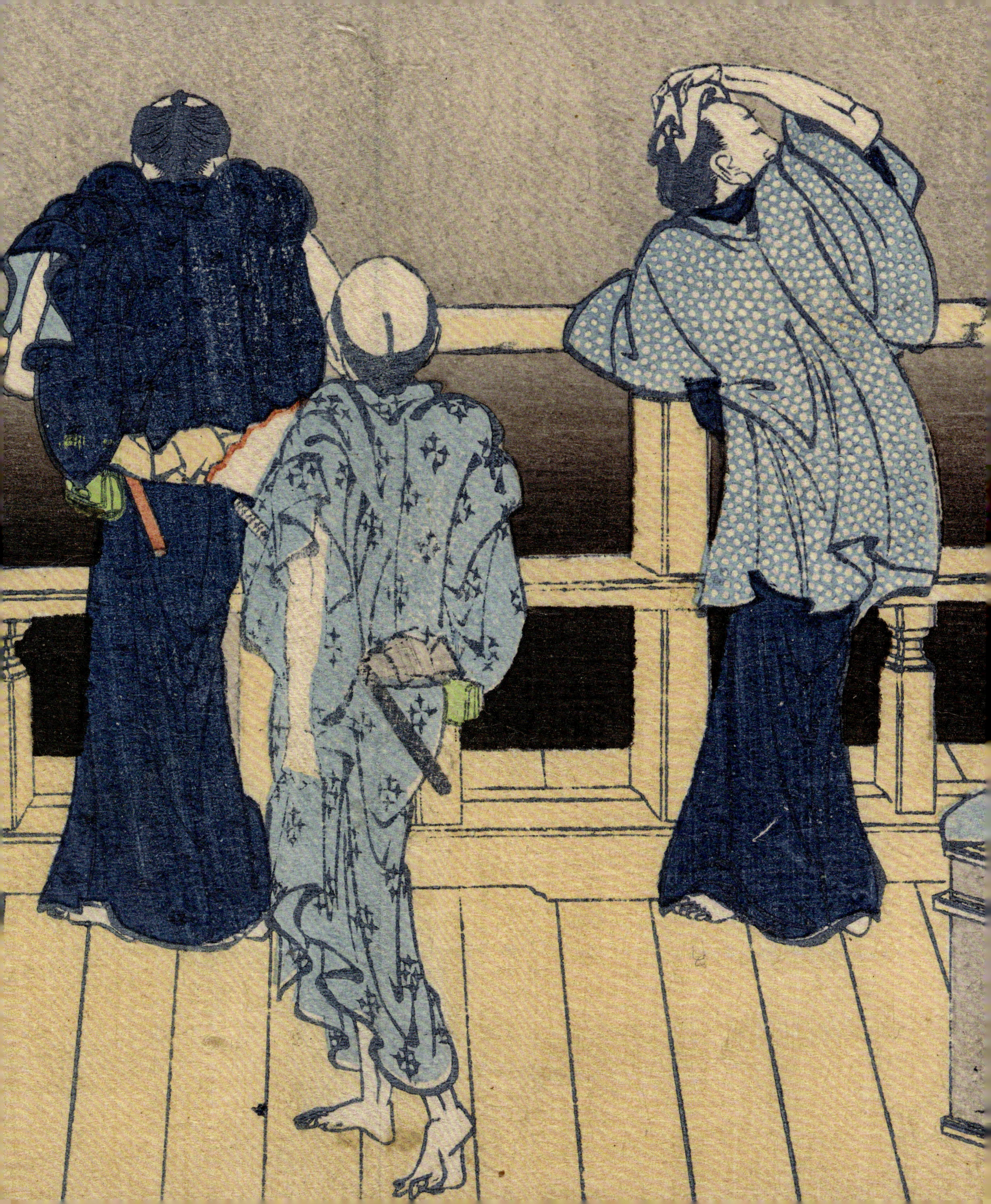

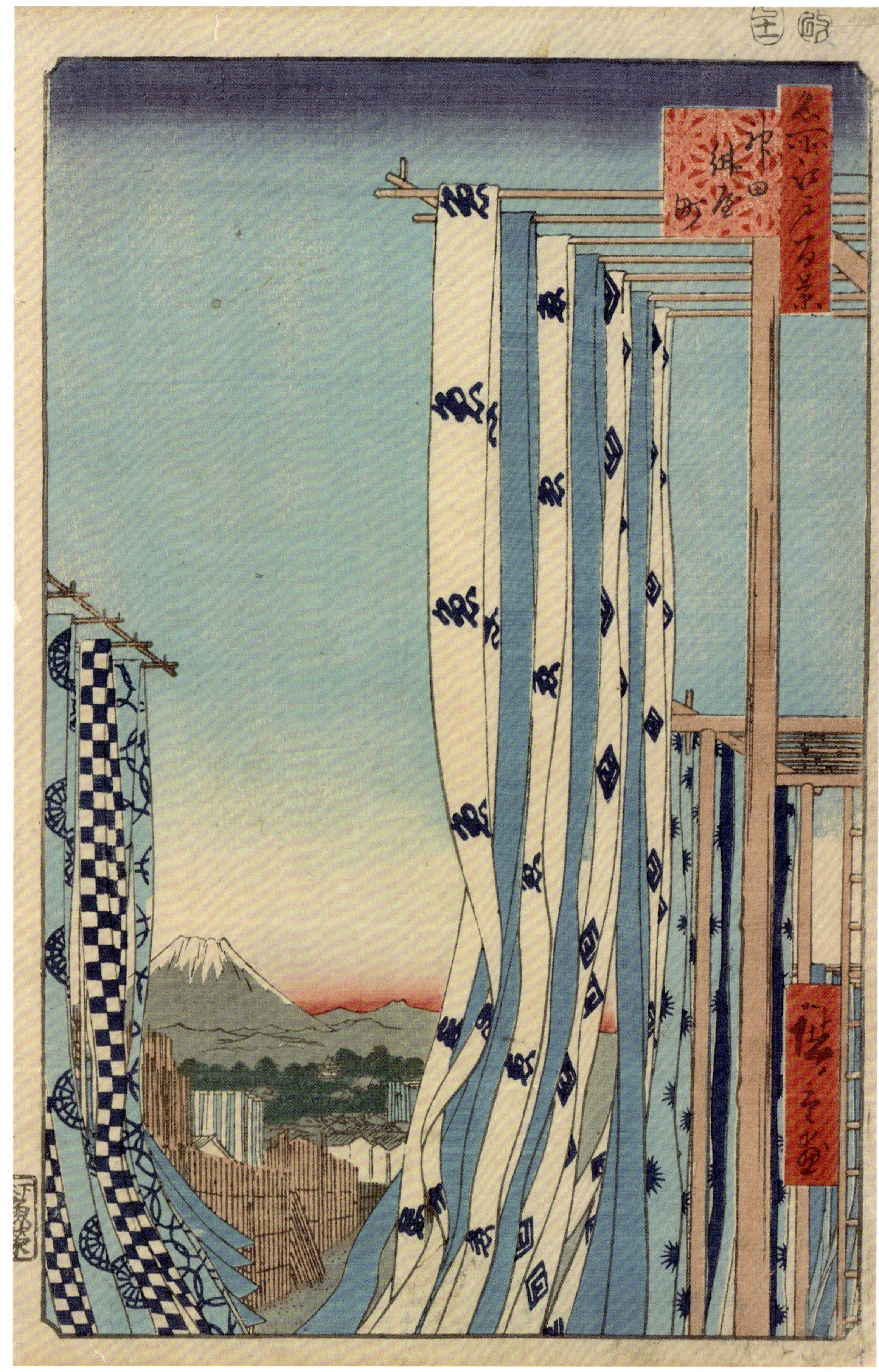

名所江戸百景
神田紺屋町
廣重画

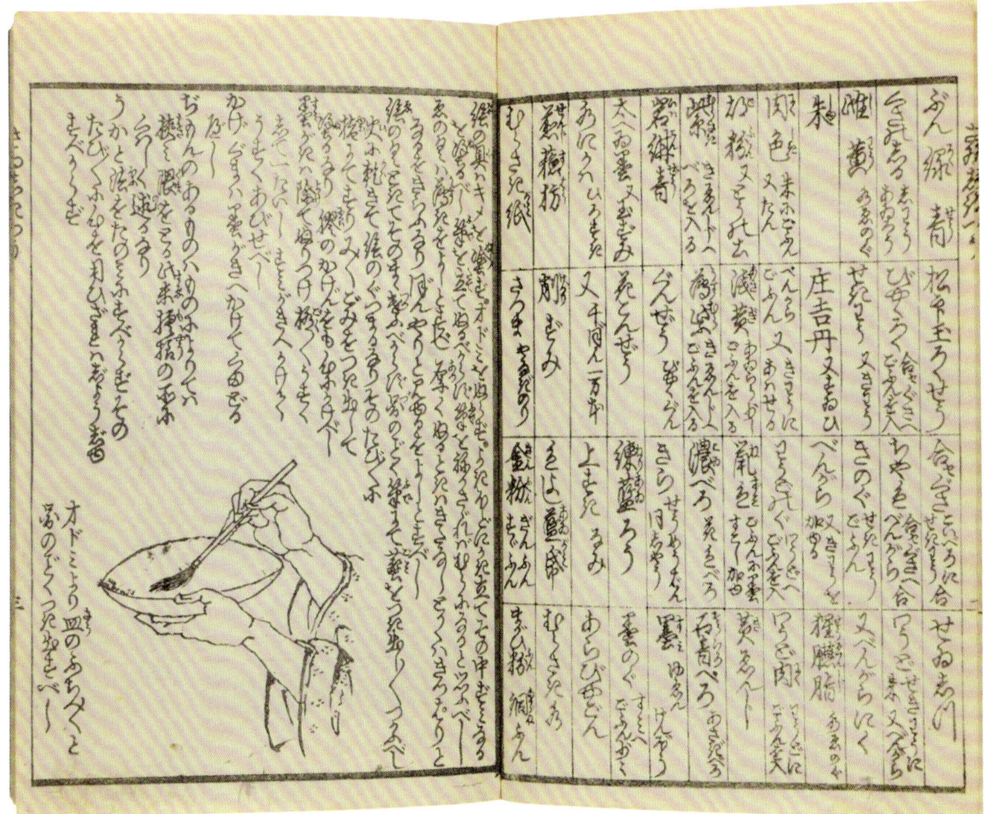

Fig. 6
Utagawa Hiroshige, *The Dyers' Quarter in Kanda* (*Kanda kon'ya-chō*), from the series *One Hundred Famous Views of Edo*. Edo period, 1857, 11th month. Woodblock print; ink and color on paper; 33.9 × 22.6 cm.

Fig. 7
Katsushika Hokusai, *Picture Book on the Use of Coloring*, vol. 1. Edo period, 1848. Woodblock-printed book (2 vols.); ink on paper; paper covers; 18.5 × 12.7 × 0.8 cm.

絵本彩色通) (1848), which begins with a long list of mineral and organic pigments and offers detailed instructions on how to remove impurities from liquid pigments by using a brush to move any sediment to the edge of a dish (fig. 7). It also contains many schematic illustrations that indicate where in a composition to apply different pigments. For instance, one page directs aspiring painters to use Berlin blue for the realistic shading of a hawk's eye—the accompanying text explaining that the fine particles allow for such precise application (fig. 8). The use of Berlin blue became more widespread through Hokusai's printers, as the unusually dense and vivid green used in his landscape series subsequent to *Thirty-Six Views*, such as *A Tour of Waterfalls in Various Provinces* (*Shokoku taki meguri* 諸國瀧廻り), was created by mixing Berlin blue with orpiment yellow (*sekiō* 石黄) (fig. 9). Hokusai was so determined that his pigments be an exact hue and consistency that he required his daughter Katsushika Ōi's 葛飾応為 (ca. 1800–ca. 1866) help in preparing them; Ōi's expertise is confirmed by an extant letter in her hand that describes the preparation of an oil-based red pigment.[29]

Like many pigments in the early modern period, Berlin blue was not only used by artists but also has a parallel history as a chemical compound used by pharmacists. Indeed, throughout the Edo period, most imported goods passed through the trading port at Nagasaki, and import records from that trading port detailing the amount of Berlin blue entering the country listed it within the category of medicine, rather than associating it with artistic pursuits.[30] At that time, pharmacies supplied life-prolonging medicines, occasionally claiming that they had legendary qualities. Hokusai acquired

Fig. 8
Katsushika Hokusai, *Picture Book on the Use of Coloring*, vol. 1. Edo period, 1848. Woodblock-printed book (2 vols.); ink on paper; paper covers; 18.5 × 12.7 × 0.8 cm.

Fig. 9
Katsushika Hokusai, *The Falls at Aoigaoka in the Eastern Capital* (*Tōto Aoigaoka no taki*), from the series *A Tour of Waterfalls in Various Provinces*. Edo period, 1833. Woodblock print; ink and color on paper; 38.4 × 26.3 cm.

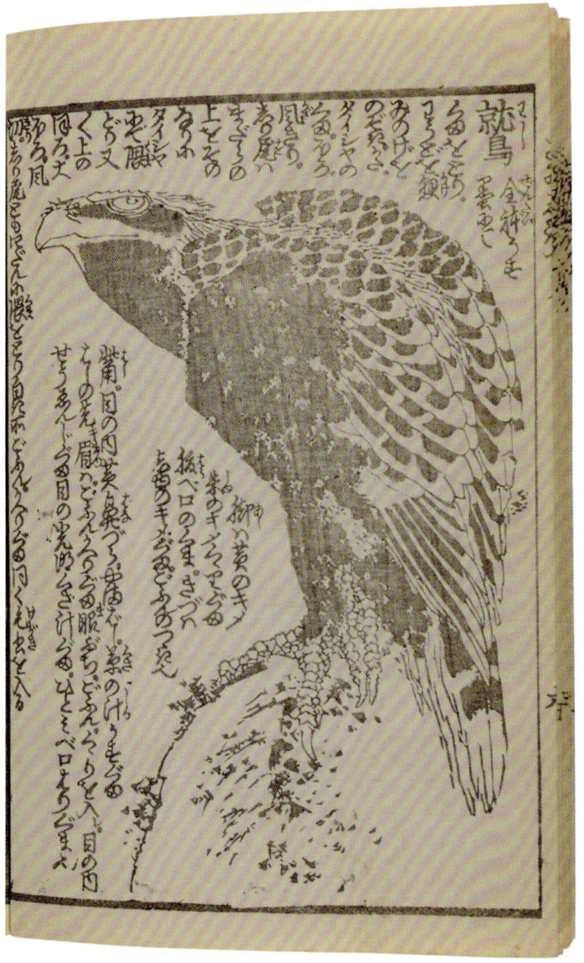

many of his pigments through pharmacists, and his interest in chemical properties has an unexpected linkage to the primary subject of the *Thirty-Six Views* series: Mount Fuji. There has been a long-held belief in Japan that an elixir of immortality can be found within the mountain, with textual sources as early as the ninth-century fictional prose narrative *The Tale of the Bamboo Cutter* (*Taketori monogatari* 竹取物語). This belief was also manifest in other literary genres: for example, in the noh play *Mount Fuji* (*Fujisan*) a Chinese emperor travels to Japan in search of the mystical elixir that lies within the heart of the volcano. This latter narrative was based on a historical mention in the Chinese first-century BCE text *Records of the Grand Historian* (*Shiji* 史記), where the court sorcerer Xu Fu 徐福 was sent overseas by his emperor to find it. Mount Fuji is surmised as a likely spot for such a substance, given that a close homonym of “Fuji” is “*fushi*” 不死, or “deathless.”

Hokusai was interested in both Mount Fuji and life-extending medicines. An extant letter by Hokusai provides a recipe of his own invention for a longevity elixir involving longan nuts, sugar, and the grain alcohol *shōchū* 焼酎, which he credits for his robust eighty-eight years of life.[31] Further, the author of the preface to the third volume of Hokusai’s *One Hundred Views of Mount Fuji* writes that Hokusai’s youthful

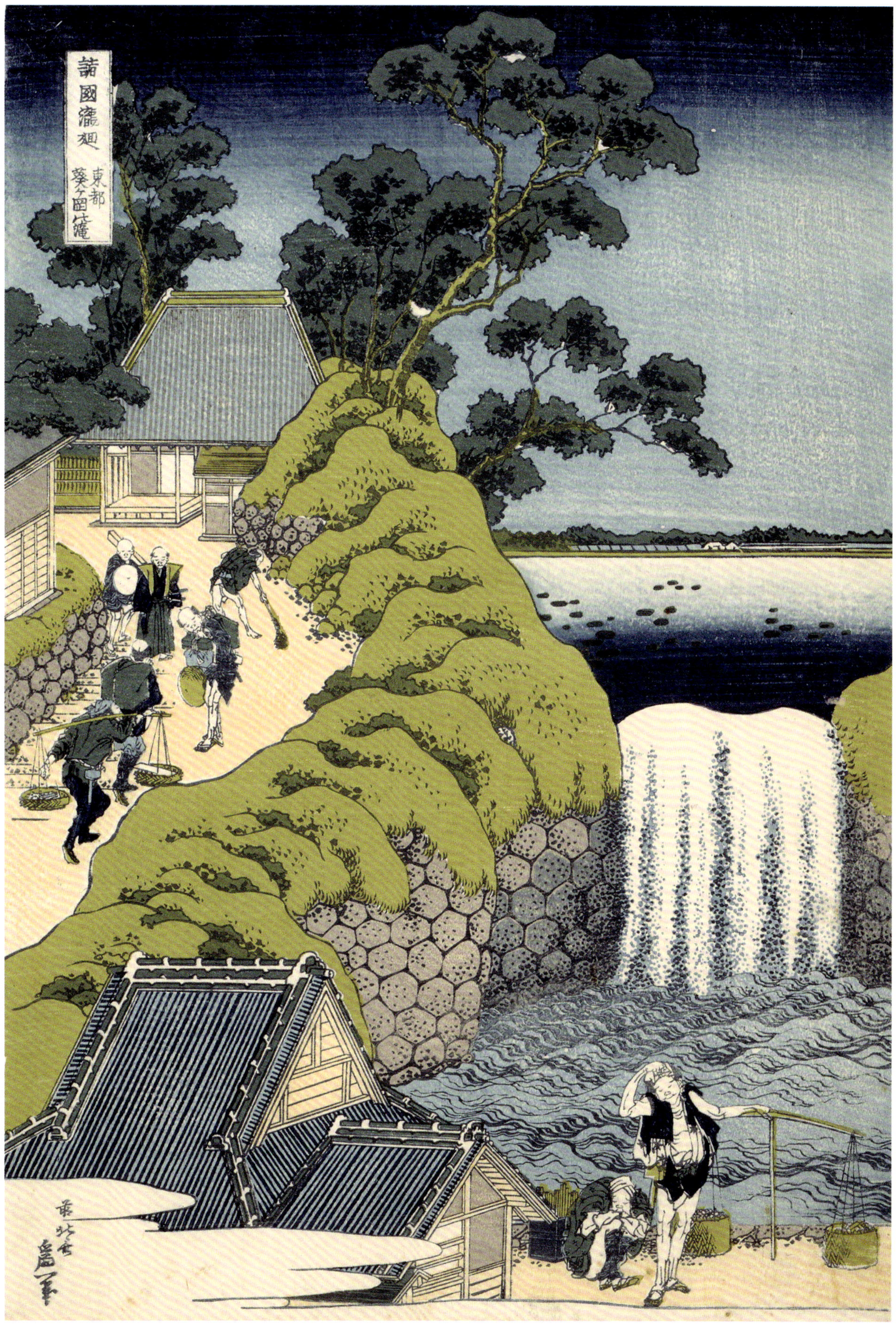
諸國瀧廻
東都
葵ケ岡の瀧

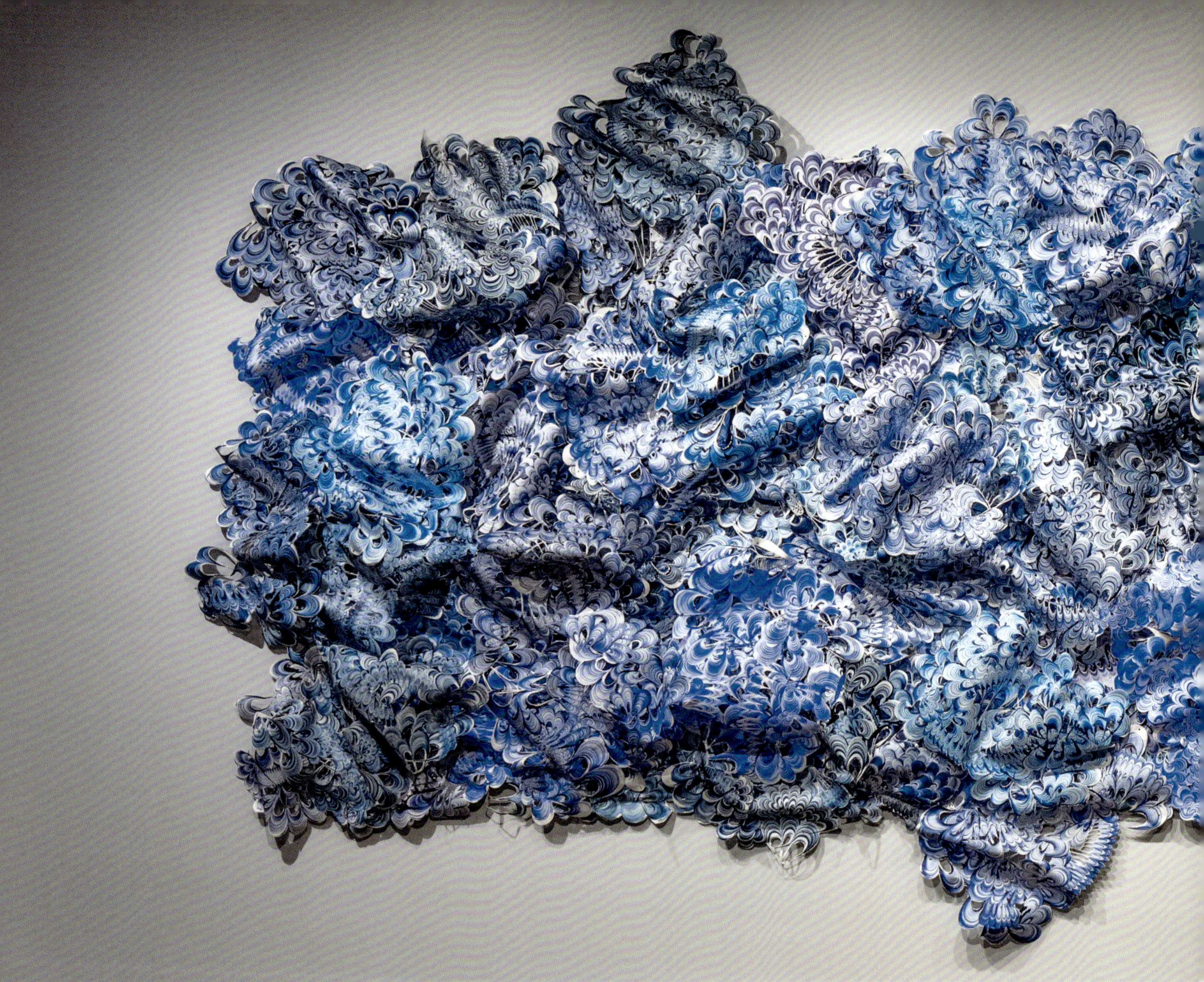

brushwork seems to suggest that the artist had actually obtained the "secret elixir of the Immortals on this miraculous mountain."[32] While this is surely a rhetorical flourish, it confirms that this belief was known to Hokusai and is here connected to the artist's practice. Although Hokusai died before reaching his target age of one hundred years, one of the prints in the *Thirty-Six Views* series, *Under the Wave off Kanagawa*, has become perhaps the most recognized artwork in the world today, endlessly reproduced, adapted, and modified, from T-shirts and underwear to the back of one-thousand-yen banknotes. No one would deny Hokusai achieved artistic immortality *through* the miraculous mountain of Mount Fuji, though this appears to have been via the use of blue pigment, and not imbibing its legendary elixir.

The risk that publisher Nishimura Yohachi took to print the series primarily in blue seems to have paid off, reflecting not only Hokusai's interests but also the tastes of the

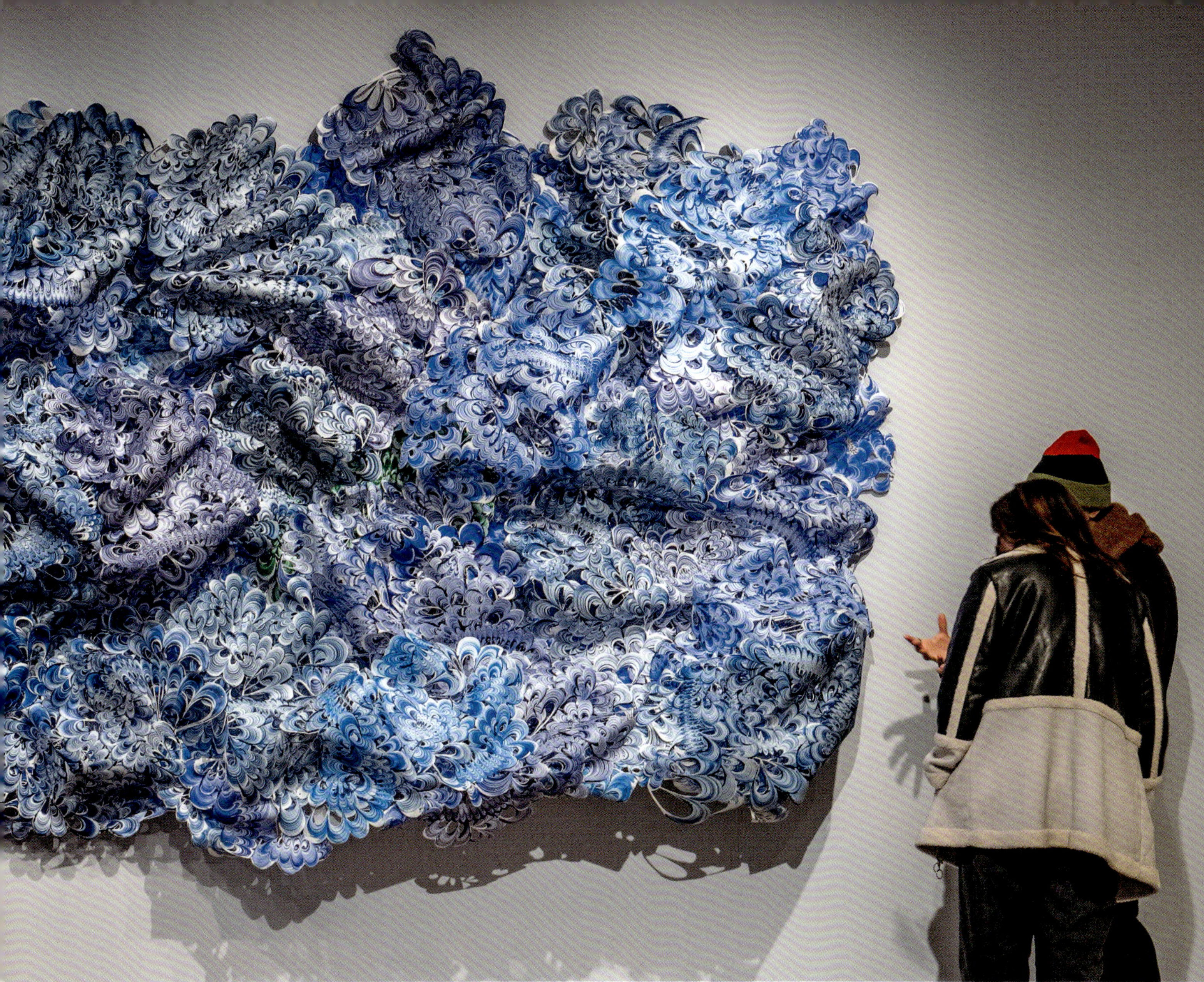

Fig. 10
Taiko Chandler, *Blue Surge*. United States, 2021. Monotype print on Tyvek; 183 × 610 × 30.5 cm.

print-buying public. The color palette remains one of the most discussed aspects of the works almost two hundred years later. Indeed, although many pigments can fascinate, blue does seem to hold people in particular thrall. To name but a few examples: the French term *indigomanie* was coined for impressionist painters and their "unhealthy" passion for blue; the essayist Maggie Nelson wrote an intimate memoir of her search for meaning through the color in *Bluets* (2009); a glimpse of Tiffany blue evokes visions of jewelry, elegance, and Audrey Hepburn; and Yves Klein's painting *Relief Éponge bleu sans titre (RE 49)* sold for almost twenty million dollars in June 2022. Hokusai's blue has inspired generations. Recently, the Japanese artist Taiko Chandler (b. 1963) in her *Blue Surge* (2021), a rippling mass of small prints on Tyvek formed a three-dimensional panorama of mesmerizing ripples that evokes swirling pools (fig. 10). Blue pigment seems to be an eternal, intoxicating elixir of its own.

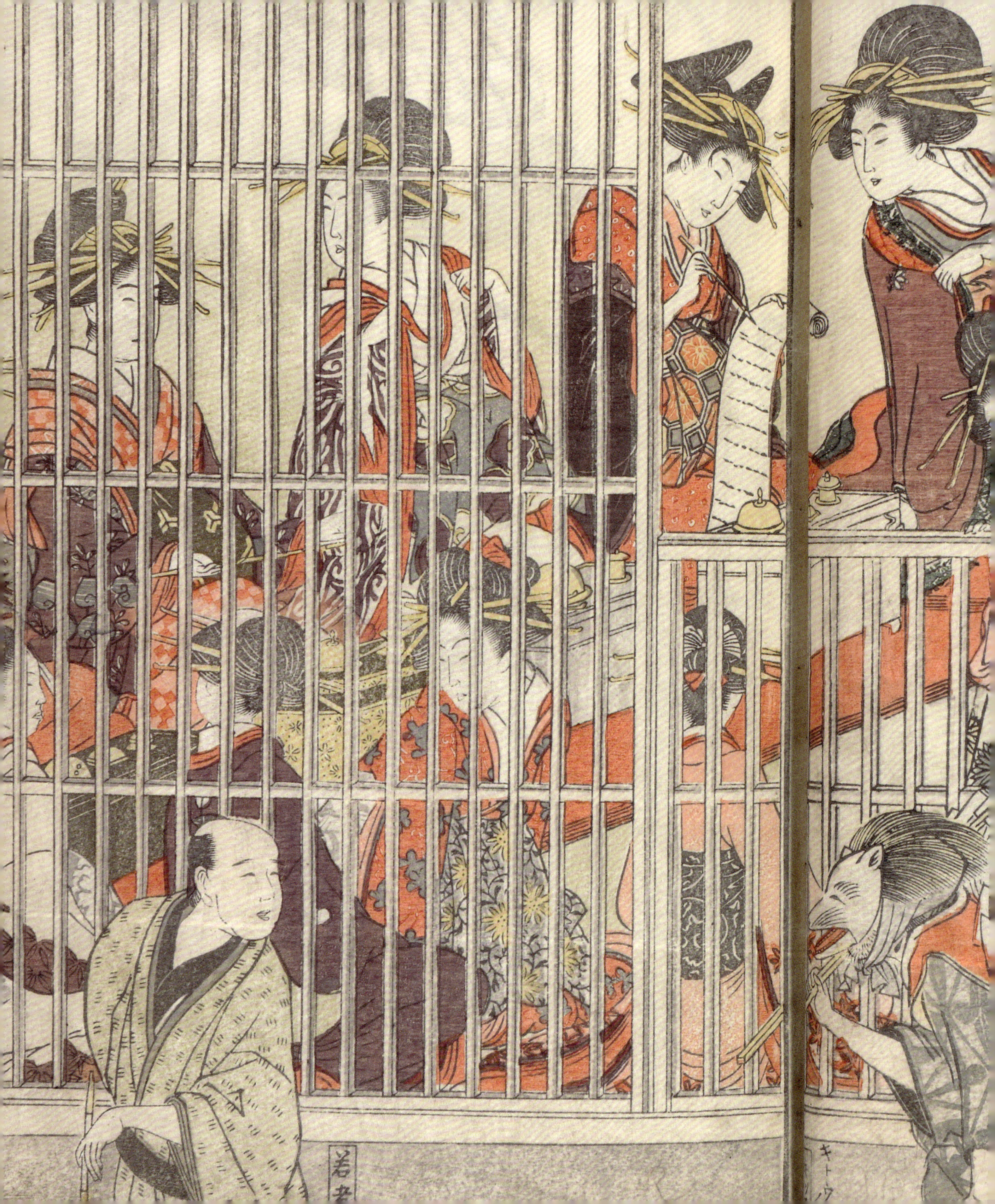
若
キトウ

RESTRICTION

Would viewers of different genders have viewed Hokusai's print in the same way? Many aspects of the feudal, class-structured society of the Edo period were restrictive to its inhabitants. However, as can be said of many cultures and time periods, this was especially true for women. Several compositional elements within *The Sazaidō of Gohyakurakanji* allude to these restrictions, in ways that would have been palpable to contemporary viewers.

One of these restrictions is suggested by the structure of the balcony itself. Excluding *The Sazaidō of Gohyakurakanji*, views from elevated platforms in ukiyo-e almost invariably offer glimpses from the interiors of the two-story establishments within the Yoshiwara 吉原, Edo's licensed sex district (fig. 1).[33] A bustling city with approximately a million residents by 1700, Edo was largely a single-story city of wood and paper. Higher structures, such as temple halls and pagodas, theaters, and brothels, were reserved for specific functions. As a consequence, tall buildings were associated primarily with the fringes of society, beyond the "ordinary" functions of residence, governance, and commerce. Most of these buildings would have had only limited access for admittance to their upper levels—that is, if individuals outside those professions could gain entry at all. Nonetheless, though actually patronizing the Yoshiwara would have been beyond the financial and social means of many Edo residents, its sights and conventions were familiar to all through the idealized versions presented in woodblock prints and books. The eroticized fantasy in these images provided consumers with the simulated perspective of a paying guest seated in revelry among such elevated company, or the conceit of privileged access to the secret lives of these desirable women when no men were present. The views from these balconies often depict, beyond the railings, glimpses of cherry blossoms—the tips of branches belonging to

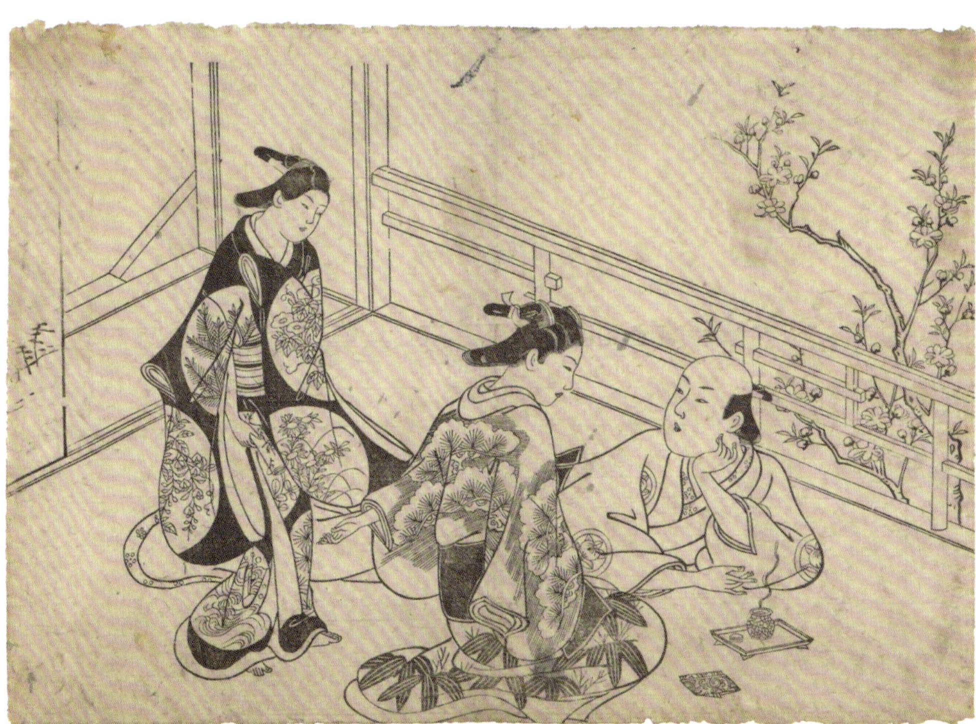

Fig. 1
Okumura Masanobu, *Ichimura Takenojō Reclining on a Balcony with Two Women*. Edo period, ca. 1715. Woodblock print; ink on paper; 26.2 × 37.3 cm.

Fig. 2
Attributed to Keisai Eisen, *Drippings from Flowers* (*Hana no shizuku*), vol. 1. Edo period, late 18th to mid-19th century. Woodblock-printed book (3 vols.); ink and color on paper; 23 × 15.6 × 1.2 cm.

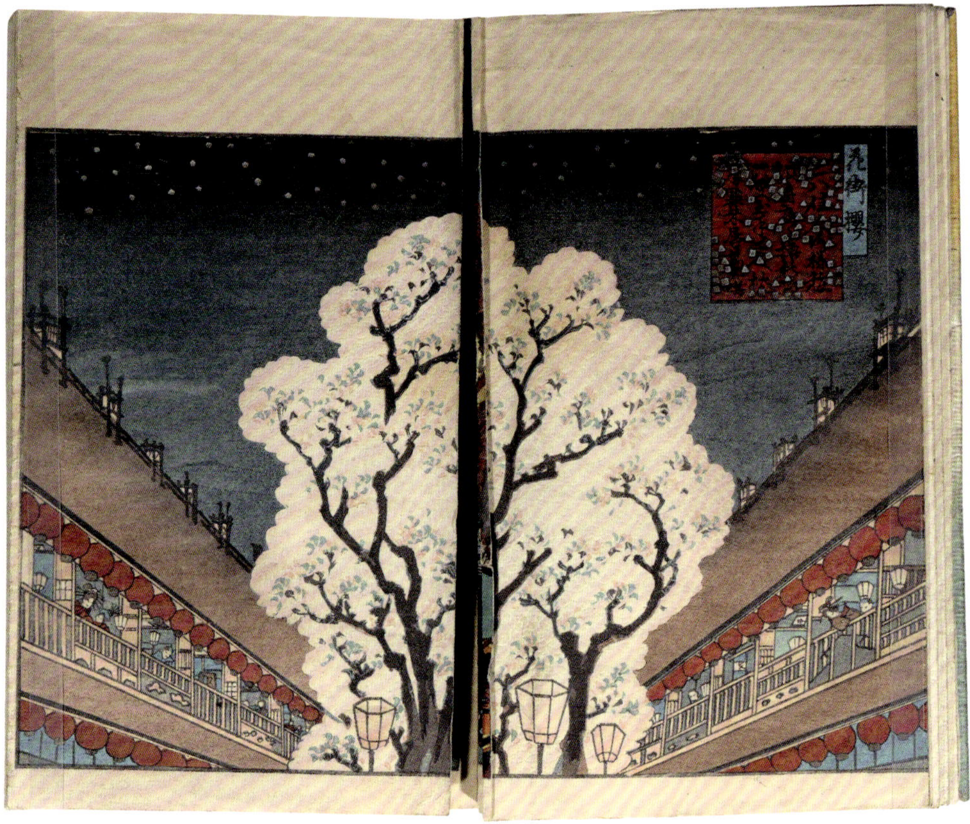

the trees that were temporarily transplanted annually along the central avenue of the Yoshiwara during the spring months and removed when their blossoms were over (fig. 2).[34] Since cherry blossoms bloom briefly, early in the calendar year, they have long been considered symbolic of female beauty, which is viewed as similarly youthful and transient—and presumably, as in the case of the Yoshiwara blooms, replaceable. As such, cherry blossoms in ukiyo-e are often suggestive of the Yoshiwara, and their inclusion within the background of a balcony view is sufficient to suggest the location of the sex district as a whole as well as the female indentured sex workers who were confined there until their contracts were completed (fig. 3). Whistler includes what appear to be cherry blossoms in his *Variations in Flesh Colour and Green—The Balcony*, and although he may have been aware of their association in Japan with feminine beauty, it is unlikely he intended associations with the dehumanizing conditions that many female sex workers endured, kept on display behind wooden lattices, like birds in a cage (fig. 4).

Images of the Yoshiwara provided access to the restricted spaces of sex work that would have been unattainable for general audiences. Analogously, Hokusai's *The Sazaidō of Gohyakurakanji* provides a degree of visual access to the distant, elegant peak of Mount Fuji—the focal point of the print and of the entire *Thirty-Six Views* series—while the balcony railing suggests another type of restrictive barrier that would have affected women viewers of the print. Regardless of gender, visiting Fuji would not have been a viable option for many members of the population because of the

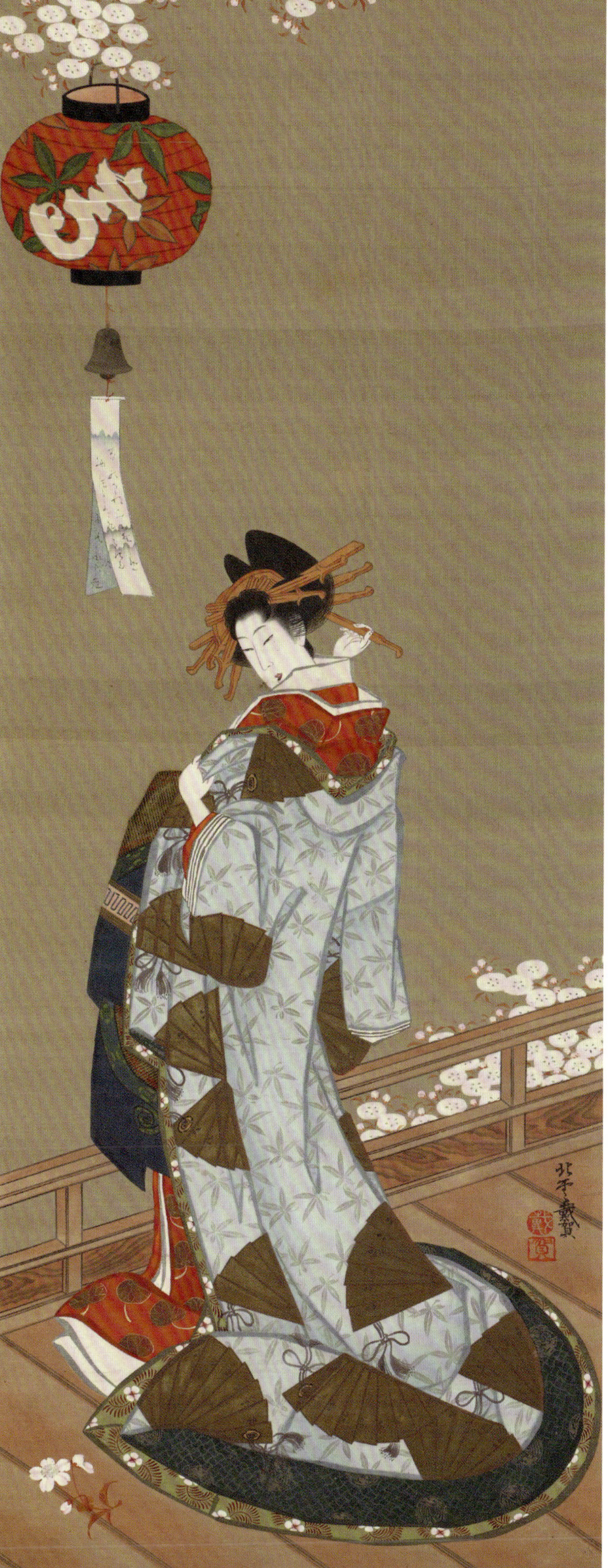

Fig. 3
Katsushika Hokuun, *Courtesan Takao Standing on a Verandah*. Japan, Edo period, early 19th century. Color and gold on silk; 87.1 × 33.8 cm.

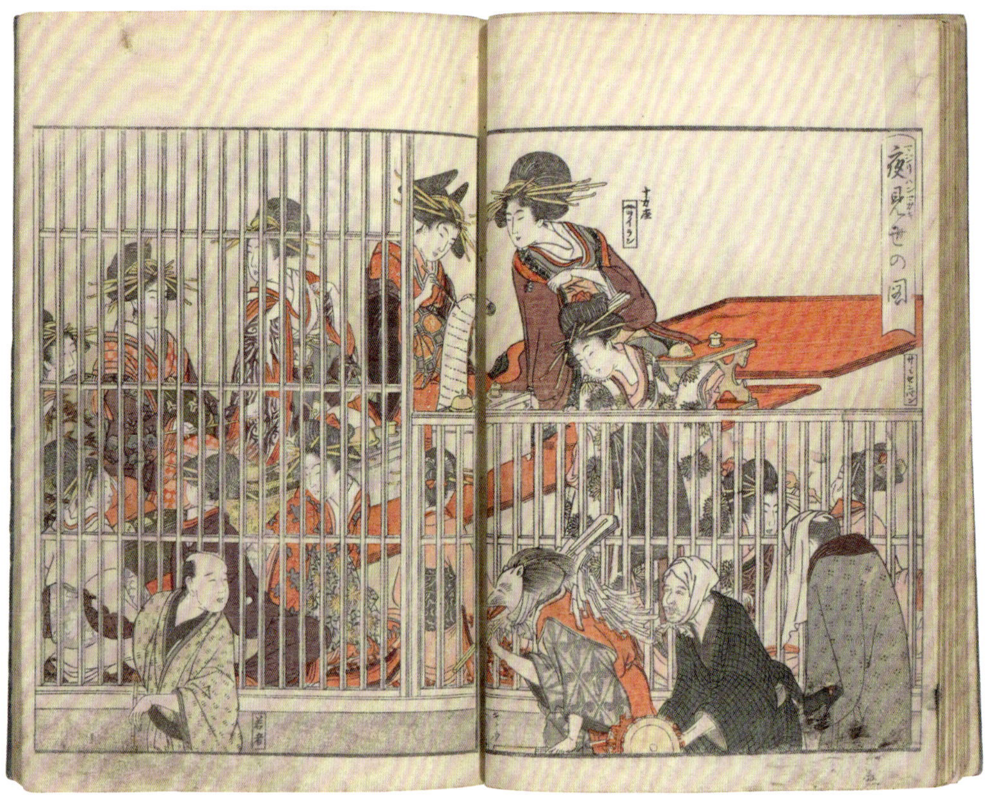

Fig. 4
Kitagawa Utamaro, *Yoshiwara Picture Book of New Year's Festivities* (*Seirō ehon nenjū gyōji*), vol. 1. Japan, Edo period, 1804. Woodblock-printed book (2 vols.); ink and color on paper; 22.7 × 15.9 × 1 cm.

obstacles imposed by physical and economic hardship. Travel was tightly regulated and monitored by the shogunal military government during the Edo period, though pilgrimage to sacred peaks like Mount Fuji was one reason for which permission might be granted.[35] However, throughout Hokusai's lifetime, women were forbidden from climbing the sacred summit of Mount Fuji because of the perception that their bodies were inherently unclean. Menstrual fluid was regarded as evidence of impurity—distilled sin—and its mere presence would "pollute" any sacred site. That perspective was shared by both Buddhism and Shinto, the primary forms of religious belief in Japan throughout much of its history. The resulting policy of women's exclusion from sacred sites (*nyonin kekkai* 女人結界) was widespread at this time, and restrictions against women's ascent to the summit of Mount Fuji were not lifted until 1860.[36]

An unusual strategy for circumventing such restrictions was the practice of constructing "mini Fujis"—replicas known as *Fujizuka* 富士塚 (literally "Fuji hills")—around the city of Edo, which could be climbed as a surrogate for the real thing (fig. 5).[37] *Fujizuka* were at the peak of their popularity in the later eighteenth century, and at the time the *Thirty-Six Views* series was completed, there were approximately ten such structures in Edo. They were occasionally built using rocks and plants transplanted from the real Mount Fuji as a means of capturing the spiritual authority invested in the original. Although at a vastly reduced size, the builders of these hills would also attempt to mirror the volcano's form by including the zigzagging, switchback trail used to reach the actual summit. Completing a miniaturized pilgrimage along the route of

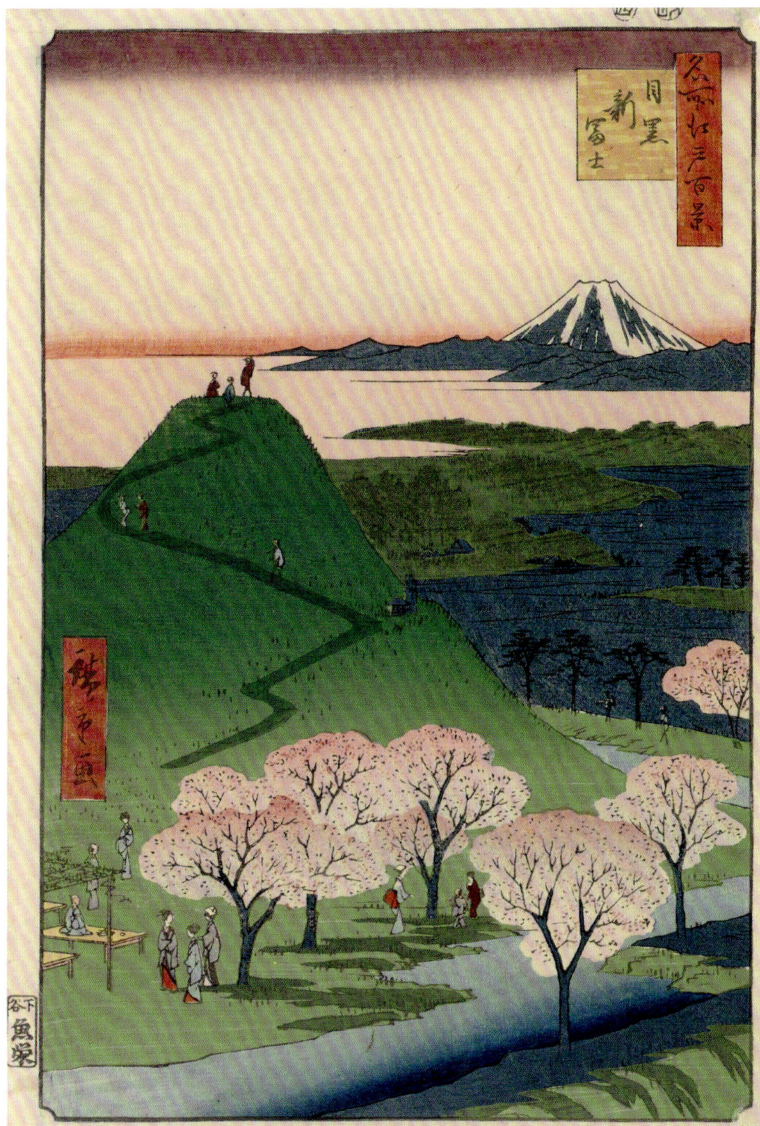

Fig. 5
Utagawa Hiroshige, *New Fuji, Meguro* (*Meguro Shin-Fuji*), from the series *One Hundred Famous Views of Edo*. Edo period, 1857, 4th month. Woodblock print; ink and color on paper; 35.3 × 24.2 cm.

a *Fujizuka* appears to have worked in a similar manner to the operation of a Buddhist prayer wheel. These spindles are mounted with the complete text of a sutra, and the mere action of spinning the wheel ostensibly generates just as much karmic merit as a serious examination and recitation of the text. Likewise, the gestural completion of a *Fujizuka* miniature pilgrimage would have provided the only viable substitute for women, the impoverished, or the infirm. A similar type of miniaturized process was already present within Gohyakurakanji's Sazaidō and the scaled Kannon pilgrimage circuits contained within (see **site**).

The effort taken to construct these mini Fujis reflects the importance of Mount Fuji in the popular imagination. It was the charismatic leader of one of the folk cults centered on Mount Fuji, known as *Fujikō* 富士講 (or "Fuji associations"), who had originally suggested the idea of *Fujizuka*. In an ironic twist, many of the activities of

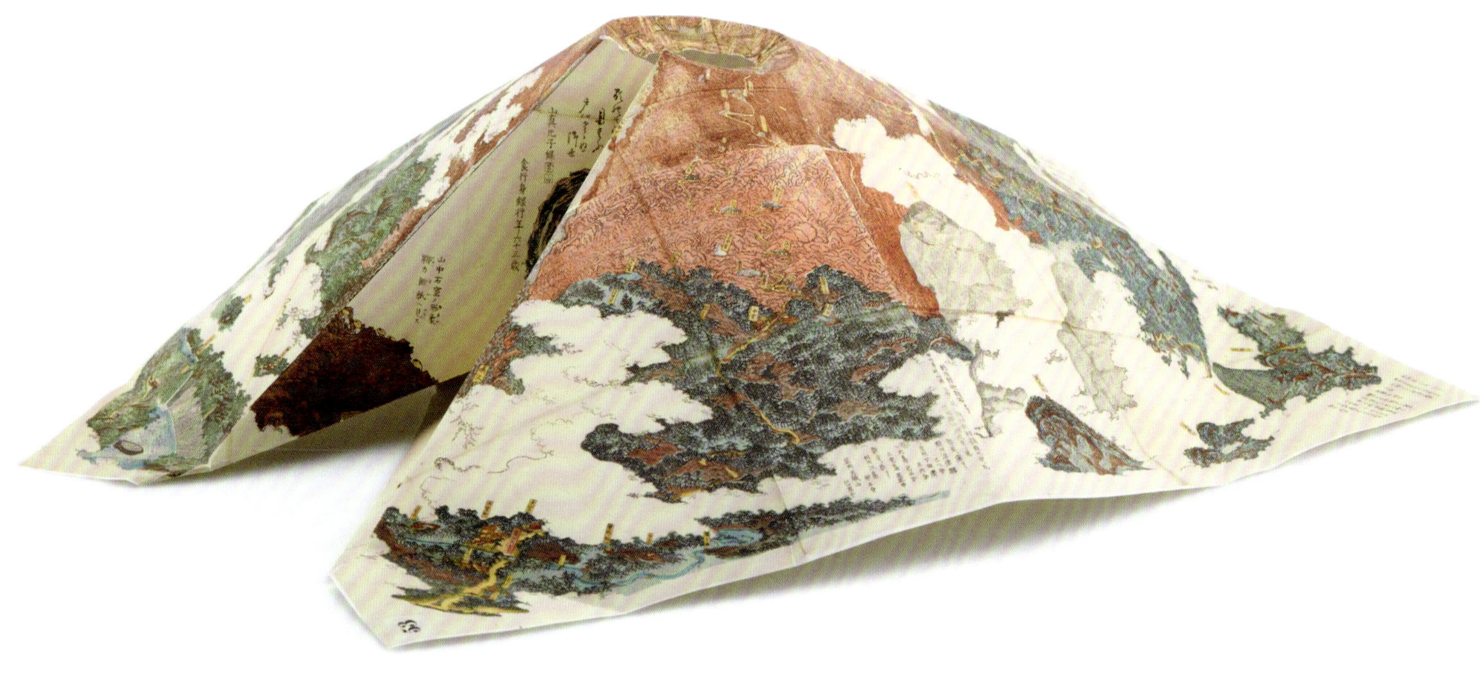

Fig. 6a
Utagawa Sadahide, *Complete Map of the True Shape of Mount Fuji* (*Fujisan shinkei zenzu*), shown constructed. Japan, Edo period, 1848. Woodblock print; ink and color on paper; 97.8 × 97.3 cm.

the *Fujikō* were centered around perceived "female" energies. It is almost as though ritualized performances by male practitioners were somehow able to reconcile the pervasive anxieties about women's bodily functions. One such element was the Womb Cave (*Tainai* 胎内), now known as the Funatsu Lava Cave (fig. 6a–c).[38] This cavern did not simply provide refuge for the climbers as they made the long and arduous ascent, but it was believed that pilgrims would pass through it and be reborn through this symbolic and physical womb. Despite the inconsistency with prohibitions against actual women accessing the site because of their corrupting fluids, the notion of mountain as gestational mother was carried even further: ardent (male) pilgrims would drink the liquid that dripped from the cave's tubular lava stalactites, a form of nourishment for the metaphorical newborns (fig. 7). The essence of Mount Fuji is perceived to be female because the deity of the mountain, Konohanasakuya-hime 木花咲耶姫, is female. The deity was herself born inside the Womb Cave and is still enshrined there today. Hokusai was certainly aware of Konohanasakuya-hime, depicting her as the very first image in his three-volume work *One Hundred Views of Mount Fuji* (fig. 8). Whether Hokusai ever made a pilgrimage to Mount Fuji is not known; but it has been suggested that he may have been a member of one of the numerous cults centered around Fuji worship at the time, despite his primary affiliation with the Nichiren sect of Buddhism.[39]

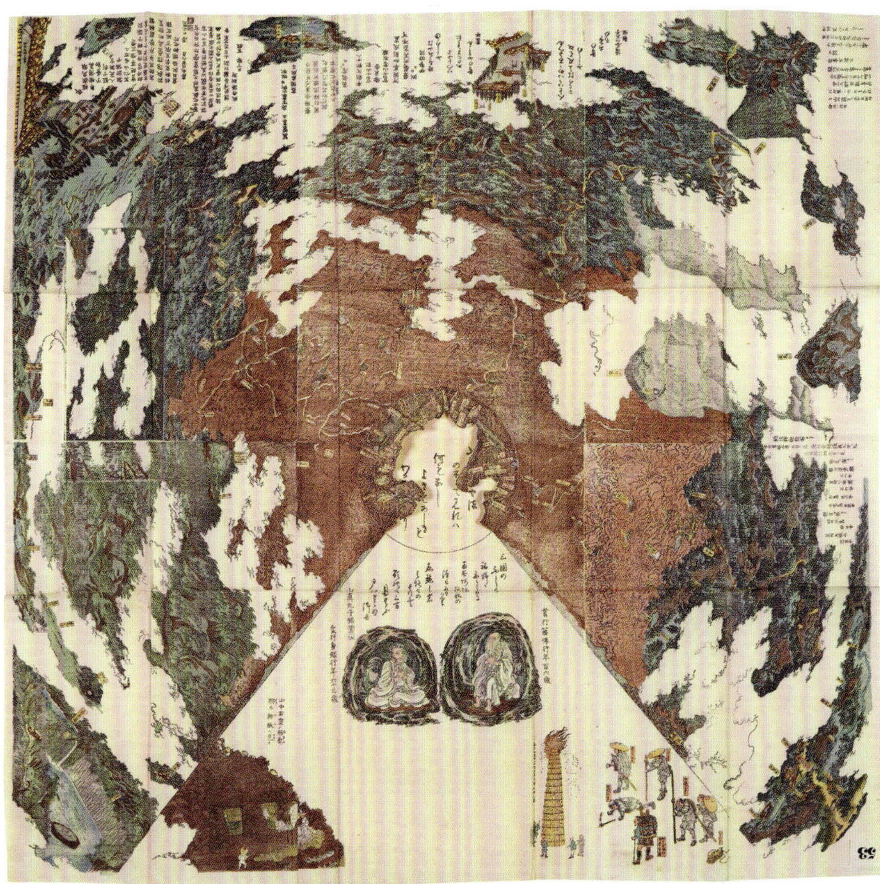

Fig. 6b
Map in fig. 6a, shown flat.

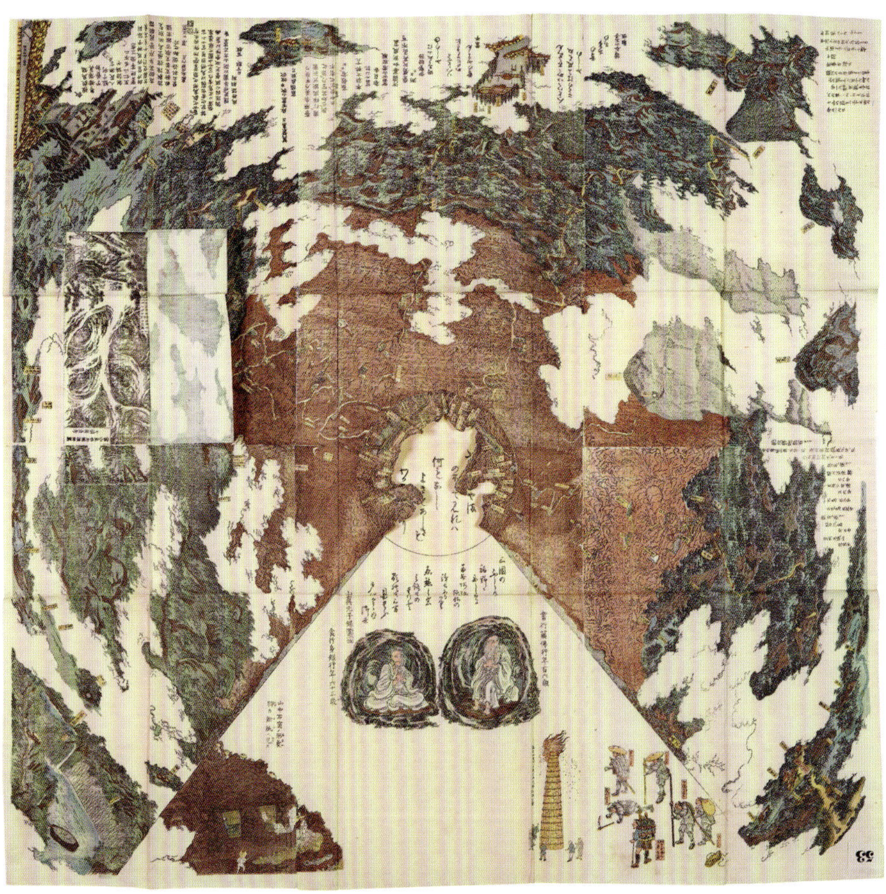

Fig. 6c
Flap of map in fig. 6b lifted to reveal Womb Cave, upper left.

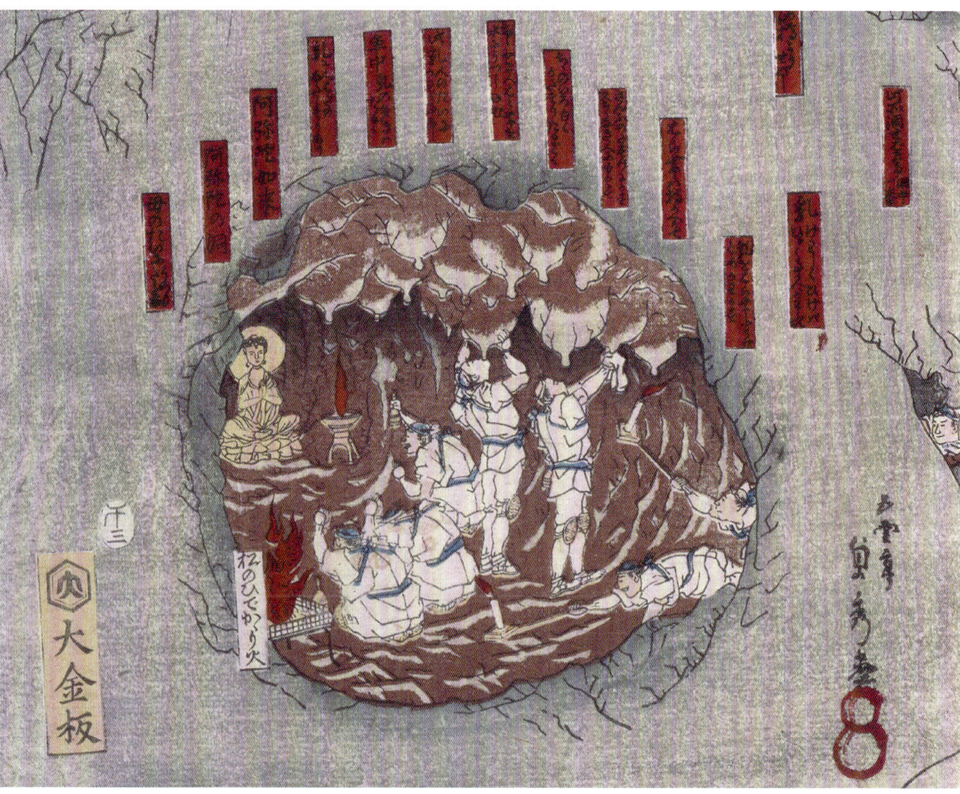

Fig. 7
Utagawa Sadahide, *Pilgrims in the Womb Cave on Mount Fuji* (*Fujisan tainai meguri no zu*) (detail). Edo period, 1857. Woodblock-printed triptych; ink and color on paper; 35.4 × 24.4 cm (each sheet).

Fig. 8
Katsushika Hokusai, *The Deity Konohanasakuya-hime* (*Konohanasakuya-hime no mikoto*), from *One Hundred Views of Mount Fuji*, vol. 1. Edo period, 1834. Woodblock print; ink and color on paper; 22.9 × 15.8 × 1 cm.

Hokusai's numerous illustrated books, prints, and colophons dedicated to Mount Fuji reveal an almost obsessive interest in the volcano. This makes it improbable that Hokusai was unaware of the prohibition against women in place at this time, particularly given his close working relationship with his third daughter, Ōi. As Hokusai's pupil, painting assistant, and traveling companion for many years, she accompanied him on several journeys between Edo and the northern town of Obuse 小布施 (in present-day Nagano Prefecture), a route that would have given them a view of Mount Fuji. Though she would have been forbidden from joining him on a pilgrimage to the summit, certain tourist attractions, like the *Fujizuka*, allowed Edo women the opportunity to transgress socially and religiously imposed boundaries, within a regulated space that ultimately did not disrupt the social order.

Although Gohyakurakanji did not contain a *Fujizuka* within its precincts, a different kind of miniaturized Fuji is provided by the distant peak in Hokusai's print. Like the Yoshiwara, Gohyakurakanji lay on the outskirts of the city, but the temple offered a form of spiritual escape rather than bodily confinement.[40] Contemporary women viewers of the print might recall the Yoshiwara balconies usually depicted in ukiyo-e, but by contemplating the small Fuji visible from the Sazaidō's viewing platform, they would now have different associations, of tourism and spiritual journeys. Although the women in our print are looking out over a different balcony railing, we might imagine they are staring beyond the restrictions of their lives—gazing at a site, or a life, forever out of reach.

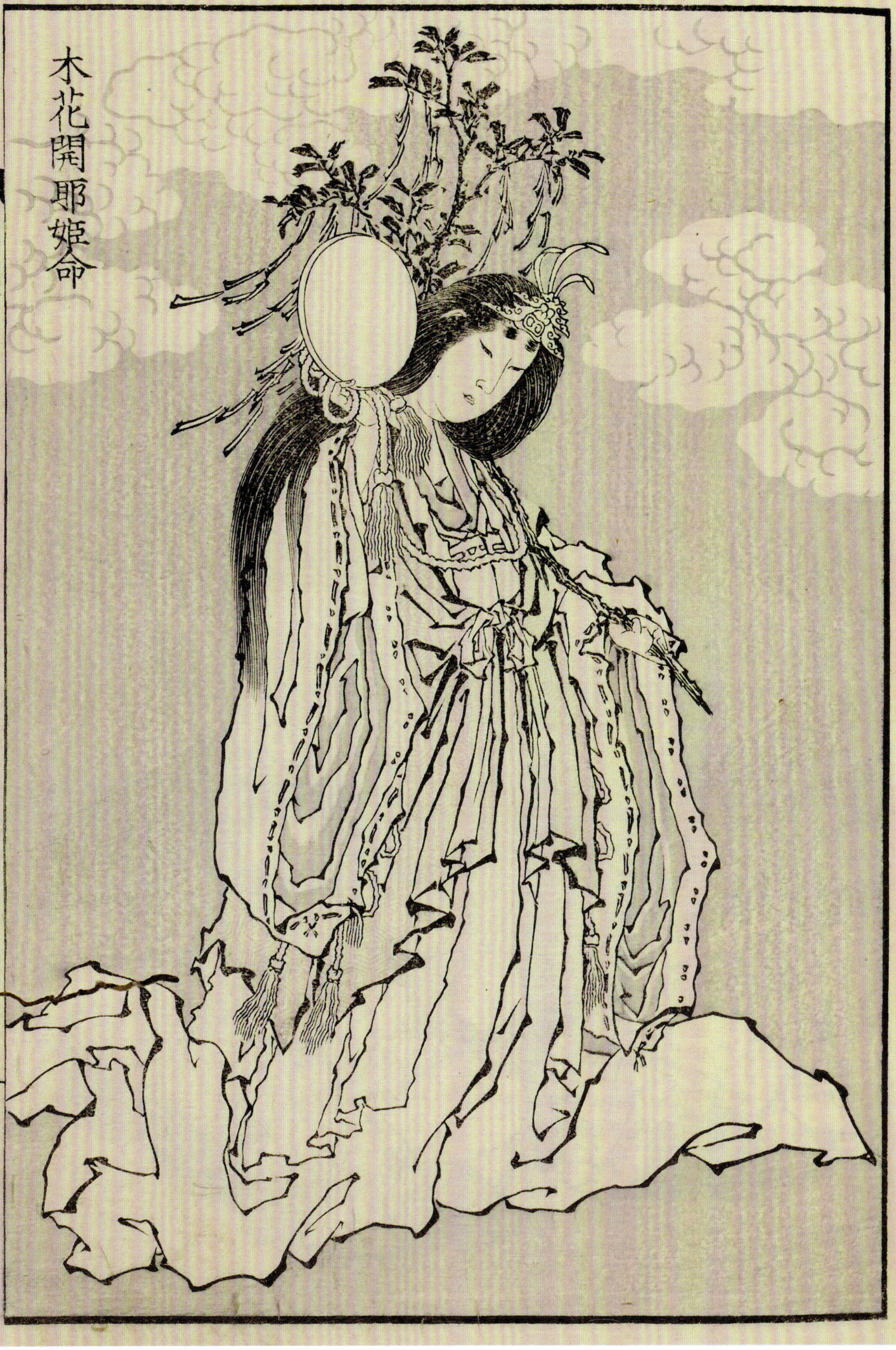

木花開耶姫命

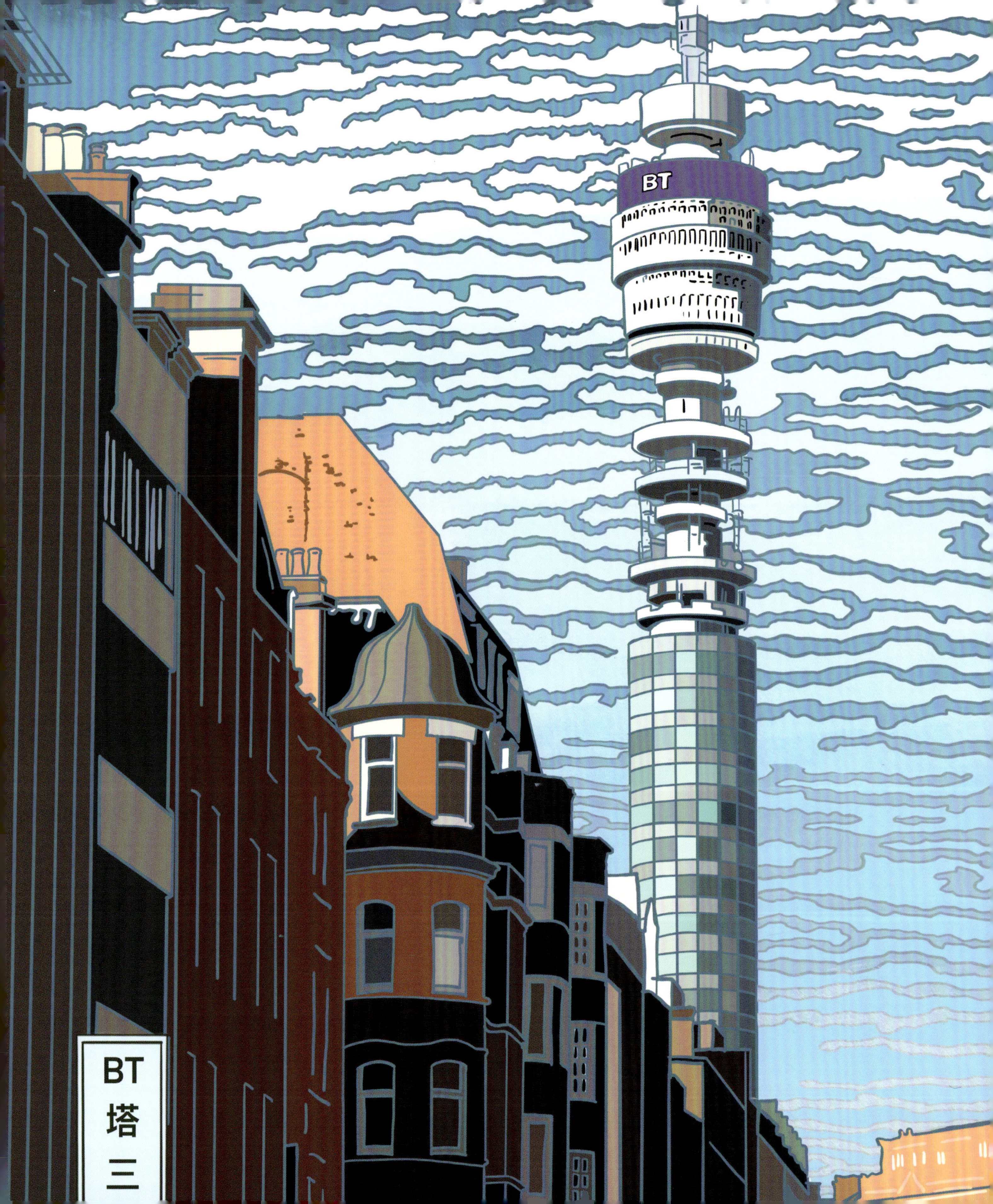
BT
BT
塔
三

(FREER) ASSOCIATION

How much does an object's history of ownership or appreciation determine its future resonance? Following a series of natural disasters in the second half of the nineteenth century, the original Gohyakurakanji complex was destroyed. The temple was eventually reestablished in the 1980s in a modern building at its current location in Tokyo's Meguro district, and 305 of the original 500 arhat sculptures are now enshrined at the site. Although the physical structure of the Sazaidō viewing platform does not survive, a sense of the experience that its vista offered is preserved through Hokusai's treatment in *The Sazaidō of Gohyakurakanji*. The genesis of this book was the juxtaposition of two works in the collection of the National Museum of Asian Art associated with the museum's founder, Charles Lang Freer (1854–1919). Freer ultimately decided to purge his collection of his impression of *The Sazaidō of Gohyakurakanji*, although another copy later entered the museum by different means. Although the *Gohyakurakanji* print and Whistler's *Balcony* remain connected, the absence of Hokusai's print from Freer's personal collection encourages us to be "freer" in our interpretations of the balcony than a strictly provenance-based analysis would usually encourage.

The impression of *The Sazaidō of Gohyakurakanji* currently in the Freer Gallery of Art was acquired through the posthumous collection bequest of the journalist and activist Agnes Ernst Meyer (1887–1970), who was a loyal friend of Freer and one of the museum's first trustees. Freer himself had also once owned many designs from the *Thirty-Six Views* series, including an impression of the *Gohyakurakanji* print, which records indicate he purchased from the dealer Yamanaka & Company's London branch in June 1904 for sixteen dollars.[41] Like many American collectors of this period, Freer owned a significant number of Japanese color prints, woodblock-printed books, and *surimono* (privately sponsored and circulated prints). By the time Freer acquired his own *Gohyakurakanji* impression in 1904, it is almost certain that he had seen the design before and may possibly have purchased alternate impressions.[42] Freer and many of his fellow collectors gained further exposure to Japanese prints by a series of exhibitions on the subject at the Grolier Club in New York, which were organized by the statesman, businessman, and art collector Shugio Hiromichi 執行弘道 (1853–1927) (fig. 1). As the director of the Kiryū Kōshō Kaisha 起立工商会社 (First Manufacturing and Trading Company), a government-established company for the export of Japanese art, Shugio was an important conduit of Japanese aestheticism at this time. He has certainly earned a pivotal place in the history of the museum, as Freer himself attributed the beginning of his Japanese art collecting to his exposure to Japanese prints at Shugio's exhibitions, which alerted him to the "points of contact" between the works of Hokusai and Whistler's etchings.[43] This observation would form the basis of his entire aesthetic philosophy. Both men were members of the Grolier Club, and in 1896 Freer had lent some of his Japanese prints to an exhibition that Shugio had organized there (fig. 2).[44] This confirms that Freer had acquired Japanese prints by this time, although unfortunately those purchases do not appear to have been recorded.[45] However, Freer attended the show, where an impression of the *Gohyakurakanji* print is listed in the catalogue of exhibits.[46]

Of all Japanese artists, Freer most admired Hokusai, and the paintings he collected have made the museum's collection of Hokusai's works one of the most renowned in the world. It is also possible that Freer was exposed to the artist during 1892–1893 at the Museum of Fine Arts, Boston, at the first exhibition of Hokusai's art to be held

Detail of fig. 5

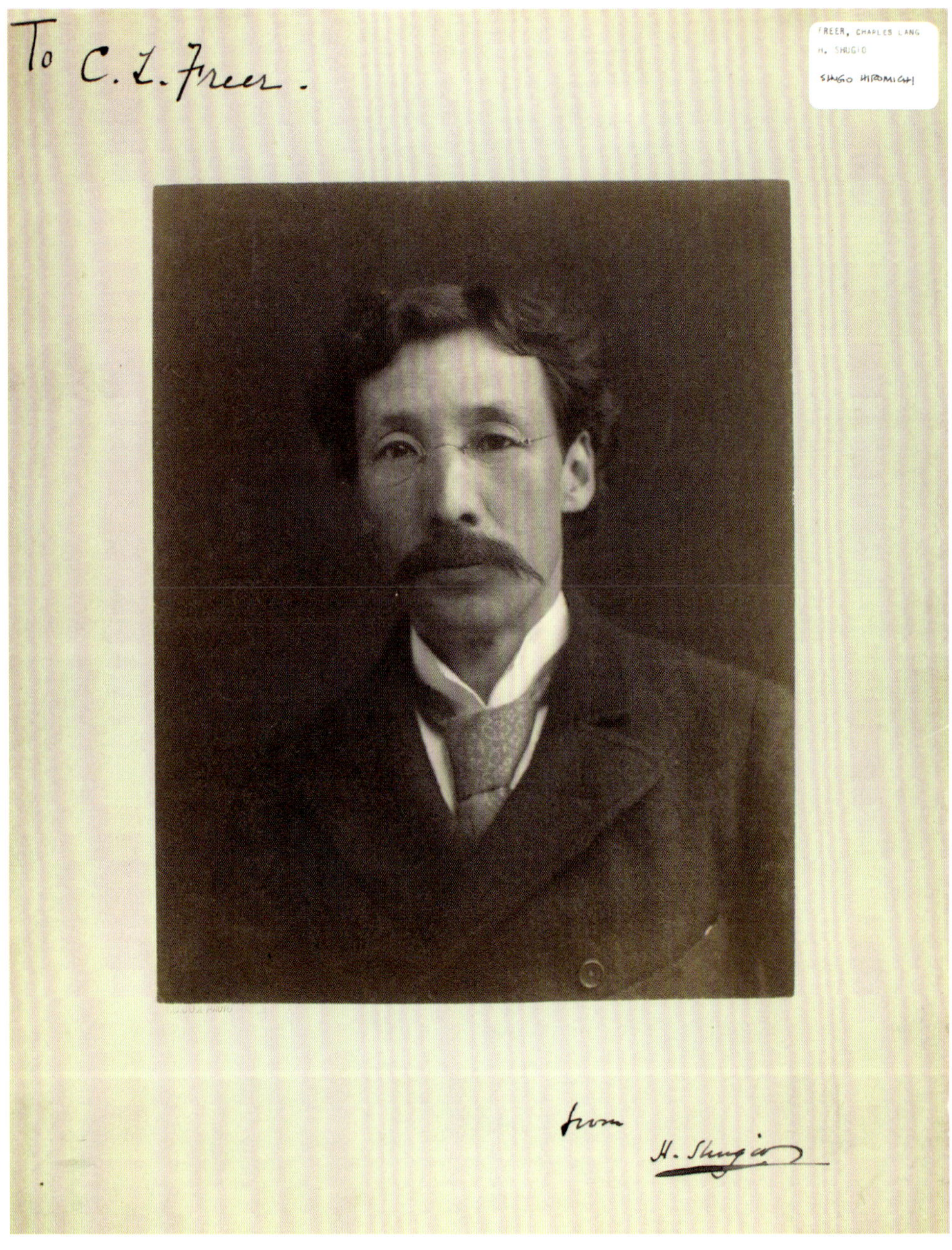

Fig. 1
George C. Cox, photographic portrait of Shugio Hiromichi. United States, undated. Platinotype on gray card mount; 35.6 × 28 cm.

anywhere in the world.[47] At this time, Hokusai's reputation had already been established as the apotheosis of Japanese design, when the art historian Louis Gonse (1846–1941) devoted an entire chapter of his 1883 survey of Japanese art, *L'Art japonais*, to Hokusai alone.[48] In the same year the Hokusai exhibition opened at the Museum of Fine Arts, Freer also saw and acquired Whistler's painting *Variations in Flesh Colour and Green—The Balcony*. There is a clear visual resonance between the two works—those aesthetic points of connection that Freer so appreciated as his guiding philosophy for art collecting. Whether Whistler modeled the composition of his painting on

Hokusai's print is unclear, as it is not known if Whistler also owned an impression of the *Gohyakurakanji* print. However, given Hokusai's important place in France during the Japonisme boom from the 1860s and the popularity of the *Thirty-Six Views* series at that time, it is very likely that Whistler at least *saw* an impression when frequenting East Asian art dealers during his time in Paris, if not later again in London. Whistler is known to have possessed other Japanese prints, including impressions from Torii Kiyonaga's 鳥居清長 (1752–1815) series *Twelve Months in the South* (*Minami jūni kō* 美南見十二候), which also shares striking compositional similarities with his *Balcony* (see **Roeder's restriction**). Freer may also have picked up on the visual similarity with the Whistler painting, as one design in the series is likely the one described as Kiyonaga's "Three Girls on a Balcony" in the catalogue of Shugio's 1896 print exhibition, which Freer lent to and attended (fig. 3).[49]

Whatever resonances Freer may have found between Whistler's *Balcony* and Hokusai's print, they ultimately proved insufficient for his grand aesthetic vision. While he chose to keep *The Balcony* painting, Freer sold his copy of *The Sazaidō of Gohyakurakanji* as he did with most of his other Japanese prints. In 1906, Freer's proposed gift to the

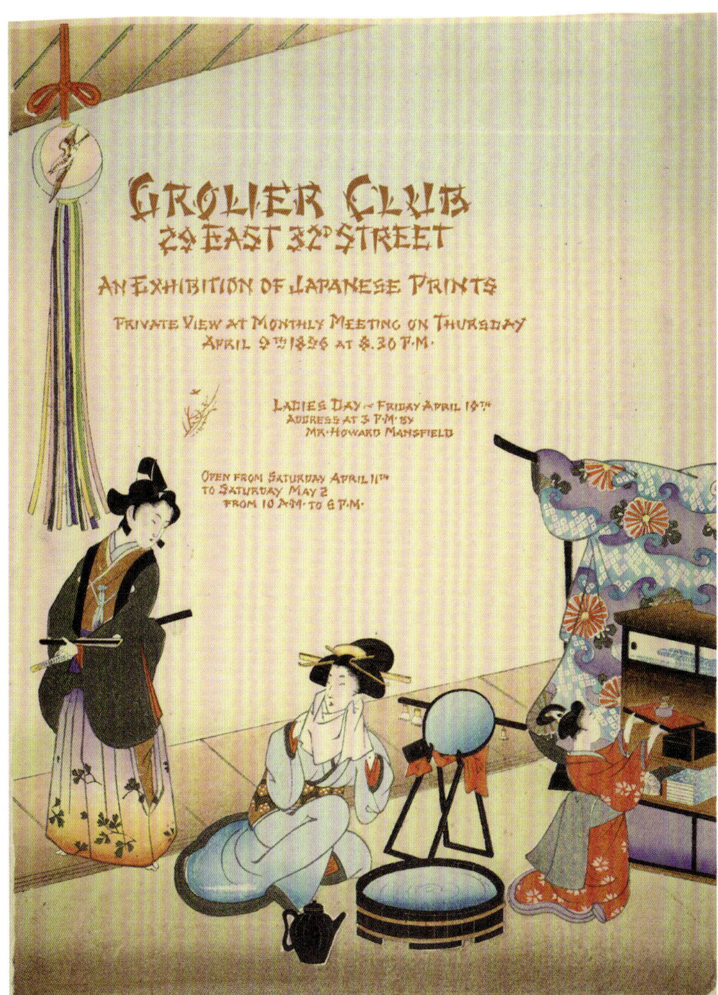

Fig. 2
Poster from 1896 Grolier Club print show. United States, 1896. Ink and color on paper; dimensions unknown.

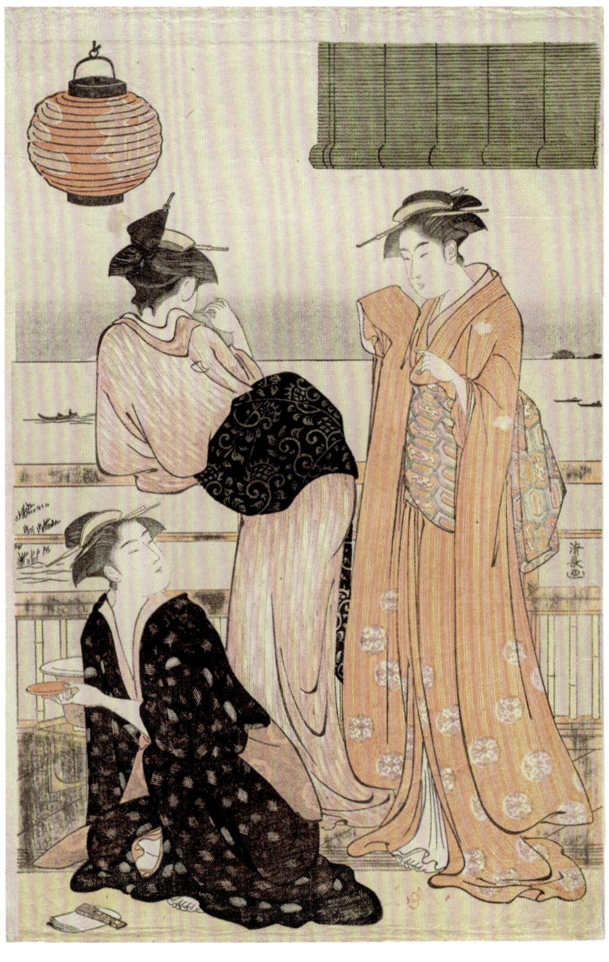

Fig. 3
Torii Kiyonaga, *The Sixth Month* (*Rokugatsu*), from the series *Twelve Months in the South*. Japan, Edo period, ca. 1784. Woodblock print; ink and color on paper; 39.9 × 25.9 cm.

nation, of American, Asian, and Near Eastern artworks to be housed in a dedicated museum, was accepted by the Smithsonian. Anticipating this decision, Freer had already begun purging works that did not reach his perceived standard of worthiness for a national institution. Most of his Japanese prints were sold in 1905, although a few appear to have been gifted to his associates.[50] Freer's precise reasons for doing so are unclear, though it seems he wished the works in his museum to reflect the direct traces of the artist's hand. Japanese woodblock prints are essentially reprographic in nature, with the original sketch of the artist mediated through the hands and tools of carvers and printers.[51] Freer could not have known that fifty years after his death, the death of his friend Agnes Meyer would occasion another impression of *The Sazaidō of Gohyakurakanji* entering the museum's collection. Whistler's painting and Hokusai's print have been exhibited many times in the intervening years, both separately and together, seen by new generations of visitors with perspectives, frames of reference, and evaluative standards of artistic merit different from those Freer held. He also would not have anticipated that another fifty years later, a book would be written that simultaneously brings the works together while also trying to pull them apart. It is here that we leave Freer behind.

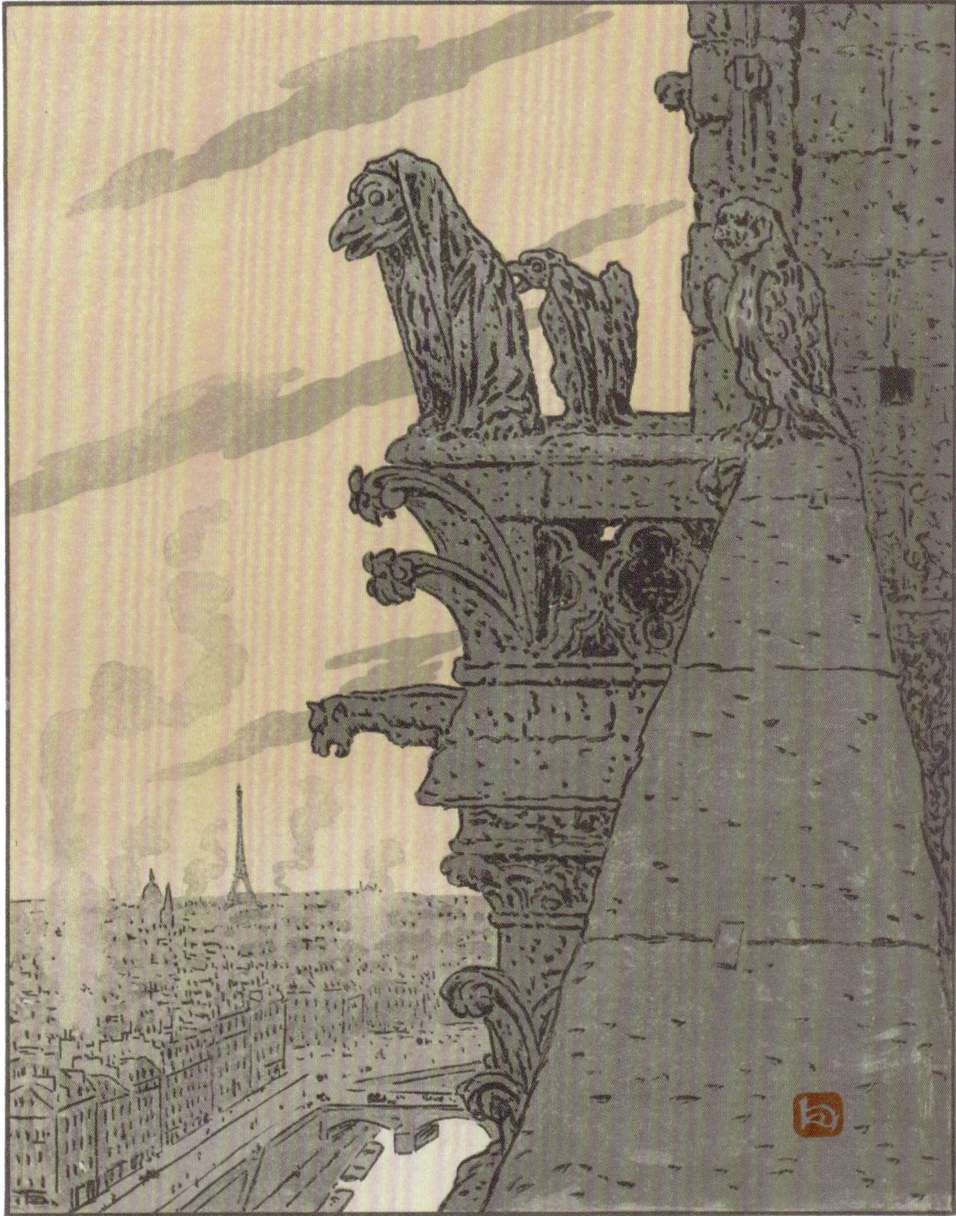

Fig. 4
Henri Rivière, *Thirty-Six Views of the Eiffel Tower*, plate 9. France, 1882–1902. Illustrated book with thirty-six lithographs; 26.7 × 22.8 cm (each sheet).

The Japonisme aesthetic to which Whistler subscribed in works like *The Balcony* has been characterized as a shallow artistic movement, being based on a mimicry of form rather than a conscientious consideration of the context of the original works being referenced (see **Roeder's view**). The implementation of Western perspectival systems in Japan is often similarly and simplistically characterized as an unquestioning and unreflective adoption of vanishing point perspective (see **perspective**). However, such reductive, influence-based models of the transmission of artistic idioms from one cultural context to another further contribute to flattening the specificities of each artwork and deemphasizing the implicit assumptions and visual languages

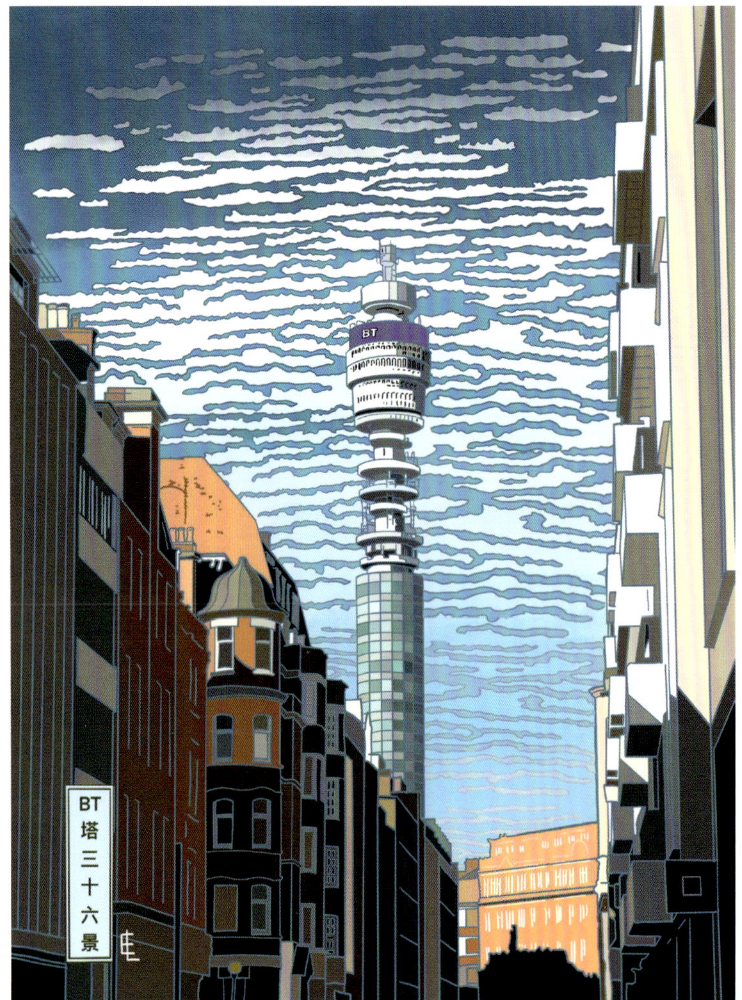

Fig. 5
Edward Luper, *"Autumn Clouds": BT Tower by Omotesando Café*, from the series *36 Views of the BT Tower*. United Kingdom, 2020. Ink and color on paper; 60.5 × 48 cm.

familiar to each audience. Although a reductive model may apply for some elements and interpretations, there are others that demonstrate a conscious recombination and adaptation of underlying mechanisms and motifs for a new context. More recent, culturally specific analyses have examined how such artistic interactions are not always a simple case of mimesis, but rather can be a *catalyst*, allowing an artist to broaden their toolkit of artistic approaches available in their immediate context.[52] For example, the framework of Hokusai's *Thirty-Six Views* series was adopted by the French artist Henri Rivière (1864–1951) for his *Thirty-Six Views of the Eiffel Tower* (*Les Trente-six vues de la Tour Eiffel*), centered on a man-made Parisian icon as a replacement for Mount Fuji (fig. 4). More recently, the London-based illustrator Edward Luper (b. 1988) created *36 Views of the BT Tower*, drawing from the aesthetics of Hokusai and Hiroshige to present the British Telecommunications tower in its role as a lodestar in central London for the city's residents (fig. 5). The composition of Hokusai's print has also been interpreted as a knitted garment, whereby viewers are now positioned to look through the wearer onto an imagined Mount Fuji beyond (fig. 6). Other examinations, such as those in this volume, can reveal hidden resonances between the works that may

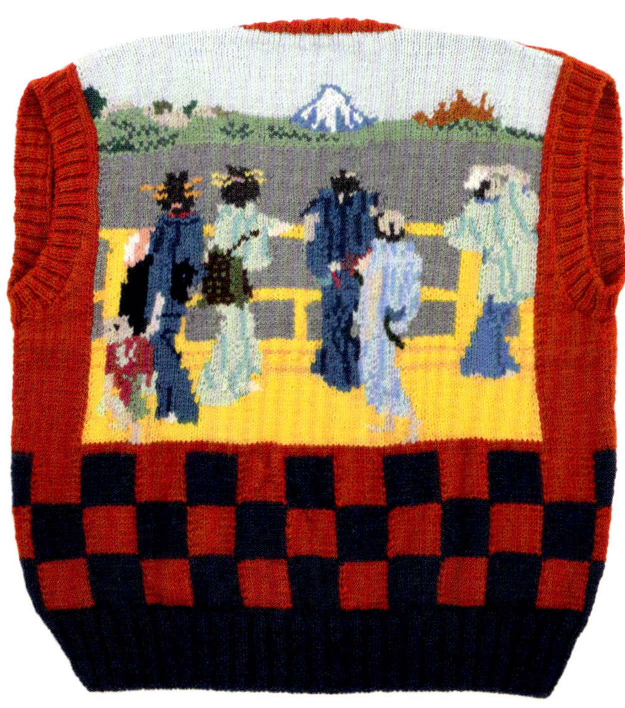

Fig. 6
Nishiyama Terumi, Gohyakurakanji vest. Japan, ca. 2023. Wool; 65 × 58 cm (approx., men's size medium).

have been unconsciously apprehended by the artists, or not known at all—discovered, ironically, by those looking past superficial similarities.

Beyond Hokusai and the immediate influences of the *Thirty-Six Views* series, the compositional and heuristic device of a balcony is well-suited to the type of recombinant configurations of motifs and styles that are common in cases of intercultural aesthetic influence. The device also makes clear that there is a very particular perspective—that of the balcony's implied or depicted occupant—being adopted. As we saw with Murasaki Shikibu in **view**, balcony views in artworks open up possibilities for a reflection on positionality. An example of the self-conscious adoption of an *opposing* perspective to the artist is foregrounded in a "balcony" view by the Japanese American artist Roger Shimomura (b. 1939) in his work *American Infamy #2* (fig. 7). Shimomura was confined to the Minidoka concentration camp by the US government at the age of two, and the experiences he and other Japanese Americans shared at such camps created generational trauma that remains unresolved. Shimomura's view offers a different kind of lofty perspective than that of Hokusai's *Gohyakurakanji*, as the viewer now shares the perspective of the armed military personnel observing the incarcerated Japanese citizens, a group that includes the artist. With a compositional framing that evokes the panels of a Japanese folding screen and incorporates the plump clouds found in Japanese narrative painting, the balcony has become a surveillance turret, and the viewer now shares the perspective of this sinister purpose.

By their nature, balcony views in art privilege interpretations that generate questions about the viewer's perspective and the vista that is presented. This volume is not intended to restrict the viewer only to a comparison of two works by Whistler and Hokusai, or to Freer's collecting, but to encourage the reader to make their own connections, between these two works but also to others far beyond. Although the

Fig. 7
Roger Shimomura, *American Infamy #2*. United States, 2006. Acrylic on canvas; 182.9 × 304.8 cm.

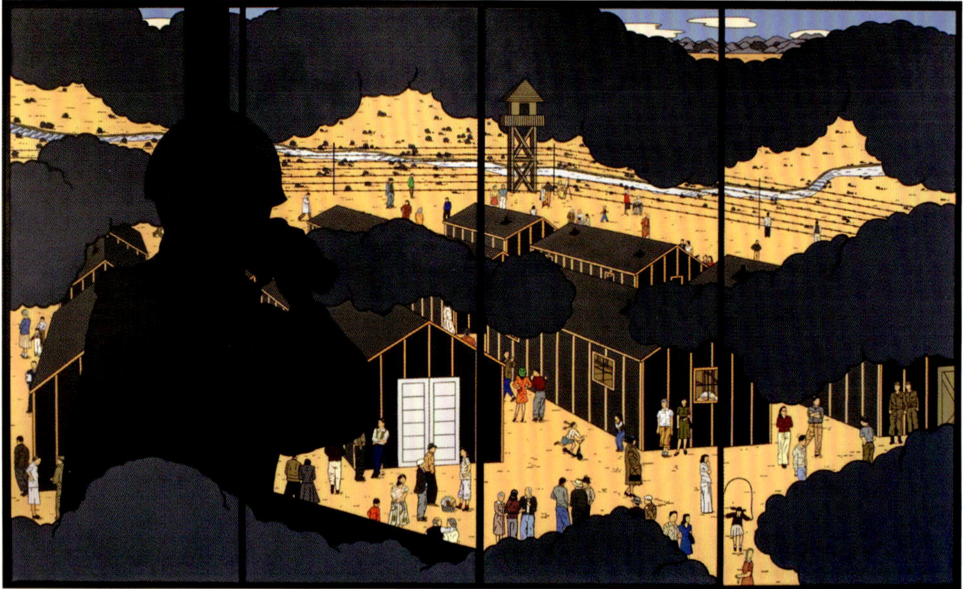

interpretative contextual angles discussed in this volume can enrich our appreciation of the *Gohyakurakanji* print, it is perfectly possible to enjoy the image in terms of its considerable visual appeal. And perhaps the most desirable outcome is to do both. After ascending many levels of Gohyakurakanji's history, we stand like Hokusai's temple visitors, exhausted by the climb—but exhilarated by the view.

Notes

1. This placement is relatively unusual, as compositions by the print's artist, Katsushika Hokusai, usually locate Mount Fuji to the right of the center line, which gives primacy to the mountain in conventional Japanese right-to-left reading order. Henry D. Smith II, "Hokusai and the Mountain of Immortality," in *One Hundred Views of Mt. Fuji* (New York: George Braziller, 1988), 8.
2. The official, formal name of the temple was Ten'onzan Gohyakurakanji 天恩山五百羅漢寺. The temple was badly damaged during the Great Ansei Earthquake of 1855. It was rebuilt in Honjo Midori-chō in 1887 with some of the extant sculptures, but many of the buildings, including the Sazaidō depicted by Hokusai, were entirely destroyed. In 1908, the temple was moved to its present location in Meguro, Tokyo.
3. Honjo was not even officially considered a part of Edo proper until 1719 and was often included as an inset or addendum to many city maps. The history and layout of Gohyakurakanji, its unusual qualities, and its function within the Edo psyche were brought to the fore by Timon Screech, "The Strangest Place in Edo: The Temple of the Five Hundred Arhats," *Monumenta Nipponica* 48, no. 4 (1993): 407-28. Screech has recently revisited the subject with a summary in his recent volume, *Tokyo Before Tokyo: Power and Magic in the Shogun's City of Edo* (London: Reaktion Books, 2020), 112-27.
4. This term was introduced by Mary Elizabeth Berry, *Japan in Print: Information and Nation in the Early Modern Period* (Berkeley: University of California Press, 2007), 15.
5. See Screech, "Strangest Place in Edo." As a whole, the Honjo area, where Gohyakurakanji was located, was associated with strange or uncanny events, and a series of supernatural tales of ghosts and shape-shifting animals developed into the Seven Wonders of Honjo (*Honjo nana fushigi* 本所七不思議).
6. This support system was unusual but not unique. The first Tokugawa shogun, Ieyasu 家康 (1543-1616), granted tracts of land for the rebuilding and establishment of Nishi Honganji 西本願寺 and Higashi Honganji 東本願寺 temples in Kyoto to reward the abbots for their loyalty to him over his military competitors.
7. Soejima Hiromichi, "Tōkyō to Rakanji no butsuzō: Chōsa kenkyū hōkoku," *Odai Shigaku*, no. 3 (2008): 39.

8. The platform was at a height of 58 shaku. A shaku is a traditional form of Japanese measurement, equivalent to approximately 30.3 centimeters.
9. Since Tani Bunchō inscribed his work with "W. Van Royen 1725," it has also been speculated that the original paintings may have been by the hand of Willem Frederiksz van Royen (ca. 1645–1723). However, as Willem Frederiksz van Royen died the year after the commission, the paintings were probably completed by someone else. Screech, "Strangest Place in Edo," 425.
10. Unfortunately, the van Royen paintings do not survive. Large-scale, framed oil paintings do not adhere to the formats or mounting traditions that are accommodated by traditional Japanese display alcoves (*tokonoma* 床の間). With limited alternate options, it is likely that the van Royen works displayed at Gohyakurakanji were hung in the buildings' eaves, the paintings' oil-pigmented surfaces degraded by wind, rain, and humidity until nothing remained.
11. Hokusai used many names throughout his career. See summary list in Frank Feltens, *Hokusai's Brush: Paintings, Drawings and Sketches by Katsushika Hokusai in the Smithsonian Freer Gallery of Art* (Washington, DC; Kyoto: Smithsonian Books; Seigensha Art Publishing, 2020), 154–55.
12. *Oranda no soroban keiko* おらんだの十露盤けいこ. See Asakura Haruhiko, *Ryūtei Tanehiko nikki* (Tokyo: Akiyama Shoten, 1979), 140. For this anecdote and an analysis of Hokusai's use of geometrical principles, see Christine M. E. Guth, "Hokusai's Geometry," *Review of Japanese Culture and Society* 20 (2008): 120–32.
13. In his later years, Hokusai was an instructor to the wealthy merchant Takai Kozan 高井鴻山 (1806–1883). Hokusai provided instructional drawings on grids that Kozan could transfer to his own gridded sketches, now in the collection of the Takai Kozan Memorial Museum, Obuse.
14. See Tony Cole, Robert Tauxe, and Ann Herring, "Japanese Woodblock-Printed Dioramas," *Andon*, no. 110 (2020): 36–55.
15. For a recent analysis of *meisho*-e, see Quintana Roo Irigon Heathman, "Beyond Landscape: Imagining Place in Later Edo Print Culture" (PhD diss., University of Pennsylvania, 2018).
16. Pierre Loti, *Madame Chrysanthème* (Paris: North Star Editions, 2016), 54.
17. The Japanese version of the website for the current incarnation of Gohyakurakanji states that Shōun carved the sculptures; the English version is more emphatic in insisting that he carved them alone (http://rakan.or.jp/, accessed December 5, 2022).
18. Yan Yang, "Japanese Edo Rakan Sculptures by Shōun Genkei at Ten'on-zan Gohyaku Rakan-ji" (unpublished manuscript, December 2019).
19. For reproductions of Kōriki Enkōan's sketches, see Nagoya-shi Hakubutsukan, *Hokusai taiga sokusho saizu: Onna yōkyoku saiyōshū* (Nagoya: Nagoya-shi Hakubutsukan, 2004).
20. Handbill in Nagoya-shi Hakubutsukan collection.
21. Smith II, trans., "Hokusai and the Mountain of Immortality," 7.
22. "*Darusen*" is an abbreviation of "Daruma Teacher" (*Daruma-sensei* 達磨先生). Nagoya-shi Hakubutsukan, *Hokusai taiga sokusho saizu*, 106; Gian Carlo Calza, *Hokusai* (London: Phaidon, 2003), 192.
23. The advertisement is placed at the end of volume 12 of an illustrated novel also published by Nishimura's firm, *Stories in Promptbook Form* (*Shōhon jitate* 正本製). The advertisement is translated in a groundbreaking essay by Henry D. Smith II, "Hokusai and the Blue Revolution in Edo Prints," in *Hokusai and His Age: Ukiyo-e Painting, Printmaking, and Book Illustration in Late Edo Japan*, ed. John Carpenter (Amsterdam: Hotei, 2005), 254, to which much of this section is indebted.
24. One of the earliest uses of Berlin blue in Japan has been confirmed by visible reflectance spectroscopy (VRS) in one painting in Itō Jakuchū's 伊藤若冲 (1716–1800) *Colorful Realm* (*Dōshoku sai-e* 動植綵絵) ensemble, completed between 1757 and 1766. Hayakawa Yasuhiro, "On the Colorants," in Yukio Lippit, *Colorful Realm: Japanese Bird and Flower Paintings by Itō Jakuchū* (Washington, DC: National Gallery of Art, 2012), 212.
25. The date of Eisen's work is based on a suggestive note in the volume *Masaki no kazura* 正木葛 by the Edo-period book dealer Seisōdō. This note is translated and analyzed in Smith II, "Hokusai and the Blue Revolution," 236.
26. Smith II, "Hokusai and the Blue Revolution."
27. Capucine F. Korenberg, Lucia Pereira-Pardo, Peter J. McElhinney, and Joanne Dyer, "Developing a Systematic Approach to Determine the Sequence of Impressions of Japanese Woodblock Prints: The Case of Hokusai's 'Red Fuji,'" *Heritage Science* 7, no. 9 (2019): 6.
28. For example, Higuchi Kazutaka, "Aizuri ukiyo-e hanga ni kansuru ichi kōsatsu: Katsushika Hokusai to Keisai Eisen no beroai-zuri fūkeiga o megutte," *Idemitsu Bijutsukan kanpō*, no. 90 (1994): 15n2; Carolina Retta, "Hokusai's Treatise on Colouring: Ehon Saishikitsū," in *Hokusai Paintings: Selected Essays*, ed. Gian Carlo Calza (Venice: The International Hokusai Research Centre, University of Venice, 1994), 237–46; selections from Hokusai's original text are translated by Ryoko Matsuba in *Mad about Painting* (New York: David Zwirner Books, 2023), 40–145.
29. Timothy Clark, *Hokusai: Beyond the Great Wave* (New York; London: Thames & Hudson; British Museum, 2017), 301. The letter is in the collection of the Hokusai Museum, Obuse.
30. See Miyashita Saburō, "Jinkō konjō (purushian burū) no mozō to yunyū," in *Ronshū Nihon no yōgaku*, ed. Arisaki Takamichi and Asai Mitsuaki, vol. 3 (Osaka: Seibundō, 1995), 131–34.
31. Smith II, "Hokusai and the Mountain of Immortality," 21.
32. Smith II, 212.
33. Following the Meireki fire in 1657, the location of the Yoshiwara was moved out of central Edo to the northeast of

the city beyond the Sensōji temple complex. Though technically this restored location earned the site the name "Shin-Yoshiwara" 新吉原 (literally "New Yoshiwara"), this volume follows convention and uses the term "Yoshiwara" when referencing the second locale.

34. For a discussion of terminology used to describe these women that is more appropriate for twenty-first-century discourse, see Julie Nelson Davis, *Picturing the Floating World* (Honolulu: University of Hawai'i Press, 2021), 36-37; and Amy Stanley, *Selling Women: Prostitution, Markets, and the Household in Early Modern Japan* (Berkeley: University of California Press, 2012).
35. For an overview on travel in the Edo period, see Constantine Vaporis, *Breaking Barriers: Travel and the State in Early Modern Japan* (Cambridge, MA: Council on East Asian Studies, Harvard University, 1994).
36. See Miyazaki Fumiko, "Female Pilgrims and Mt. Fuji: Changing Perspectives on the Exclusion of Women," *Monumenta Nipponica* 60, no. 3 (2005): 339-91. Most restrictions against women visiting sacred sites were lifted in 1872, although some continue even today. See Lindsey E. DeWitt, "Envisioning and Observing Women's Exclusion from Sacred Mountains in Japan," *Journal of Asian Humanities at Kyushu University* 1 (2016): 19-28.
37. See Melinda Takeuchi, "Making Mountains: Mini-Fujis, Edo Popular Religion and Hiroshige's 'One Hundred Famous Views of Edo,'" *Impressions* 24 (2002): 24-47.
38. See Miyazaki Fumiko, "An Artist's Rendering of the Divine Mount Fuji," in *Cartographic Japan: A History in Maps*, ed. Kären Wigen, Sugimoto Fumiko, and Cary Karacas (Chicago: University of Chicago Press, 2016), 98-101.
39. For a discussion of Hokusai's spirituality with regard to Mount Fuji, see Smith II, "Hokusai and the Mountain of Immortality."
40. Screech claims that Honjo was suggested as a site for the relocation for the Yoshiwara in the 1650s. Screech, "Strangest Place in Edo," 409.
41. Thirty prints from the *Thirty-Six Views* series were purchased from Yamanaka on this occasion (NMAA Archives, Charles Lang Freer Papers, FSA.A.01, "List of Prints owned by Charles L. Freer," Y44, 30). The impression currently in the collection has been trimmed and appears to be a later impression. For information on the different states of this design, see Matthi Forrer, *Hokusai: Prints and Drawings* (Munich: Prestel, 1991), no. 22.
42. According to the timeline provided by Wayne State University, Freer had also purchased prints by Hokusai in 1894 (http://peacockroom.wayne.edu/timeline).
43. Royal Cortissoz, "Freer Museum Soon to Be Built in Washington," *New York Tribune*, December 15, 1915.
44. The list of exhibits is recorded in Shugio Hiromichi, *Catalogue of an Exhibition of Japanese Prints at the Grolier Club: April, 1896* (New York: The Grolier Club, 1896). The eight works lent by Freer are described in his March 16, 1896, letter to Howard Mansfield, who jointly organized the exhibition.
45. It has been suggested that Freer bought prints directly from Shugio. Ingrid Larsen, "'DON'T SEND MING OR LATER PICTURES': Charles Lang Freer and the First Major Collection of Chinese Painting in an American Museum," *Ars Orientalis* 40 (2011): 10.
46. Hiromichi, *Catalogue of an Exhibition of Japanese Prints*, 20, no. 154.
47. Although Freer's diaries do not explicitly confirm his attendance at this exhibition, his diaries for 1892-1893 include several visits to Boston on dates that coincide with the exhibition period. The lack of confirmation is not unusual, as Freer's diary entries around this time are limited mostly to the city where he was located on any given day as well as any business expenses incurred. Moreover, Freer owned a copy of the catalogue, which is now in the museum's library (Museum of Fine Arts, *Hokusai and His School: Catalogue of Special Exhibition Number One* [Boston: Alfred Mudge and Son, 1893]).
48. See Inaga Shigemi, "The Making of Hokusai's Reputation in the Context of Japonisme," *Japan Review*, no. 15 (2003): 77-100.
49. Hiromichi, *Catalogue of an Exhibition of Japanese Prints*, 13, no. 74.
50. Freer sold the majority to Tod Ford of Pasadena, California, as recorded in his letter to Ford on March 10, 1905 (NMAA Archives, Letterpress book, vol. 16, January 7-March 15, 1905, nos. 388-90). In this same letter, Freer recalls that although he had at one time hoped to build a "representative" print collection, it was difficult to find high-quality impressions, and over time, he found himself far more inclined to paintings than prints.
51. There are a small number of Japanese prints remaining in Freer's collection, and several blocks. Freer may have intended these to serve an educational purpose. Freer did not divest his collection of Whistler's prints. This may have been for sentimental reasons (Whistler died in 1903, and Freer had been aiming to assemble the "definitive" Whistler collection); or this may have been because he considered that Whistler's prints were less "mediated," since he played an active role in manipulating the ink on the plate to create different tonal effects.
52. For a fascinating account of how the Chinese iconography of a plowing ritual was adapted into the creation of a French Republican festival, see Ryan Whyte, "Turned Earth: The Chinese Plowing Ritual in the Age of Enlightenment," *The Art Bulletin* 104, no. 1 (2022): 78-97.

Do you remember the view from your childhood bedroom?

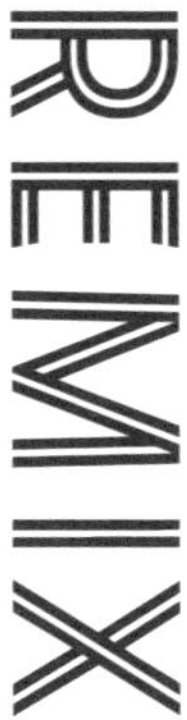

Drawing can be a powerful tool for unlocking memory. Once you start drawing, you may remember more things than you would have recalled using words alone.

You may want to start with the window frame. Was it plastic, or wood? Did the window have one pane of glass, or several? Add a detail that you remember from the view. As you build the picture, try to remember textures and sensations, and incorporate them as much as possible.

draw in here

What is your ideal view from a balcony?

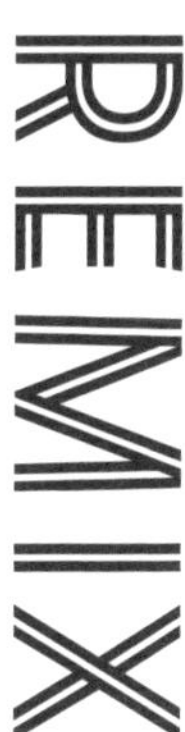

Start assembling materials for a collage, which can be gathered from magazines, printed from the internet, or even cut from the pages of this book. What kind of view are you trying to create? One that relaxes, or inspires? Creating a harmonious color palette may strengthen your intention, especially if you use colors that are symbolic or have a meaning that is special to you. Your view might be a fantasy location or perhaps a real place you have not yet visited. Are there any people in your view?

collage in here

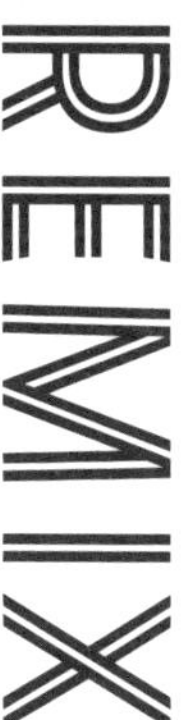

Can you picture yourself in the artist's place?

What colors would you use in this scene? How would you populate this balcony? What would you include in the landscape, and what would you exclude?

*You may want to photocopy the line drawing before you begin so that you can try this activity more than once.

draw and color in here

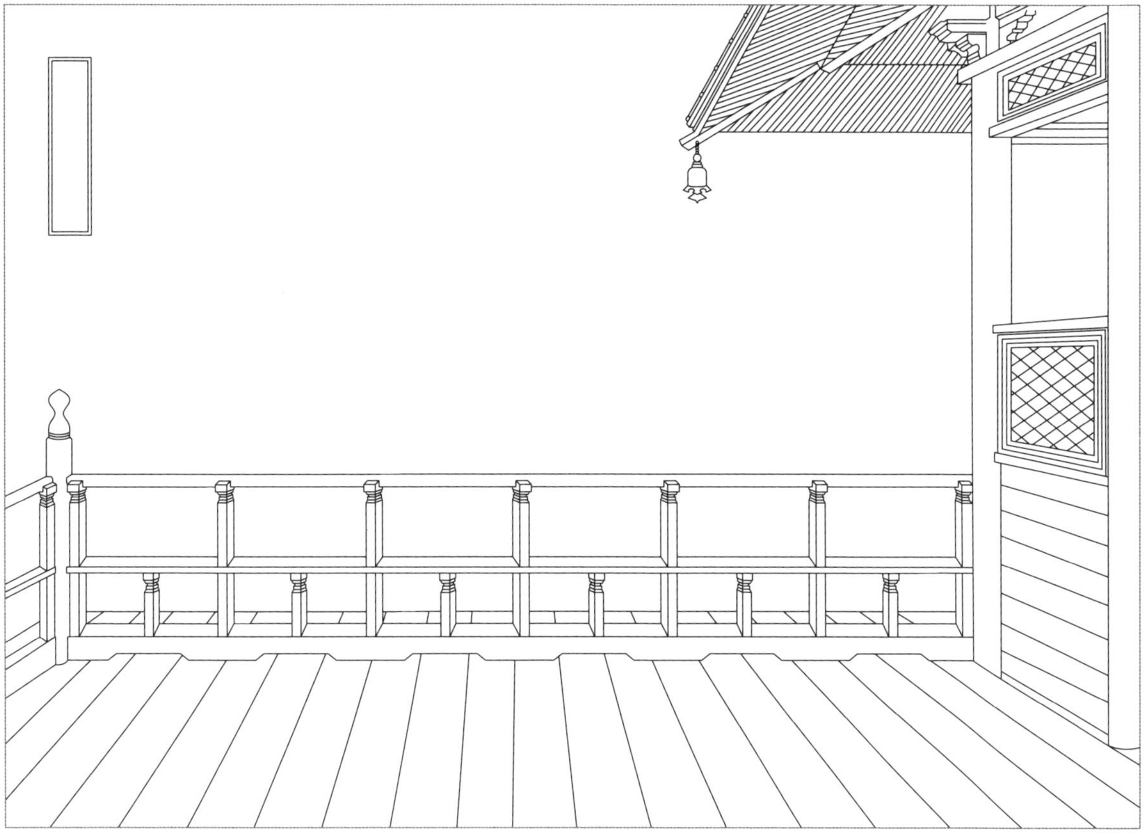

Can you build your own gate? Hokusai pop-out (diorama)

This type of paper diorama, which was cut out and assembled by the consumer, became very popular in mid-nineteenth-century Japan. A small black-and-white drawing in the lower left corner illustrates how the finished diorama should look. This scene shows a fight between visitors to the Kaminarimon 雷門 (literally "Lightning Gate") at the entrance to the temple of Sensōji in Asakusa, in northeast Tokyo. Although only this design is known today, there may originally have been other sheets as part of a set showing the various elements of this temple compound. What else would you add?

Remove the pop-out elements along the perforations and fold as instructed on the reverse.

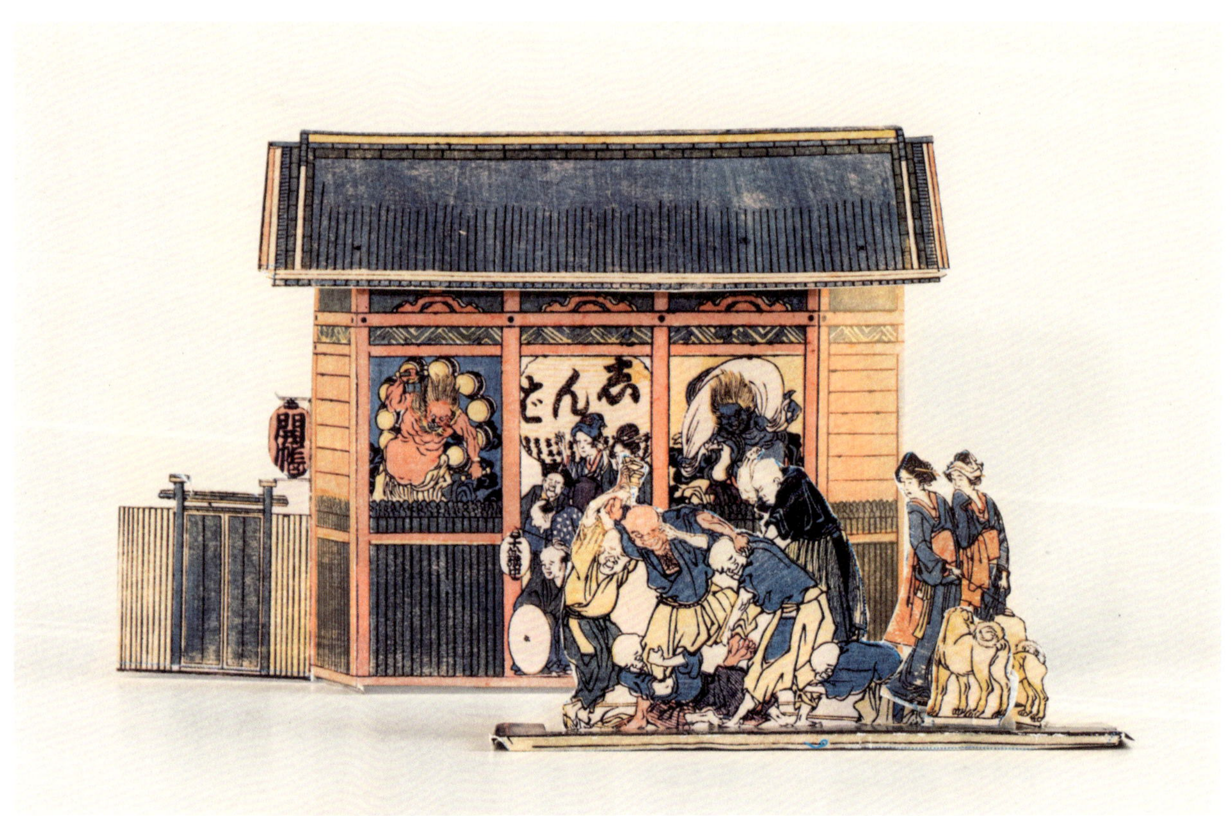

Katsushika Hokusai, single sheet from *The Kaminarimon at Asakusa Sensōji.*

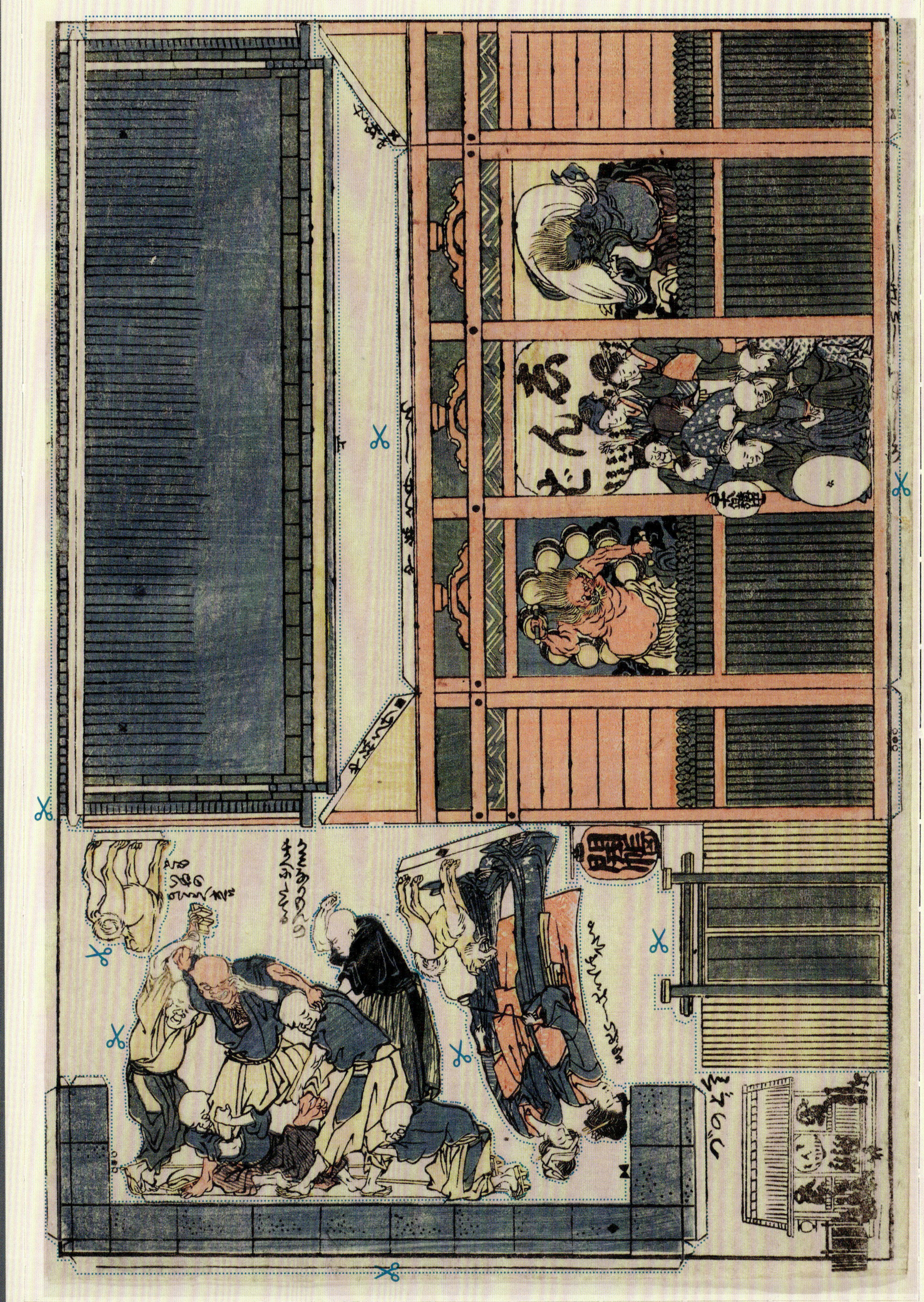

Fold backward

Position this element over the middle of the gate, with this edge as the top of the roof

Fold backward

Fold forward

Place piece in front of gate

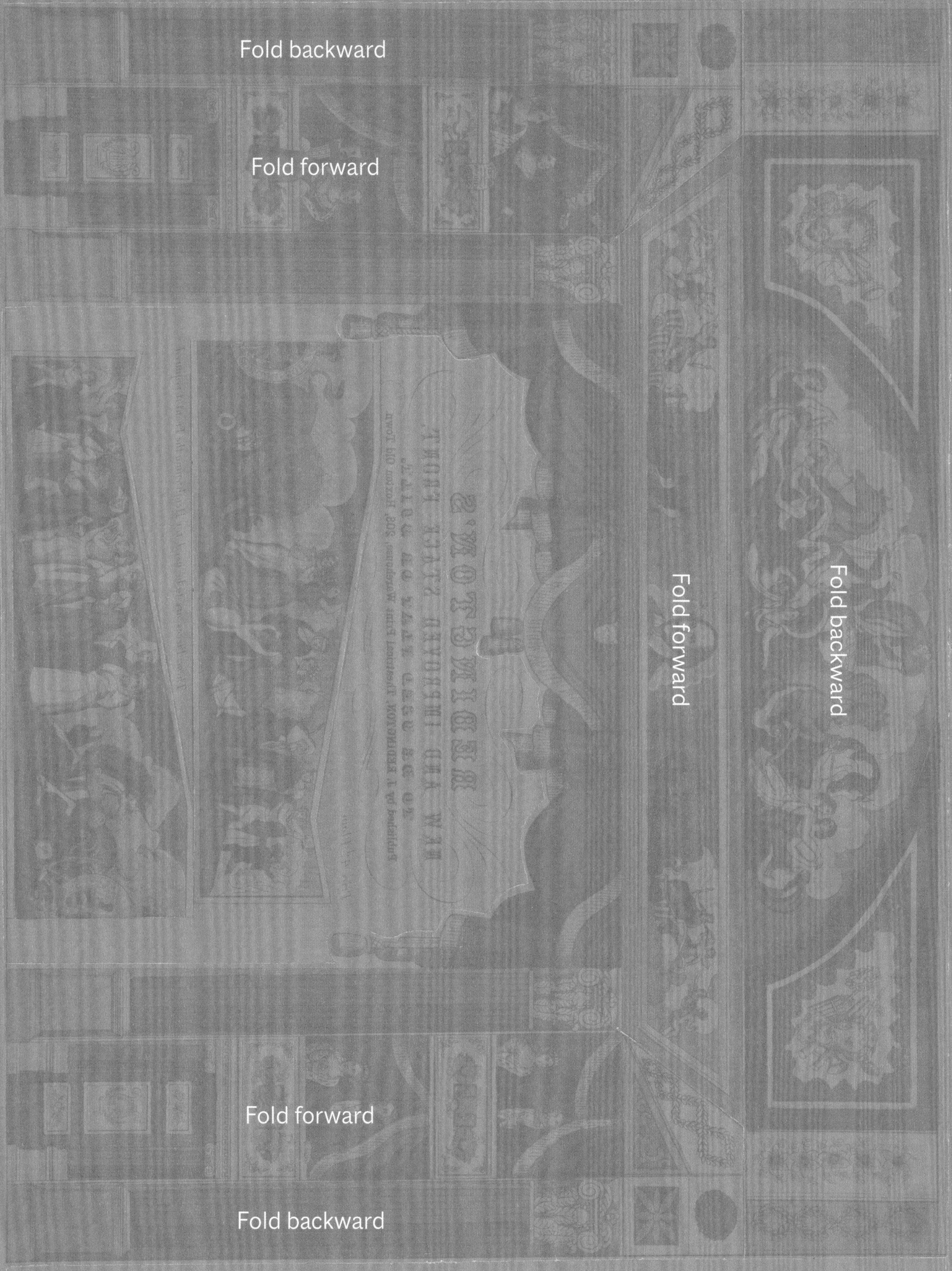

Fold backward

Fold forward

Fold forward

Fold backward

Fold forward

Fold backward

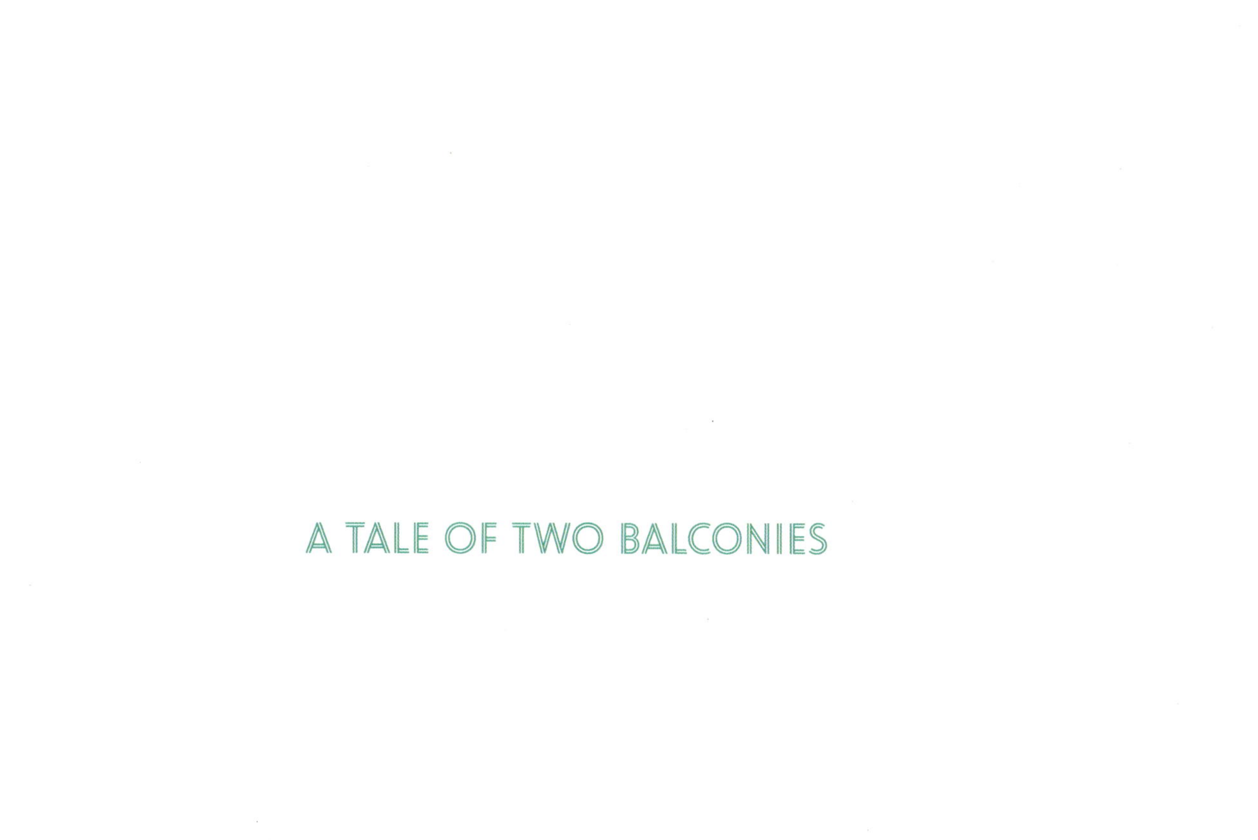

A TALE OF TWO BALCONIES

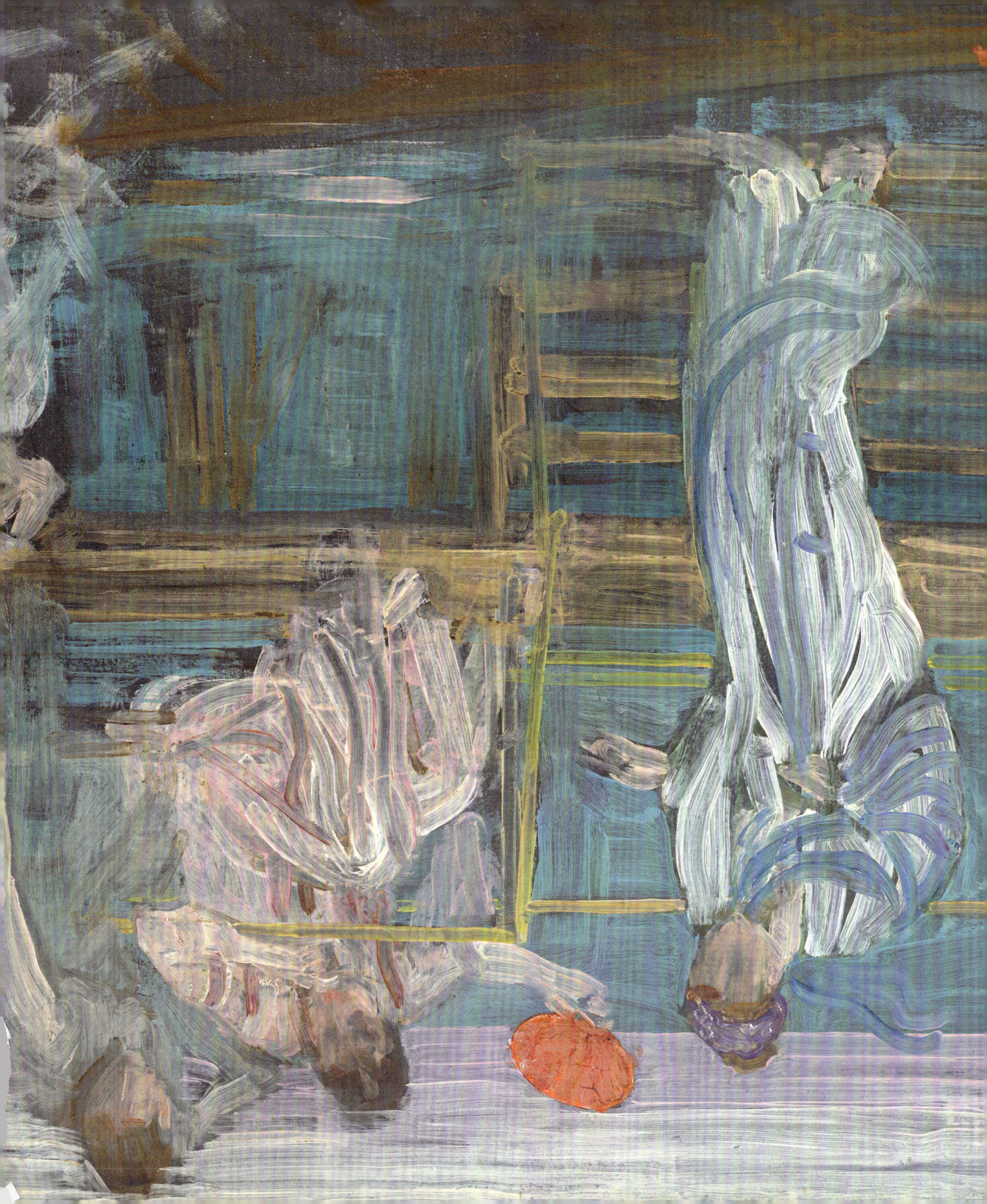

A TALE OF TWO BALCONIES

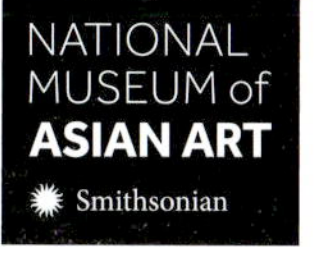

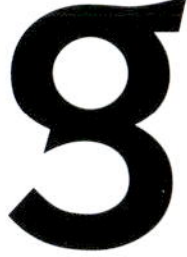

National Museum of Asian Art, Smithsonian Institution in association with D Giles Limited

National Museum of Asian Art,
Smithsonian Institution
1000 Jefferson Drive SW
Washington, DC, 20560

First published in 2024 by GILES
An imprint of D Giles Limited
66 High Street
Lewes, BN7 1XG, UK
gilesltd.com

Library of Congress Cataloging-in-Publication Data
LCCN: 2024016123

ISBN: 978-1-913875-82-4

Support for *A Tale of Two Balconies* is provided by the Anne van Biema Endowment Fund

For the National Museum of Asian Art:
Managing Editor, Judy Lee
Publication Assistant, Sophie Loring
Editor, Akiko Yamagata

For D Giles Limited:
Proofreader, Jenny Wilson
Designer, Alfonso Iacurci
Printed and bound in China

All measurements are in meters and centimeters.

Image credits

Front cover
James McNeill Whistler / National Museum of Asian Art, Smithsonian Institution, Freer Collection, Gift of Charles Lang Freer, F1892.23a-b

Frontispiece
James McNeill Whistler / National Museum of Asian Art, Smithsonian Institution, Freer Collection, Gift of Charles Lang Freer, F1903.177a-b

Pop-out model
National Museum of Asian Art, Smithsonian Institution: Photograph © Cory Grace

Image Copyright © The Metropolitan Museum of Art
27, Image source: Art Resource, NY, 67.241
29, Image source: Art Resource, NY, 29.100.10
43, Image source: Art Resource, NY, 30.117

Museum of Fine Arts, Boston
33, The Hayden Collection—Charles Henry Hayden Fund, 10.35
52, 1951 Purchase Fund, 56.147

National Museum of Asian Art, Smithsonian Institution, Freer Collection
2 (detail), **39**, James McNeill Whistler / Gift of Charles Lang Freer, F1903.177a-b
5 (detail), **38**, James McNeill Whistler / Gift of Charles Lang Freer, F1902.138a-b
6 (detail), **8-9** (detail), **10**, James McNeill Whistler / Gift of Charles Lang Freer, F1892.23a-b
12, **22** (detail), Katsushika Hokusai / Gift of the family of Eugene and Agnes E. Meyer, F1974.63
14, James McNeill Whistler / Gift of Charles Lang Freer, F1904.75a
16, James McNeill Whistler / Gift of Charles Lang Freer, F1906.105
18 (detail), **25**, James McNeill Whistler / Gift of Charles Lang Freer, F1902.249a-b
19, James McNeill Whistler / Gift of Charles Lang Freer, F1898.264
26 (detail), **35**, James McNeill Whistler / Gift of Charles Lang Freer, F1905.212
36 (detail), **40**, James McNeill Whistler / Gift of Charles Lang Freer, F1903.179a-b
41, James McNeill Whistler / Gift of Charles Lang Freer, F1903.178a-b
44, James McNeill Whistler / Gift of Charles Lang Freer, F1903.147a-c
47, James McNeill Whistler / Gift of Charles Lang Freer, F1903.91a-b
48 (detail), **49**, James McNeill Whistler / Gift of Charles Lang Freer, F1902.97a-b
54 (detail), **57**, James McNeill Whistler / Gift of Charles Lang Freer, F1905.129a-b
61 (detail), Gift of Charles Lang Freer, F1903.208
69, James McNeill Whistler / Gift of Charles Lang Freer, F1904.61
71, Gift of Charles Lang Freer, F1908.243

Other Collections
13, Library of Congress Geography and Map Division
15, © National Portrait Gallery, London / Art Resource, NY, D37559
20, The Miriam and Ira D. Wallach Division of Art, Prints and Photographs: Print Collection, The New York Public Library. New York Public Library Digital Collections
21, © The Hunterian, University of Glasgow, GLAHA_46359
23, RBKC Local Studies and Archives
28, © RMN-Grand Palais / Art Resource, NY, 10-541559
30, "Perspectief II. Het balkon van Manet" by René Magritte, MSK Gent, www.artinflanders.be, photo Cedric Verhelst, © 2024 C. Herscovici / Artists Rights Society (ARS), New York
31, © Tokyo Fuji Art Museum / DNPartcom
32, Artizon Museum, Ishibashi Foundation, Tokyo
34, **81**, The Jerome Robbins Dance Division, The New York Public Library. New York Public Library Digital Collections
53, Richard S. Zeisler Fund, National Gallery of Art, Washington 2009.39.1.1-560
55, Photograph reproduced with the kind Permission of the Russell-Cotes Art Gallery & Museum, Bournemouth, BORGM 01536
56, Harvard Art Museums/Fogg Museum, Gift of Grenville L. Winthrop, Class of 1886, 1942.203
58, The J. Paul Getty Museum, Villa Collection, Malibu, California, 56.AD.17
63, Gilbert and Sullivan Archive, Collection of John Sands
64, National Galleries of Scotland. Dr Camilla M. Uytman Gift 1981 / Purchased 1980, D 5102.48
65, National Galleries of Scotland. Purchased 1980, PG 2467
66 (detail), **73**, © Hannah Rothstein
67, Haviland-Heidgerd Historical Collection, Elting Memorial Library, New Paltz, New York
68, Detroit Evening News
72, Courtesy of Darren Waterston and DC Moore Gallery, New York. Photo by National Museum of Asian Art, Smithsonian Institution

Tate
24, Purchased 1940, N05216. Photo: Tate
37, Purchased with assistance from the Friends of the Tate Gallery 1980, T03064. Photo: Tate
50, Presented by W. Graham Robertson 1940, N05065. Photo: Tate

© The Trustees of the British Museum. All rights reserved
45, 1874,0305.65
60, 1949,0409,0.66.1-2

Victoria and Albert Museum, London
46, CAI.8
59, C.935-1910
62, S.133:418-2007

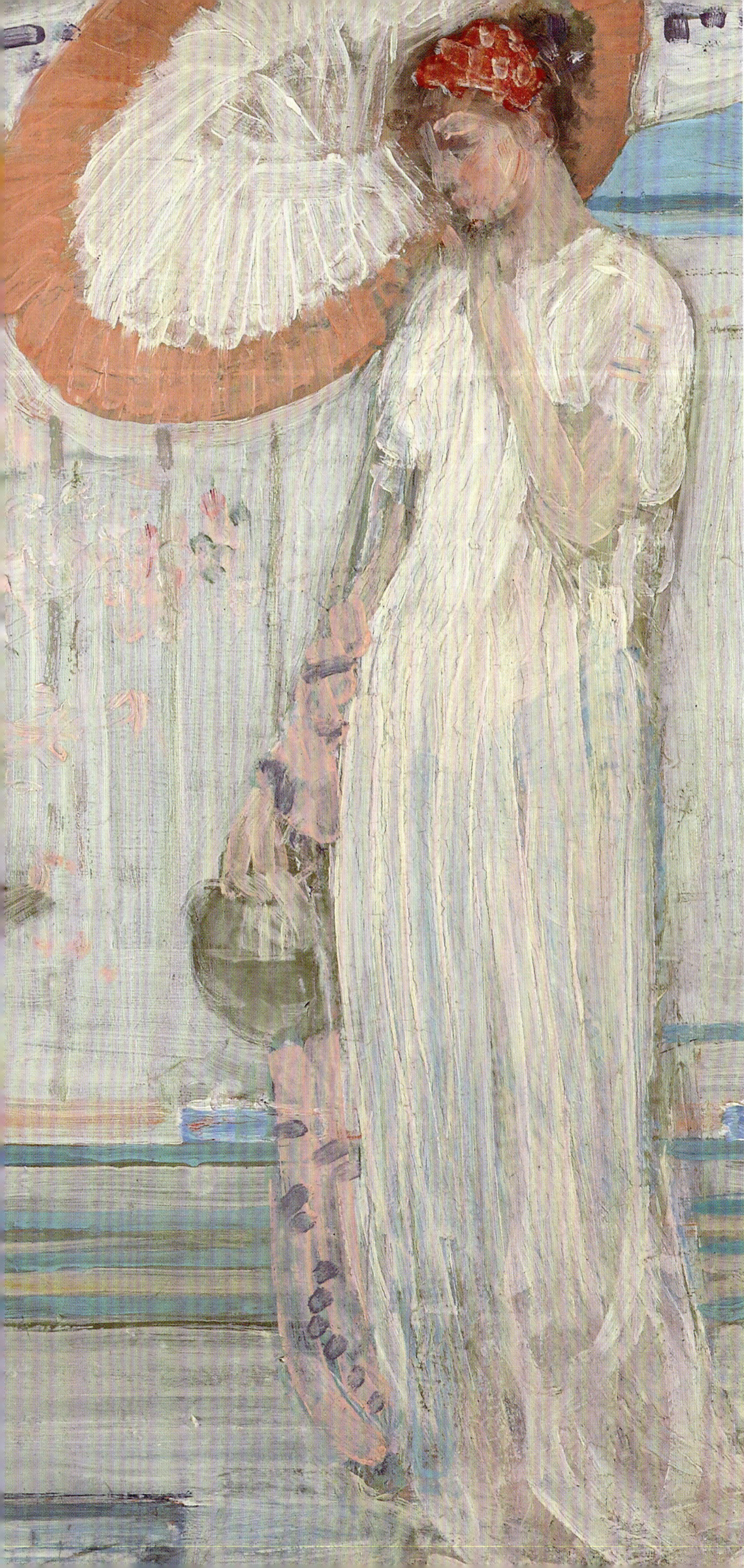

CONTENTS

WHISTLER
KATHERINE ROEDER

APPROACH

As you sketch out a view from a balcony—what do you see? How much is memory and how much is fantasy in that self-constructed reality? How do balconies define our relationship to our surroundings? Within an image, a balcony can present the viewer with a space that is, at once, private and public, and the geometry of its architecture creates a picture within a picture. It constructs a view, defined by the building and the location, that provides an opportunity to visualize and juxtapose different worlds. Railings, barriers, balustrades—these separate the intimate space of viewers from their environment but also present artists with the opportunity to bend reality and create the perspectives they want us to see.

This book examines two specific balcony views, Katsushika Hokusai's *The Sazaidō of Gohyakurakanji* and James McNeill Whistler's *Variations in Flesh Colour and Green—The Balcony* (fig. 1), with a center section providing prompts for readers to make their own balcony-inspired creations. It is an exercise in complementary analysis—although the two works have previously been linked by their compositional similarities, each work is examined here on its own terms using parallel analytical categories. The intent is not to compare them to each other, but to provide a comparable treatment of each separately. Utilizing a mirrored presentation that divides the book into two equal parts,

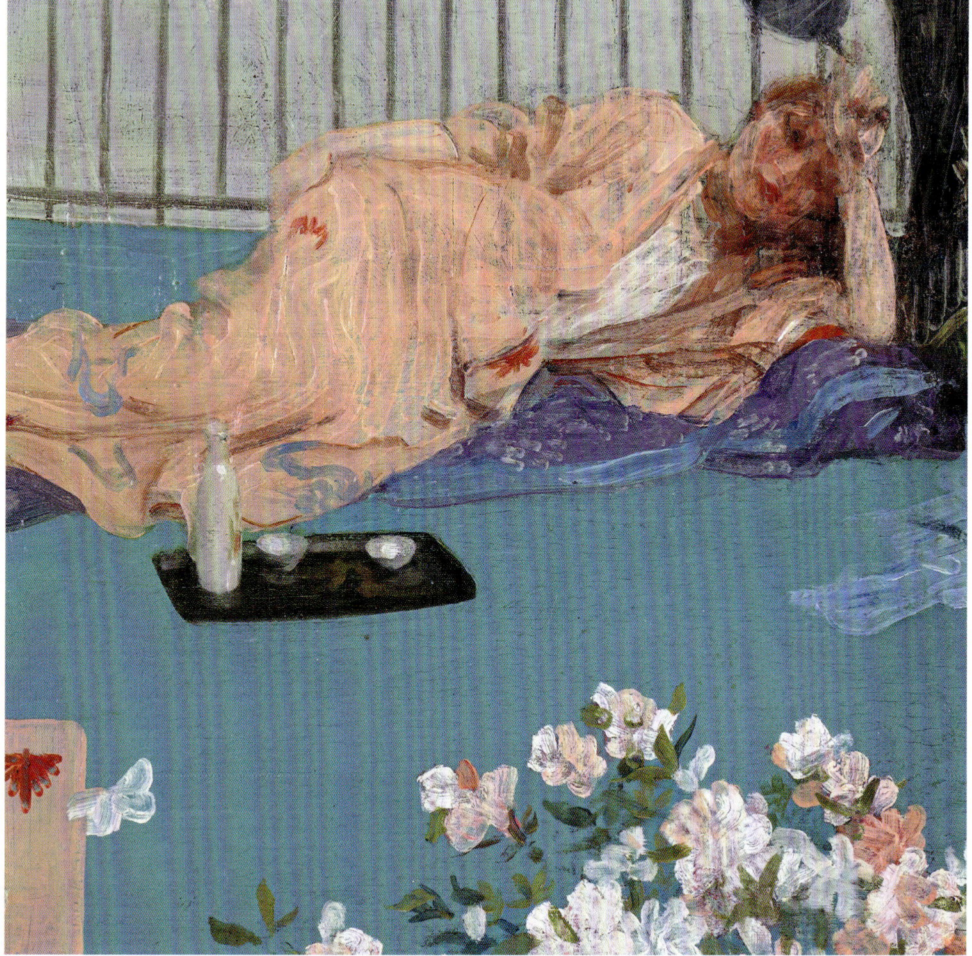

Fig. 1 James McNeill Whistler, *Variations in Flesh Colour and Green—The Balcony* (detail). England, 1864-1870, additions 1870-1879. Oil on wood panel; 61.4 × 48.5 cm.

by two different authors, this publication explores the individual history of each work and what makes it distinctive, with particular emphasis on the context of its reception and the particularity of the location it depicts. As images of balconies, the two works can be immersive for the viewer and offer a space for self-referential looking, as if we are tacitly included as part of the group of figures depicted within the scenes. The reader can start here, or at the opposite end.

Hokusai's *The Sazaidō of Gohyakurakanji* is often eclipsed by his *Under the Wave off Kanagawa*, another print within the same series of views of Mount Fuji. Whistler's work is often understood as an instance of Japonisme—a late nineteenth-century trend for Western artists to incorporate and appropriate aspects of Japanese art and design, which was newly available in this period. However, this book is *not* a book about Hokusai, or Whistler, or Japonisme. It is an attempt to move beyond reductive narratives of influence and propose a new model for comparative art historical explorations. Each artist made careful choices about what to include, discard, or adapt, based on a variety of possibilities, their artistic practices, and contemporary currents in their own artistic traditions. As much as a balcony is a physical structure, it is also a compositional and intellectual framework that can be applied to many artworks and contexts.

A Tale of Two Balconies is physically divided into two halves with a parallel organizational structure. Mirrored sections—**view**, **site**, **perspective**, **figure**, **pigment**, **restriction**, and **(freer) association**—examine the details of each work by taking the reader through the specificities of the geographical location depicted in the background, the pictorial devices, innovations, and pigments used, the visual strategies incorporated by each artist, and the significance of the balcony as a framing device for representing landscapes that combine the real and the imagined. Additionally, the sections address broader concerns that likely lay beyond the conscious attention of these artists, such as race and gender dynamics, tourism and urbanization, globalization, and the circulation of ideas and materials. These ideas may not be explicit in the image, but embedded clues can help reconstruct the assumptions of a contemporary viewer. The section headings are far from an exhaustive list of possible angles of interpretation but are, rather, generative prompts to trigger alternate perspectives. The headings are like balcony railings—guide rails, but not impassable. They are also flexible, as the authors have taken the same prompt in different directions for each of the works. Throughout, readers are encouraged to make their own expansive reflections regarding the compositions, culminating in the shared central section, **remix**, which contains several creative exercises to provoke construction of their own balcony scenes. Embarking on such a close consideration allows us to appreciate each work's own particular features as well as provide an arsenal of interpretive approaches to interrogate other images or create new ones.

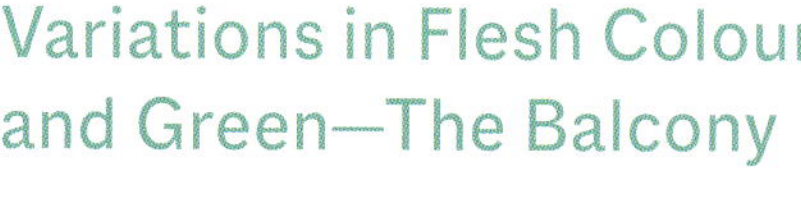

Variations in Flesh Colour and Green—The Balcony

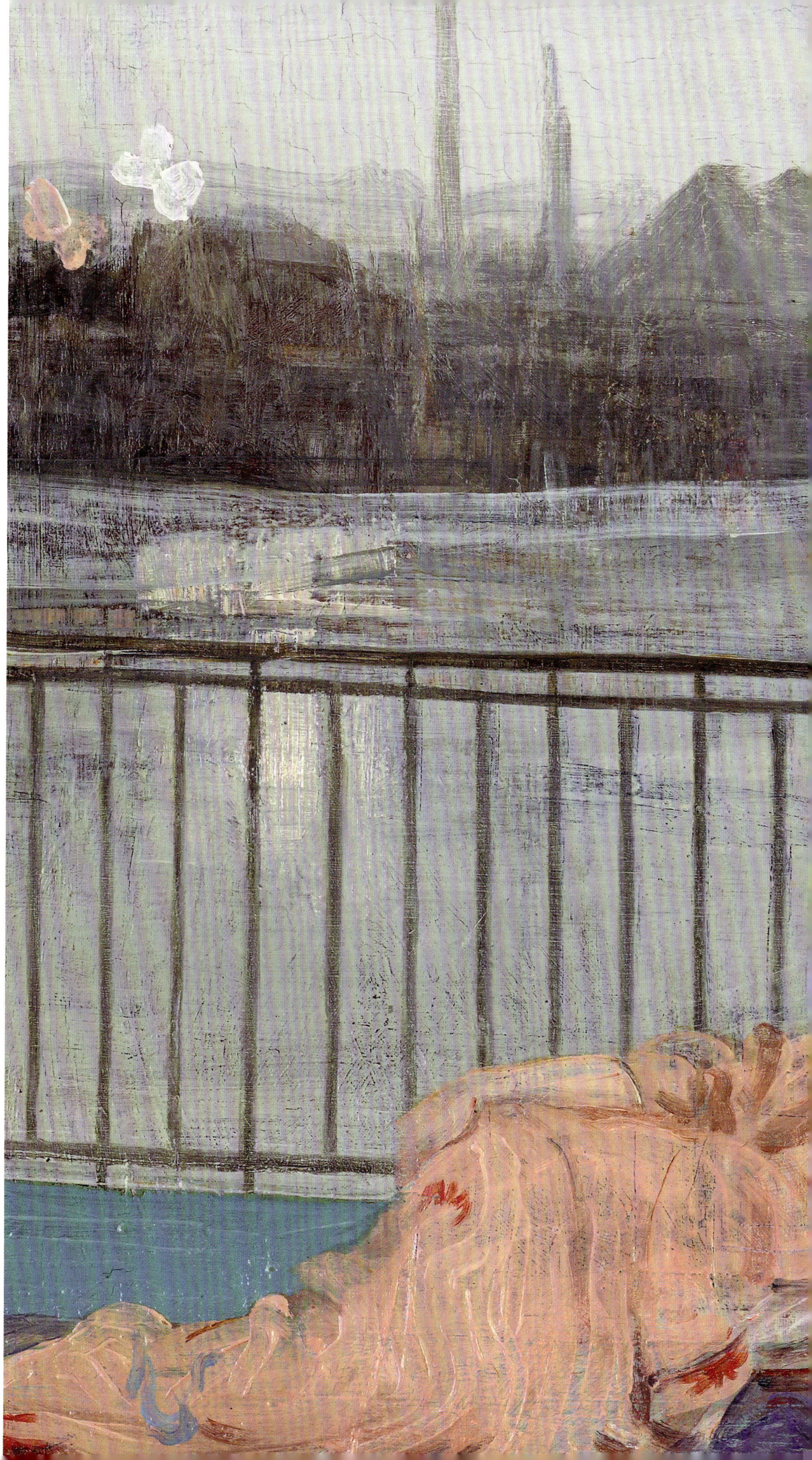

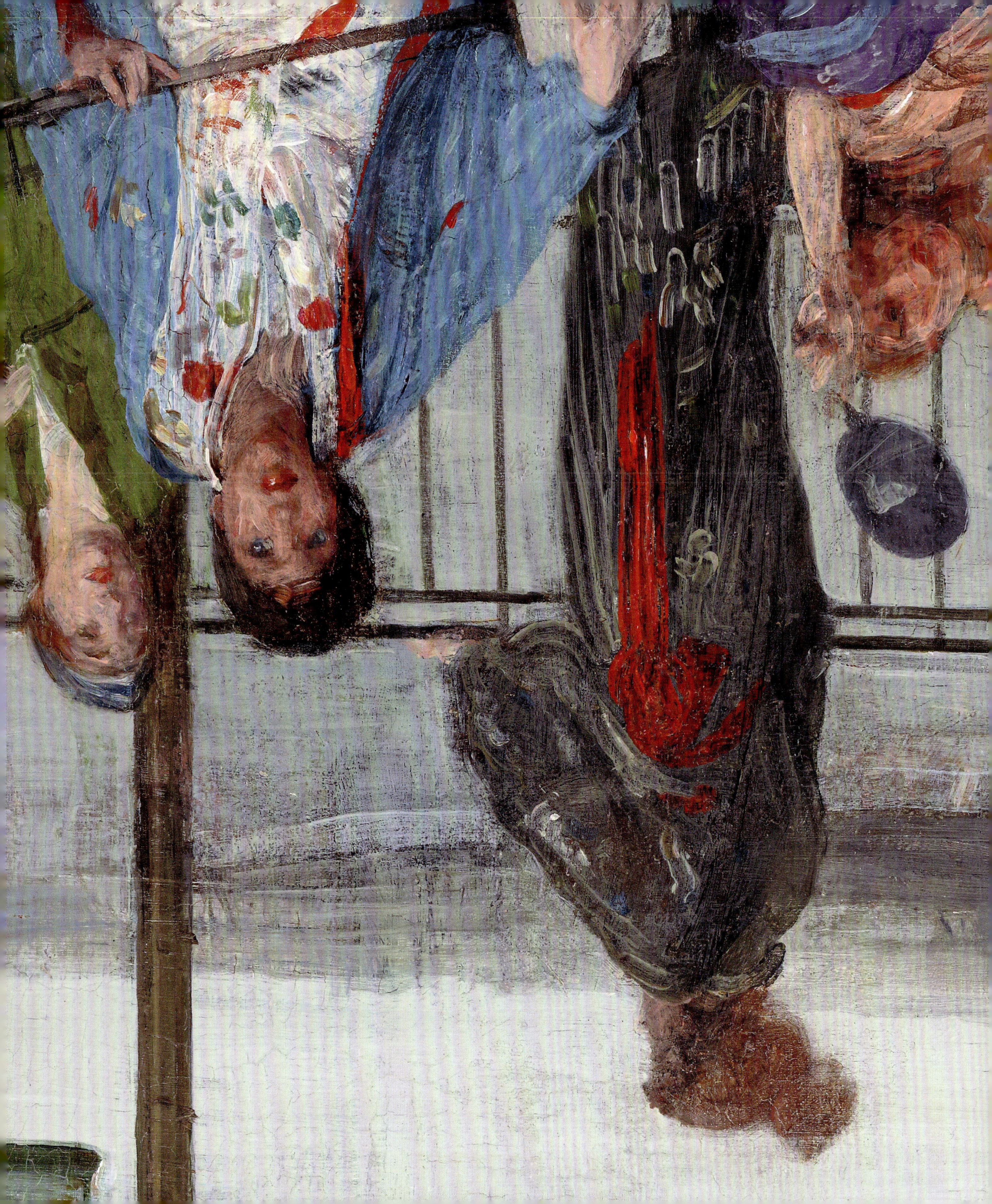

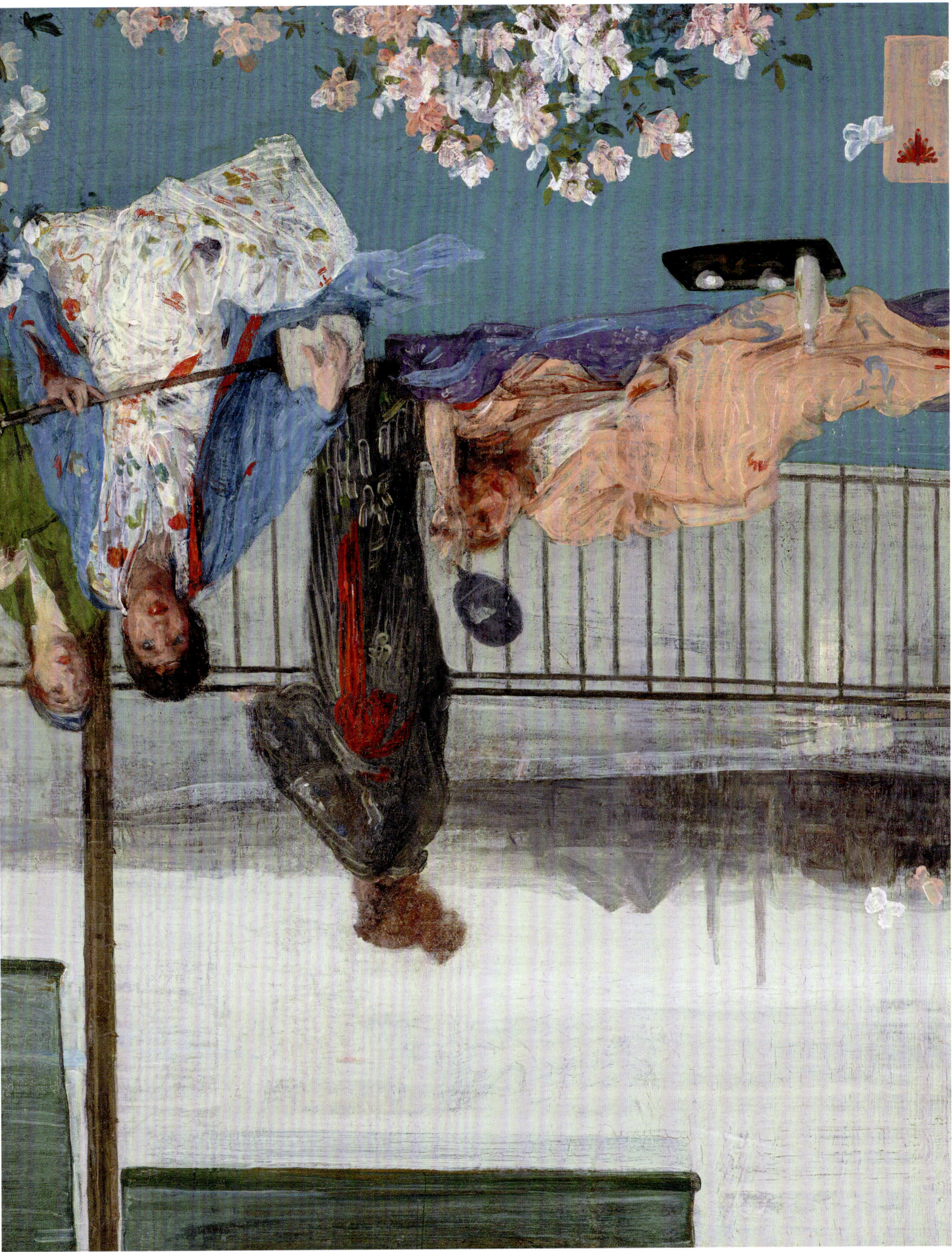

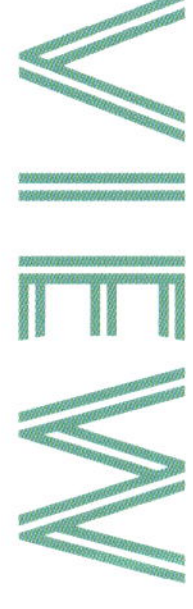

What are the visual cues and physical structures that signal to us that a view is worthy of our attention? Balconies create views by design: they not only define the area to be looked at, they also position viewers to emphasize their relationship to their surroundings. With *Variations in Flesh Colour and Green—The Balcony*, an early-career painting by American-born artist James McNeill Whistler (1834–1903), the horizontal expanse of a balcony railing divides a colorful foreground from a monochrome landscape, generating a composition that emphasizes both the view and the vantage point (fig. 1).

Precursors to Whistler's composition include *The Sazaidō of Gohyakurakanji* (*Gohyakurakanji Sazaidō* 五百らかん寺さざゐどう) by Katsushika Hokusai 葛飾北斎 (1760–1849), a Japanese artist whose work Whistler collected and whom he referenced by name in his aesthetic manifesto, the 1885 "Ten O'Clock" lecture (fig. 2).[1] Too often, discussions of Western artists' collecting of Japanese prints have relied on an unbalanced framework that prioritizes the trajectory of European painting. Divorced from their original viewing contexts, the Japanese works are considered inert upon their arrival on Western shores, serving only as a repository of exotic motifs and colors for artists to exploit and explore. This volume attempts to avoid such reductive traps. Rather than merely comparing these two works, it develops sustained parallel inquiries into both using a series of thematic prompts. Readers are welcome to approach the text however and wherever they see fit and are invited to engage in further creative exploration in the discursive zone at the center of the book.

The starting point is **view**, which situates both the artwork and the stakes of this cross-cultural exercise. Moving from the balcony to the **site** of Victorian London affords a window into how the industrialized landscape and its environmental degradation in *The Balcony* are both realized and obfuscated by Whistler's brushstrokes. The balcony's **perspective** is a function of privilege and necessitates a discussion of the ways public and private spaces were gendered in Victorian society. The biases and assumptions of a "flesh color" in Whistler's title for this painting, and the racism they reveal, are addressed in **pigment**. Whistler's conflation of Greek and Japanese references elucidates how each culture performed a role as an imaginary ideal **figure** for the artist. The politics of that cultural exchange are further complicated by Whistler's depiction of Western women wearing kimono, as the painting simultaneously appropriates Japanese clothing while offering the painting's female Western viewers freedom from the **restriction** of contemporary dress expectations. Finally, **(freer) association** delves into this object's life beyond Whistler's brush—from its acquisition by Charles Lang Freer (1854–1919) to its various afterlives. The liminal space between the texts on Hokusai and Whistler creates room for readers to experiment, explore, and remix their own creative practice, reflecting upon balconies and the positionality of the viewers depicted as well as upon the viewing experience.

Approaching the text from the opposite side of the book, you will find Kit Brooks excavating *The Sazaidō of Gohyakurakanji* using the same prompts but exploring entirely different themes and contexts. Just as the physical structure of the balcony railing becomes a compositional device that artists work with and around, the seven thematic prompts provide this volume with a common framework to play with and expand upon. Just as we make space for readers to explore their creative impulses, we challenged ourselves to find new ways of interacting with objects, history, and culture.

Fig. 1 James McNeill Whistler, *Variations in Flesh Colour and Green—The Balcony*.

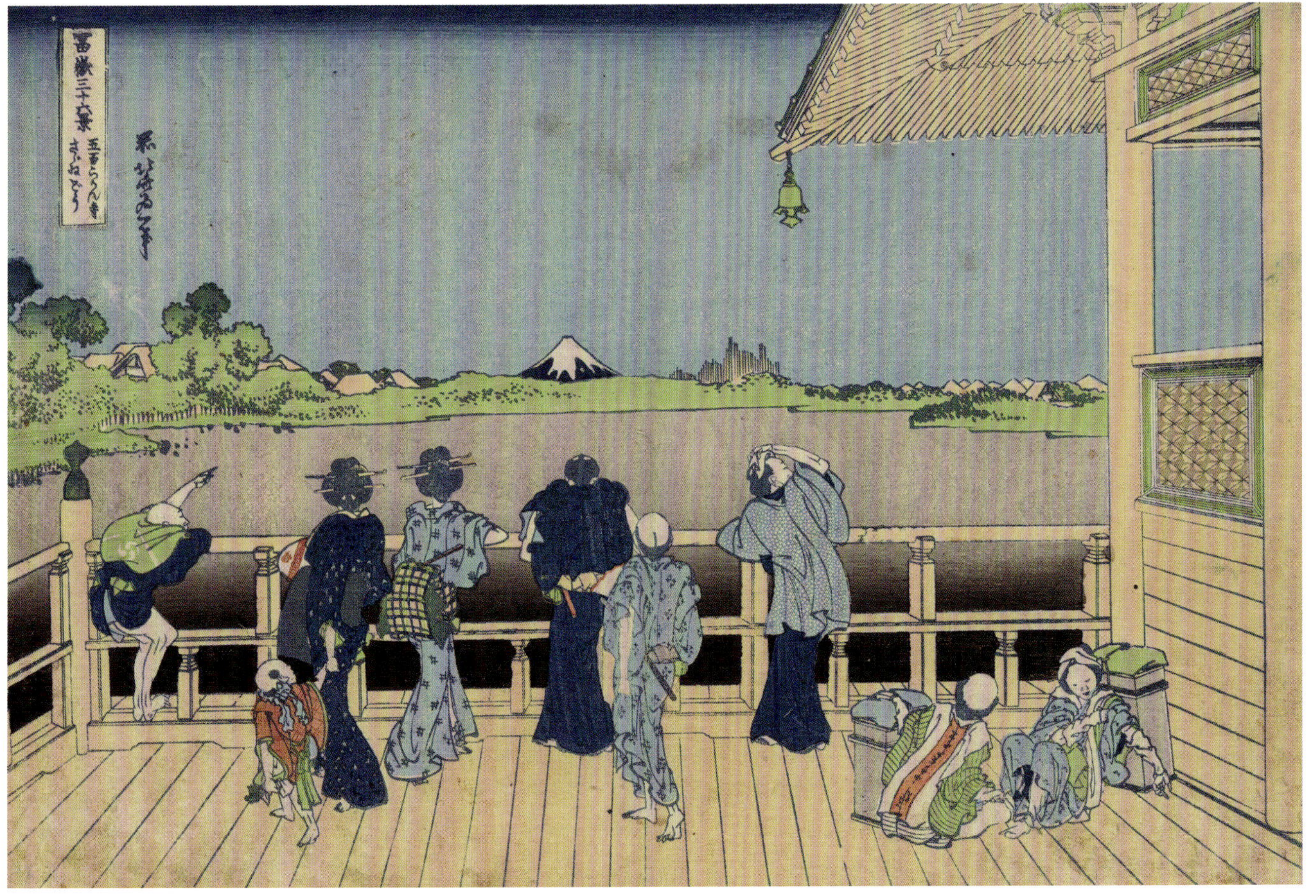

Fig. 2
Katsushika Hokusai, *The Sazaidō of Gohyakurakanji*, from the series *Thirty-Six Views of Mount Fuji* (*Fugaku sanjūrokkei*). Japan, Edo period, ca. 1830–1831. Woodblock print; ink and color on paper; 24.5 × 37 cm.

Any viewer of Whistler's painting is positioned as though they were themselves standing on the balcony depicted, which was attached to the artist's home studio on Lindsey Row (now Cheyne Walk), in Chelsea, west London, looking out over the Thames with a view of Battersea, where industry flourished on the south bank (fig. 3). Though born in Massachusetts, the artist spent most of his career in Britain, within walking distance of the Thames riverfront. The river features in several of his prominent early paintings. In *The Balcony*, the river and sky are similar in tone, bisected by the monochrome brownish grays of the Battersea factories and slag heaps lining the horizon. The rigidity of the balcony railing creates a visual divide between the languid reverie of the kimono-clad women in the foreground and the working river behind them. Only one woman looks out at the world beyond their vantage point; the three remaining women face the viewer.

The women are engaged in various leisure activities, both active and passive. They are resting, looking, performing, and listening to music. A woman in a pinkish-peach kimono reclines on the ground, a sake set in front of her, with one raised arm holding a fan, seemingly shading her face from the sun. The fan also blocks her vision. Standing behind her is a woman with reddish hair who looks out from the balcony toward the right. A woman in a blue kimono plays a Japanese stringed instrument known as a shamisen, while the woman in green next to her listens. Collectively, the grouping

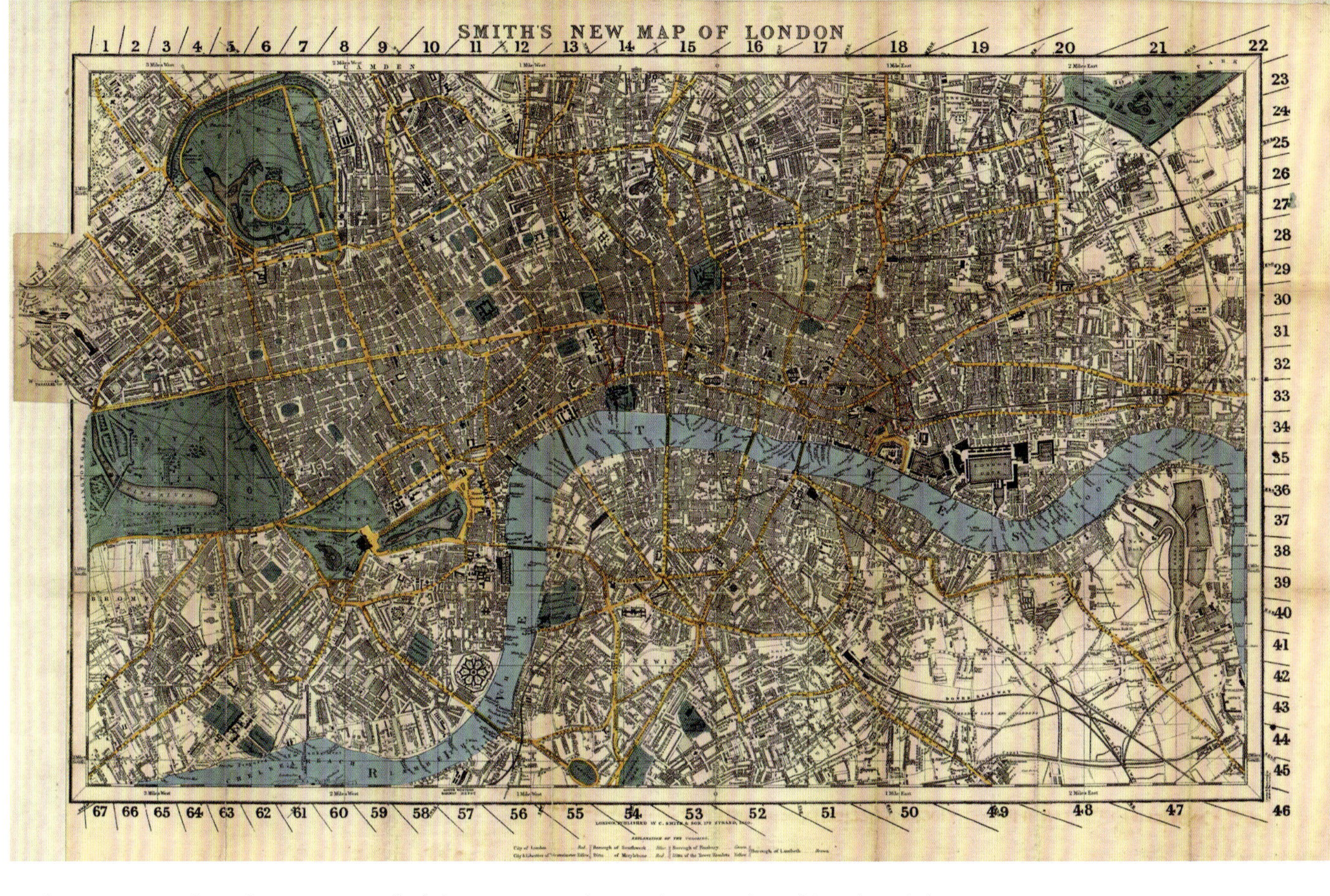

Fig. 3
C. Smith & Son. *Smith's New Map of London*. England, 1860. Hand-colored map; 36 × 63 cm.

makes an appeal to the senses—of sight, taste, and sound—completed by the pink blossoms in the foreground perfuming the air. Rendered predominantly in tones of pink, peach, and greenish blue, with select areas of red and purple providing spots of contrast, the women exist in a world divorced from the polluted Thames and grimy industry indicated by the vertical smokestacks and mountain of slag across the river. Nevertheless, the inclusion of Japanese items would not have been possible without the massive expansion of global trade and industry in the nineteenth century that these unpleasant landscape elements portend, linking the besmirched background and fantasized foreground inextricably together.

Whistler would have first been exposed to Japanese art when he lived in Paris from the end of 1855 until May 1859, when his social circle included French realist painters Henri Fantin-Latour (1836–1904) and Édouard Manet (1832–1883). His Japanese art collecting began at this time, and he was among the vanguard when he arrived in London in 1859. Interest in Japan began to rise precipitously in his new city several years later, when a Japanese art display was included in the International Exhibition of 1862 held there.[2] Though formed largely from the private collection of the first British consul general to Japan, rather than through the Japanese government's direct involvement, the designated section for Japanese objects was the first to be featured in a world's fair.[3] Immediately after the exhibition, the retail firm of Farmer & Rogers

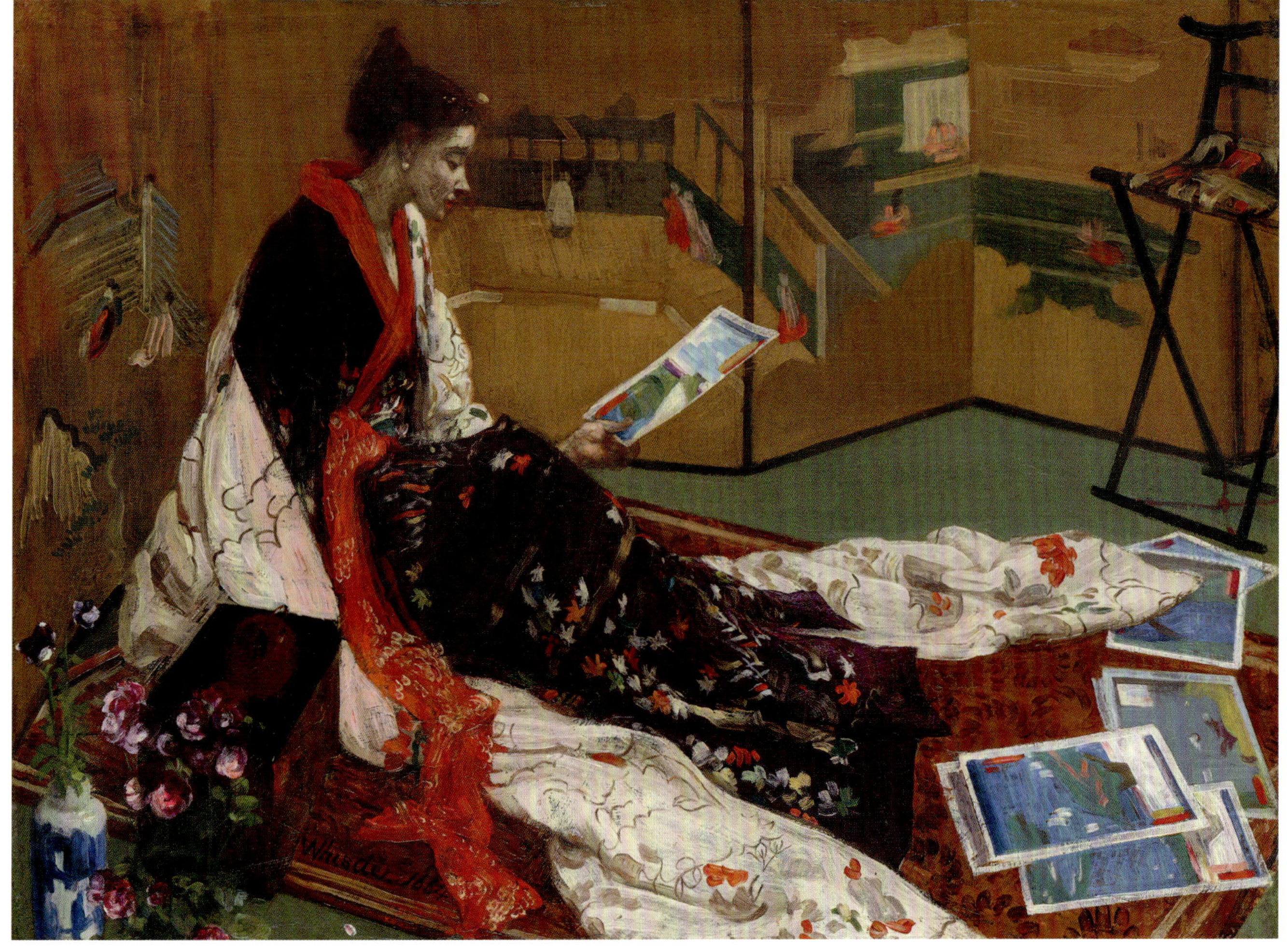

Fig. 4
James McNeill Whistler, *Caprice in Purple and Gold—The Golden Screen*. 1864. Oil on wood panel; 50.1 × 68.5 cm.

began selling the pieces from the display to dealers and collectors.[4] Soon after, Dante Gabriel Rossetti (1828–1882), the Pre-Raphaelite painter whom Whistler befriended upon his arrival in London, published two articles on Japanese art, helping to further fuel the craze among British artists and collectors. In 1863, Whistler moved to 7 Lindsey Row in Chelsea, the location of the studio where he would soon begin work on *The Balcony*. Describing this workspace, Whistler's first biographers noted, "In his house in Chelsea, facing Battersea Bridge … he had lovely blue and white [porcelains], Chinese and Japanese. The only decorations, except the harmony of colour, were the prints on the walls, a flight of Japanese fans in one place, in another shelves of blue and white."[5] Whistler began using Japanese and Chinese objects and dress as elements in a series of costume pictures soon after, as in *Caprice in Purple and Gold—The Golden Screen* (fig. 4).

This environment, where Whistler both gravitated to the working river but surrounded his home with objects of faraway beauty, was the genesis for *The Balcony*, and the painting was significant enough that it was mentioned in a letter written by his mother to a friend in 1864. Anna McNeill Whistler (1804–1881), Whistler's mother

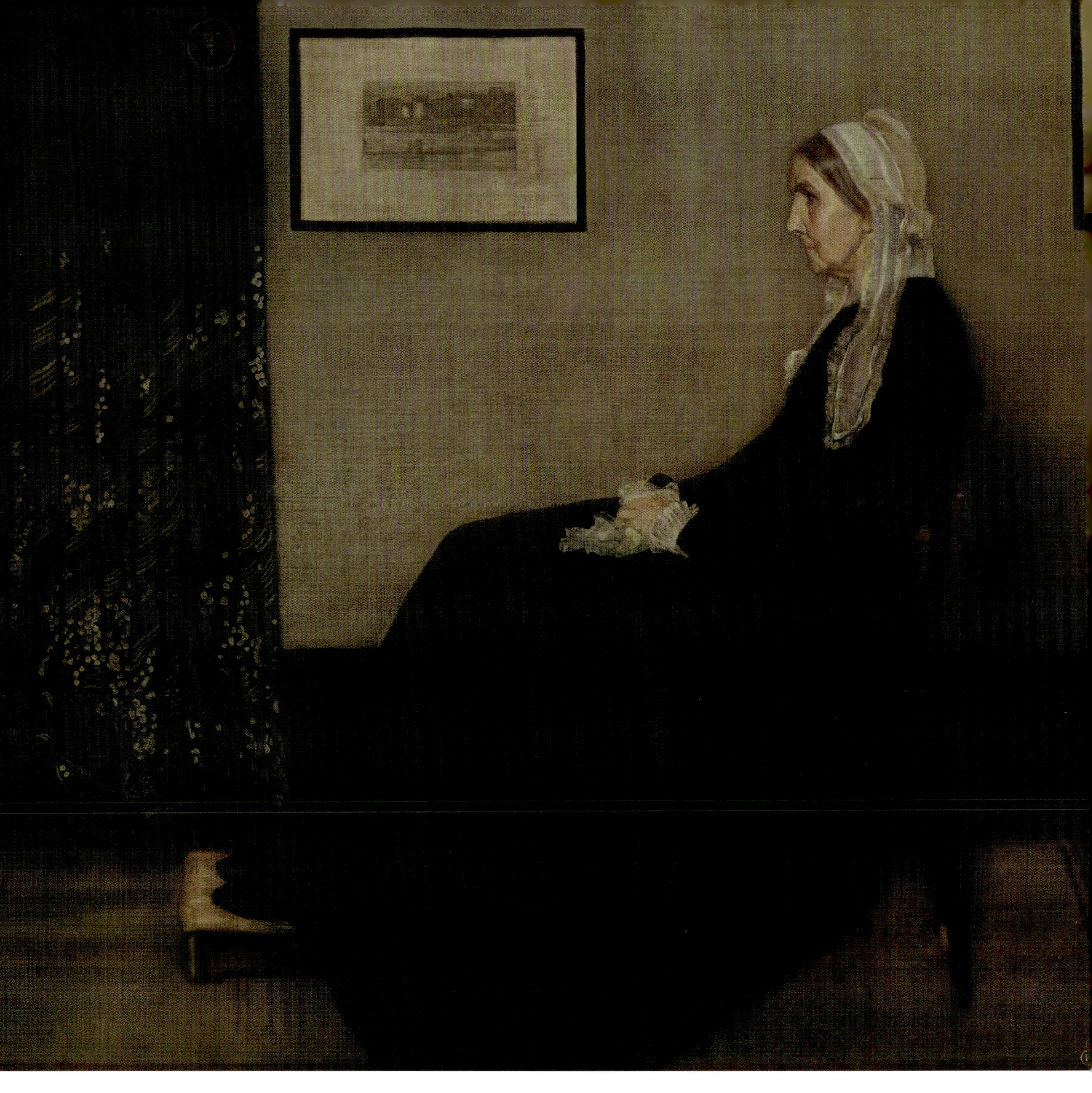

Fig. 5
James McNeill Whistler, *Arrangement in Grey and Black No. 1*. 1871. Oil on canvas; 144.3 × 163 cm.

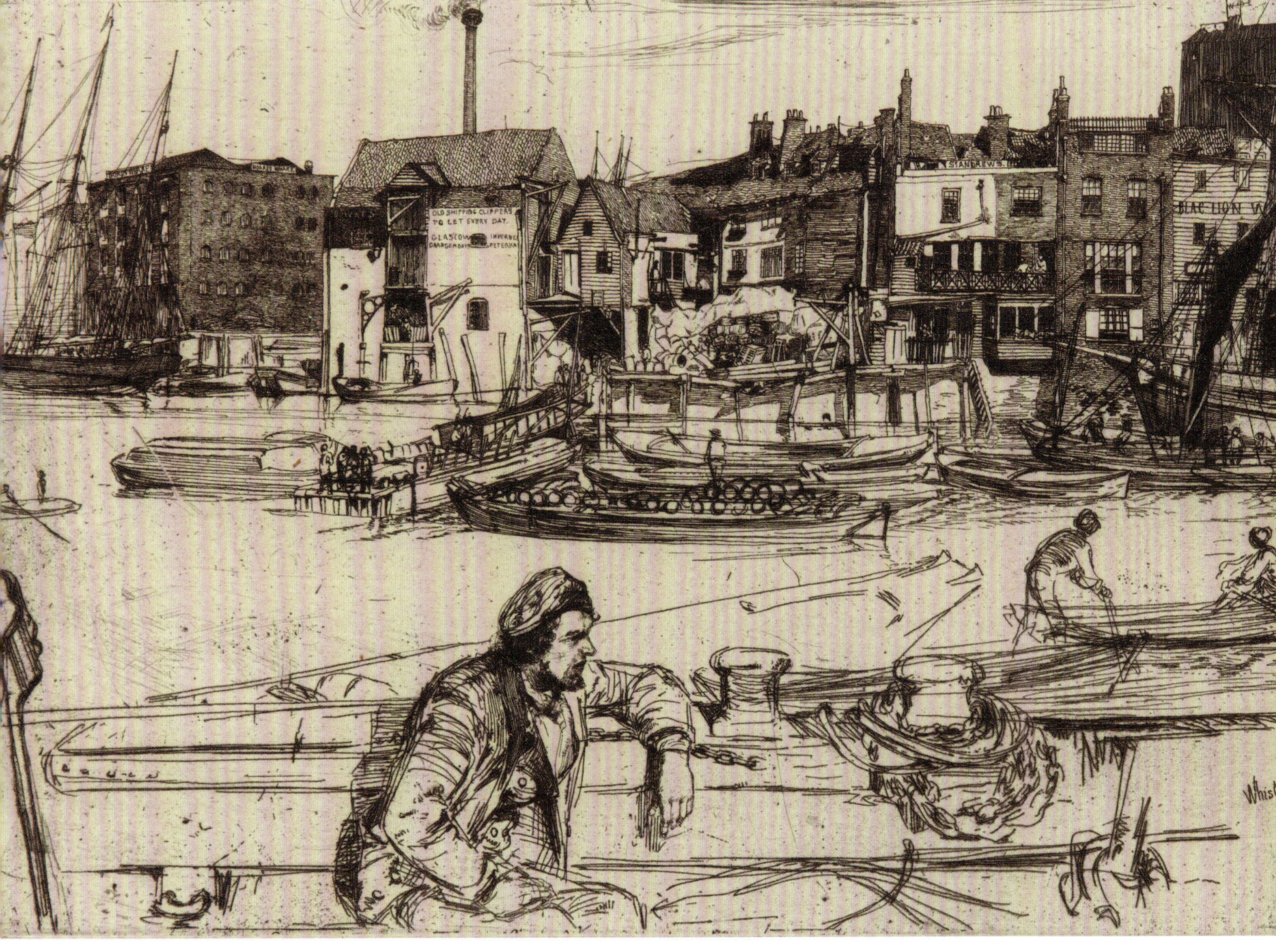

Fig. 6
James McNeill Whistler, *Black Lion Wharf*. 1859. Etching on paper; 15.1 × 22.7 cm.

and the subject of his most well-known painting, had moved in with her son in 1863. *Arrangement in Grey and Black No. 1*, like *The Balcony*, features a woman in the act of looking in a domestic space, with an industrial riverscape in the background (fig. 5). In this case, the outside world is represented by a framed print of *Black Lion Wharf* (fig. 6) hanging on the wall. Whistler's mother described his Chelsea studio as being

> ornamented by a very rare collection of Japanese & Chinese [porcelain], he considers the paintings upon them the finest specimens of Art & his companions (Artists) . . . get enthusiastic as the[y] handle & examine the curious subjects pourtrayed [*sic*], some of the pieces more than two centuries old, he has also a Japanese book of painting, unique in their estimation . . . his oriental paintings which are ordered & he has several in progress: One portrays a group in Oriental costume on a balcony, a tea equipage of the old China, the[y] look out upon a river, with a town in the distance.[6]

Whistler's mother misreading a sake set as tea equipment is indicative of the large gaps in knowledge about the Japanese objects Whistler collected and their usage. The art objects that Whistler acquired were divorced from their contexts and the customs they depicted, as his primary concern was surface and form. Nevertheless, the paintings contained references that contemporary Japanese viewers would have understood.

The Balcony was begun in 1864, a formative moment when Whistler was actively collecting and surrounding himself with Japanese art. However, the painting was reworked and revisited over the next fifteen years, indicating that Whistler's own view and artistic persona were neither settled nor static. In this vein, this volume offers the reader pathways for working through different interpretations of the work as well as the space to create and reflect.

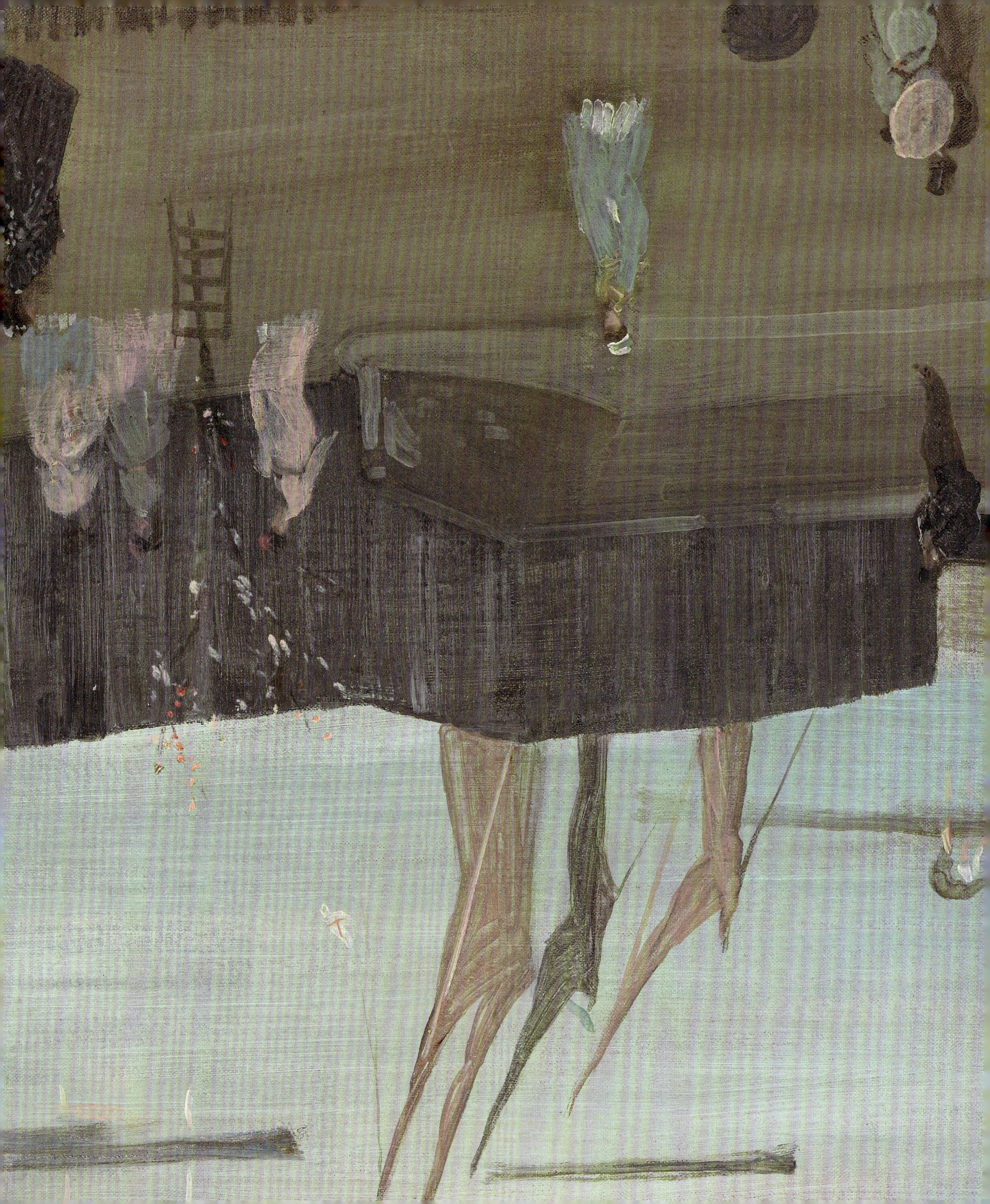

SITE

How do we reconcile the uneasy juxtaposition of beauty and ugliness in Whistler's paintings? The manufacturing and trade on London's waterfront, which polluted the Thames and degraded the environment, also created the economic prosperity that made Whistler's success possible.[7] The Thames in Whistler's work is not just a compositional device: as a conduit for the British empire, it also situates the artwork within the context that propelled its production. Yet when noxious factory fumes are rendered as painterly atmosphere and factory waste is transformed into landscape features, does the painting draw viewers' attention to these issues? Or does it aestheticize and insulate Whistler's patrons from industry's costs?

The operations of nineteenth-century industrialization were embedded in James McNeill Whistler's early life from the outset, and perhaps it stands to reason that London's industrial character would come to preoccupy the artist for most of his career. Born in the mill town of Lowell, Massachusetts, he was directly impacted by the churning global economy during his upbringing. When he was eight, his father moved the family to Russia after being offered a position as an engineer involved in the construction of a railway between St. Petersburg and Moscow. During this period, the young Whistler would also occasionally visit his half sister who lived in London. As a teenager, after his father's death, Whistler returned to America, where he briefly (and unsuccessfully) attended the military academy at West Point and learned to etch while working as an artist for the US Coast Survey. Whistler was discontented with his government position, however, and left after a matter of months, fleeing to Paris to study art in 1855. He relocated to London in 1859, drawn partly by his family connections. His half sister, Deborah, was married to an etcher, Francis Seymour Haden (1818–1910), who convinced Whistler that he would find success with the city's burgeoning art market. By the mid-nineteenth century, rapid industrial growth in London had created an economically prosperous middle class, who were eager to decorate their homes with etchings, drawings, and even oil paintings. Whistler would later proclaim that England "welcomes young artists with both hands."[8] Over the course of his career, he spent extended periods of time in other cities, including

Fig. 1
James McNeill Whistler, *Thames Warehouses*. 1859. Etching on paper; 7.6 × 20.3 cm.

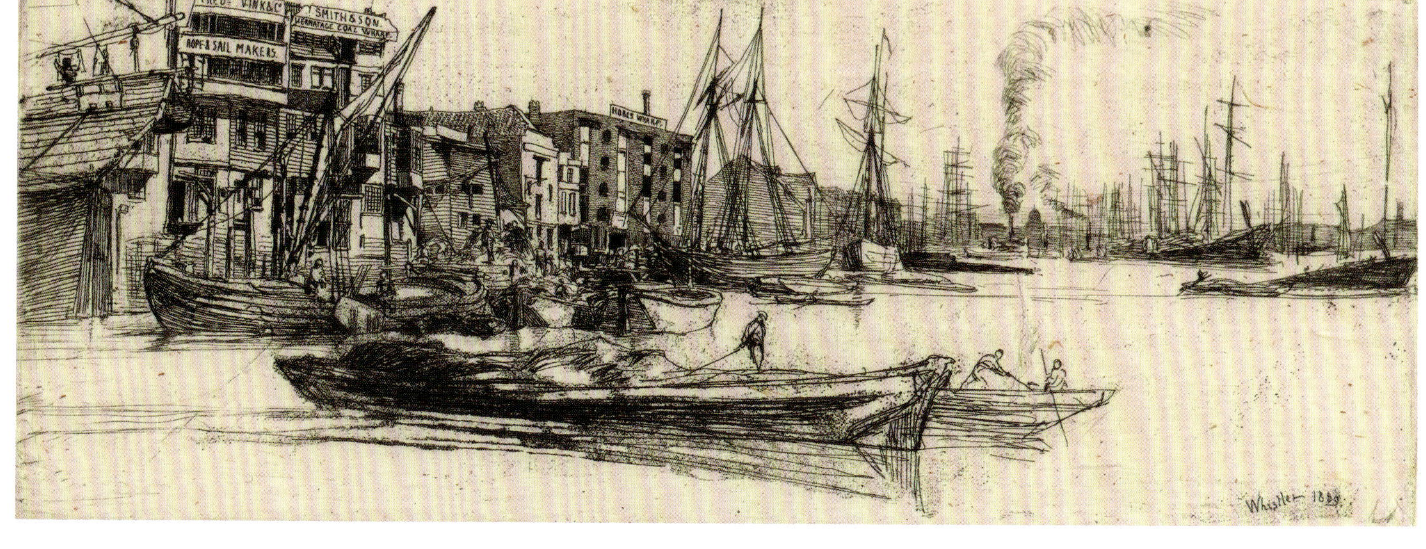

Detail of fig. 7

Paris and Venice, but London would be his primary residence for the rest of his life. According to Whistler, London was "the only city in the world fit to live in."[9]

Upon his arrival in London, Whistler was immediately attracted to the Thames's bustling riverfront. He developed a friendship with Walter Greaves (1846–1930), the son of a boat builder, who introduced him to the working river and the lives of the watermen bound to it. His early works document the docks, wharves, and barges as seen from the ground level, as opposed to the elevated viewpoint of *The Balcony*. Whistler's mother declared that her son was "charmed with the life on the Thames."[10] For at least twenty years, the river was a major source of inspiration for a variety of works, from the Thames Set of etchings, begun upon his arrival in the city, through to his experimental Nocturnes of the 1870s. *Thames Warehouses* from 1859 was among his first etchings following his relocation to London. Its emphasis on the river's

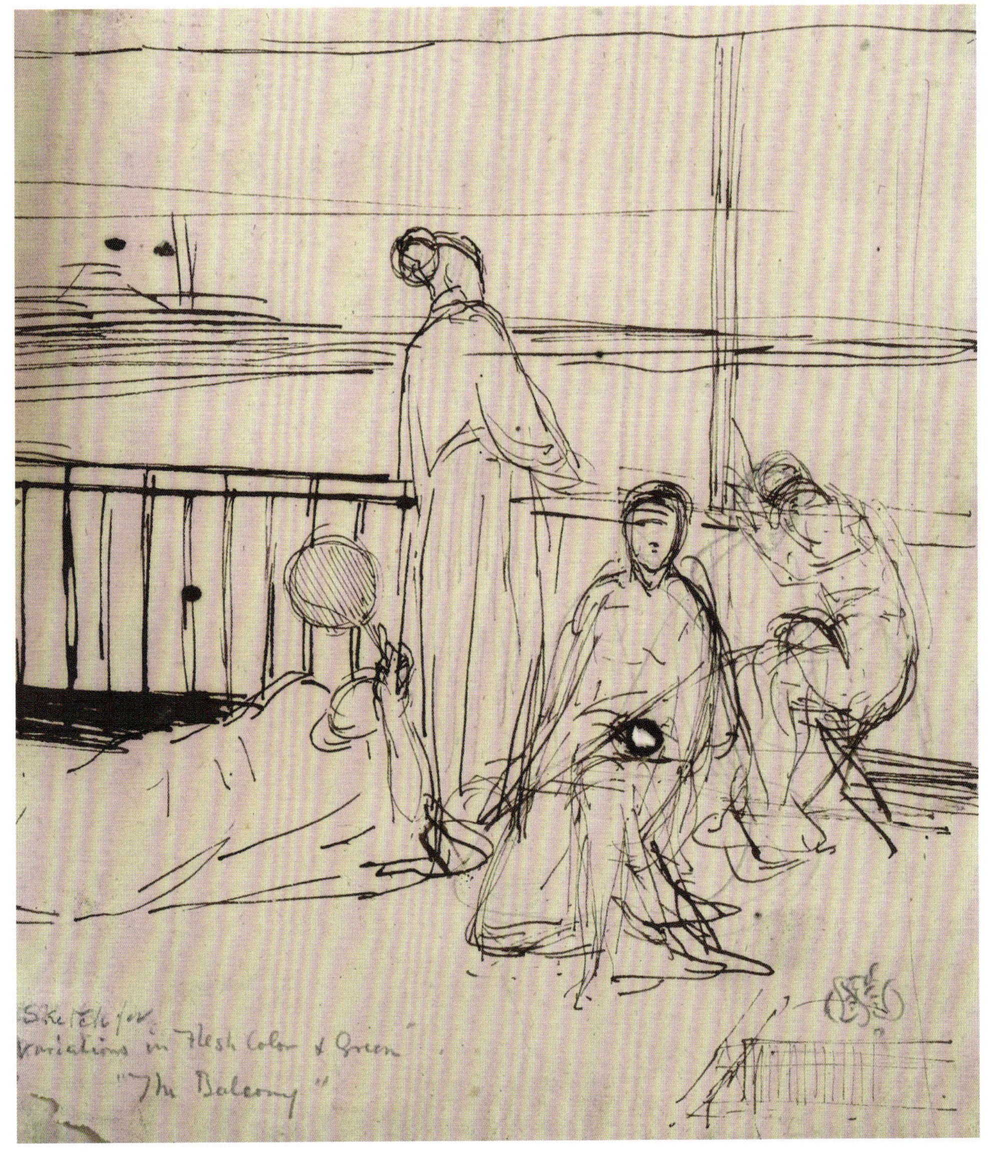

Fig. 2
James McNeill Whistler, sketch for *Variations in Flesh Colour and Green—The Balcony*. 1867–1868. Ink on paper; 21.5 × 18.9 cm.

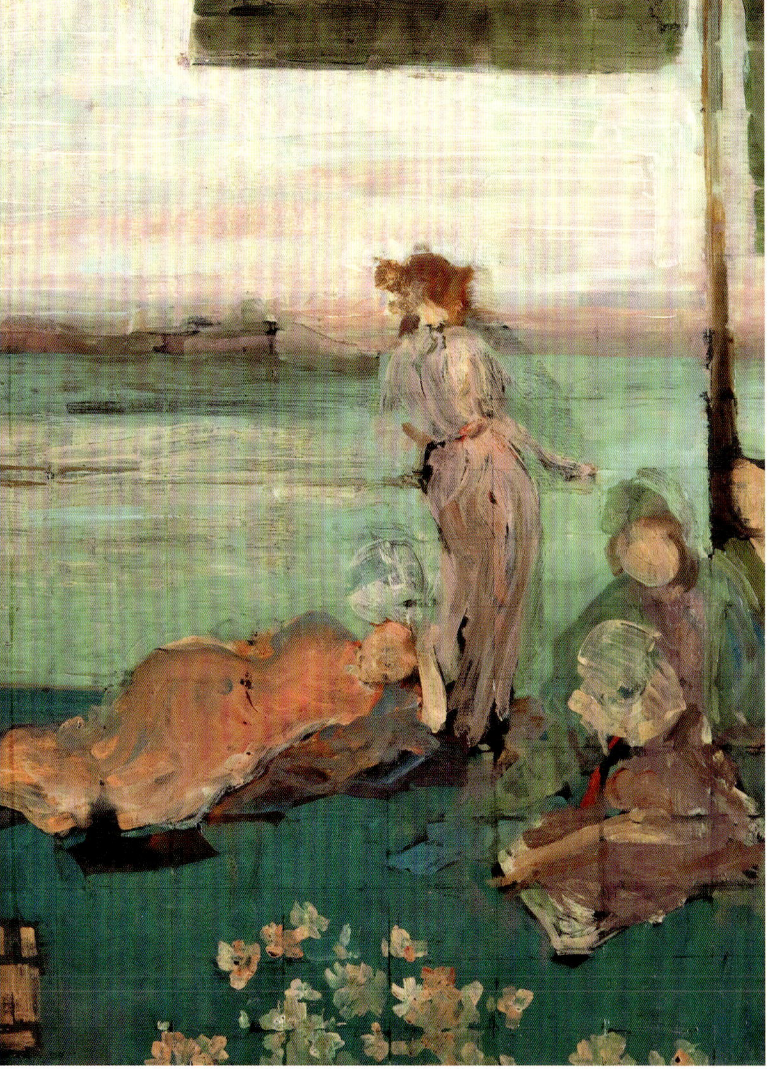

Fig. 3
James McNeill Whistler, sketch for *The Balcony*. ca. 1867. Oil on panel; 61 × 48.2 cm.

commercial nature, with a focus on warehouses and smokestacks, would prove to be a lifelong preoccupation (fig. 1). The bifurcated composition of Whistler's *Balcony*, with its monochrome view of the Thames and the industrial Battersea neighborhood framed as a picture within a picture by the balcony railing, references the Thames Set etchings, which were similarly focused on industrial landscapes. In this way, Whistler knits together two distinct moments in his career, his early London etchings and the "costume" paintings of the 1860s, which feature Western women in kimono surrounded by East Asian objects.

Although the painterly qualities of Whistler's *Balcony* obscure the more obvious markers of industrial labor, they are nonetheless just below the surface. The painting itself was a product of prolonged labor: Whistler first embarked upon the project in 1864 and made subtle changes over the next fifteen years but did not complete it until 1879. Evidence of the time and attention that Whistler gave to this composition can be seen in several studies undertaken by the artist in the 1860s. The New York

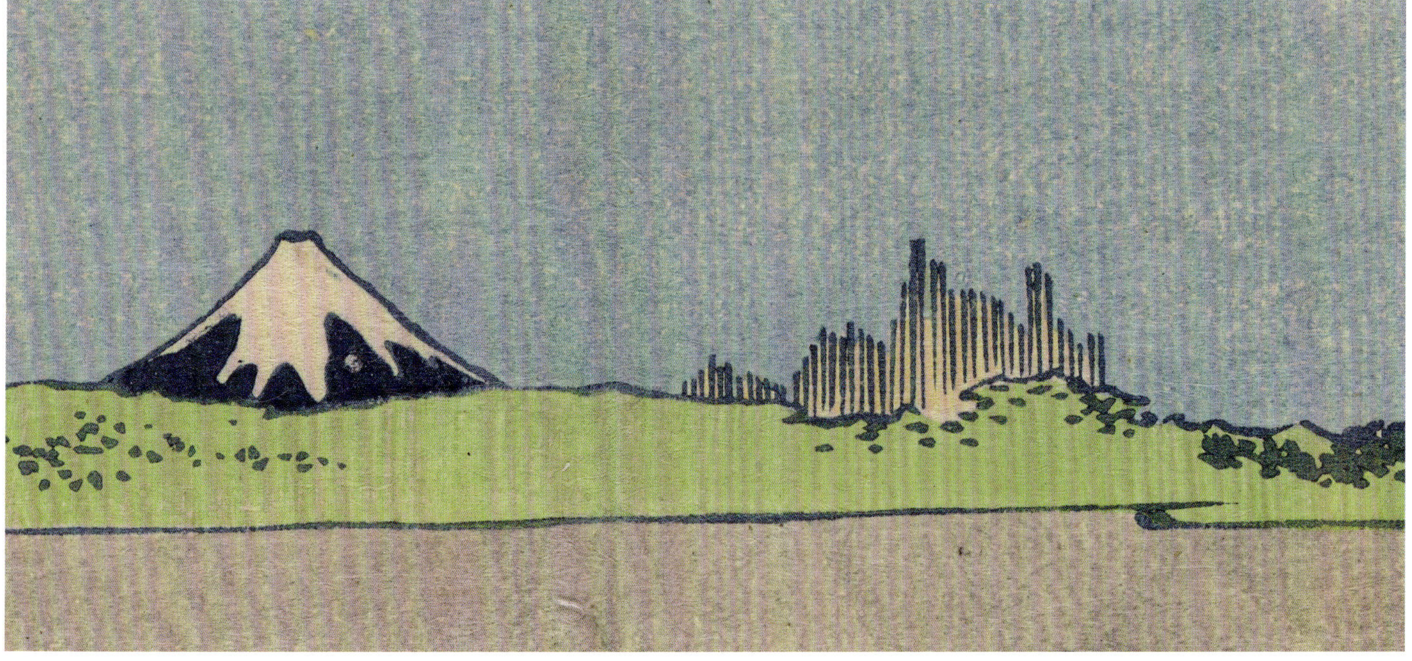

Fig. 4
Katsushika Hokusai,
The Sazaidō of Gohyakurakanji (detail).

Public Library owns a pen-and-ink sketch of the composition dated to 1867–1868; and the Hunterian at the University of Glasgow possesses a large watercolor study and a small oil on panel, both dated to ca. 1867 (figs. 2, 3). The oil painting is squared up, meaning that a grid has been applied as a scaling tool to help the artist transfer the composition to a larger canvas. These related works reveal that the artist spent time working and reworking the scene, with the unrealized ambition of enlarging the composition even further, and he had considered producing a larger version for submission to the Salon in 1867.[11] He also made further changes to the original painting. He added the butterfly signature in 1870 and added a new frame in 1878. He also mentioned touching it up on multiple occasions and saw these modifications as having economic value, as he wrote in an 1878 letter to John Cavafy (1861–1923), son of the painting's original owner: "I borrowed it several times from your Father — and each time I worked upon it and added to its worth until at last I had more than quadrupled its value — In the end I also ordered for it a new frame — and elaborately painted and ornamented it."[12] Labor is thereby tangibly present, embodied in the extended period of the painting's creation and alluded to in the industrial setting.

Whistler's composition features the balcony of his home studio on Lindsey Row in Chelsea overlooking the Thames, with a view of Battersea on the south bank of the river. The serene figures in the foreground form an idyllic counterpoint to the background featuring the polluted Thames and grimy industry, signaled by the vertical smokestacks rising from coal-burning factories and the mountain of industrial waste across the river. Curator and author George H. Birch (1862–1917), described how the "stench arising from the mud-banks at low water and their disgusting appearance were long a standing reproach to London."[13] Two of the most prominent Battersea factories located across the river were devoted to heavy metals and chemicals.

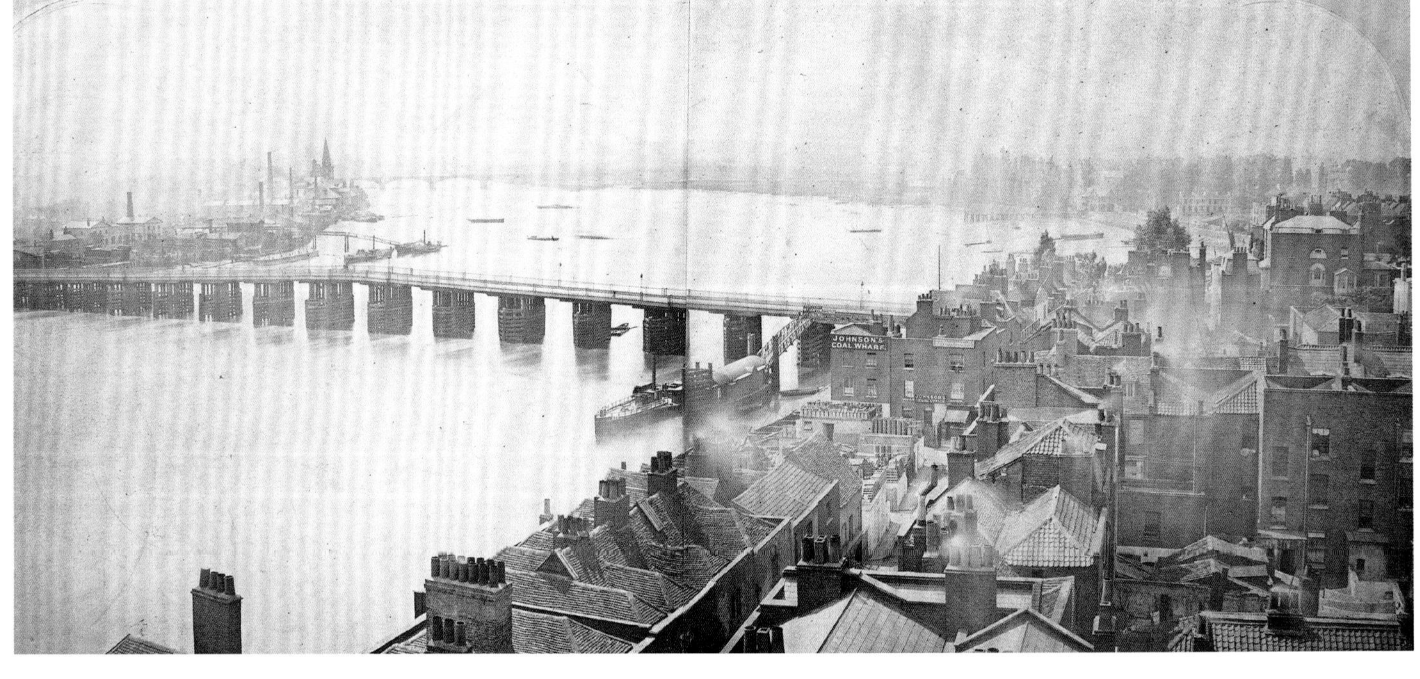

Fig. 5
James Hedderly, Panorama of the Thames at Chelsea and Battersea. England, ca. 1870. Photograph; 20.5 × 42 cm.

May and Baker moved to Battersea in 1861, and there they produced chemicals for pharmaceutical products. Patent Plumbago Crucible Company (later Morgan Crucible Company) occupied a nearby site from 1856 onward. At the time, they were the world's largest manufacturer of industrial crucibles—ceramic containers used for melting metal at high temperatures. The pyramidal shapes to the right of the smokestacks are the heaps of slag waste created by their manufacturing process. The slag heaps become the modern, industrial counterpart to depictions of Mount Fuji as a timeless natural wonder in the background of Katsushika Hokusai's series *Thirty-Six Views of Mount Fuji*. However, upon closer examination of the background of *The Sazaidō of Gohyakurakanji*, a jagged, pointy structure can be seen next to Fuji (fig. 4). It is likely the Fukagawa lumberyards. Thus, the ukiyo-e print's landscape also implicitly references a premodern form of industry and construction and cannot be reduced to a binary counterpoint to Whistler's adaptation.

Photographer James Hedderly (1815–1885), who lived on Duke Street, not far from Whistler's Lindsey Row studio, documented Chelsea and the active Thames riverfront in a series of photographs taken in the 1860s–1870s (fig. 5).[14] These images attest to the crowded and commercial character of the river, but they also reveal how Whistler altered and subdued elements of the industrial landscape to achieve his desired composition. Walter Greaves, who had introduced Whistler to the waterfront, became a longtime studio assistant of Whistler and an artist in his own right. He painted the level section of the Thames riverfront known as Battersea Reach as well, providing in his 1870 painting a more representational perspective on the busy river (fig. 6).

The development of the Chelsea embankment in 1874 led to the destruction of several working-class neighborhoods, as part of a process of urban renewal that echoed the dramatic remaking of Parisian boulevards under the direction of Baron

Fig. 6
Walter Greaves, *Battersea Reach*. England, ca. 1870.
Oil on canvas; 64.1 × 76.8 cm.

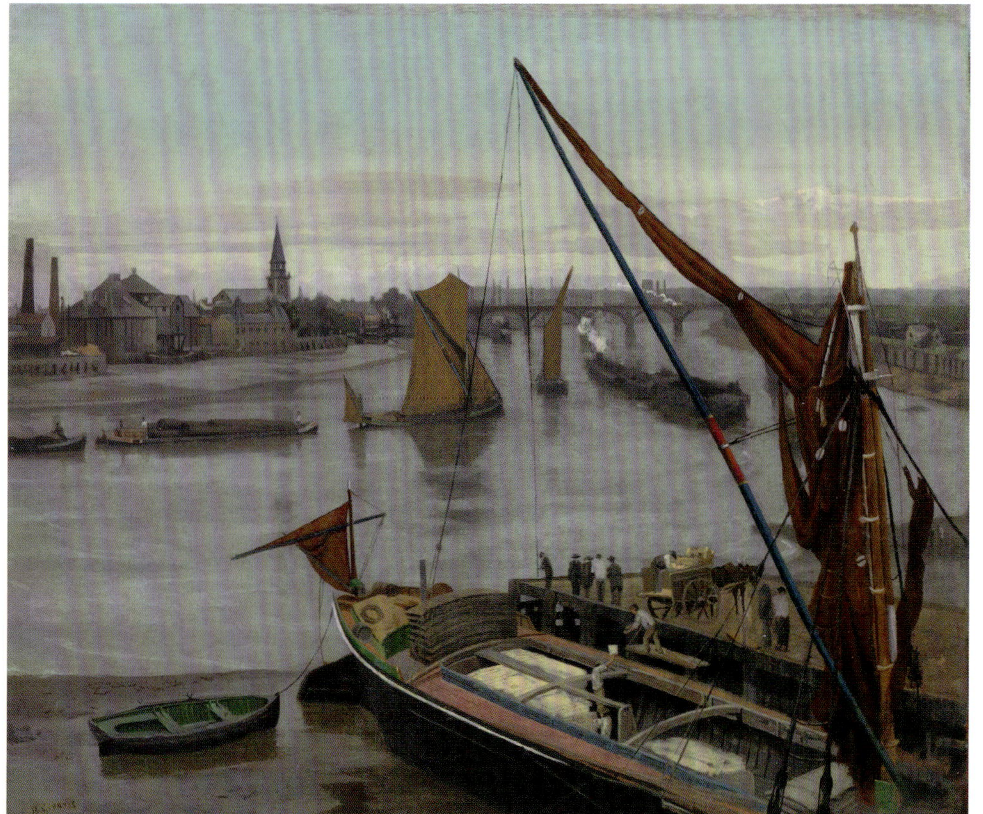

Georges-Eugène Haussmann (1809–1891) between 1853 and 1870. The embankment project created an expansive walkway along the river but demolished older storefronts and residential areas in the process. Many of Whistler's works from this period detail the local shops and businesses that were in danger of disappearing in a swiftly developing city. They do not, however, level any implicit political commentary on this transformation. Though his renderings of storefronts are inherently tinged with nostalgia, Whistler focuses not on subject matter but the primacy of paint on canvas. *Variations in Pink and Grey—Chelsea* (fig. 7) shows the construction fencing in place, as the riverfront was being redeveloped with modern sewers and granite-walled pedestrian walkways. The bird's-eye view was likely drawn from Whistler's second-story window or the balcony of his Chelsea home studio. Whereas the Greaves composition places the viewer on the muddy banks of the river, the elevated perspective in Whistler's painting flattens and abstracts the view. Battersea Reach is visible, a band of dark gray paint along the composition's elevated horizon. But the hallmarks of industry, from smoke and smog to the docks and barges, indicated by streaks, are rendered as decorative elements of color and line. Site in Whistler's work thus manages to be both specific and obscured, at once local and generic.

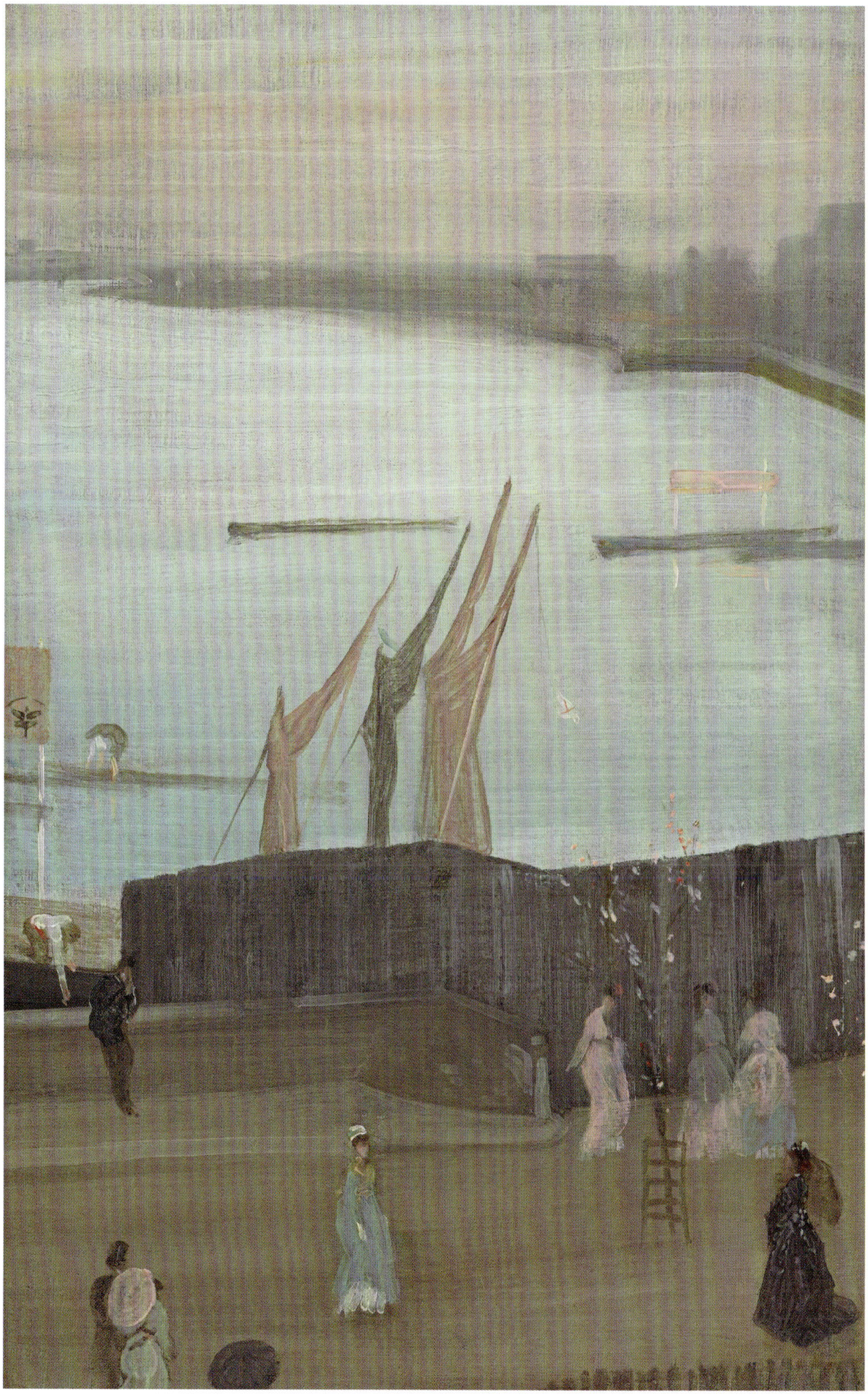

Fig. 7
James McNeill Whistler,
Variations in Pink and Grey—Chelsea. 1871-1872.
Oil on canvas; 82 × 62.7 cm.

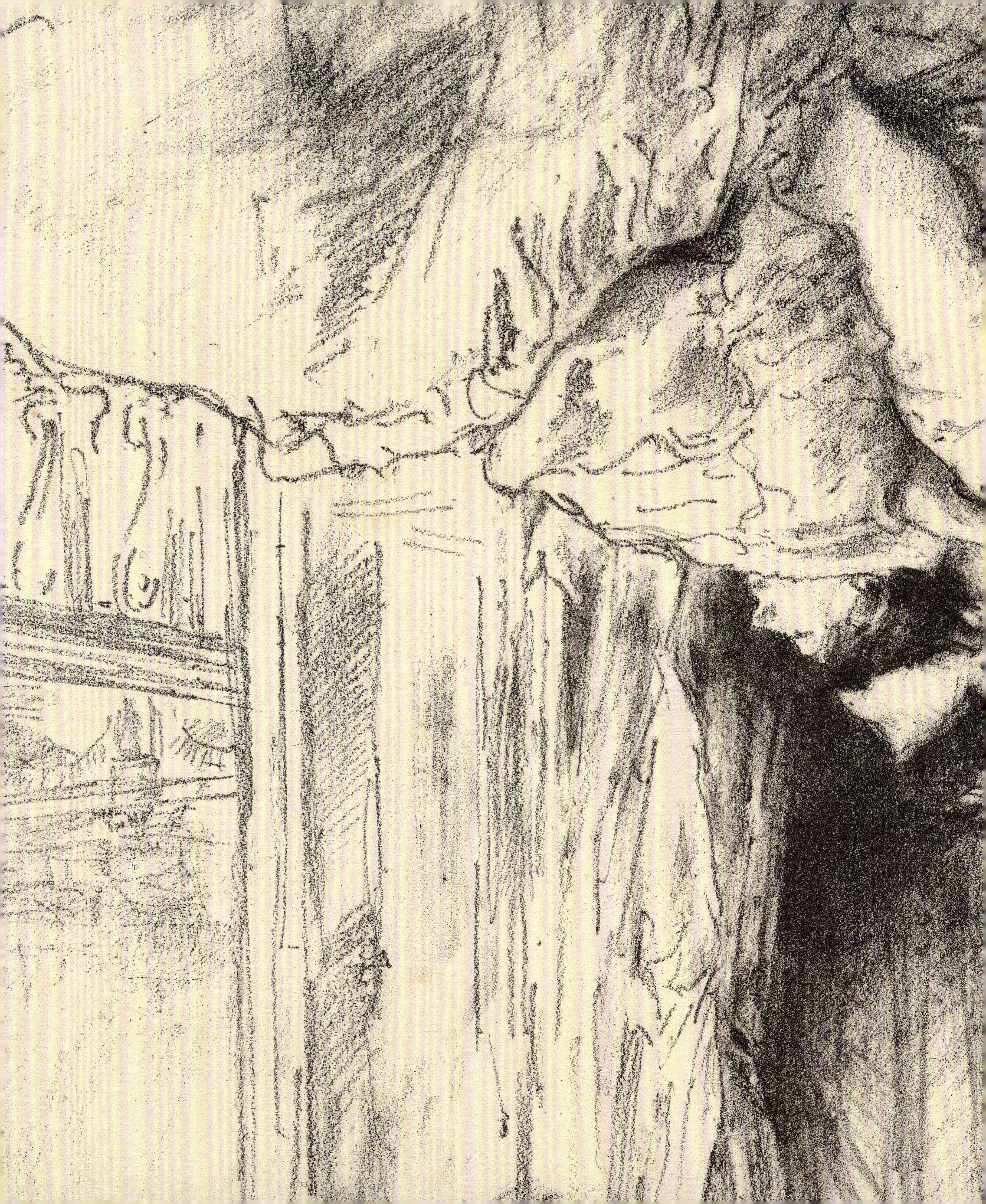

PERSPECTIVE

In what ways does a balcony offer distinctive perspectives on and physical experiences of our surroundings? As an architectural feature, a balcony provides an advantaged point of view, elevating the viewer and offering the prospect of surveilling one's surroundings. When attached to apartment buildings and private homes, it can create an interstitial space that is both public and domestic and is therefore able to straddle two different social realities. As European cities grew denser because of exponential urbanization and industrialization in the second half of the nineteenth century, balconies allowed wealthy urban dwellers an elevated and detached perch to take in the changing world around them. Perhaps it is no wonder that the balcony held appeal, not only to Whistler but also to French artists like Claude Monet (1840–1926), Édouard Manet, and Berthe Morisot (1841–1895), all of whom explored the contours of public and private life in rapidly evolving nineteenth-century Paris.

In discussing *The Sazaidō of Gohyakurakanji*'s impact on European painters, scholars typically point to Monet's *Garden at Sainte-Adresse* (*Jardin à Sainte-Adresse*) (1867) as work incorporating a similar design scheme (fig. 1). Indeed, like the woodblock print, Monet's painting shows several figures, some seated and others positioned by a horizontal railing that bisects the space, dividing the picture plane between the relaxed genre scene in the foreground and the waterscape of the background. The two flagpoles providing vertical framing for the scene were also a feature of Ōbaku Zen temples like Gohyakurakanji (see **Brooks's site**). Like Whistler's *Balcony*, Monet sets up a contrast between the world of leisure and that of industry—the latter indicated by the smokestacks and steamships in the distance. Incidentally, these landscape features are also markers of the same industrial developments and maritime trade

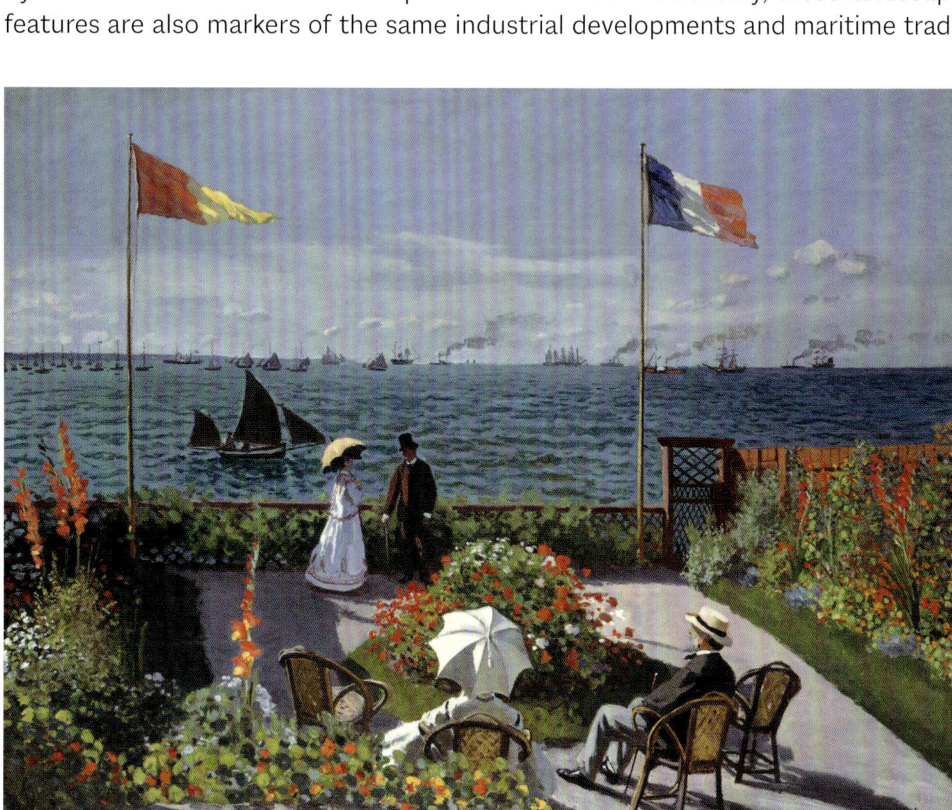

Fig. 1
Claude Monet, *Garden at Sainte-Adresse*. France, 1867. Oil on canvas; 98.1 × 129.9 cm.

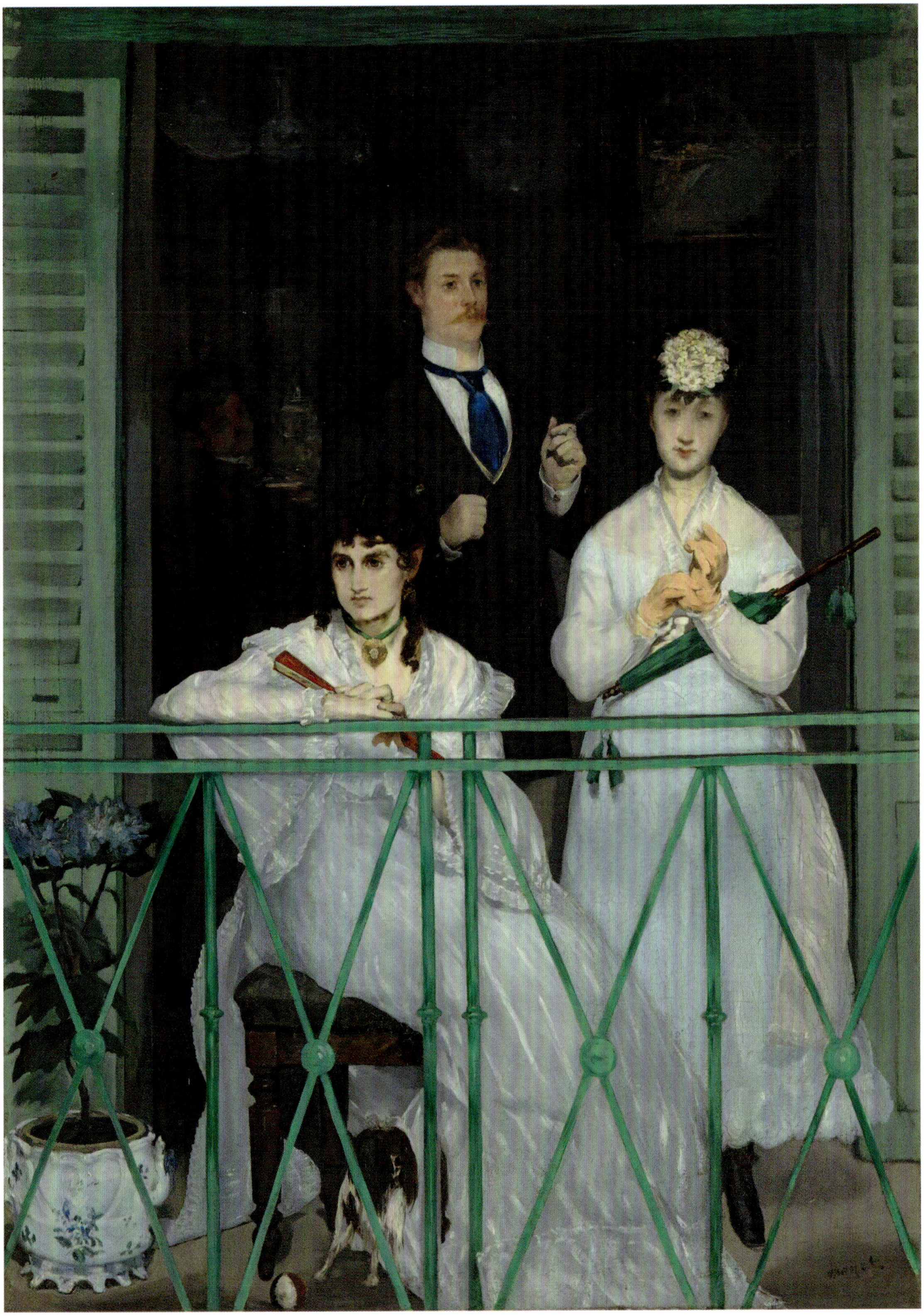

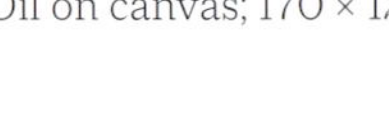

Fig. 2
Édouard Manet, *The Balcony*. France, 1868.
Oil on canvas; 170 × 125 cm.

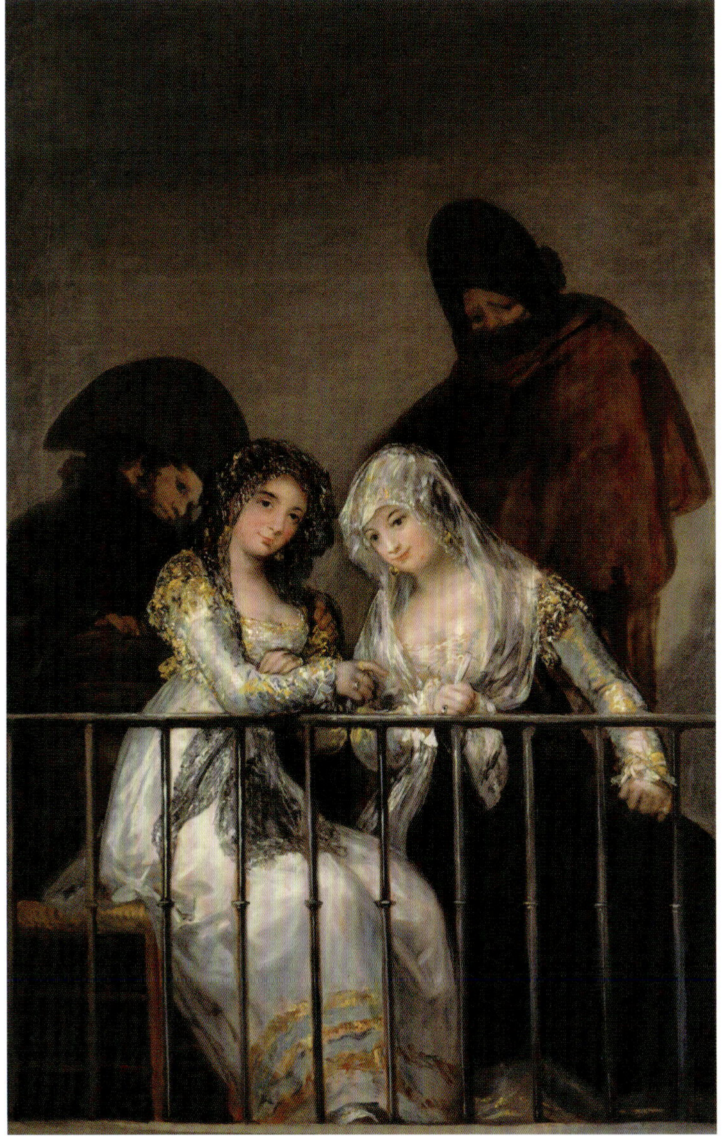

Fig. 3
Attributed to Francisco Goya, *Majas on the Balcony*. Spain, ca. 1800-1810. Oil on canvas; 194.9 × 125.7 cm.

routes that enabled Monet to encounter Hokusai's work. The acceleration of global trade occurred after Commodore Matthew Perry arrived in Japan in 1853 and demanded a trade treaty with the United States, opening the door to treaties with other nations as well. As a result, Japanese goods became increasingly available in Europe in the late nineteenth century. Although there is some dispute over the precise date that Monet began collecting Japanese prints, it is confirmed that by the end of his life he had assembled a collection of 231 impressions in his home in Giverny.[15] Significantly, his collection included a copy of *The Sazaidō of Gohyakurakanji*, which was noted to be damaged, perhaps indicating that it was among his earliest, well-worn purchases.[16] Monet's painting, however, depicts a terrace rather than a balcony; so although it contains the same interstitial resonance as a threshold between two worlds, it does not position the viewer from the same elevated perspective.

Édouard Manet's *The Balcony* (*Le Balcon*), painted in 1868 and exhibited at the Paris Salon of 1869, was arguably the best-known painting of a balcony produced in France (fig. 2). It would also prove to be influential on this circle of modernist and impressionist painters. The canvas remained in the artist's studio until his death in 1883. Whistler had met Manet in Paris in 1861, and the two artists corresponded regularly after the American artist moved to London. One can surmise that Whistler would have seen the *Balcony* painting and its angular, architectural composition for himself during a visit to Manet's studio. However, Whistler's own *Balcony* was begun before Manet took up the subject, and the paintings are dissimilar: Manet's composition places the viewer on a level plane, looking *at* the balcony, rather than in a position *on* the balcony looking outward. Manet, on this occasion and several others, took his cues from the Spanish romantic painter Francisco Goya (1746-1828), whose attributed *Majas on the Balcony* (*Majas al balcón*) similarly features two women, one of whom rests a bent arm upon the balcony railing, with two male figures in the background (fig. 3). Like the women in Yoshiwara balcony scenes (see **Brooks's restriction**), Goya's women are sex workers. They meet the world with a

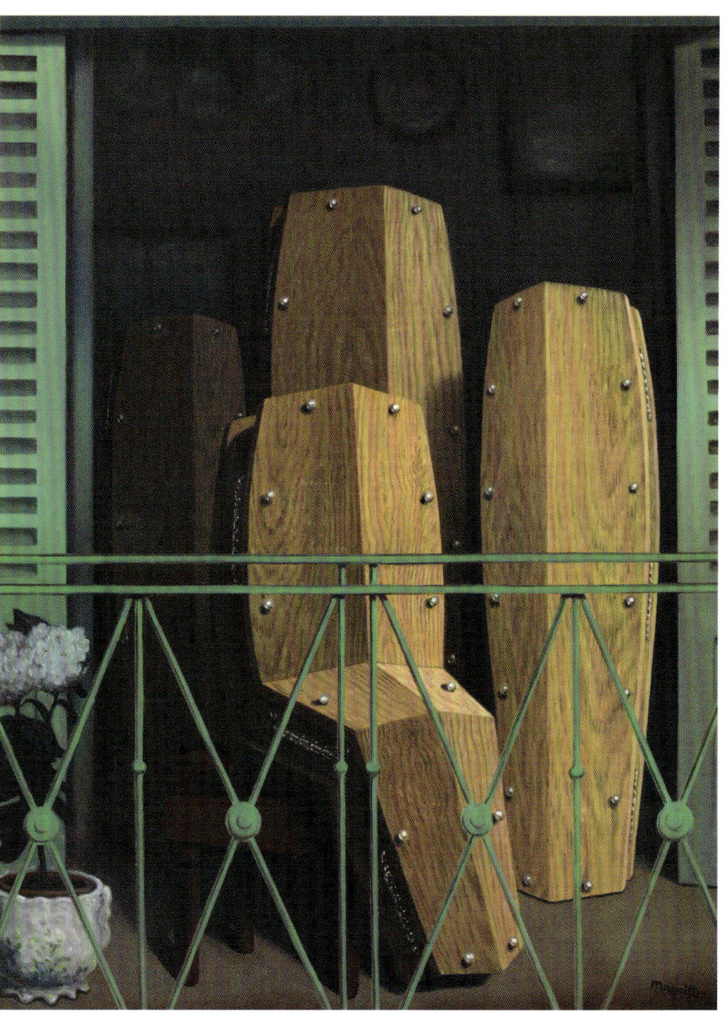

Fig. 4
René Magritte, *Perspective II: Manet's Balcony*. France, 1950. Oil on canvas; 84 × 65 cm.

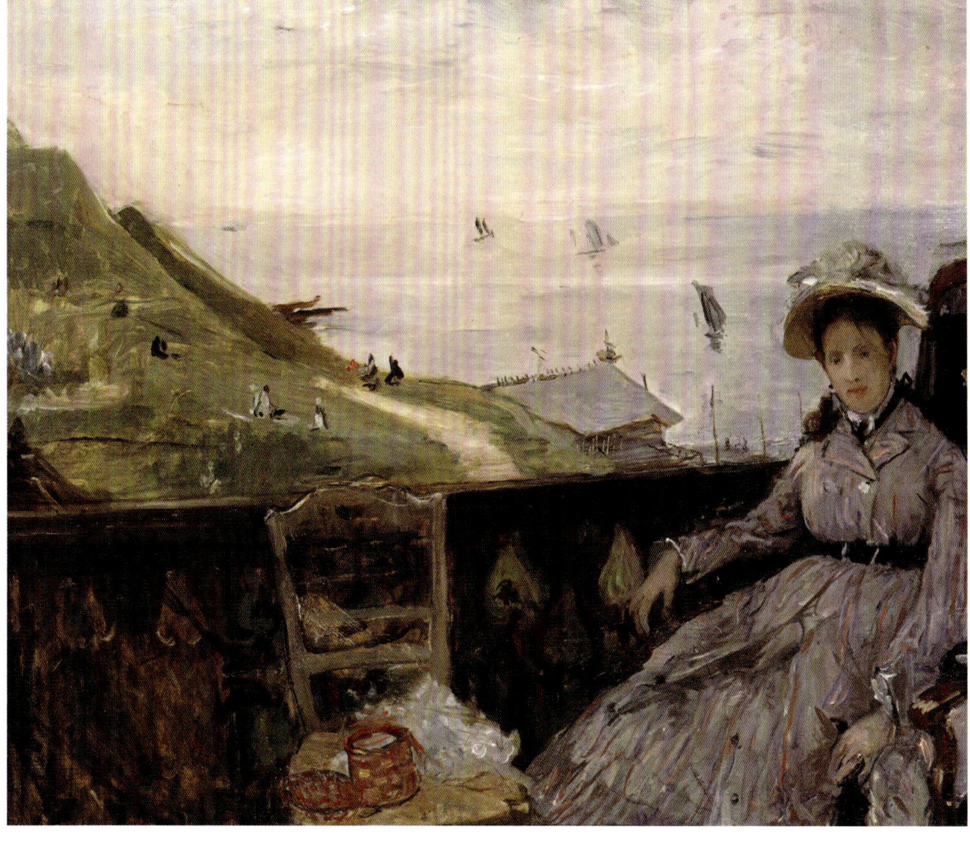

Fig. 5
Berthe Morisot, *On the Terrace*. France, 1874.
Oil on canvas; 45 × 54 cm.

direct and appraising gaze. By contrast, Manet's bourgeois models are more detached, and as in Whistler's composition, the figures share a physical space but are seemingly emotionally disconnected from each other.

The woman on the left of Manet's *Balcony* is Berthe Morisot. A fellow painter and friend of Manet, Morisot eventually married the artist's brother, Eugène, six years later. This painting elicited criticism upon its exhibition at the Salon in 1869: critics referred to Manet's color scheme as discordant and claimed the figures looked "morose" and "disagreeable."[17] Yet it would continue to exert influence on Manet and his circle for decades to come, hanging near his (in)famous *Olympia* (1863–1865) in the artist's studio. The impressionist painter Gustave Caillebotte (1848–1894) purchased Manet's *Balcony* upon the older artist's death and displayed it in his home before donating it to the French state. The surrealist René Magritte (1898–1967) would later recreate the composition but replaced the figures with coffins in his 1950 painting *Perspective II: Manet's Balcony* (*Perspective II: Le Balcon de Manet*) (fig. 4). Magritte's painting was part of a series called *Perspective*, in which he copied paintings by well-known French painters like Manet and Jacques-Louis David (1748–1825) and replaced figural subjects with coffins, as if to comment on the inevitability of mortality or, perhaps, the deadliness of French polite society. Here, the substitution also takes the critique of Manet's "morose" figures to its logical conclusion. However, Manet's depiction of Morisot is more active than the Magritte's rigid coffins would suggest. She is leaning slightly forward with her arm resting on the railing and looking pensively off to the

Fig. 6
Berthe Morisot, *Woman and Child on the Balcony*. 1872.
Oil on canvas; 61 × 50 cm.

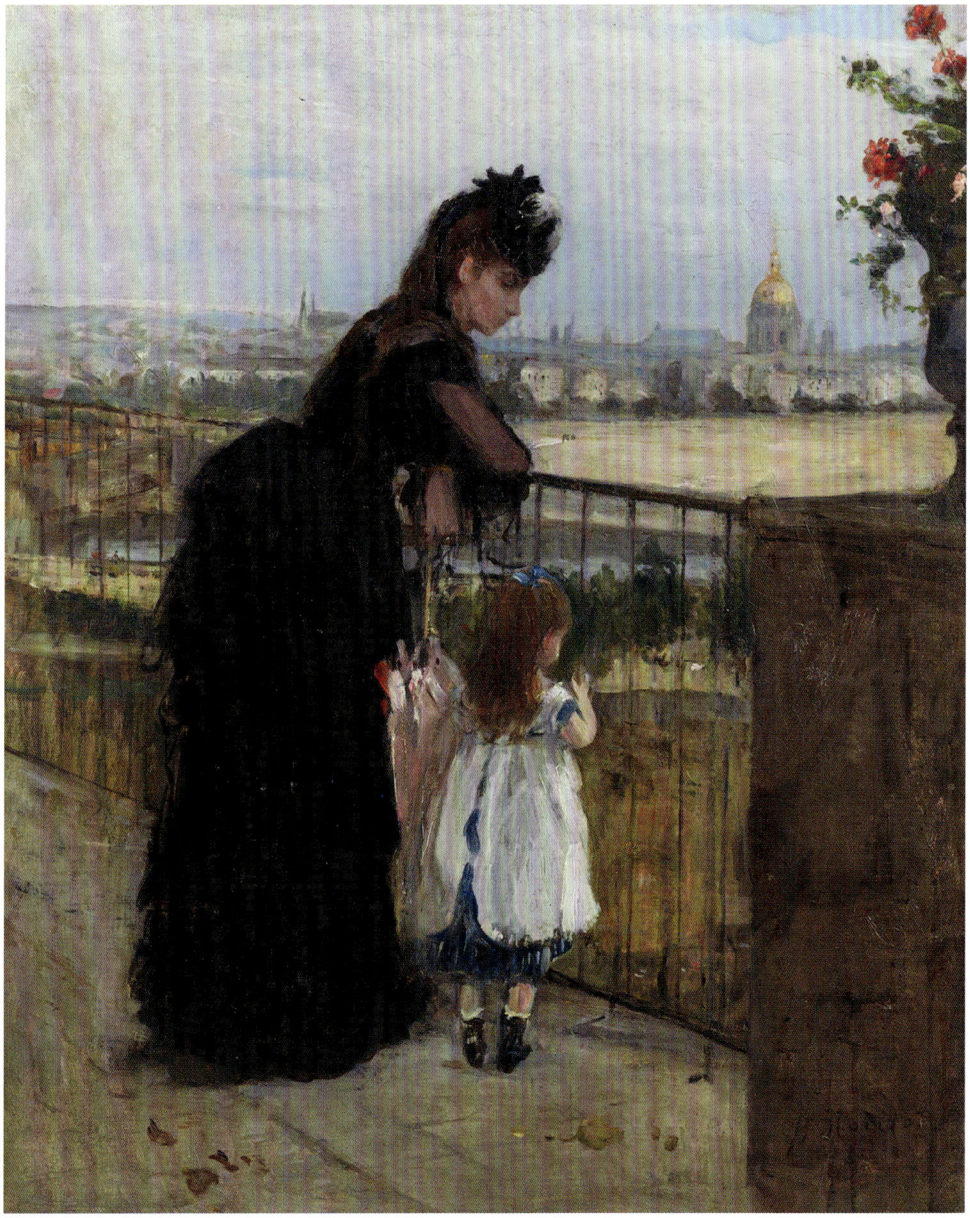

left. Morisot's fixed stare from her semipublic position has allowed scholars to posit that the painting makes a case for the possibility of a *flâneuse*, a female observer of modern life.[18] *Flâneurs* were, by definition, men of wealth and power who were able to casually surveil Parisian life from a position of privilege. Morisot on the balcony is an argument for how women found alternate pathways to public life.

Berthe Morisot painted balcony subjects herself on several occasions, but always from the vantage of the balcony or threshold and looking outward to the land or cityscape beyond. Indeed, the art historian Cindy Kang has identified the preponderance of windows, balconies, and verandahs in Morisot's work as a thematic constant and suggests that, given the limited access women artists had to the public spaces of

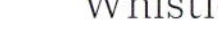

Paris, balconies offered access to a greater world while remaining grounded within a domestic context.[19] In *On the Terrace* (*Sur la terrasse*) from 1874, Morisot paints a woman seated upon an upholstered chair perched upon a balcony (fig. 5). She looks dispassionately at the viewer, while ignoring the lively landscape in the background. The empty chair to her left reads as an ambiguous invitation for a viewer of the painting to join her on the balcony. A railing bisects the picture plane, dividing the domesticity of the foreground from the landscape dotted with figures and boats in the background. As in Whistler's *Balcony*, the horizon line is elevated. This choice can be attributed to these artists' exposure to Japanese ukiyo-e prints, while also speaking to the way these elevated perspectives collapse distance and compress the view. By orienting the subject's back to the vista, the composition presents *her*, as well as the scenery, for our viewing pleasure. Morisot's *Woman and Child on the Balcony* (*Femme et enfant au balcon*), from 1872, on the other hand, suggests a more active mode of engagement (fig. 6). Here, the balcony is framed at an angle, with the railing forming a diagonal line that adds a dynamic element to the scene. An urn of flowers on a pedestal is mostly cropped out of the picture, placing the viewer firmly on the ledge together with the painting's subjects. A woman in black leans upon the handrail, looking down at the young girl by her side. The child is peering off in the distance, but holding the railing's balusters as though they were prison bars, perhaps anticipating the way her future

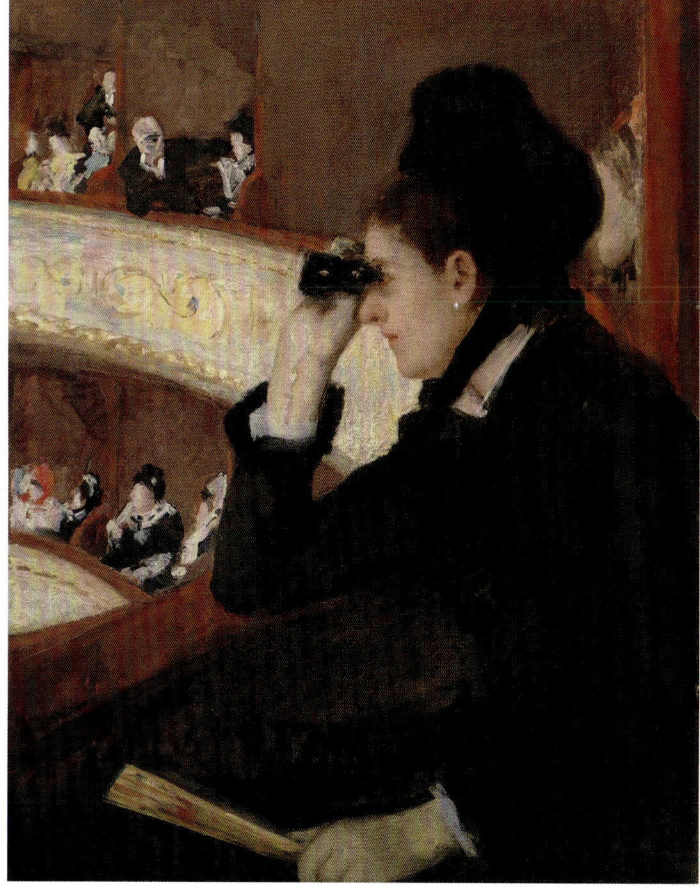

Fig. 7
Mary Cassatt, *In the Loge*. France, 1878.
Oil on canvas; 81.3 × 66 cm.

public life will be restricted by forces outside of her control. As a woman painter often discredited, disparaged, or forbidden from full participation in the art world of her time, Morisot fully understood these constraints. The railing plays a similarly decisive demarcation between private and public space in Whistler's *Balcony*. However, his composition is unusual in that only one figure peers off in the distance. The three other women sprawled on the balcony face away from the vista and instead direct their attention to either the artist or the viewer, who is positioned looking out towards the balcony and the river. All of the three seated figures look up, as though their individual reveries have been disturbed by the arrival of an unexpected visitor.

Other impressionist women likewise explored similar tensions in the more public realms of theater and opera houses. Mary Cassatt (1844–1926) and Eva Gonzalès (1849–1883) each depicted women navigating Parisian society at a remove, in the intimate, cocooned space of opera loges and theater boxes, as in Cassatt's *In the Loge* (fig. 7). The painting of a woman peering through opera glasses at the stage, while simultaneously being looked at by a man in a neighboring box, showcases this interior balcony as a dynamic, unsettled space for seeing and being seen. Victorian toy theaters (see **remix**), which were miniature paper reproductions of European theaters collected by children and adults alike as souvenirs of theatrical performances, allow us to replicate the environment on a small scale (fig. 8).

The glimpse of public space that is both tantalizingly close and completely out of reach also calls to mind a late lithograph by Whistler titled *By the Balcony* from 1896 (fig. 9). The rare print (there are only six known impressions) is among Whistler's most deeply personal compositions. It shows Beatrix Whistler (1857–1896), the artist's

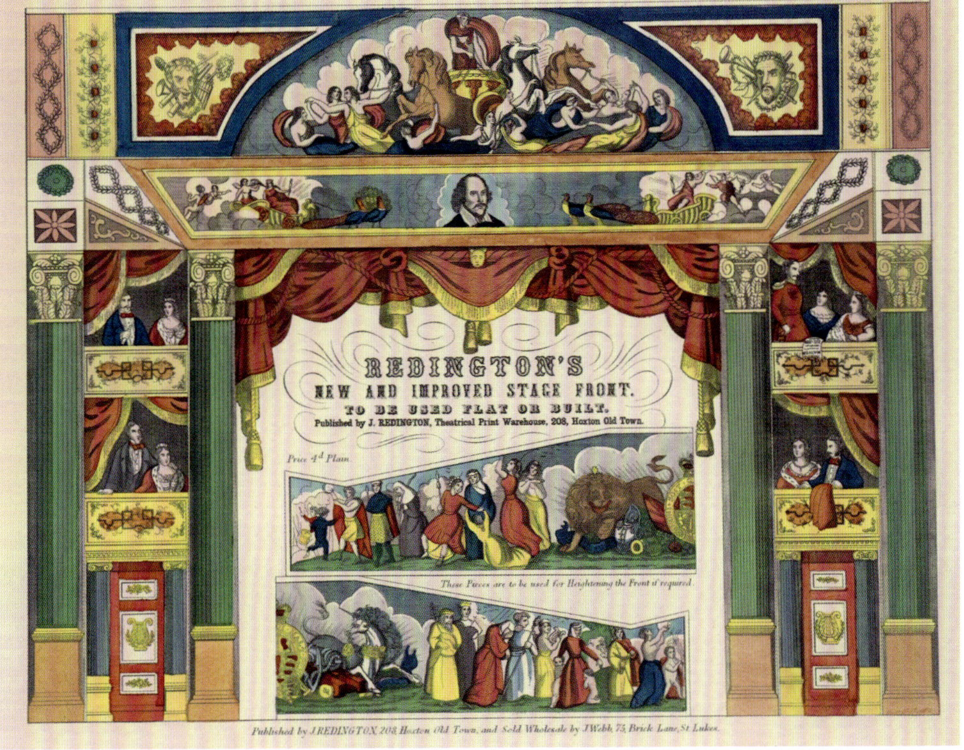

Fig. 8
Redington's new and improved stage front. England, 1800–1899. Hand-colored etching and engraving on paper; 52 × 65 cm.

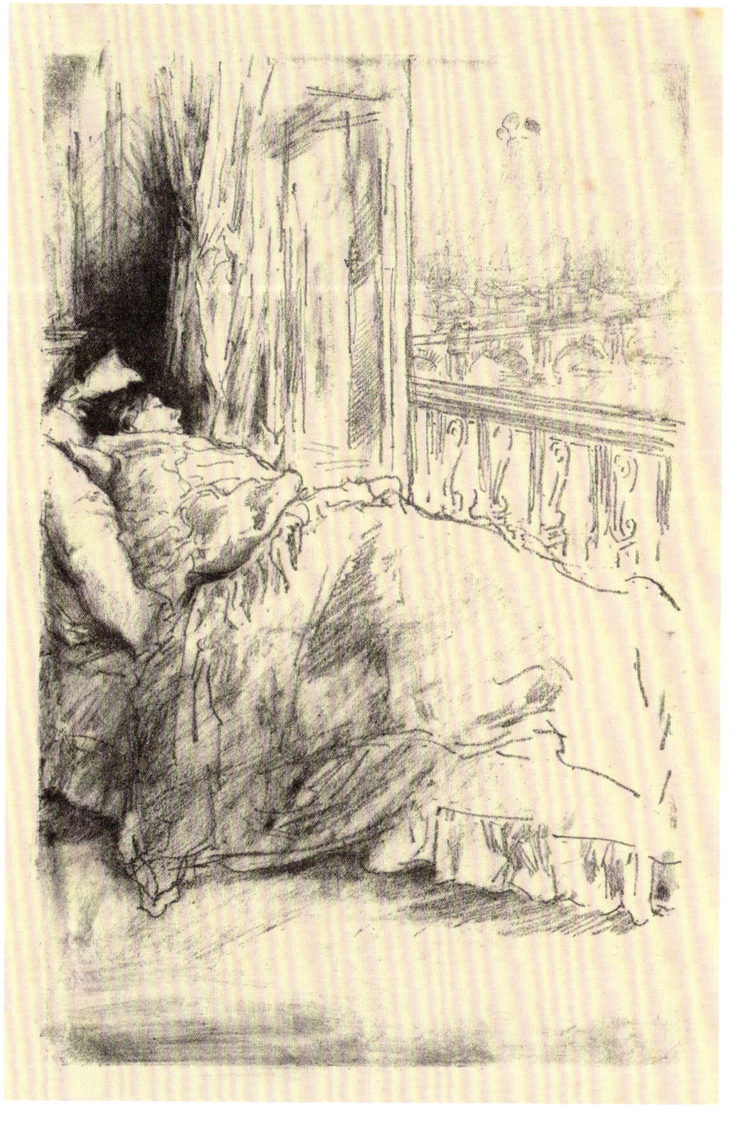

Fig. 9
James McNeill Whistler, *By the Balcony*. 1896. Lithograph on paper; 21.6 × 14 cm.

wife, as she lay dying of cancer; in the background is an oblique view of the Thames. Dark shadows gather at the head of the bed, drawing attention to Beatrix's profile but also serving as a reminder of the ever-present specter of death. Lying in bed, she looks toward the view with her arm extending outward but without breaching the threshold that separates her from the busy city beyond. Whistler's monogram floats in the sky on the right side of the composition, aligned with the world of the living. The angles of the balcony railing and the distant bridge over the river appear as though they could converge, though their meeting is curtailed by the hanging curtain at the left. Here, the balcony serves as an access point to the life of a city and a world that Beatrix was on the cusp of leaving behind. While the lithograph is visually dissimilar in composition and scale from *The Balcony* painting he began in 1864, it represents an end-of-life return—for both himself and his wife—to the locations and vantage points that were so important to his career.

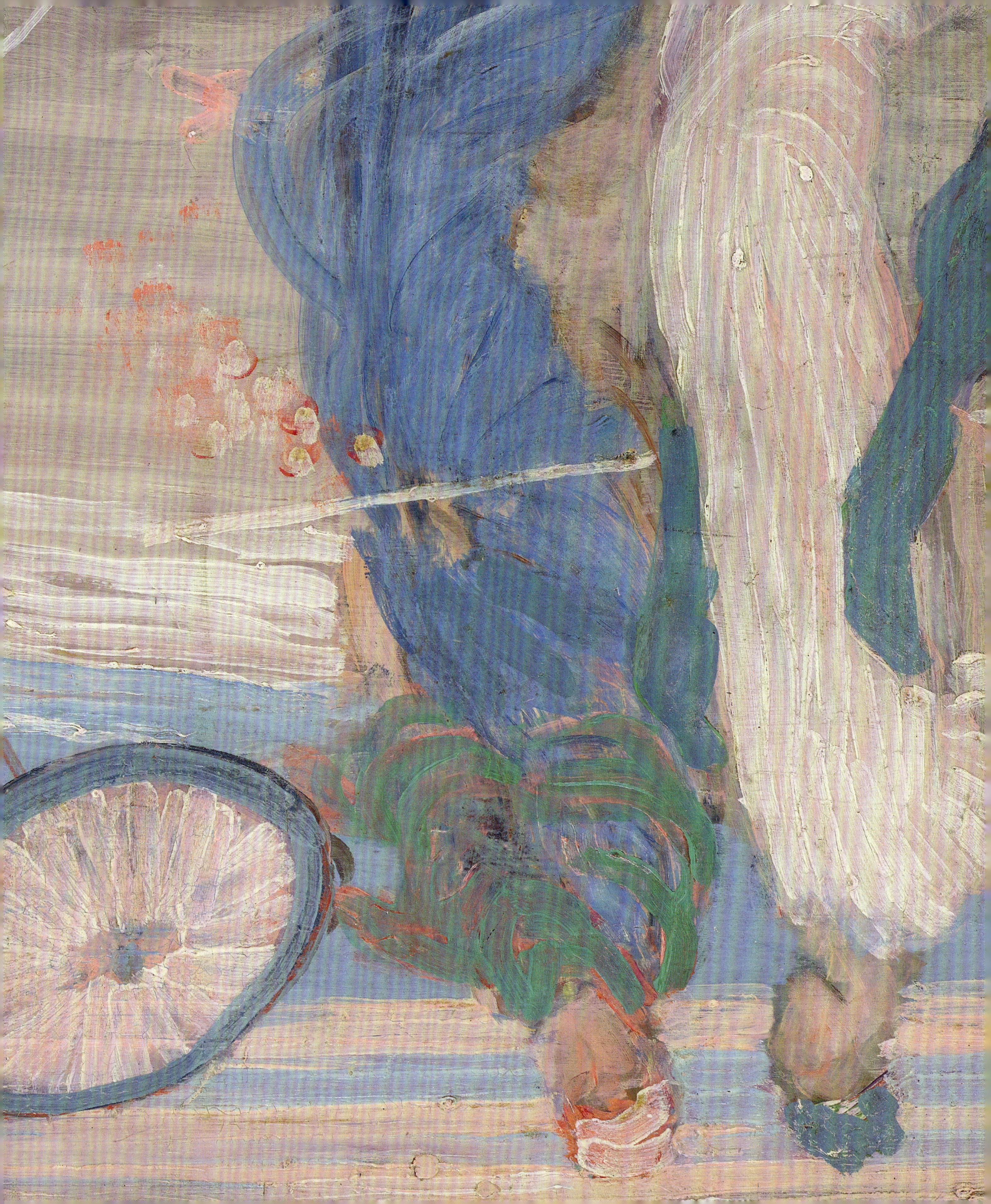

Why does Whistler invoke Greece and Japan with such frequency in his compositions? "The story of the beautiful is already complete—hewn in the marbles of the Parthenon, and broidered, with the birds, upon the fan of Hokusai—at the foot of Fusi-hama."[20] These oft-quoted remarks came from Whistler's "Ten O'Clock Lecture," an hour-long speech that he delivered on February 20, 1885, at the Prince's Hall in Piccadilly, London, which was subsequently reproduced and circulated as an artist's manifesto of sorts. Foundational to his argument about art and beauty were Whistler's interests in ancient Greek and Japanese art, motifs that appear in his work repeatedly and at times converge upon one another. Whistler's anachronistic conflations of these two foreign cultures are particularly apparent in his treatment of female figures.

In 1865, Whistler began a close friendship with the neoclassical painter Albert Moore (1841–1893), who encouraged Whistler's interest in ancient Greece (fig. 1). Moore's own interest in classicism is commonly linked to the display of the Parthenon

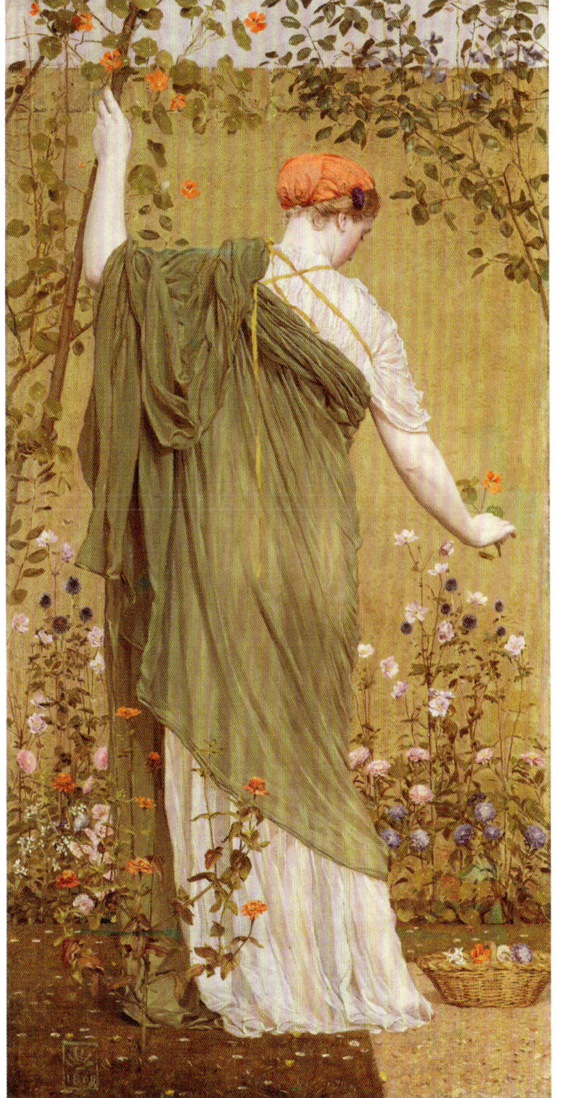

Fig. 1
Albert Moore, *A Garden*.
England, 1869. Oil on canvas;
174.6 × 87.9 cm.

Detail of fig. 4

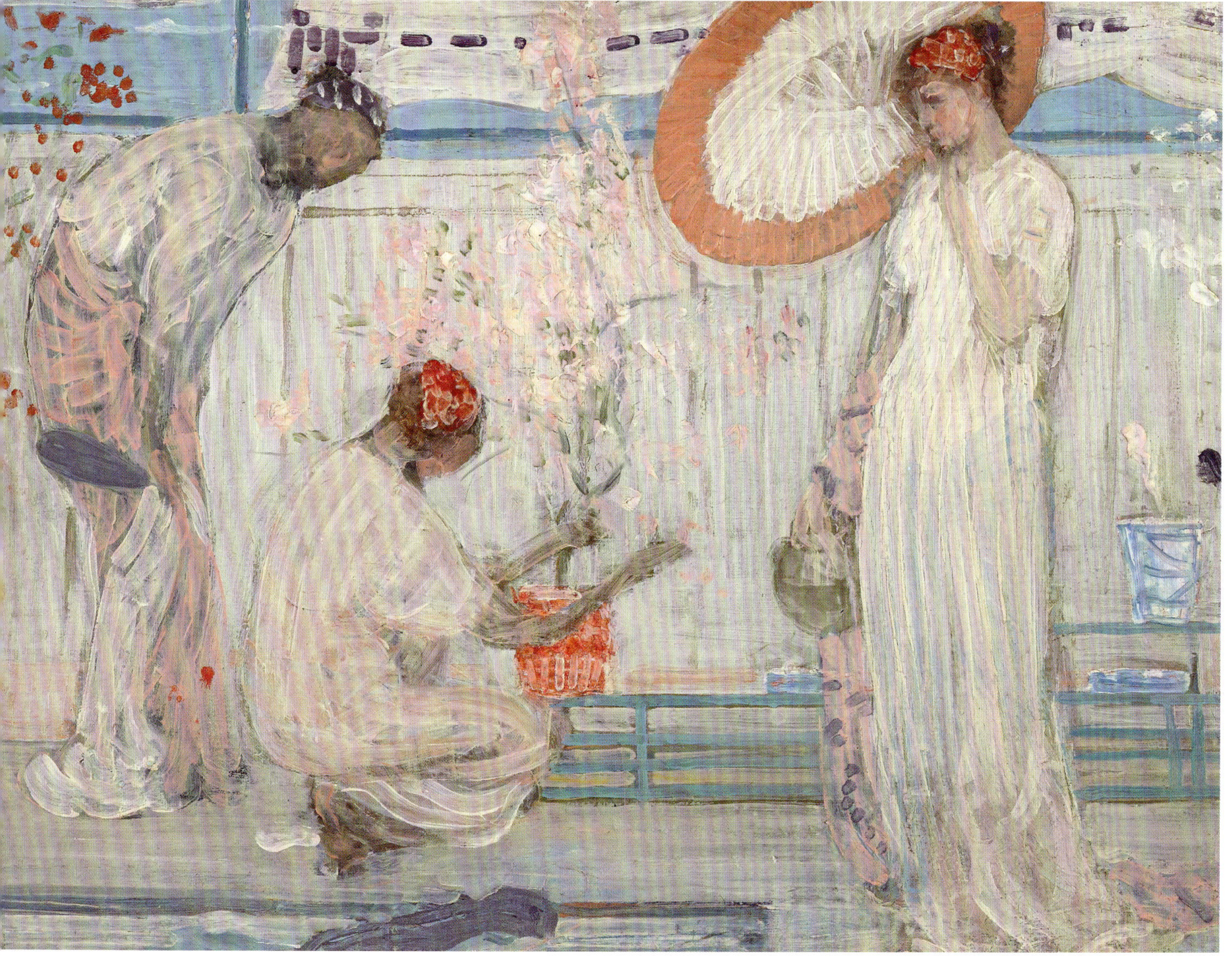

Fig. 2
James McNeill Whistler, *The White Symphony—Three Girls*. ca. 1868. Oil on millboard mounted on wood panel; 46.4 × 61.6 cm.

marbles in London in the 1860s.[21] By 1868, Whistler was sharing a studio at 62 Great Russell Street, just across the street from the British Museum. Moore lived in the vicinity, and the two would visit the museum together to sketch from the marbles and other ancient sculpture.[22] It was during this period that Whistler embarked on a commission for his primary patron, Frederick Leyland (1831–1892), a painting titled *The Three Girls*. The work was never realized because Whistler's ambitious scheme for the Peacock Room, the immersive aesthetic space initially decorated for Leyland and now on permanent view at the National Museum of Asian Art (see **restriction**), led to a falling out with his patron. However, a remaining preparatory oil sketch, known as *The White Symphony—Three Girls*, demonstrates how Whistler was absorbing classical influences from his visits with Moore and combining them with his own explorations of Japanese aesthetics (fig. 2). These combined influences can be seen in

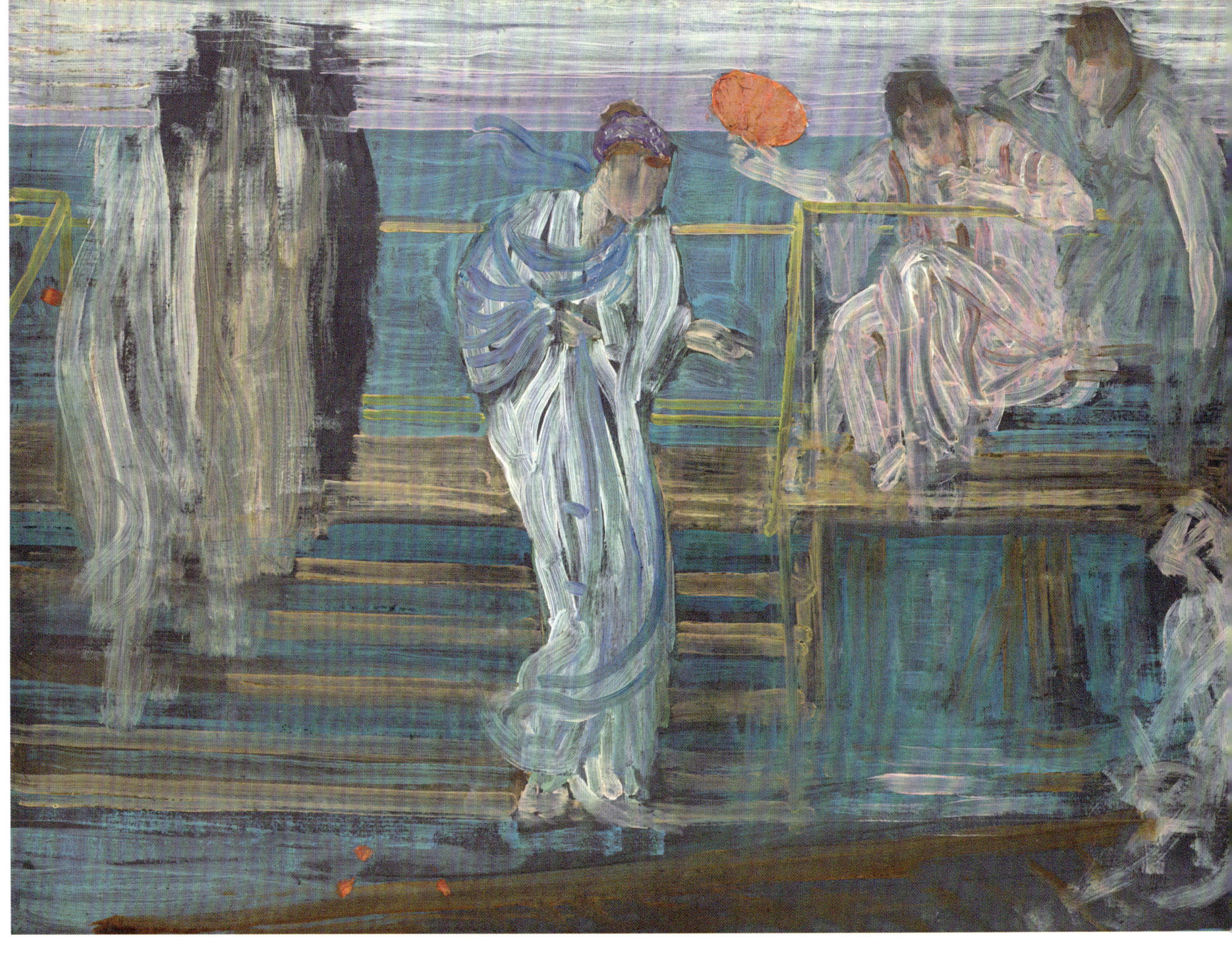

Fig. 3
James McNeill Whistler, *Symphony in White and Red.* ca. 1868. Oil on millboard mounted on wood panel; 46.8 × 61.8 cm.

another unfinished project, now known as the *Six Projects* series, that he was working on at the same time. Although only sketches survive, including *Symphony in White and Red* and *Symphony in Blue and Pink*, these works also featured women in Greek drapery, carrying fans and parasols arranged in a shallow, linear space reminiscent of a Japanese print (figs. 3, 4).[23]

Whistler's anachronistic conflation of ancient Greece and Edo-period (1603–1868) Japan was part of a larger cultural phenomenon known as Japonisme, which scholar Christopher Reed links to the "perceptions of Japan as a civilization paradoxically exotic and familiar."[24] In an ultimately patronizing view, Whistler was repelled by Japan's absorption of contemporary Western practices. By aligning nineteenth-century Japanese culture with Greek classicism, Whistler effectively fixed Japan in amber as an ancient culture worthy of veneration, thereby denying its reality as a dynamic

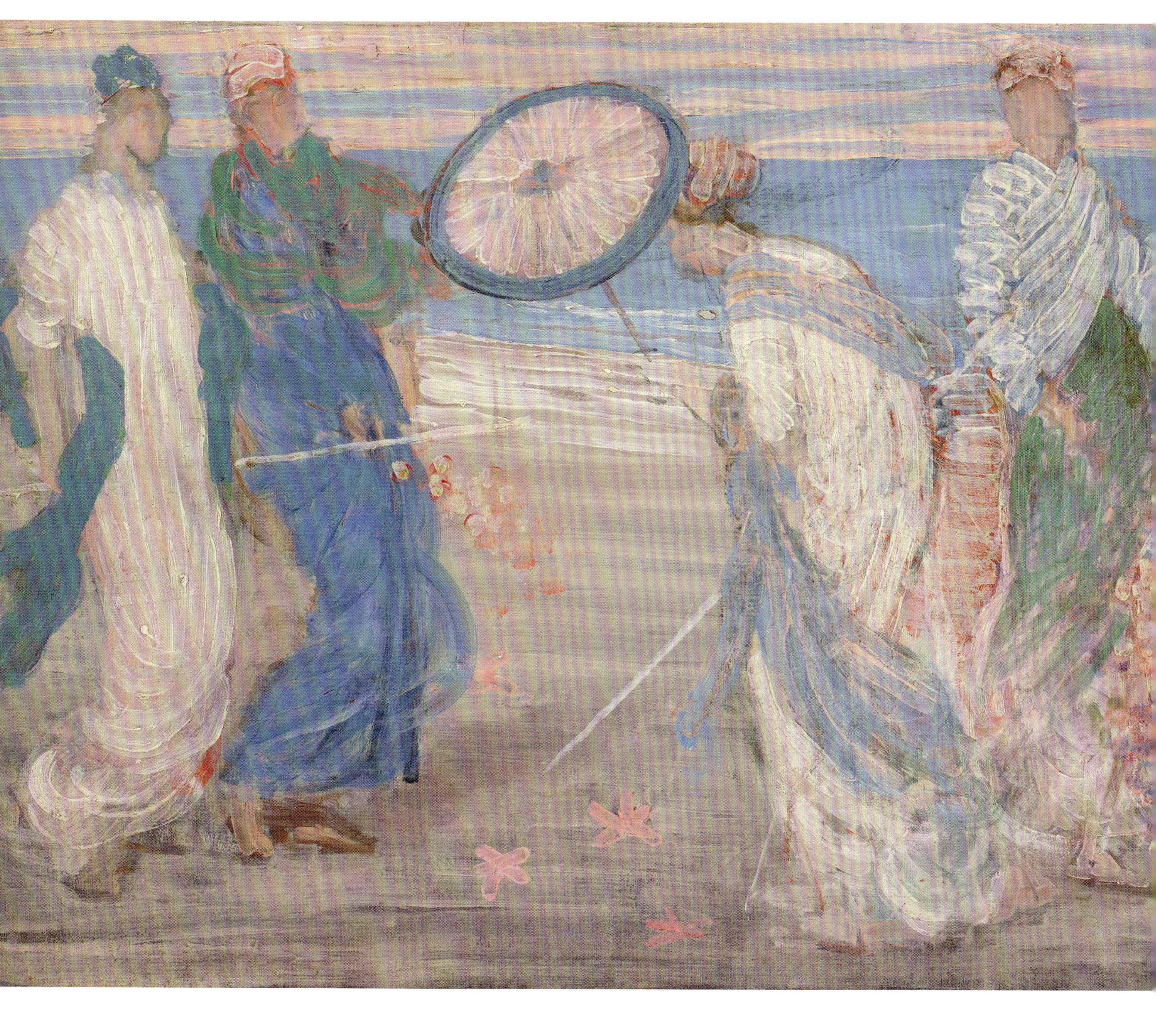

Fig. 4
James McNeill Whistler,
Symphony in Blue and Pink.
ca. 1868. Oil on millboard
mounted on wood panel;
46.7 × 61.8 cm.

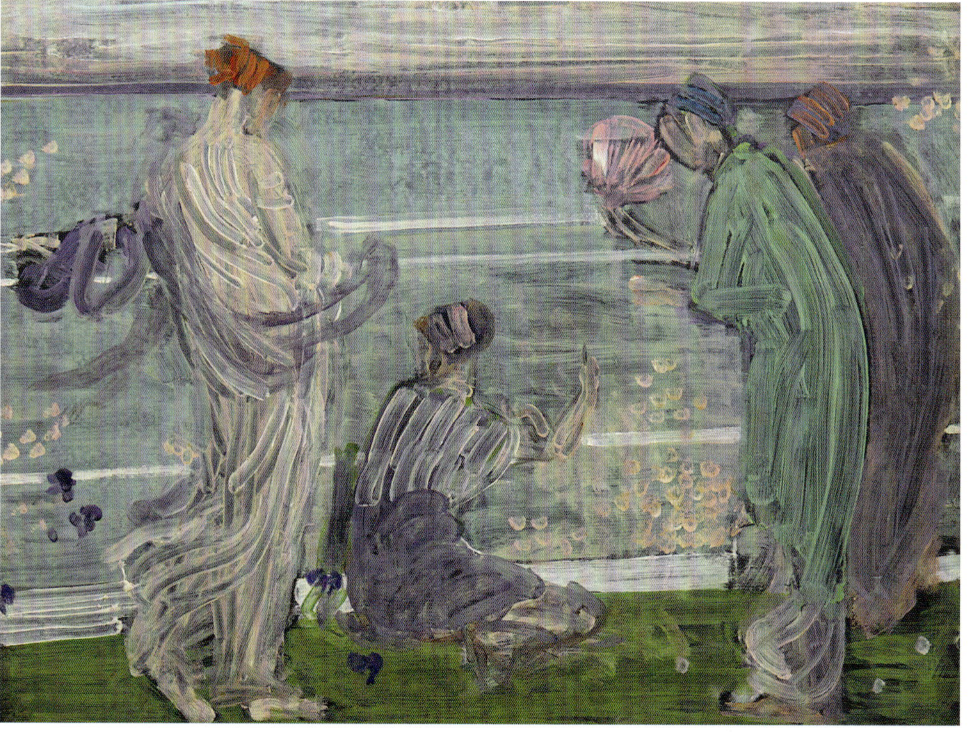

Fig. 5
James McNeill Whistler, *Variations in Blue and Green.* ca. 1868. Oil on millboard mounted on wood panel; 46.9 × 61.8 cm.

and evolving modern nation. A comparison of maps of London and Edo (pre-1868 Tokyo) shows that both cities were dense and rapidly modernizing by the nineteenth century. As early as the eighteenth century, a million people lived in Edo, making it the largest city in the world at that time. London's population did not surpass Edo's until the nineteenth century, when it grew to three million by 1870.[25] Unlike Whistler's emphasis on grimy industry, Hokusai's view in *The Sazaidō of Gohyakurakanji*, situated on the outskirts of the city, suggests a more bucolic scene, though he does include the Fukagawa lumberyards on the horizon line with Mount Fuji. While not as polluting as a chemical factory, the timber yard's presence acknowledges the growing need for construction materials in a rapidly expanding Edo, a city constructed largely of wooden buildings. Whistler never traveled to Japan himself, thus allowing him to preserve his fantasy of a country untouched by industrialization and urban sprawl.

For Whistler, references to Japan and Greece came to represent idealized and otherworldly forms that transported the figures in his paintings from their own dreary reality. Whistler's classically inspired oil sketches from the late 1860s, such as *Variations in Blue and Green* (fig. 5), correspond in several ways with *The Balcony*. All feature an arrangement of four or five women lounging in a geometrically defined, shallow space. The figures in the aforementioned *Six Projects* sketches are also located on a balcony, where the geometry of the railing and horizon line is contrasted by the soft, curvilinear forms of the draped figures. However, unlike *The Balcony*, where the women wear kimono, here the women are dressed in long, flowing gowns, which call to mind a genre of ancient Greek sculpture known as Tanagra statuettes (fig. 6).

Mass-produced Hellenistic statuettes made of terracotta, Tanagra figurines were named for a city in ancient Boeotia, which was excavated in the nineteenth century.[26]

The small statues date to fourth-century BCE Athens and feature men, women, and children. However, the figures unearthed in Tanagra were mostly women, in a range of elegant poses and often holding a wreath or fan and wearing flowing garments (a chiton, which was a tunic, and/or a himation, or mantle). They were constructed from multiple concave clay molds, with separate molds for the front, back, legs, arms, head, and base. The separate pieces were then assembled and painted with white slip prior to being fired in a kiln. After firing, they were colorfully painted with water-soluble mineral or vegetable pigments, and traces of these paints are occasionally found on their surfaces. The British Museum began acquiring and displaying Tanagra figurines in the mid-1860s. Indeed, "Tanagramania" took hold of Britain in this period, and between eight and ten thousand Hellenistic tombs were looted to meet the demand. Forgeries became commonplace and were produced using local clay and molds taken from genuine figures, making them harder to identify as fraudulent.[27]

Archaeologist Malcolm Bell highlights the emphasis on clothing and pose, claiming: "Tanagra figures are thus by nature drapery studies, and much is ruled out, including any overt narrative or religious content."[28] The emphasis on form devoid of meaning must have appealed to Whistler, who actively rejected narrative interpretations of his work, and Whistler's pastel sketches seem to deliberately invoke the Tanagra (fig. 7). It was Moore who, in addition to accompanying Whistler on visits to the British Museum, had encouraged Whistler to experiment with pastels as a way to explore color and form in a more organic and direct way, by sketching the outlines of figures with rudimentary strokes of color and adding details later.[29] Whistler preferred brown kraft paper for his pastels, which give a textured backdrop to the image. Moreover, the harmony of the brown paper, white chalk, and abbreviated areas of color resembles the surface of Tanagra figurines, with remnants of white slip and hints of pigment on the terracotta (fig. 8).

Despite his aesthetic preferences for ancient art, Whistler did have connections to contemporary Greece, which is a latent presence in *The Balcony* painting and its provenance. Not long after Whistler moved to London, he became associated with two prominent and closely linked families of Greek merchants then living in England. The patriarchs of the Cavafy and Ionides families originally emigrated from Constantinople (now Istanbul) to Manchester.[30] They opened an import-export business that grew to include offices in Alexandria, London, Liverpool, Manchester, and Constantinople.[31] As the business expanded, the families formed marriages and alliances with each other and other Greek mercantile families in the region. The family's second generation included George John Cavafy (1805–1891) and Alexander Constantine Ionides (1810–1890). Ionides had expanded the business into banking, and by 1860 he was also director of the Crystal Palace Company and the consul general for Greece.[32] They were assimilated into British social circles through their art patronage. Both men acquired paintings by Whistler and considered him a friend.[33] In July 1862, the critic and satirist George du Maurier (1834–1896) said of Whistler that he was "painting river pictures for the Greeks," in reference to the patronage of Cavafy and Ionides; he also cynically referred to them as "very useful acquaintances," as if to underscore the transactional nature of their friendship.[34] It was the income from these sales that enabled Whistler to upgrade his accommodations and move to a home studio with a river view, at 7 Lindsey Row (now 101 Cheyne Walk).[35] This location was

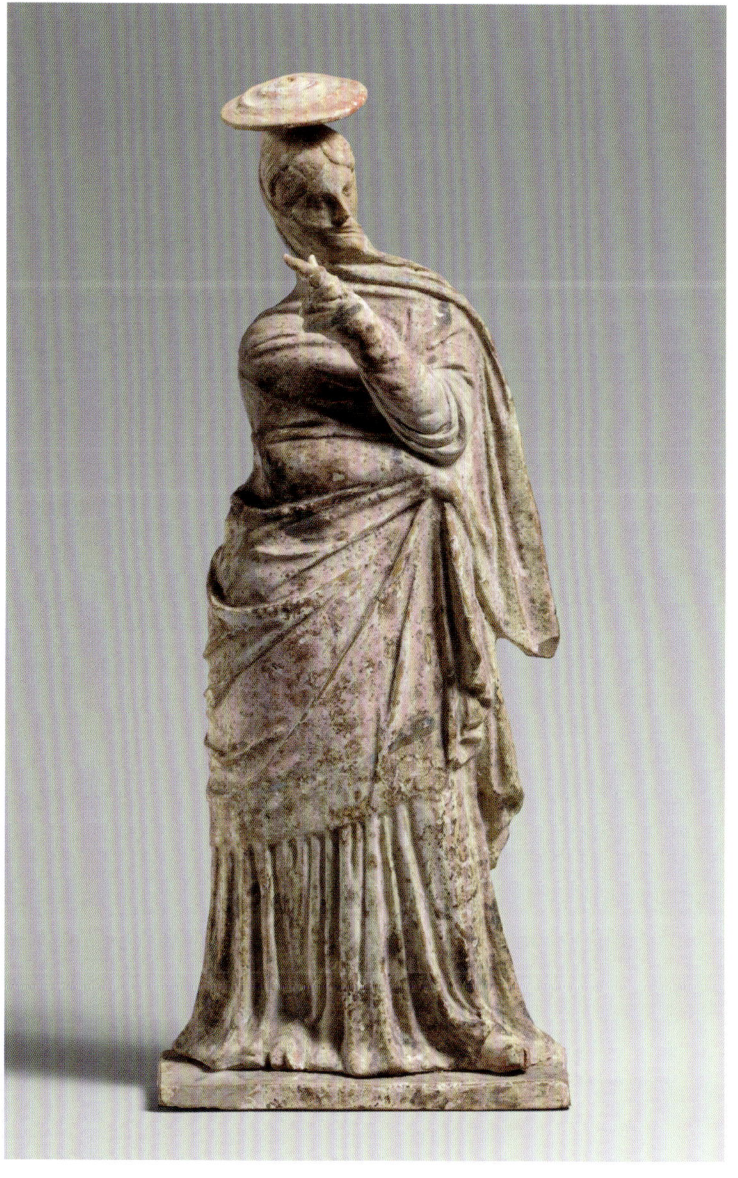

Fig. 6
Hellenistic terracotta statuette. Greek, perhaps Asia Minor, Hellenistic period, 2nd century BCE. Terracotta; H: 29.8 cm.

where Whistler had painted *The Balcony*, which was purchased by George Cavafy for thirty guineas.[36] Cavafy's firm, Cavafy and Company, imported Egyptian cotton and exported Manchester textiles, and this affinity for fabric may have drawn him to *The Balcony*'s draped figures. The loose kimono and Grecian drapery found in Whistler's compositions of this time demonstrate how he gravitated to forms across cultures and time periods. Tanagra and kimono were both appropriated symbols, each with their own distinct meanings and associations that are subordinated here in service of Whistler's aesthetic agenda. The kimono are just colors, the Tanagra are drapery and form, the women are figures without recognizable features.

Alexander Ionides's lavish home at 1 Holland Park became a gathering place for Pre-Raphaelite artists, writers, and diplomats. Like the heady mix of people and

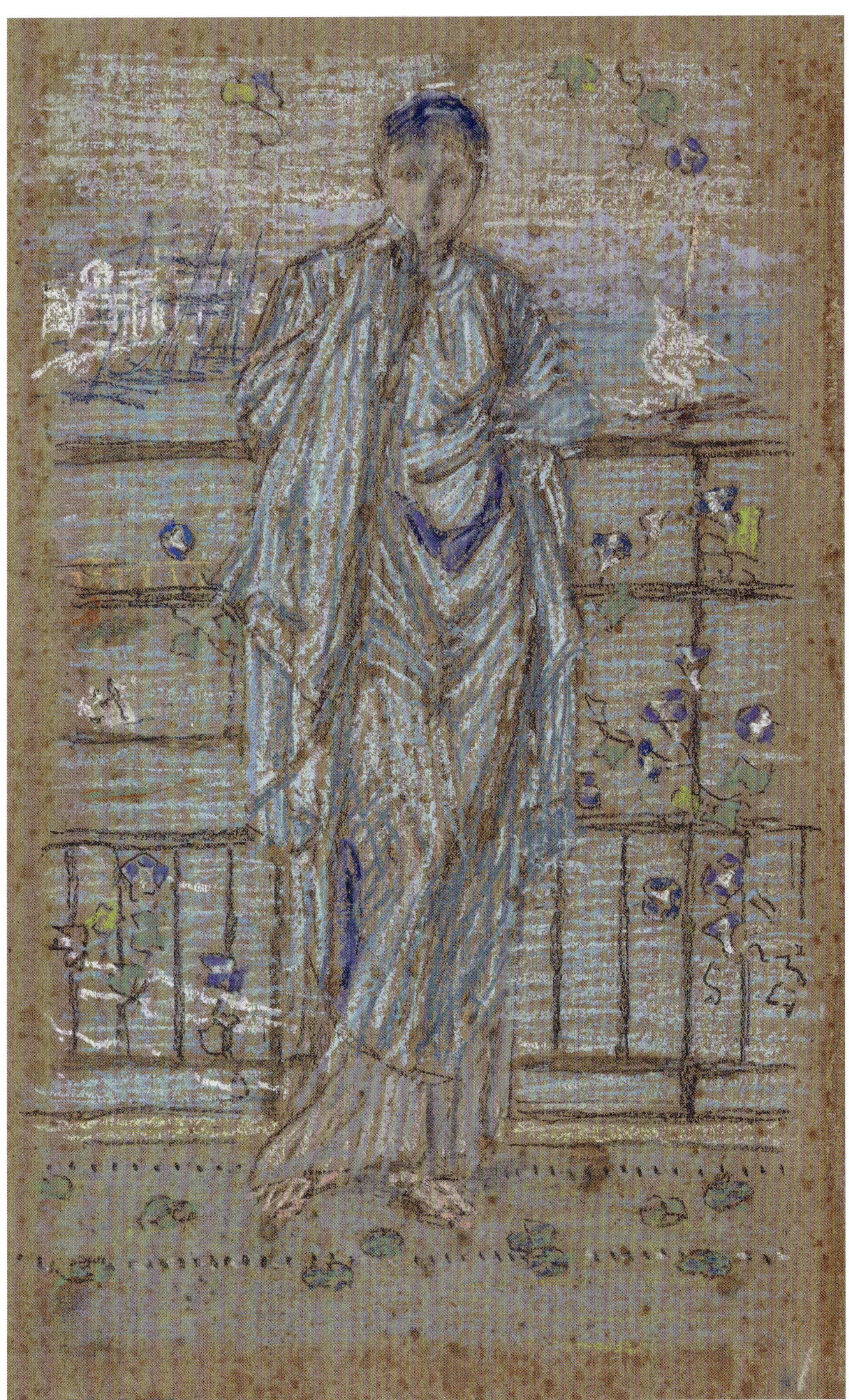

Fig. 7
James McNeill Whistler,
Morning Glories.
1871–1873. Chalk and
pastel on brown paper;
26.1 × 16.2 cm.

cultures that filled the space, the home itself showcased a global art collection, including an array of British paintings, Japanese lacquer, Persian tiles, and a substantial collection of Tanagra figurines, which Whistler not only had access to but also owned a photographic catalogue of.[37] According to Caroline Dakers, the Ionides family and their friends "appeared exotic to many of the artists."[38] The young women of the family modeled for several of the artists: Aglaia Ionides Coronio (1834–1906), her cousin Maria Zambaco (1843–1914), and their friend Marie Spartali (1844–1927) all modeled for Dante Gabriel Rossetti (1828–1882), George Frederic Watts (1817–1904), and Edward Burne-Jones (1833–1898), whose painting *The Mill* features all three (fig. 9).

Greece and Japan collide again in the figure of *The Princess from the Land of Porcelain* (*La Princesse du pays de la porcelaine*), the painting prominently featured

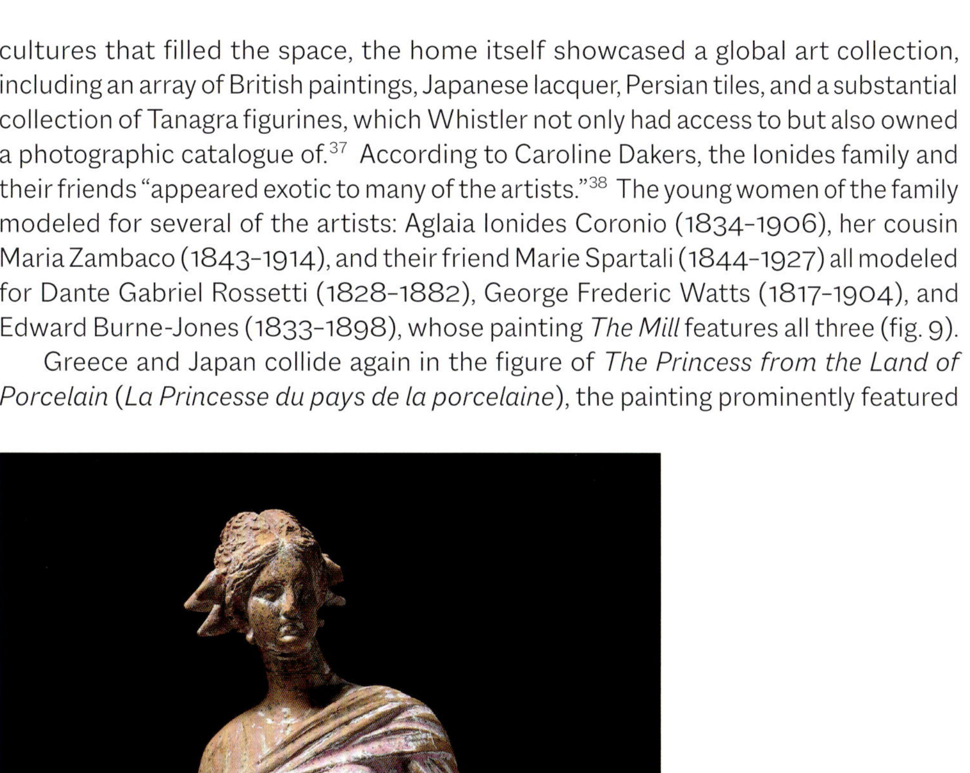

Fig. 8
Hellenistic figure. Greece, Hellenistic period, ca. 260 BCE–ca. 190 BCE. Terracotta; H: 20.5 cm.

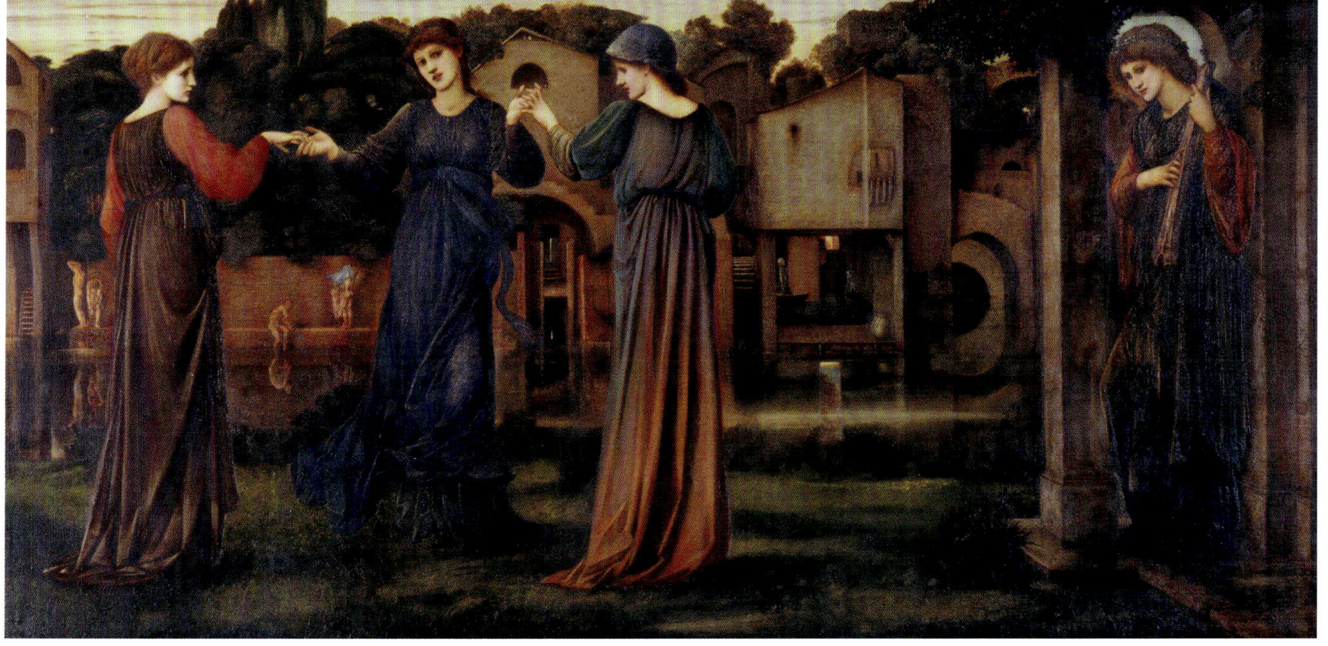

Fig. 9
Edward Burne-Jones, *The Mill: Girls Dancing to Music by a River*. England, 1870. Oil on canvas; 91.3 × 198.1 cm.

in Whistler's Peacock Room above the fireplace (fig. 10). The central figure is a young Greek woman clad in a peach kimono adorned with red floral motifs, likely the same kimono of this color that appears in *The Balcony*, since Whistler was known to have reused his props. Not everyone, however, approved of Whistler using these things as "neutral" in his paintings, even in his own time. The model for the painting was Christina Spartali, sister of Marie Spartali (who became an artist herself) and friend of the Ionides and Cavafy clans. Her father, Michael Spartali, succeeded Alexander Ionides as consul general to Greece.[39] Whistler had hoped that Christina's father would purchase the painting, but apparently "he objected to it as a portrait of his daughter."[40] Spartali's comment speaks to his daughter's role in the painting, not as an autonomous subject or representing a specific person but as an element of beauty personified, treated no differently than the rug or the painted screen. The princess of the painting's title might as well be an animated Tanagra figure, a human embodiment of Whistler's interests in Greek and Japanese cultures brought together as fantasy, a living doll.

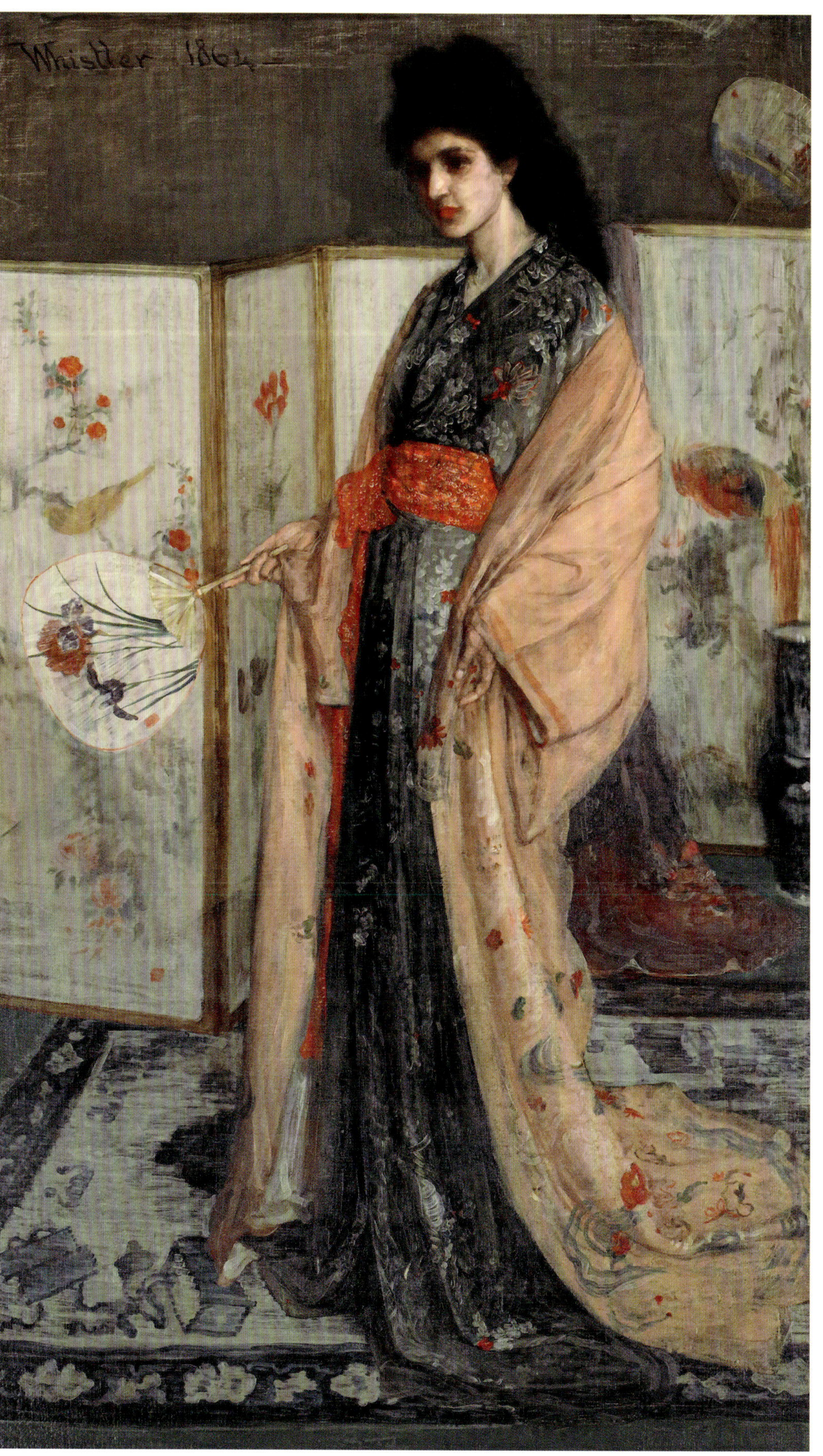

Fig. 10
James McNeill Whistler,
The Princess from the Land of Porcelain. 1863-1865.
Oil on canvas; 201.5 × 116.1 cm.

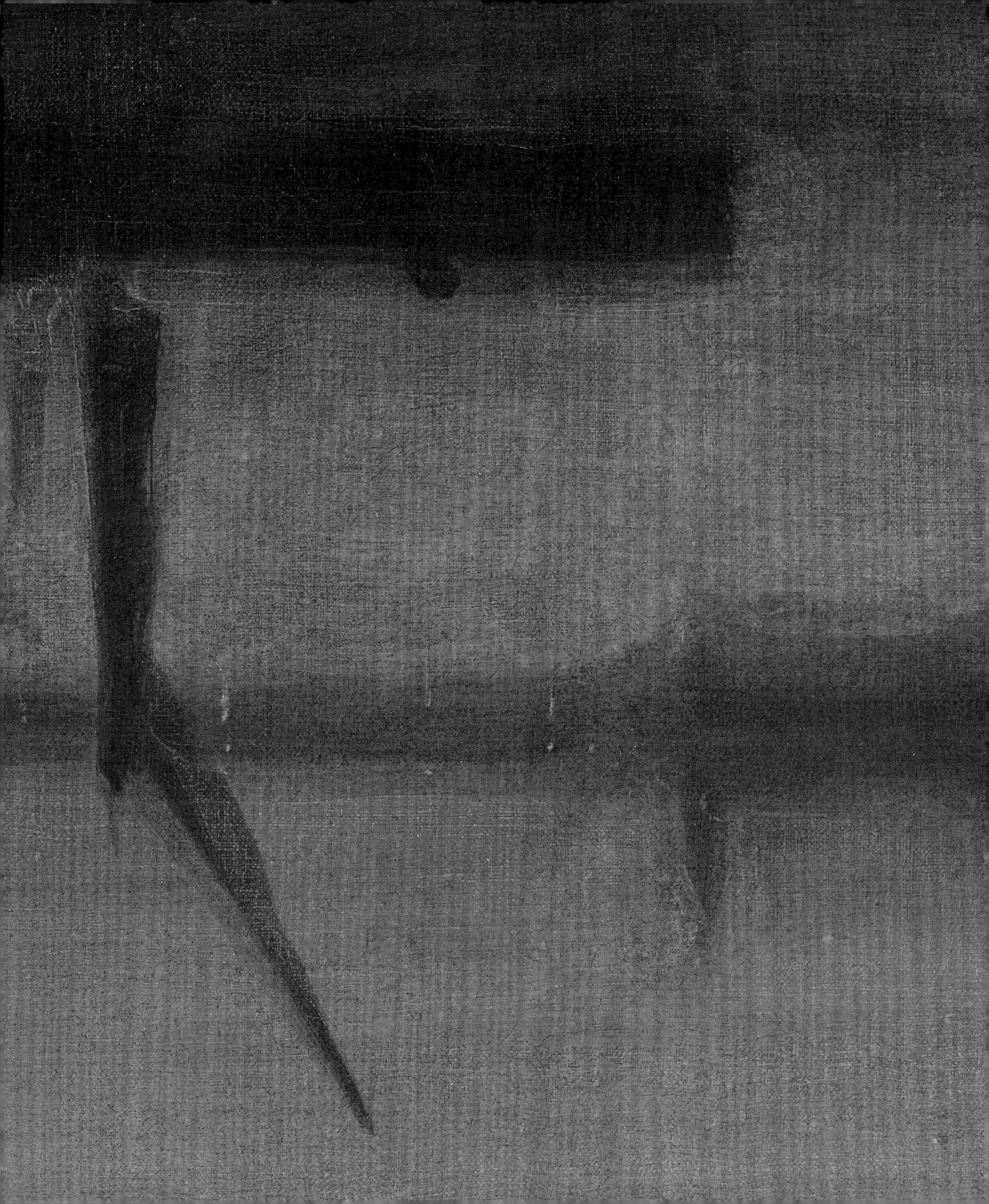

PIGMENT

What do the titles of artworks reveal about an artist's priorities and implicit assumptions? The lengthy titles Whistler assigned to his paintings were not mere afterthoughts—they were deliberately crafted to emphasize his aesthetic agenda. He famously prioritized pigments rather than subject matter, as in works like *Arrangement in Grey and Black No. 1*, *Nocturne: Blue and Gold*, and *Symphony in White, No. 1*. Much has been written about Whistler's systematic use of musical terms such as *symphonies* and *arrangements*, to draw parallels between his paintings and the abstract, expressive qualities of music. Indeed, the full title of the painting that is the demi-subject of this book is one such example, *Variations in Flesh Colour and Green—The Balcony*, with *variations* here referring to a repeated, yet altered, melody. For the sake of expediency, the secondary title, *The Balcony*, is most often used to refer to the artwork, including throughout this volume. However, this familiar abbreviation obscures the uncomfortable assumptions in the first part of Whistler's title. *Variations in Flesh Colour and Green* indicates the artist's attempt to guide the viewer to focus on the interplay of tonalities on the canvas, namely the green-heavy colors of the balcony setting and the skin tones and attire of the women. Yet referring to a pale peach pigment as "flesh" presumes whiteness as the default in describing skin color, an assumption that inadvertently tells us much about how Whistler understood the world, as well as the racial politics embedded in his painting of European women wearing Japanese kimono on a balcony in Victorian London. While Whistler's work has been criticized for his orientalizing framing of Japanese and Chinese culture, there are additional ways that his work affirms whiteness and European hegemony, which require further interrogating.[41] Such a reading is certainly not the only way to understand Whistler's use of the word *flesh*, but it bears further consideration. In Whistler's attempt to deny narrative interpretation, he allows other tensions to build, which still bubble to the surface today.

The primacy of oil paint—its physical presence and its viscous materiality—was central to Whistler's artistic practice. His approach to painting began with the palette

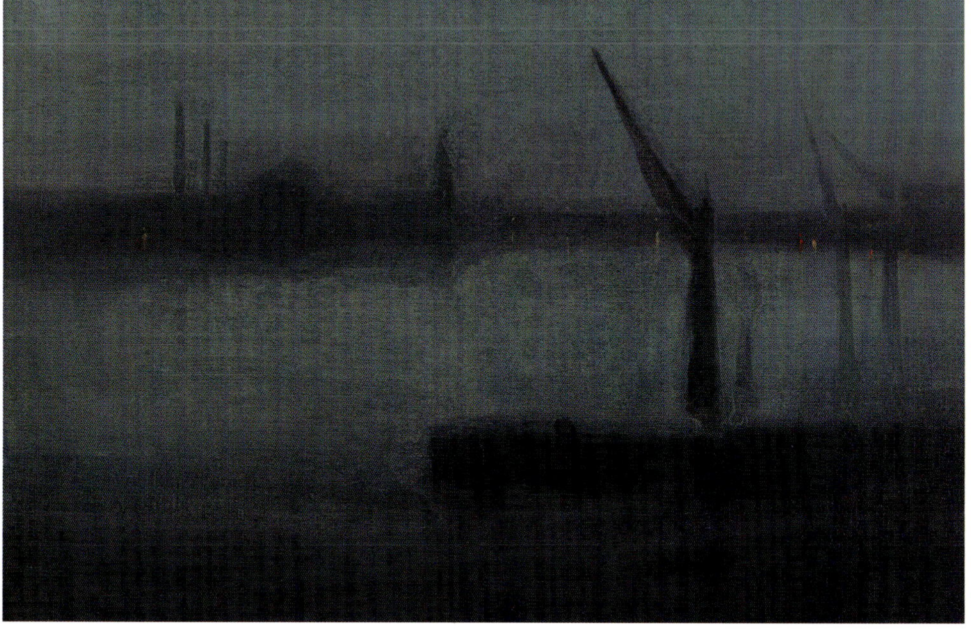

Fig. 1
James McNeill Whistler,
Nocturne: Blue and Silver—Battersea Reach. 1870-1875.
Oil on canvas; 49.9 × 72.3 cm.

Detail of fig. 1

itself. He instructed his followers on the importance of arranging pigments and using the palette to determine color relationships even prior to touching the canvas, going so far as to demand to see his students' palettes before he would look at their paintings.[42] His own paint application was characterized by the use of thin washes of a fluid paint mixture that he referred to as his "sauce." The exact components are debated; however, his assistant Walter Greaves claimed it resulted from mixing tube paint with linseed oil and turpentine.[43] These effects became most visibly pronounced in his experimental Nocturnes, where nearly translucent layers of blue-gray washes in ghostly, sepulchral works such as *Nocturne: Blue and Silver—Battersea Reach* conjure the miasma emanating from the Thames (fig. 1). While these works were intended to emphasize color and tone rather than form, critics repeatedly criticized Whistler's lack of conventional finish and decried it as "sketchy."[44] As meditations on mood, these works diminish the standard priority that is given to the paint handling and the surface of the canvas.

While Whistler was preoccupied with the physical properties of paint, he would have no reason to consider the larger implications of common terms assigned to

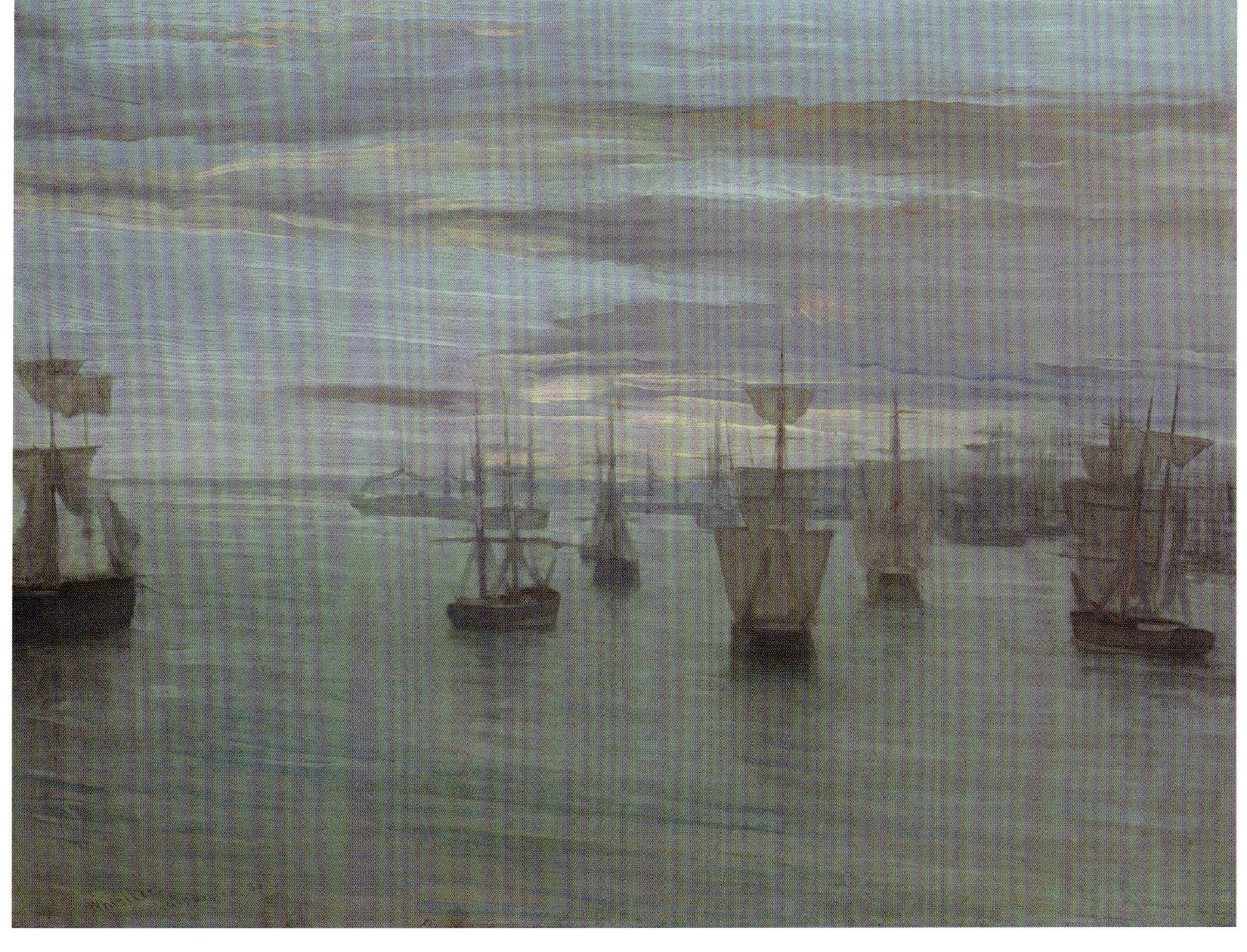

Fig. 2
James McNeill Whistler, *Crepuscule in Flesh Colour and Green—Valparaiso.* 1866. Oil on canvas; 58.6 × 75.9 cm.

commercial pigments in the nineteenth century. Nevertheless, his titles are instructive in that they point to the artist's biases and assumptions and those of the world in which he operated. The way that racism, which privileges whiteness at the expense of other races, has been institutionalized in all aspects of life is apparent even from art materials that perpetuate ideas of "flesh color." References to flesh as a "color" can be found everywhere from seventeenth-century pigment manuals to Crayola crayons, which have historically used *flesh* as a reductive term for a creamy, pinkish-white hue that necessarily excludes the full range of human skin tones. The term can be dated back to Roger de Piles's 1673 treatise, *Dialogue on Color* (*Dialogue sur le coloris*), which described the pigments needed to create what he called "flesh," the pale skin found in portraits by Rubens and Titian.[45] As critic and theorist W. J. T. Mitchell elucidates, "the association of pale colors with 'flesh tones' is just another aspect of what we might call 'normative whiteness.'"[46] Crayola began marketing light beige as "flesh" in 1949 but changed the name of the color in 1962 as a result of pressure from the Civil Rights Movement. Yet an expanded range of skin tones initially marketed as Multicultural Crayons was not launched until 1991.[47] Shockingly, many fine art material firms did not change their pigment names until the summer of 2020, when on the heels of worldwide Black Lives Matter protests, an art supplier in the United Kingdom launched a campaign calling upon manufacturers to abandon such exclusionary terminology.[48] The London-based art supply distributor Jackson's Art led the charge. They announced that their Flesh Tint oil paint would be renamed Pale Terracotta and encouraged other firms such as Faber-Castell and Winsor & Newton to make changes as well.

Whistler used the word *flesh* in his titles more than twenty times over the course of his career.[49] Many of these include other instances where his use of the word *flesh*, unconsciously or consciously on the artist's part, seems to iron over racial and cultural difference. Two years after beginning *The Balcony*, he traveled to Valparaiso, Chile, and painted a seascape titled *Crepuscule in Flesh Colour and Green—Valparaiso* (1866) (fig. 2). The color here is entirely divorced from the context of skin tone, suggesting that Whistler has the privilege of seeing "flesh color" as a neutral descriptor. Instead, he uses *flesh* to refer to the creamy pink that tinges the sky and highlights the green seas of a harbor filled with boats. The fleet depicted were British, American, and French ships that had been sent to assist Chile in its conflict with Spain, which was seeking to occupy the neighboring Peruvian-owned Chincha Islands. It is thought that Whistler's scene depicts the night before the ships withdrew upon hearing of the Spaniards' plans to bomb the city. Yet the composition features sailing ships rather than the gunboats, frigates, and steamers that were known to be on-site, an omission that strips the scene of its political tensions. The only indication of the military presence is a single French flag in the center of the composition. While the conflict itself and its roots in colonialism are muted, racial whiteness still asserts its presence by way of Whistler's title.[50]

The "flesh" mentioned in Whistler's title for *The Balcony* is most prominently featured in the peach kimono worn by the reclining woman at left. Her horizontal form is a focal point in the picture: the soft and curving figure is created with long, almost translucent strokes of paint, marking a contrast with the rigid vertical lines of the balcony railing. The woman's arms are nearly the same color, with necessary grayish contours used to indicate where the kimono ends and her limbs begin. She props herself up on a purple textile, which further draws attention to the figure.

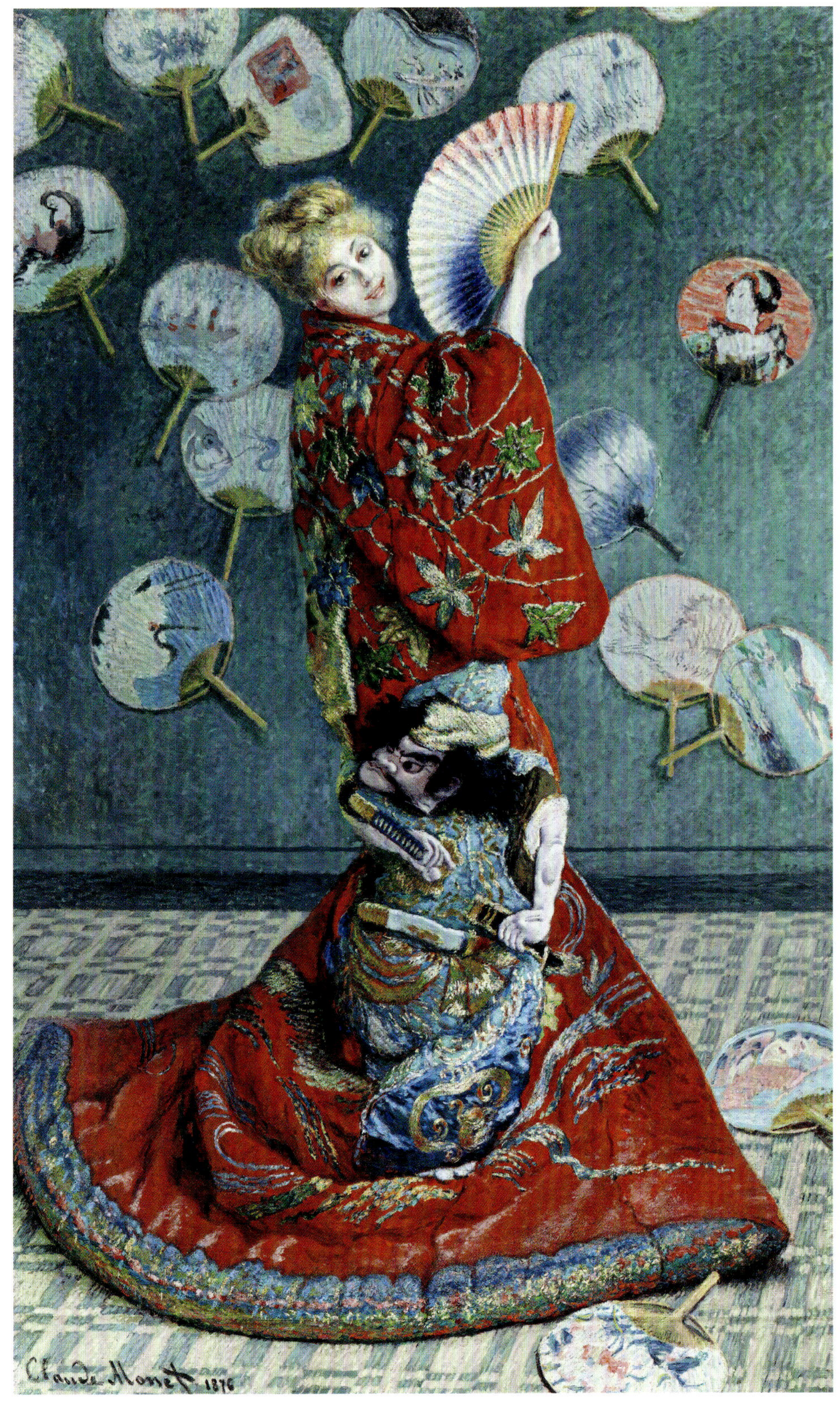

Fig. 3
Claude Monet, *La Japonaise (Camille Monet in Japanese Costume)*. 1876. Oil on canvas; 231.8 × 142.3 cm.

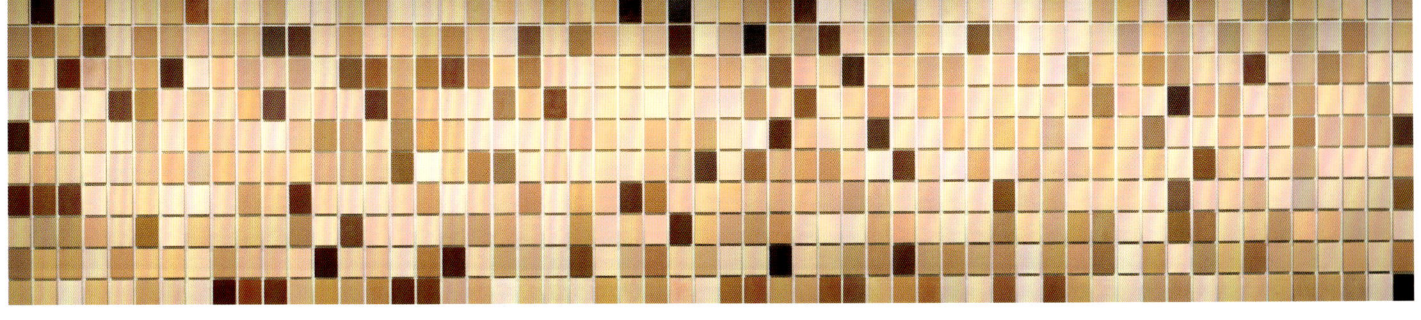

Fig. 4
Byron Kim, *Synecdoche*. United States, 1991-present. Oil and wax on plywood; each panel (overall installed dimensions variable): 25.4 × 20.3 cm.

Whistler, who never spent time in Japan, was not the only European artist to dress Western models in kimono. Claude Monet painted his wife, Camille, in an elaborately embroidered red kimono, surrounded by a display of fans in 1876 (fig. 3). She wears a blonde wig, reinforcing her status as a cultural interloper and mocking the Parisian clamor for all things Japanese.[51]

The pale peach paint is further used in the vertical seal at bottom left, where Whistler signs the painting with his brick red butterfly monogram. The artist has used this same red tone to decorate the peach kimono, faintly suggesting a pattern and further connecting the two aspects of the composition. Borrowing from the type of vermillion seals found on Chinese and Japanese paintings, prints, and other artworks, Whistler's monogram transforms his signature into yet another design element. Whistler's butterfly was based upon a stylization of his initials, using the *J* to form the insect's body, superimposed by the *M* and *W* to create the butterfly's wings. The butterfly here has been described as a symbol of transformation, reflecting Whistler's imagined occupation of two worlds within the composition, moving from the reality of London to a fantasy of Japan.[52] Within the painting, Whistler has created a binary, divided by the geometry of the railing, between masculine, harsh, gray, industrial England and his feminized fantasy of Japan, which is brightly colored, soft, and leisurely.

Recent artists are explicitly challenging the assumptions outlined in this section in ever-more confrontational ways. For example, the contemporary Korean American artist Byron Kim's work *Synecdoche*, an ongoing group portrait, dismantles the idea of race as a singular and stable category (fig. 4). His project began in 1991 and consists of over four hundred 10 × 8 inch (25.4 × 20.3 cm) panels, employing dimensions common to portrait photography. Each panel functions as an abstract portrait depicting the skin tones of Kim's friends, family, and acquaintances, with the part standing in for the whole and forming an ever-growing mosaic of varied hues. Kim's sitters, who have included other artists, museum guards, and strangers, would sit for roughly twenty minutes while Kim examined a patch of their skin and blended tones on his palette to match their flesh.[53] Like Whistler's attention to customizing his paint mixtures, Kim fashions his own medium. He carefully mixes the oil pigments with wax, which is then applied to the panel with a palette knife.[54] The technique recalls encaustic religious icons, while also bringing to mind children's wax crayons and the formative racial encoding that those art materials have produced. Nonetheless, though these conversations continue to progress, the assumptions implicit in Whistler's title remain a legacy that should not be ignored.

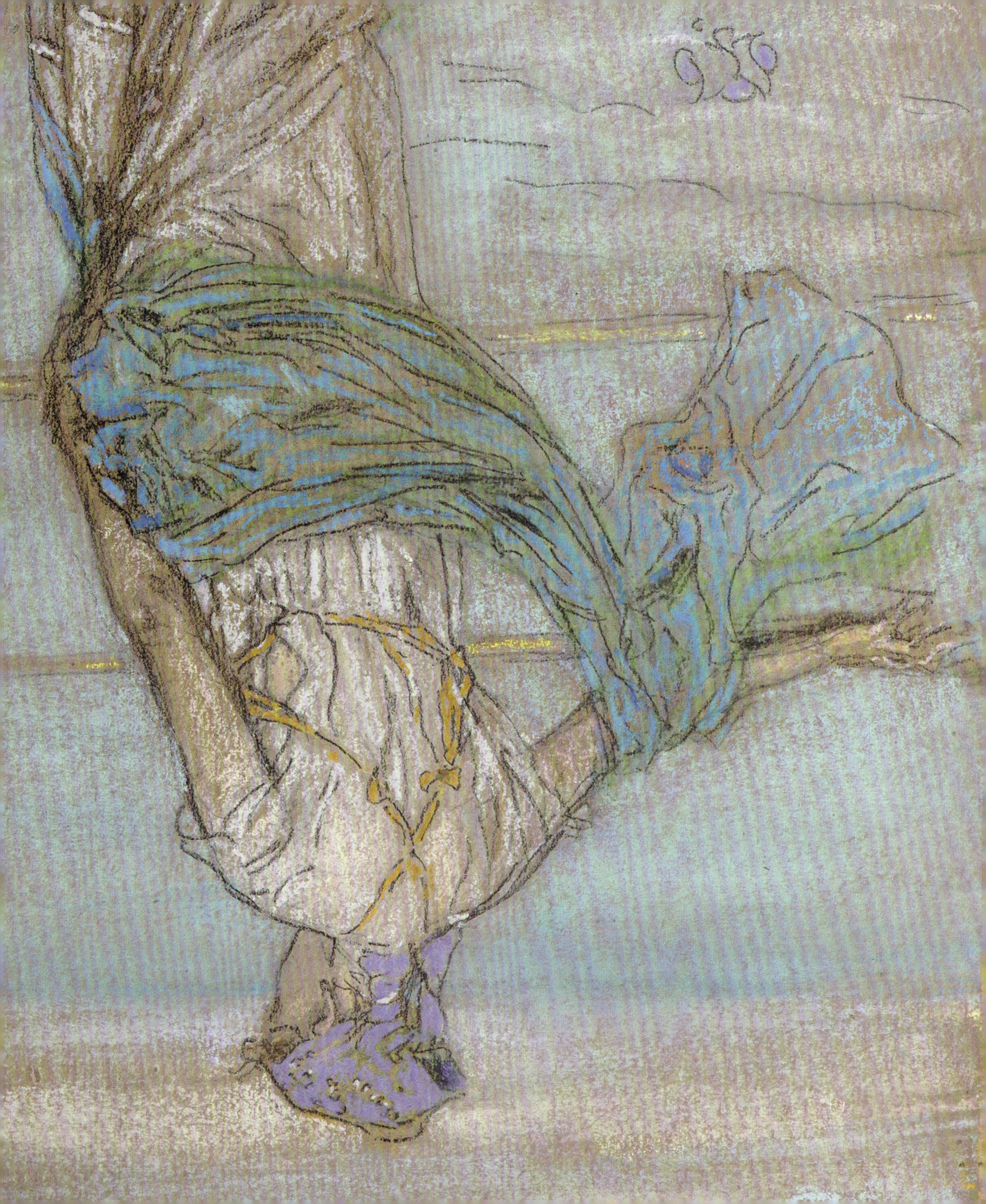

RESTRICTION

In what ways can art challenge us to think about the gender dynamics of depicted subjects and viewership? Whistler's *Balcony* includes women on a platform, physically removed from the markers of industry in the distance by the river Thames but also by the Victorian ideology of separate spheres, which confined women to domestic—rather than public—spaces. This gendered binary is made explicit by the compositional elements of the painting rendered into two distinct pictorial planes: four languid women in a range of colored kimono are shown on the balcony, their reverie in the foreground visually divided by the horizontal railing from the largely male workforce that occupied the Battersea factories that line the horizon. However, while the women are denied agency in public life, and arguably merely function as decorative objects within Whistler's composition, their manner of dress simultaneously would have offered contemporary female viewers a fashion of resistance. By the mid-nineteenth century, English feminists had embraced dress reform as a pathway to women's liberation, a cause that also found favor among artists.[55] Despite conventional assumptions that kimono are stiff, formal, and restrictive by modern standards, the kimono worn by

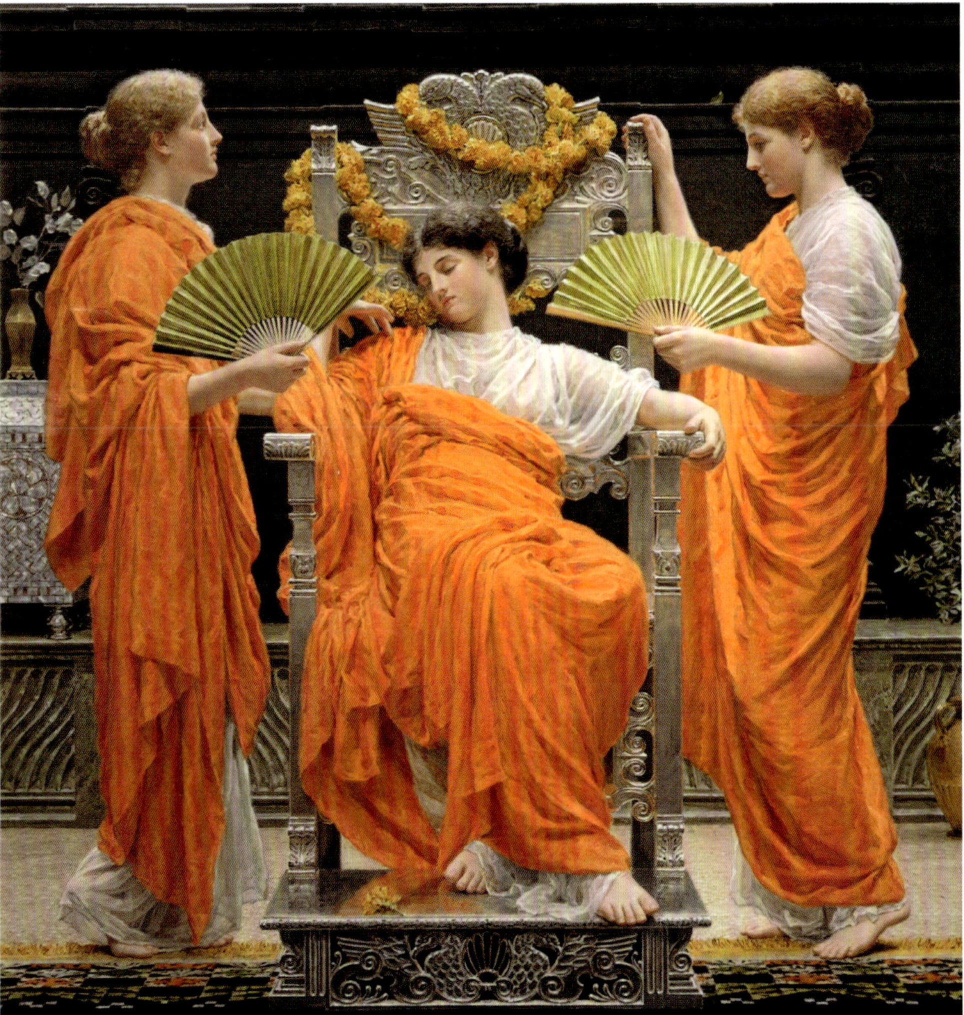

Fig. 1
Albert Moore, *Midsummer*.
1887. Oil on canvas;
155 × 148.5 cm.

Detail of fig. 3

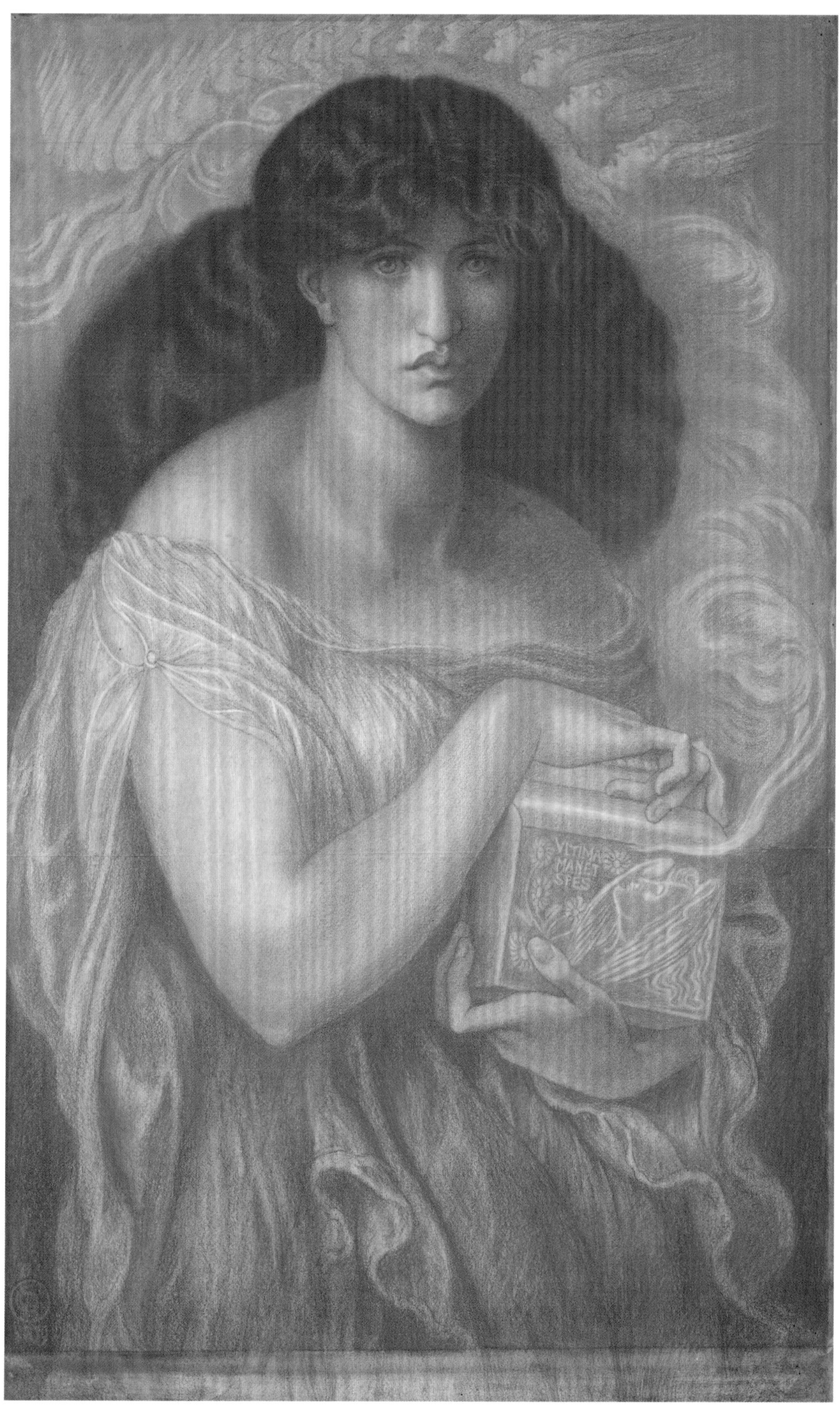

Fig. 2
Dante Gabriel Rossetti, *Pandora*. England, 1879. Colored chalks on cream wove paper; 103.2 × 62.7 cm.

Whistler's models offered a form of physical freedom, absent corsets or crinolines, to female viewers at the time, while also demonstrating how Japanese influences in Whistler's early costume pictures functioned to create an exoticized other.

Dress reform, also known as the rational dress movement, first gained momentum in England and America in the 1850s, contemporaneous with the suffrage and temperance movements, other forms of activism that sought to improve women's lives. For example, suffrage and access to the vote would have increased legal protections for women, while banning alcohol was partly an attempt to combat domestic abuse. While those movements focused on public and home life, dress reform was about bodily autonomy. Advocates were concerned that corsetry and the weight of heavily fabricated garments were not only limiting but potentially damaging to women's health. Artistic circles were

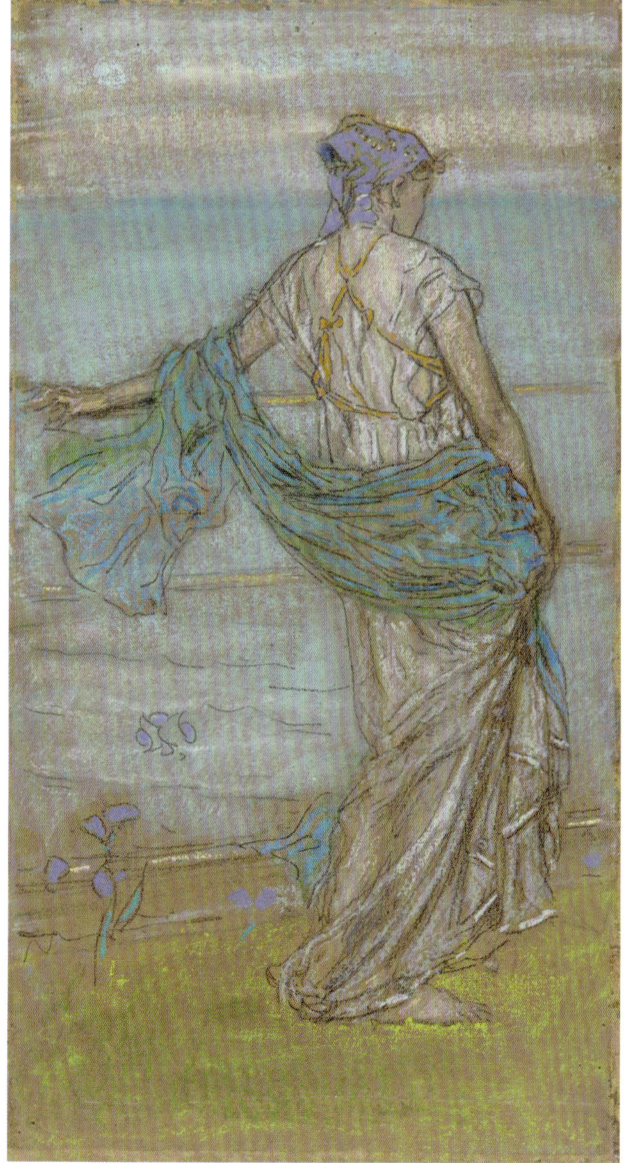

Fig. 3
James McNeill Whistler,
Annabel Lee. 1885–1887.
Chalk and pastel on brown
paper; 32.3 × 18 cm.

among the first to adopt dress reform—the Pre-Raphaelites promoted loose-fitting garments by depicting models in voluminous gowns inspired by medieval and ancient Greek clothing (figs. 1, 2). Upon Whistler's arrival in London, he became friendly with Pre-Raphaelite artists including Dante Gabriel Rossetti and Albert Moore, and his pastel balcony drawings of this period feature Grecian-inspired women in free-flowing drapery (fig. 3). They were likely inspired by Tanagra, the terracotta figurines that had become a collecting craze in Victorian England (fig. 4) (see **figure**). Simultaneously, the Arts and Crafts movement, which shared members and influences with the Pre-Raphaelite and the Aesthetic movements, began to advocate for greater attention to decorating both one's home and person in beautiful, handcrafted items as a rejection of rampant industrialization and mass production. Aesthetic dress therefore came to embody several interconnected philosophies in circulation regarding art, politics, gender, individual expression, and health.[56]

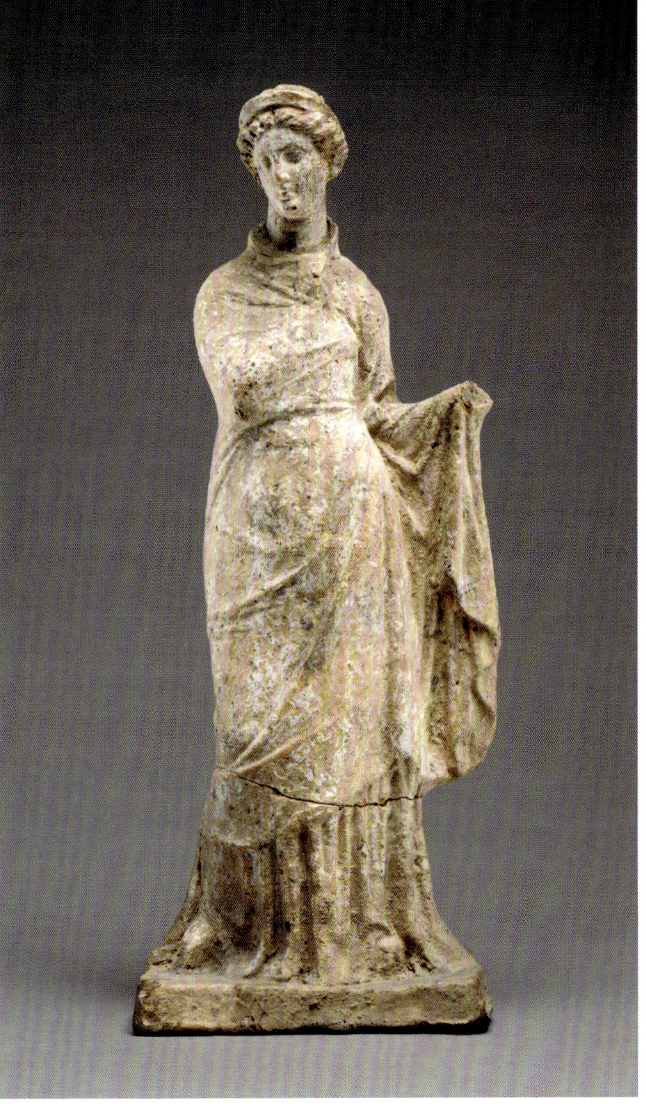

Fig. 4
Statuette of a draped female figure. Greece, 4th-3rd century BCE. Terracotta with traces of polychromy; H: 29.1 cm.

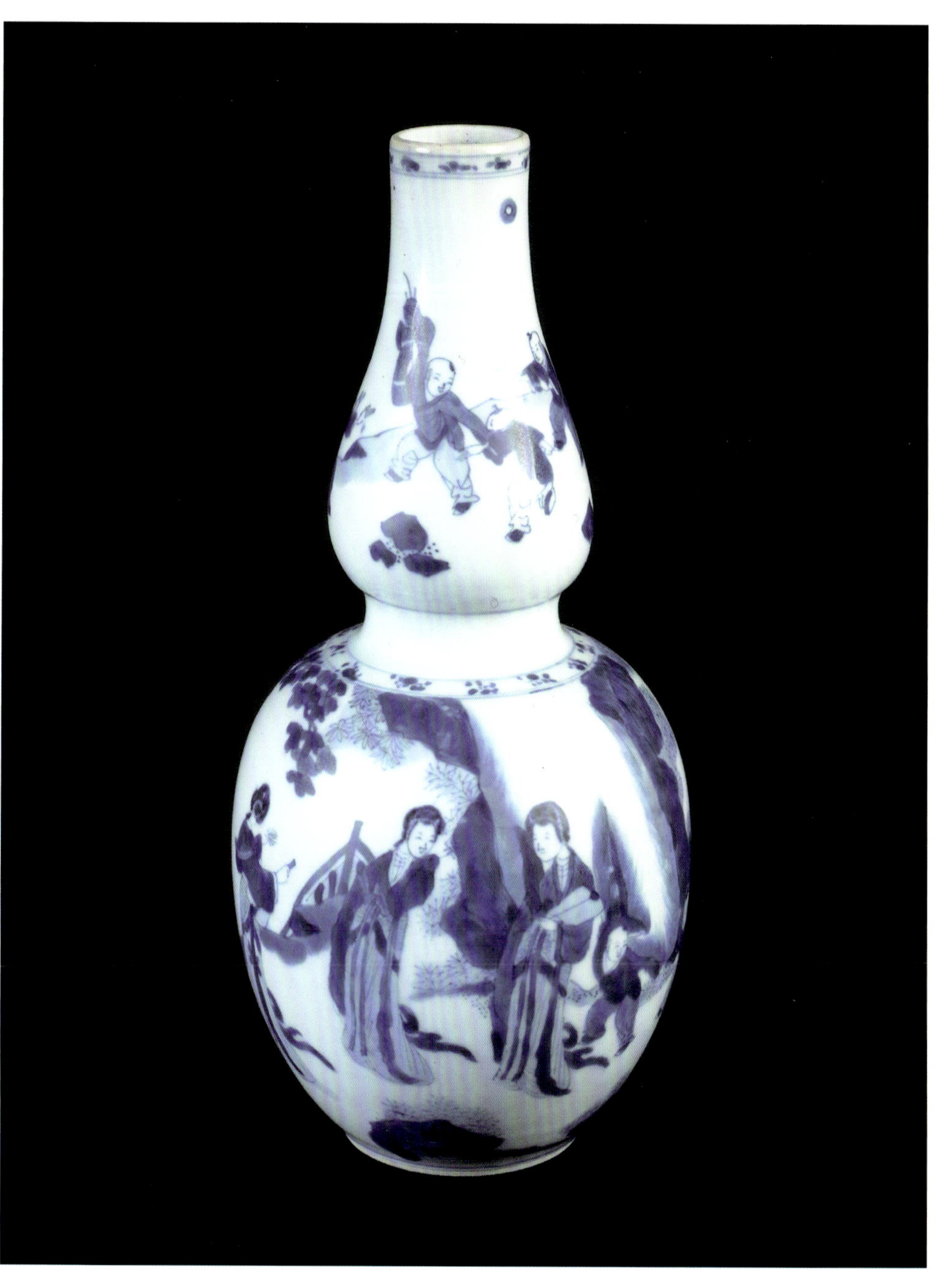

Fig. 5
Kangxi vase. China, Jingdezhen, 1662–1722. Porcelain decorated in underglaze cobalt blue; 26.8 × 13 cm.

Around this same time, Japan opened trade relations with Britain, and English artists began acquiring Japanese prints, paintings, and decorative arts, including kimono and fans. Whistler began to populate his artworks with kimono-clad women from 1863 until about 1872. Known as his "costume pictures," these works incorporated both Chinese and Japanese objects into compositions where Whistler made no attempt to distinguish between the two cultures, allowing the items to be conflated as representative symbols of an exoticized other.[57] This was exemplified in works like *The Princess from*

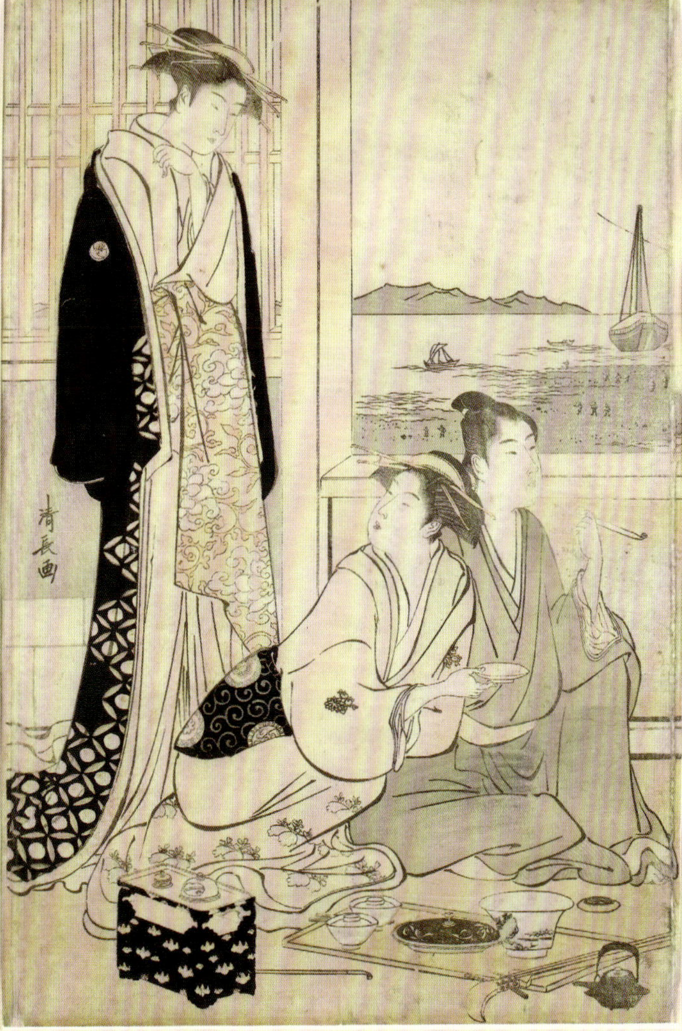

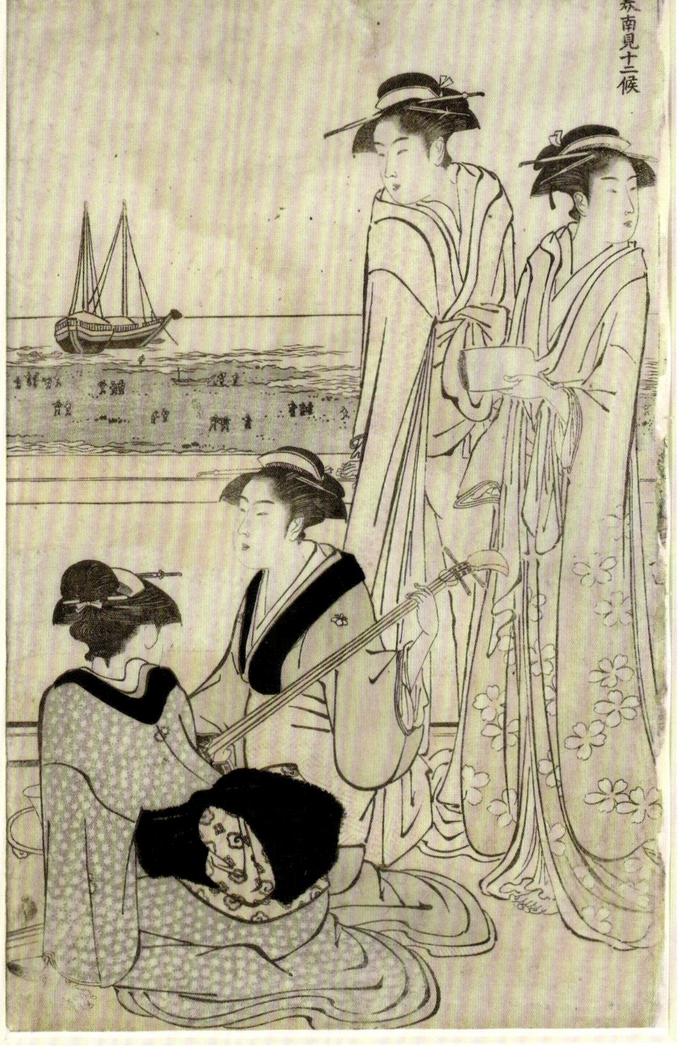

Fig. 6
Torii Kiyonaga, *The Fourth Month* (*Shigatsu*), from the series *Twelve Months in the South* (*Minami jūni kō*). Japan, Edo period, ca. 1780s. Woodblock print; ink and color on paper; 50.7 × 51.1 cm.

the Land of Porcelain, where a Greek model holds a fan and wears a peach-colored Japanese kimono (likely the same one that appears in *The Balcony*) while standing in front of a painted screen (see **figure**, fig. 10). A blue-and-white vase appears in the background, and the model's elongated form is reminiscent of the figural decorations on Chinese Kangxi ware, such as a vase that once belonged to Rossetti (fig. 5). The blue-and-whites in Whistler's and Rossetti's own collections were purchased from the dealer Murray Marks (1840–1918), who supplied industrialist Frederick Leyland with the porcelains that filled his dining room and which also prominently featured in his *Princess* painting above the fireplace.[58] Within a decade, Whistler would abandon such direct points of reference in favor of a more sophisticated process incorporating visual strategies derived from East Asian artworks.

Whistler had no personal experience of Japan and would have known how kimono were worn only through his exposure to prints by artists such as Torii Kiyonaga 鳥居清長 (1752–1815), whose prints he is known to have collected. Kiyonaga's depiction of a

mixed group of sitting and standing figures by an open window was likely one of several prints whose elements Whistler adopted in developing *The Balcony* composition (fig. 6).[59] Both works show a seated woman playing a stringed instrument, a shamisen, surrounded by a mixture of standing and lounging figures, all of whom seem to be looking in different directions. The kimono worn by Kiyonaga's women are very loose, pooling at their feet. The folds and lines of the fabric become a repeating design element in the composition. Whistler's women are similarly each engaged in distinct activities—playing music, drinking, listening, and looking—but unified by the printed, flowing robes they wear. None of the women in Whistler's *Balcony* wear a modern obi, as he was unlikely to have been familiar with how the wide sash was properly worn and tied. Only the standing figure at the railing wears a slim sash tied at the side of her hip, further suggesting Whistler's limited understanding of how kimono were secured. This omission allows the robes to appear even less restrictive than they would have been for most Japanese women in Whistler's day. In earlier periods, kimono had been worn much more loosely, as can be seen in sixteenth-century painted screens, further reinforcing that Whistler's conception of Japanese dress was drawn from art (fig. 7).

Fig. 7
Indoor Occupations (detail). Japan, Momoyama period, 1568–1615. Painted screen; ink, color, and gold on paper; 58.9 × 232.7 cm.

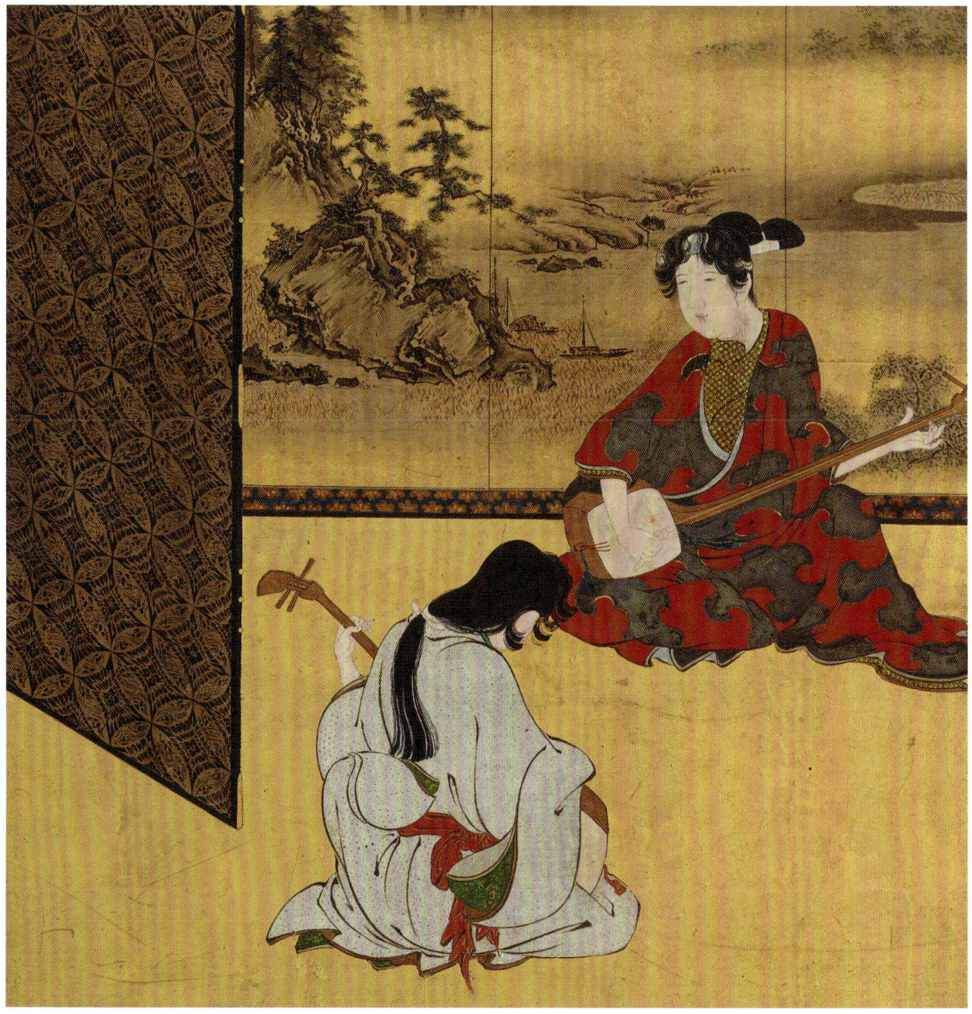

Fig. 8
Samuel Alex Walker, Photograph of Ellen Terry. England, ca. 1874. Sepia photograph on paper; 14.1 × 10.4 cm.

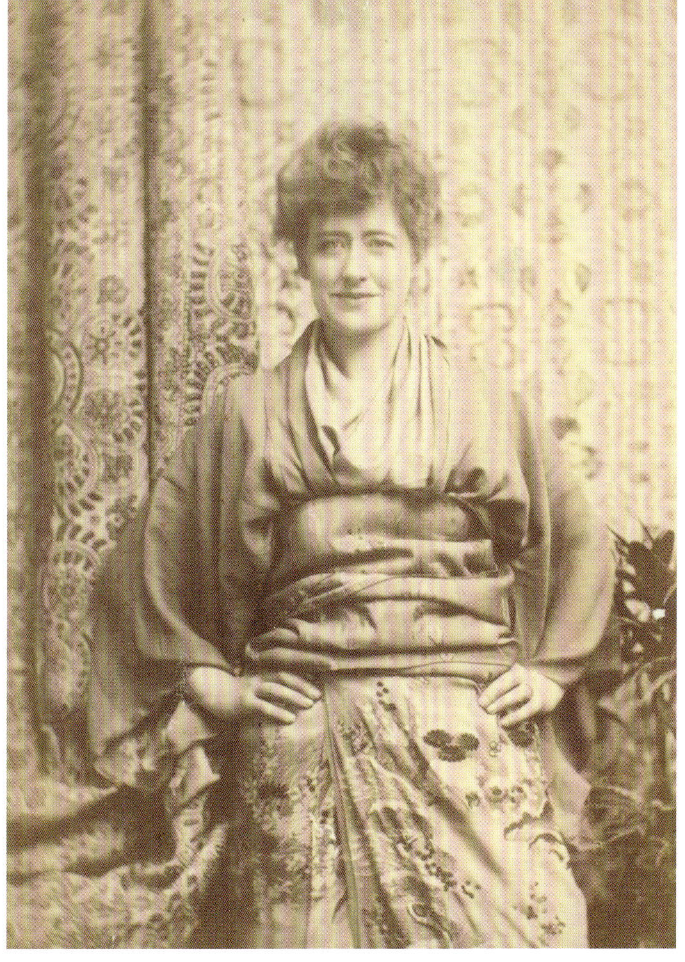

Such misunderstandings are indicative of what historian of art and fashion Adam Geczy describes as Europeans' adoption of Japanese kimono as an orientalist project, in which the robes as a generic marker of difference allowed Europeans to assert their unconventionality.[60] Whistler may have used the kimono to signal his divergence from conventional norms as well as for compositional purposes, but that does not foreclose his viewers from finding their own meanings and alternative paths to self-expression.

The Aestheticist circles that Whistler was entangled with embraced Japanese kimono as an alternative to constrictive British fashions. Oscar Wilde even delivered several lectures on women's dress, espousing Aesthetic dress reform ideals and advocating finding inspiration in Japanese and classical Greek art.[61] Among the women who were known to don kimono were French actress Sarah Bernhardt (1844–1923) and the English performer Ellen Terry (1847–1928). Among England's most famous actresses in the nineteenth and early twentieth centuries, Terry was also part of London's artistic community: she was briefly married to British painter George Frederic Watts and also had a long-term relationship with aesthetic architect E. W. Godwin (1833–1886) that produced two children. Terry was among the most photographed women in Victorian England, and although the project never materialized, Whistler

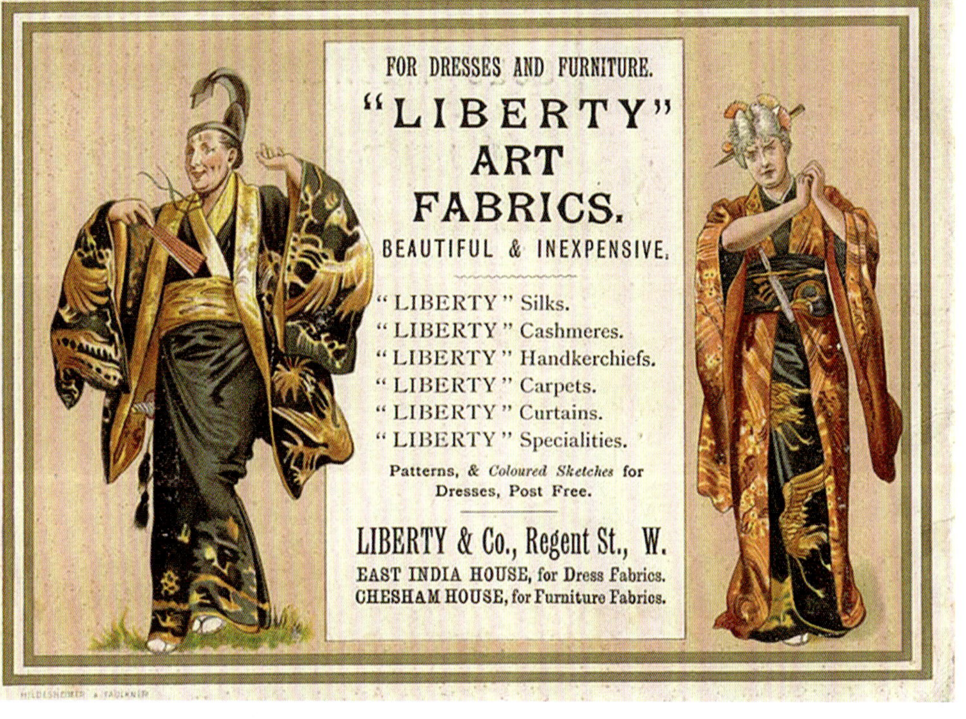

Fig. 9
Liberty's advertisement, *The Mikado* program, Savoy Theatre (England), October 7, 1885. Color print on paper; 17.4 × 12.8 cm.

discussed painting her portrait as well. This photograph of Terry in a kimono was one of many in circulation in Victorian England and would have contributed to her status as an early celebrity, known for both her acting and her unconventional lifestyle (fig. 8). Terry realized how self-fashioning could be used as a tool to advance her theatrical career. Many photographs show Terry dressed in kimono for performances, but we know she wore them in her personal life as well; furthermore, it appears that Whistler gave her daughter a kimono in 1875.[62] E. W. Godwin felt so strongly about abolishing the use of stays and corsets that he published a pamphlet on the subject. In it, he maintained that fashion shaped good health, just as architecture could be used to promote a healthy environment, and he encouraged both Terry and their daughter to wear kimono.[63] His authority on the subject led to his being named an advisor on dress to the famous department store Liberty's of London, in 1884.[64] Liberty's itself started as an enterprise to import Japanese art, design, and textiles. Godwin collaborated with Whistler on several projects, including the design of the artist's White House, a home studio that Whistler was able to live in for only a year before personal bankruptcy forced its sale. After Godwin's death, Whistler married Godwin's widow, Beatrice.

The tremendous success of Gilbert and Sullivan's 1885 comic opera set in Japan, *The Mikado*, further drove the kimono into British consciousness, and Liberty's sales catalogues began offering imported Japanese garments for sale (fig. 9). An 1898 catalogue advertised "Japanese Kimono (or Native Robe). In Silk, Satin, and Silk-Crêpe. Beautifully embroidered in characteristic designs. Charming as Tea Gowns and Fancy Costumes."[65] By the 1880s, Japan had become a distinct category in guides to costume ("fancy dress" in British) parties and balls. Visual evidence of this enthusiasm

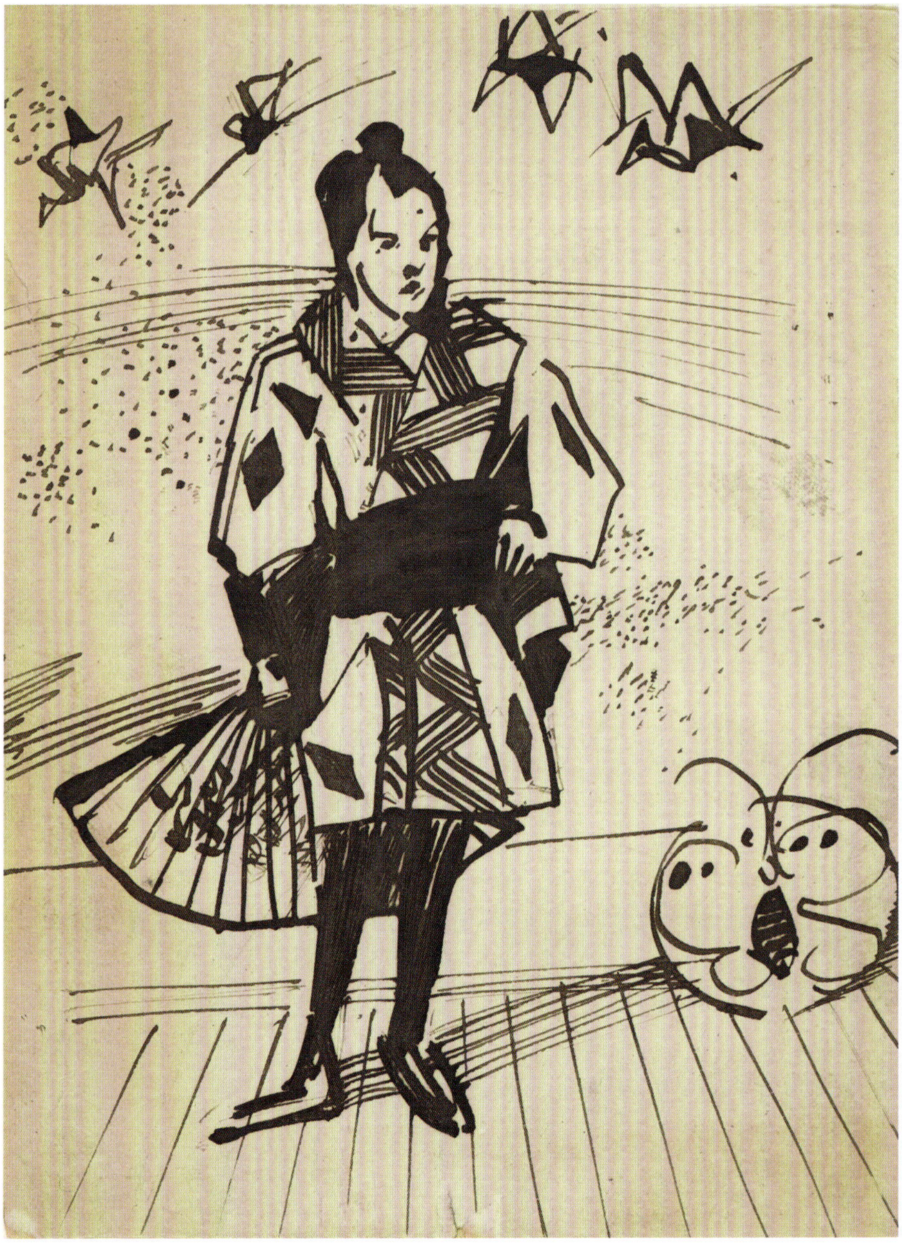

Fig. 10
Sir James Guthrie, *Edward Arthur Walton dressed as Hokusai*. Scotland, ca. late 19th century. Pen on paper; 13.8 × 10.5 cm.

for cultural dress-up can be found in a portrait of Scottish artist Edward Arthur Walton (1860–1922) dressed as Hokusai for the Glasgow Art Club's Grand Costume Ball in 1889 (fig. 10). Near Walton's feet is a monogram alluding to Whistler's famous butterfly signature. The presence of Whistler in the portrait is a reference to his role in introducing Hokusai to a generation of British artists. Indeed, Walton's costume was coupled with that of his fiancée Helen Law (1859–1945), who was intended to be a personification of Whistler's butterfly (fig. 11).

Whistler's use of kimono-clad figures can be interpreted in several ways. Understood as a gesture of cultural appropriation, the kimono has an orientalizing

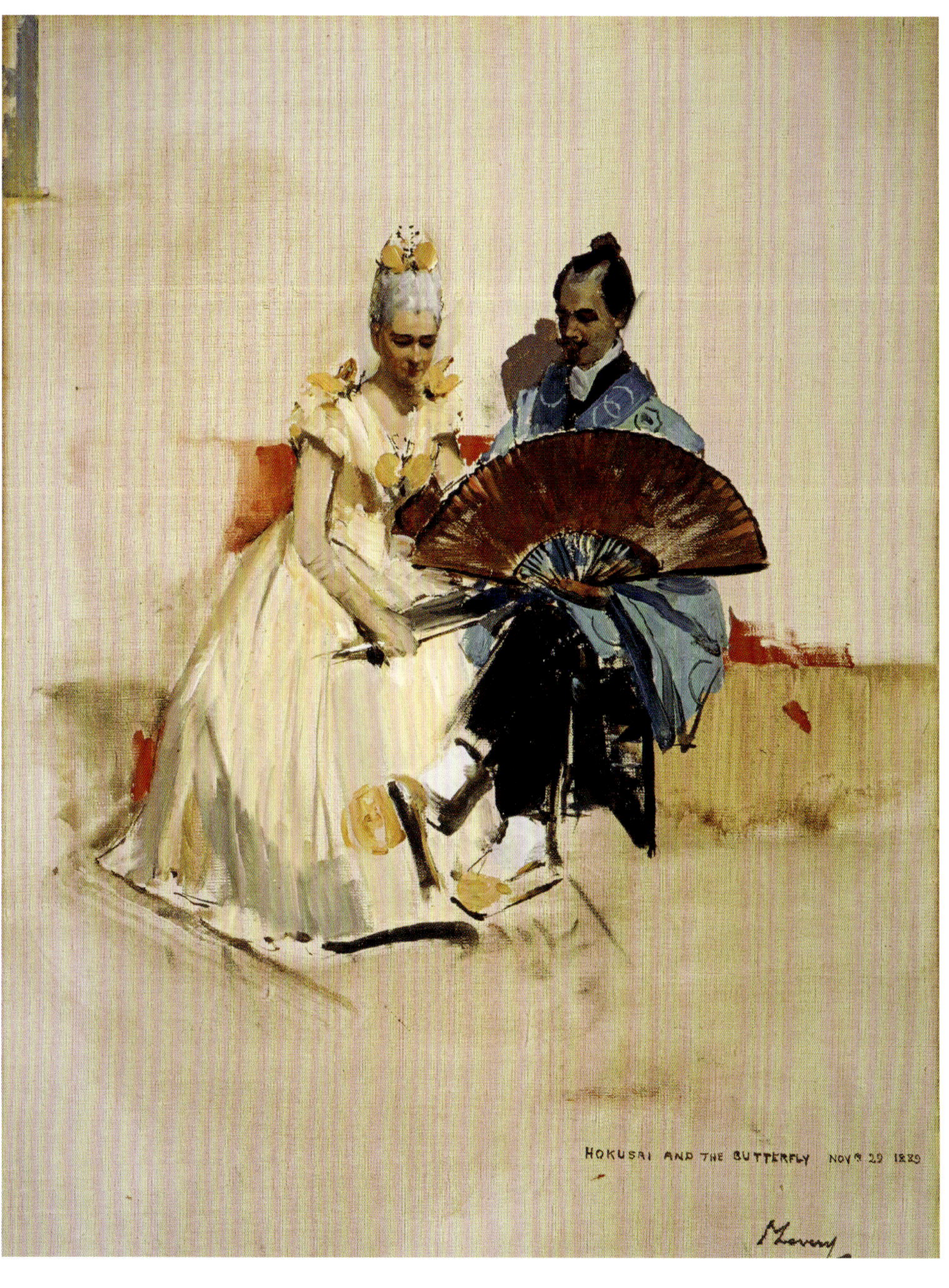

Fig. 11
Sir John Lavery, *Edward Arthur Walton with his fiancée Helen Law (Hokusai and the Butterfly)*. Scotland, 1889. Oil on canvas; 61.1 × 45.7 cm.

effect, interjecting an exotic element to an industrial landscape as a simple visual contrast that obscures the ways that Japanese society was rapidly modernizing at that very moment. However, the meanings on offer were complex and dynamic, providing alternate avenues of interpretation to different viewers. Given the larger conversations surrounding dress reform more broadly, and Aesthetic dress specifically, the message delivered by this group of women in loose, flowing robes was more fluid than the binary implied by the ideology of separate spheres that governed middle-class social operations at the time.

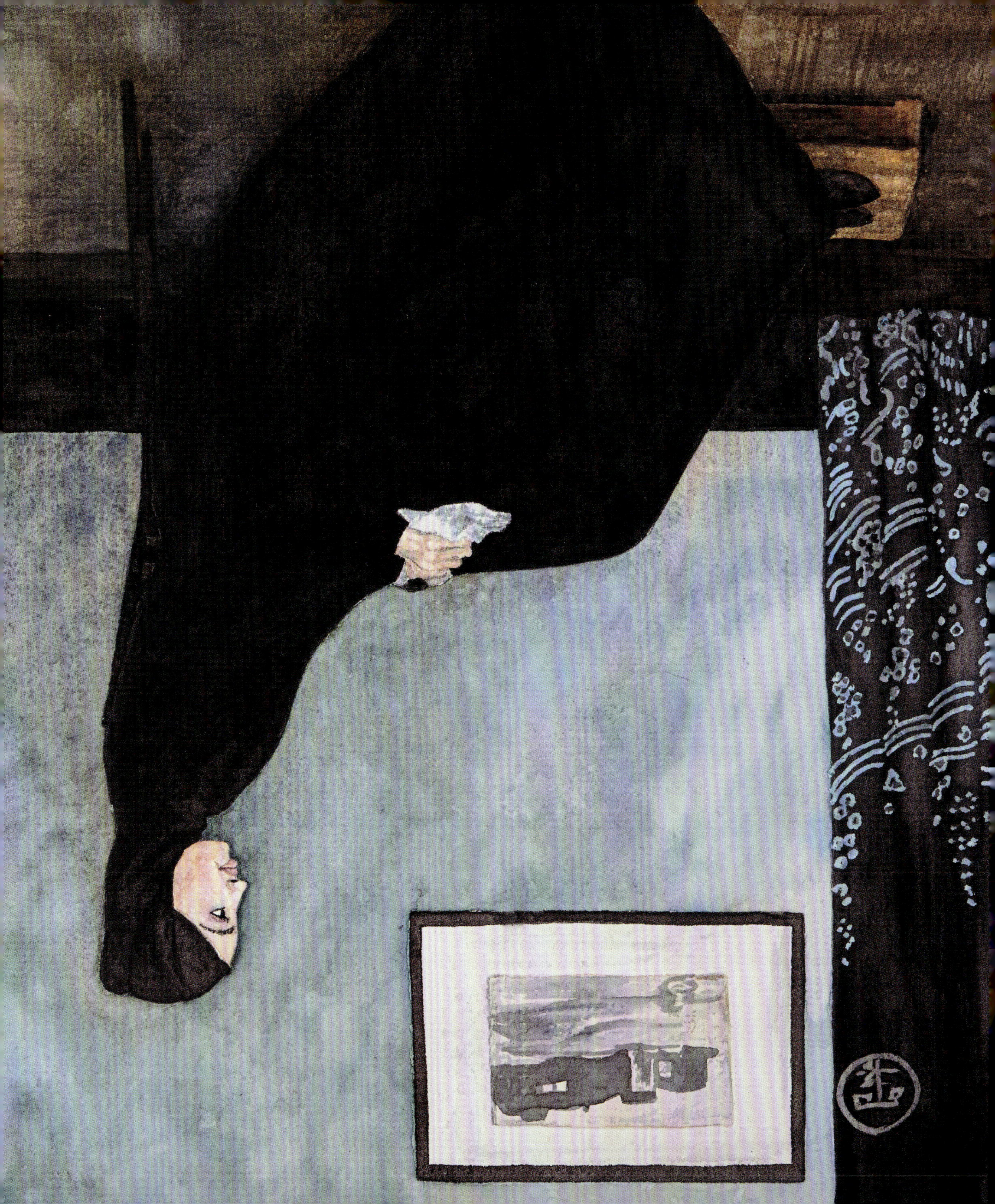

(FREER) ASSOCIATION

How does an object's ownership history impact our understanding of the artwork? How do our personal connections to art create openings for further explorations and creative experimentation? *The Balcony* was the first Whistler oil painting purchased by the industrialist Charles Lang Freer. Freer's own story is embedded in a full understanding of the painting, as objects accumulate meaning over time and through encounters with new viewers and ever-changing contexts.

Freer purchased his first etchings by Whistler in 1887, and he visited the artist in his studio in 1890. This was the beginning of a friendship that lasted until Whistler's death in 1903. Freer owed a great deal of his aesthetic sensibility to Whistler, who encouraged his interest in Japanese and Chinese art. Both men's lives were also deeply entwined with industry in formative ways. Whistler's father was an engineer who oversaw the construction of the St. Petersburg–Moscow Railway, and Whistler's early training as an etcher came as a result of his work for the US Coast Survey, whose mission was tied to the larger project of westward expansion and economic development driven by the railroad industry.[66] Freer bought *The Balcony* painting in 1892. At that time, it was the most sizeable artwork obtained by the collector after years of purchasing small-scale prints, pastels, and watercolors. Freer would eventually make it his ambition to assemble what Whistler himself referred to as "The collection" of the artist's work and to preserve his own legacy as a collector by gifting the entirety of the Asian and American art in his possession to the Smithsonian Institution.[67]

Charles Lang Freer was raised in a working-class family in Kingston, an Ulster County town in upstate New York. He left school after the eighth grade and found work at a cement factory as a teenager (fig. 1). After leaving the factory for a job as a clerk at a general store, Freer met Frank Hecker (1846–1927). A Civil War veteran, Hecker initially entered the railroad industry when he was hired by Union Pacific Railroad upon finishing his military service.[68] By 1872, Hecker was overseeing the construction

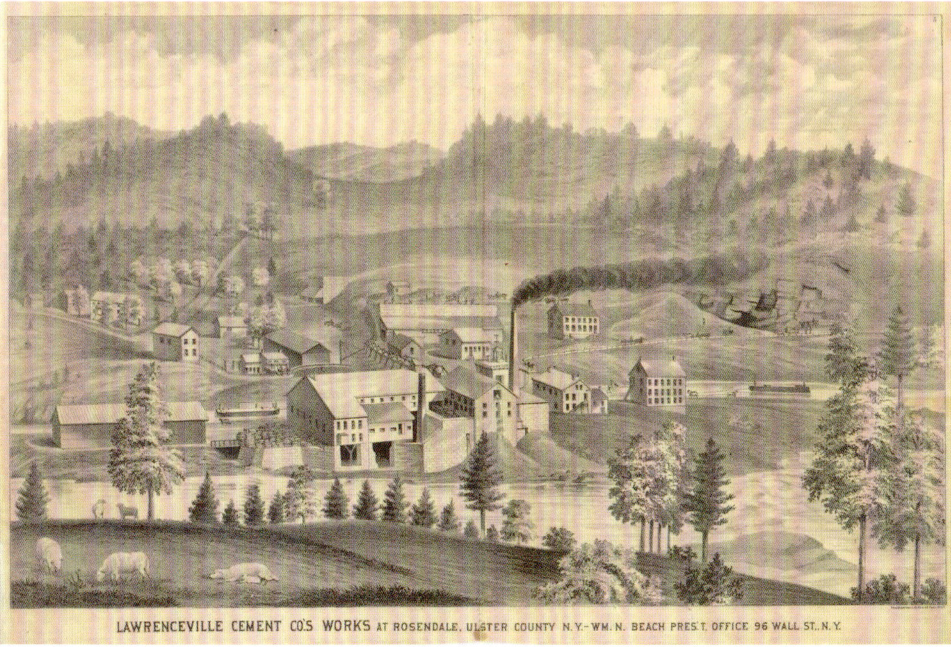

Fig. 1
Illustration of Lawrenceville Cement Works, the cement factory where Freer likely worked, in F. W. Beers, *Atlas of Ulster County, New York, From Recent and Actual Surveys and Records*, United States, 1875.

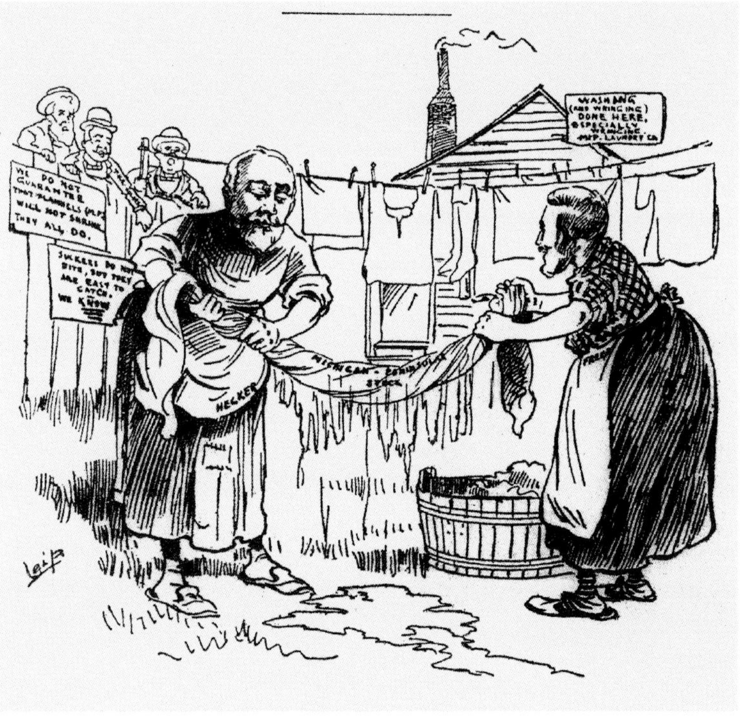

Fig. 2
"Squeezing Water Out," *Detroit Evening News*, July 27, 1897.

Fig. 3
James McNeill Whistler, *Harmony in Blue and Gold—The Peacock Room*. 1876–1877. Oil paint and gold leaf on canvas, leather, mosaic tile, and wood; 421.6 × 613.4 × 1026.2 cm.

of a local railway, the Kingston and Syracuse Railroad in upstate New York, and Freer became Hecker's accountant. The two men eventually went into business together, using Hecker's capital and funding from a group of investors from Detroit, Michigan. Freer and Hecker both relocated to the Midwestern city in 1880 and together opened the Peninsular Car Works, a train car manufacturing plant.[69]

Within five years, the company had expanded; and in 1892, the same year Freer bought *The Balcony*, the business merged with its competitor, forming the Michigan-Peninsular Car Company. Now with five thousand workers, they doubled production and created a regional monopoly. It was common for the company's employees to work twelve-hour days, six days a week, in grueling and often dangerous environments. And once the businesses merged, eliminating local competition, the laborers had little recourse to advocate for better working conditions.[70]

Freer and his partner Hecker quickly became well-known in the Detroit area and were even the subject of political cartoons, attacking them for inflating their company's value in anticipation of yet another large merger (fig. 2). In 1899, Freer succeeded in consolidating thirteen companies into a single entity that controlled 70 percent of the country's production of train cars. He even briefly entertained a scheme to expand the business into Japan and Russia, though that plan never materialized. Freer took advantage of his economic windfall and retired from the company in 1899, at the age of forty-five. He would spend the next twenty years applying the tenacity he developed as an industrialist toward building his art collection, now acquiring objects instead of companies and developing plans for his eponymous museum.

Freer's interest in Whistler was ignited upon seeing the etching collection of Howard Mansfield (1887–1938), a railroad company attorney. Freer initially purchased

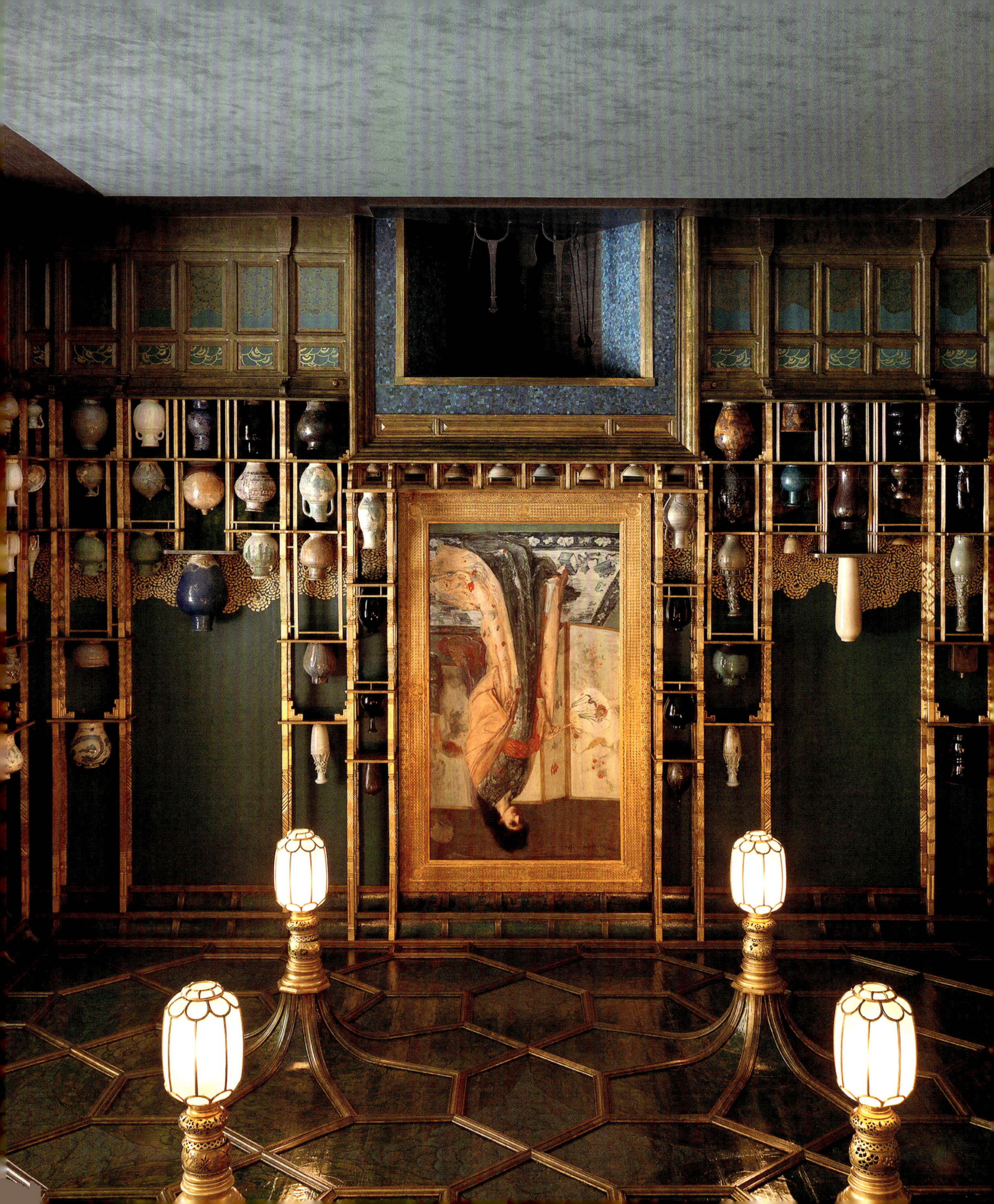

Fig. 4
Unknown artist, after Whistler's oil painting, *Variations in Flesh Colour and Green—The Balcony*. England, 19th century. Wood engraving on paper; 15.6 × 12.1 cm.

only etchings and pastels. As his success in the railroad industry grew, so did his purchasing power, and *The Balcony* was the first oil painting he acquired. As such, it surely was an important acquisition for Freer. The painting was notable for Whistler as well, in that he kept returning to it again and again, making gradual alterations over a period of fifteen years. While Whistler did occasionally sign his paintings at later dates, it was unusual for him to tinker with the composition for as long as he did with *The Balcony*, suggesting that it held a special significance to him. As we look back at Freer's origins, from his teen years at the concrete factory to his time as a captain of industry in Detroit, possible motivations for his acquisition of *The Balcony* as his first major purchase come to the fore, as does the appeal of the fantasy it offers, with its inclusion of industry at a remove and its foregrounding of an aesthetic life of the senses. The painting also significantly anticipated Freer's growing interest in acquiring art from Japan. Its juxtaposition of different cultures based on their perceived aesthetic harmonies would be a guiding principle of Freer's approach to collecting.

At the same moment in 1892, an exhibition of Hokusai's work was on view in Boston at the Museum of Fine Arts. While it is not known if Freer visited the exhibition, he certainly knew of it and acquired the catalogue for his library, and it remains in the Museum's Library collection. Freer also learned about Japanese prints from a series of exhibitions at the Grolier Club in New York organized by Shugio Hiromichi 執行弘道 (1853–1927) (see **Brooks's freer**). This exposure alerted Freer to "points of contact" between the works of Hokusai and Whistler, and this quest for aesthetic intersections became a foundational aspect of Freer's collecting philosophy.[71] In June 1904, Freer purchased *The Sazaidō of Gohyakurakanji* from the dealer Yamanaka & Company's London branch for sixteen dollars.[72] Whistler would have been much on Freer's mind at that moment. The collector had been in London the year before, when Whistler died. Freer made funeral arrangements for the artist and served as a pallbearer.[73] He also organized a memorial exhibition in Whistler's honor in March 1904. While that exhibition was on view in Boston, Freer was in discussion with Secretary of the Smithsonian Samuel Langley (1834–1906) about the future of his collection. By the summer, and concurrent with the purchase of the Hokusai print from Yamanaka, Freer was involved in negotiations to acquire the Peacock Room, the fabled immersive, aesthetic interior painted by Whistler for British shipping magnate Frederick Leyland in 1876–1877 (fig. 3). It is not hard to imagine that when Freer acquired *The Sazaidō of Gohyakurakanji*, he reflected upon Whistler and that pivotal purchase of *The Balcony*. Unfortunately, Freer divested almost his entire collection of woodblock prints in 1905, preferring to direct his attention to Japanese painting. He did acquire a wood engraving of *The Balcony* in 1908, by an unknown artist (possibly Thomas Way, Whistler's longtime printer) (fig. 4). Whistler was trained in etching and lithography but never used woodblock or wood engraving himself, despite his appreciation for the art form. The print returns the painting to the medium upon which it built its foundation, reminding the viewer of how Whistler relied on Japanese print sources to develop his composition. Meanwhile, Freer himself turned away from woodblocks in favor of artworks where the artist's hand was more physically apparent, as in a painter's calligraphic brushwork or Whistler's manipulation of plate tone in his etchings.

Freer's close confidante Agnes Ernst Meyer (1887–1970) retained her own collection of Japanese prints until her death. After Freer died, Meyer was appointed a lifetime

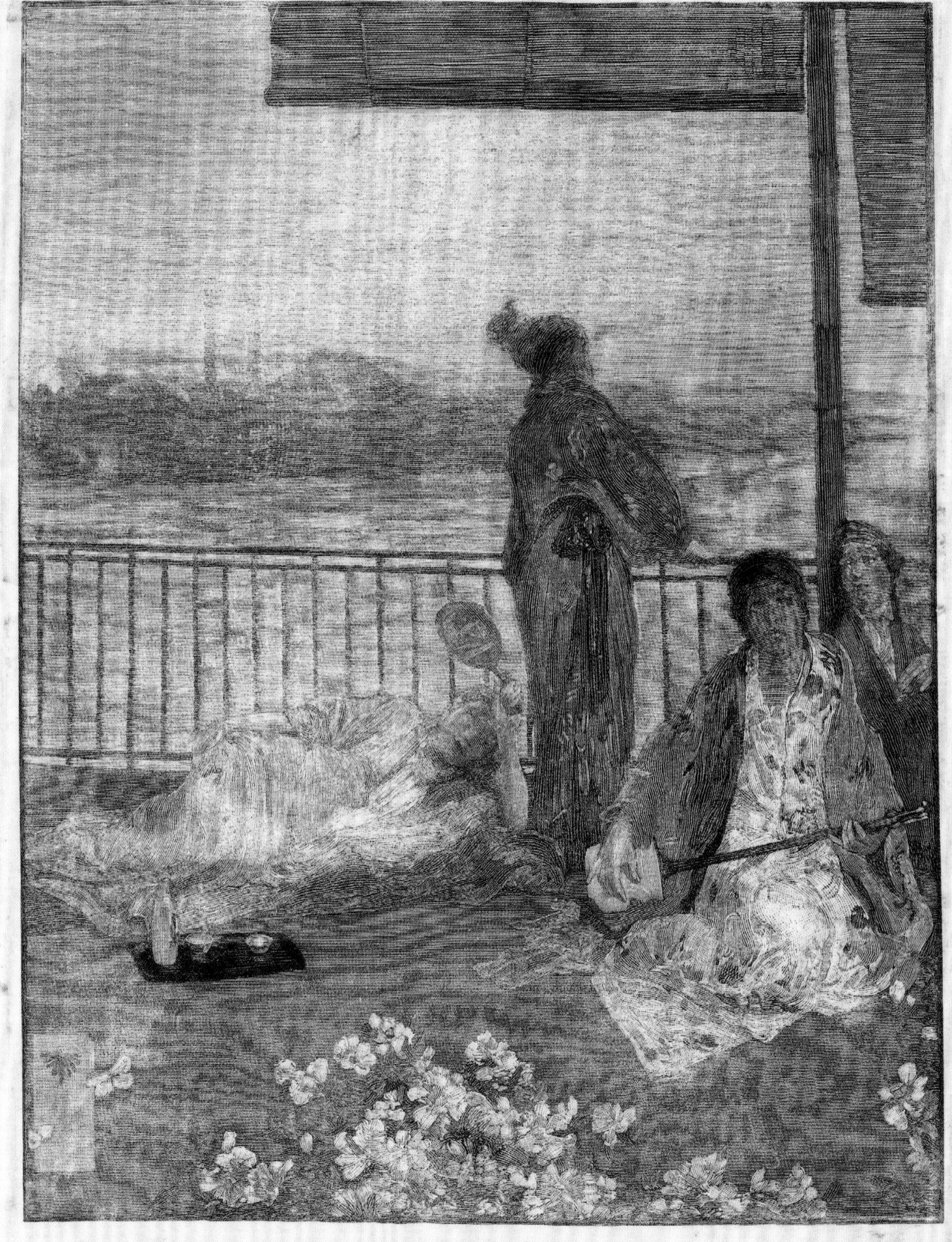

premier etat

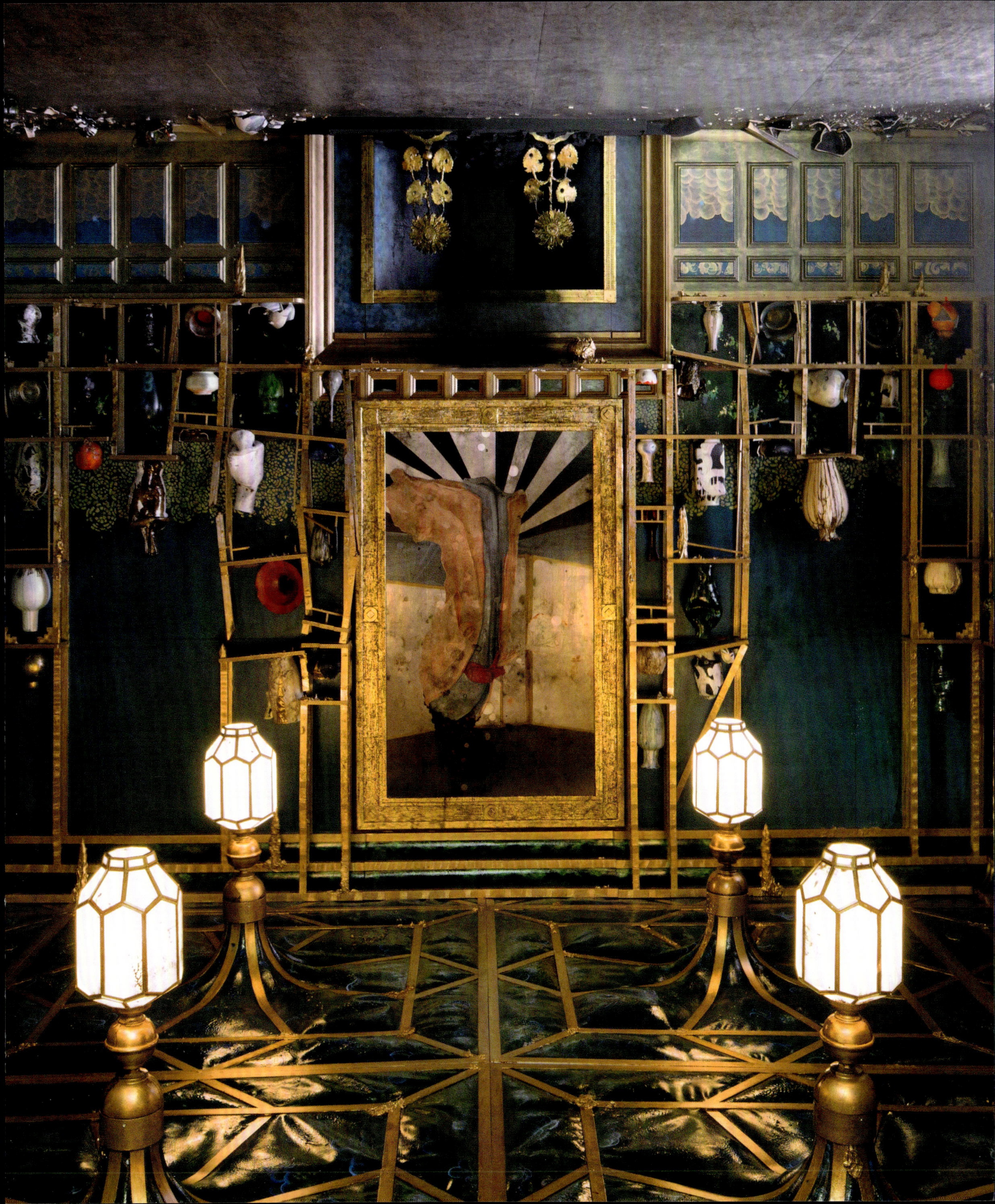

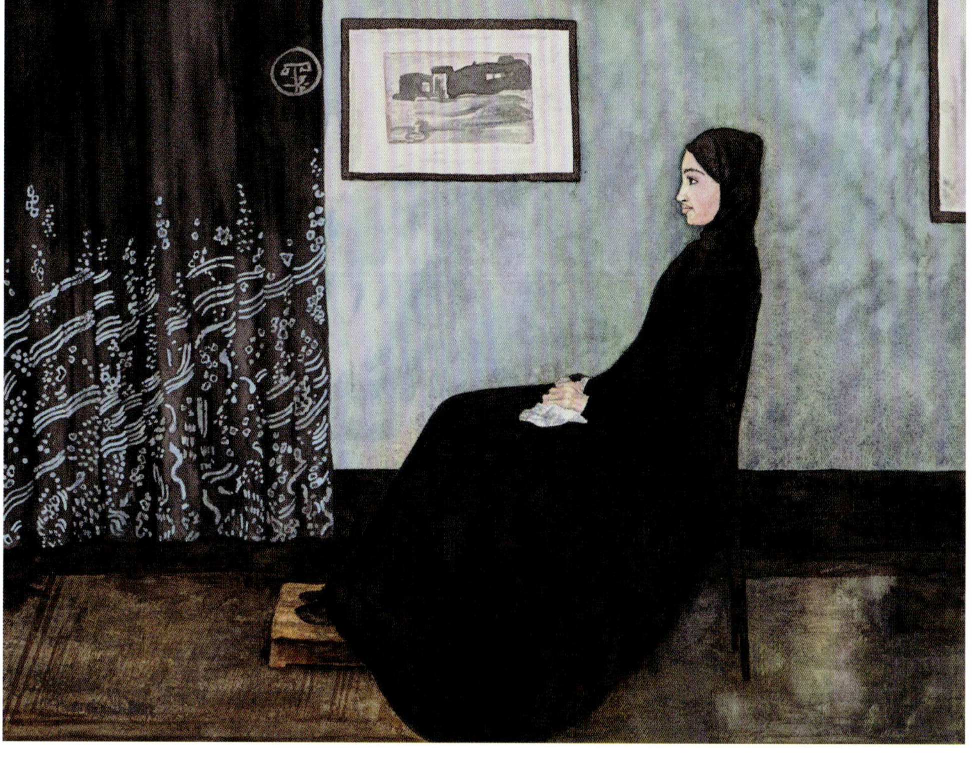

Fig. 5
Darren Waterston, *Filthy Lucre: Whistler's Peacock Room Reimagined*. United States, 2013–2014. Mixed media installation with sound; 370.8 × 929.6 × 604.5 cm (approx.).

Fig. 6
Hannah Rothstein, *Waheed's Mother*, from the series *We the People*. United States, 2019. Watercolor on paper; 30.5 × 40.6 cm.

board member of the Freer Gallery of Art, and among her gifts to the museum are nearly eighty Japanese prints, of which the museum's current impression of *The Sazaidō of Gohyakurakanji* is one. Meyer was from a middle-class background. When she enrolled in Barnard College in 1903, she earned her way through school by working as a journalist. While she became quite wealthy through marriage and became a major art benefactor, she continued to pursue investigative journalism, writing newspaper articles about racial inequity in Washington, DC public schools, and lobbied for the creation of the Department of Health, Education, and Welfare (now Health and Human Services). While living in New York, Meyer became attached to the group of modernist artists and writers surrounding Alfred Stieglitz (1864–1946) and published poetry in his journals. Her friendship with Freer began in this city and may have sprung from their shared interest in Asian art. She met her husband, the financier Eugene Meyer (1875–1959), at a Japanese art exhibition in 1908.[74] After moving to Washington in the 1920s, she organized an exhibition of Chinese art for the Corcoran Gallery of Art and published a book on the painter Li Gonglin 李公麟 (1070–1106).[75] Beyond her art patronage and scholarship, she also remained committed to education and community activism for the rest of her life. In the 1950s, she wrote an autobiography detailing her varied life experiences.[76]

The points of contact and of tension surfacing in Whistler's artwork continue to attract the attention of artists today. Darren Waterston's (b. 1965) *Filthy Lucre* installation reinterprets Whistler's Peacock Room as a ruin, collapsing under the weight of its own decadence (fig. 5). Hannah Rothstein (b. 1986) uses the iconography of Whistler's mother, which has long been misconstrued as a tribute to American

motherhood, to draw attention to the importance of pluralism. Her watercolor titled *Waheed's Mother* replaces Anna McNeill Whistler with a young woman of color in a hijab (fig. 6). The decoration on the curtain is more apparent in Rothstein's interpretation, a stylized motif of bubbles and waves that is reminiscent of the sea. The picture within a picture that hangs on the wall above her—abstracted and barely recognizable—is Whistler's etching of *Black Lion Wharf*, which was also reproduced in the original painting (**view**, fig. 6). These elements of a woman looking toward water with an industrial scene as a backdrop harken back to *The Balcony* in unexpected ways. Waterston's and Rothstein's explicit reinterpretations of Whistler's works make the assumptions implicit in the original more apparent and more alarming, encouraging us to challenge our own biases when viewing artworks in our own contemporary contexts.

Notes

1. James McNeill Whistler, "The Ten O'Clock Lecture," in *Whistler on Art: Selected Letters and Writings of James McNeill Whistler*, ed. Nigel Thorp (Washington, DC: Smithsonian Institution Press, 1994), 95.
2. For more discussion of the International Exhibition of 1862 and the rise of Japonisme in England, see Ayako Ono, *Japonisme in Britain: Whistler, Menpes, Henry, Hornel and Nineteenth-Century Japan* (London: Taylor and Francis, 2013); and Toshio Watanabe, "The Western Image of Japanese Art in the Late Edo Period," *Modern Asian Studies* 18, no. 4 (1984): 667–84.
3. Sir Rutherford Alcock (1809–1897), the British consul general whose collection was featured at the International Exhibition, would go on to publish *Art and Art Industries in Japan* in 1878. This and American art critic James Jackson Jarves's *A Glimpse at the Art of Japan* (1876) were the first books on Japanese art for English speakers. For more on this period, see Anna Jackson, "Imagining Japan: The Victorian Perception and Acquisition of Japanese Culture," *Journal of Design History* 5, no. 4 (1992): 245–56.
4. That same year, Farmer & Rogers hired Arthur Lasenby Liberty (1843–1917). He would later go on to open his own department store, Liberty's, on Regent Street in 1875. The store was known for its embrace of the Arts and Crafts movement and its imported goods from India, China, and Japan. See Rohan McWilliam, *London's West End: Creating the Pleasure District, 1800–1914* (Oxford: Oxford University Press, 2020), 291.
5. Elizabeth Robins Pennell and Joseph Pennell, *The Life of James McNeill Whistler* (London: J. B. Lippincott, 1911), 85.
6. Anna McNeill Whistler to James H. Gamble, February 10–11, 1864, Glasgow University Library, GUW #06522.
7. Margaret F. MacDonald, *An American in London: Whistler and the Thames* (London: Phillip Wilson, 2013), 10.
8. James McNeill Whistler to Henri Fantin-Latour, June 29, 1859, James McNeill Whistler Collection, University of Glasgow, GUW #08050.
9. J. M. Whistler to Deborah Delano Haden, January 1, 1880, Freer Gallery Archives, Whistler 18.
10. A. M. Whistler to Catherine Jane Palmer, November 3–4, 1871, GUW #10071.
11. J. M. Whistler to H. Fantin-Latour [September? 1867], Library of Congress, Manuscript Division, Pennell-Whistler Collection, PWC 1/33/25.
12. J. M. Whistler to John Cavafy [July/October 1878], GUW #00549.
13. George Henry Birch, *London on Thames in Bygone Days* (London: Seeley and Company, 1903), 86.
14. Hedderly shows up in Whistler's bankruptcy documents looking to be paid, which indicates that Whistler used his services on at least one occasion; see MacDonald, *An American in London*, 179n11.
15. John House, *Monet: Nature into Art* (New Haven, CT: Yale University Press, 1986), 47. Monet initially told Gustave Geffroy, a biographer, that he had purchased his first Japanese print in Holland in 1871. Later, he claimed to have purchased his first print in France in 1856. Given that Japan did not sign a commercial trade agreement with France until 1858, House asserts that the earlier date is less likely. Regardless, Monet would have encountered Hokusai's work in Paris prior to his first purchase.
16. House, 51.
17. Michael Fried, *Manet's Modernism: or, The Face of Painting in the 1860s* (Chicago: University of Chicago Press, 1996), 299.
18. Aruna D'Souza and Tom McDonough, eds., *The Invisible Flâneuse?: Gender, Public Space and Visual Culture in Nineteenth-Century Paris* (Manchester: Manchester University Press, 2006).
19. Cindy Kang, *Berthe Morisot, Woman Impressionist* (New York: Rizzoli, 2018). Kang, in turn, is drawing upon the pioneering work of Griselda Pollock on gender and the spaces of modernity. See Griselda Pollock, *Vision and Difference: Feminism, Femininity and the Histories of Art* (London: Routledge, 2003).

20. J. M. Whistler, "Ten O'Clock Lecture," 95.
21. Richard Jenkyns, *The Victorians and Ancient Greece* (Oxford: Blackwell, 1980), 133–54.
22. Daniel E. Sutherland, *Whistler: A Life for Art's Sake* (New Haven, CT: Yale University Press, 2014), 111.
23. Toshio Watanabe, *High Victorian Japonisme* (Bern: P. Lang, 1991), 243. See also Ayako Ono, *Japonisme in Britain: Whistler, Menpes, Henry, Hornel and Nineteenth-Century Japan*, 70–71.
24. Christopher Reed, *Bachelor Japanists: Japanese Aesthetics and Western Masculinities* (New York: Columbia University Press, 2016), 12–17.
25. Saitō Seiji, "Edo jidai no toshi jinkō," *Chiiki kaihatsu*, no. 240 (1984): 48–63.
26. Rosemary J. Barrow, with Michael Silk, Jaś Elsner, Sebastian Matzner, and Michael Squire, *Gender, Identity and the Body in Greek and Roman Sculpture* (Cambridge: Cambridge University Press, 2018), 49.
27. Reynold A. Higgins, *Tanagra and the Figurines* (Princeton, NJ: Princeton University Press, 1987).
28. Malcolm Bell, "Tanagras and the Idea of Type," *Harvard University Art Museums Bulletin* 1, no. 3 (1993): 40.
29. Doreen Bolger, *American Pastels in the Metropolitan Museum of Art* (New York: Metropolitan Museum of Art, 1989), 49.
30. The Ionides family was originally called Ipliktzis. They changed name when they formed their company in 1833.
31. Peter Jeffreys, *Reframing Decadence* (Ithaca, NY: Cornell University Press, 2015), 3. The Cavafy and Ionides families were linked for three generations. For example, John Cavafy's son George married Constantine Ionides's sister-in-law, and Constantine's son Alexander Ionides baptized George Cavafy's son John.
32. Caroline Dakers, *The Holland Park Circle: Artists and Victorian Society* (New Haven, CT: Yale University Press, 1999), 106.
33. Jeffreys, *Reframing Decadence*, 4. Whistler's brother, William, even married Alexander Ionides's niece Helen (Nellie) Ionides in 1877.
34. Richard Dorment and Margaret MacDonald, *James McNeill Whistler* (New York: Harry N. Abrams, 1994), 100.
35. Dakers, *Holland Park Circle*, 108.
36. Cavafy also purchased *The Last of Old Westminster* (1862) and *Battersea Reach* (ca. 1863) in 1863. Whistler gave him *Harmony in Blue and Silver—Trouville* (1865), for which the artist later demanded payment, but Cavafy refused him. *The Correspondence of James McNeill Whistler*, online edition, biography for George John Cavafy 1805–1891.
37. Nicoletta Momigliano and Alexandre Farnoux, *Hellenomania* (Abingdon, Oxon: Taylor & Francis, 2018). See also Dakers, *Holland Park Circle* for more on the Ionides home.
38. Dakers, 107.
39. Dakers, 107.
40. Elizabeth Robins Pennell and Joseph Pennell, *The Life of James McNeill Whistler*, 2 vols. (Philadelphia: J. B. Lippincott, 1908), vol. 1, 124. It was eventually purchased several years later by Frederick Leyland in 1872.
41. See Aileen Tsui, "Whistler's *La Princesse du pays de la porcelaine*: Painting Re-Oriented," *Nineteenth-Century Art Worldwide* 9 (2010).
42. Joyce H. Townsend, "Whistler's Oil Painting Materials," *The Burlington Magazine* 136, no. 1099 (1994): 690. Townsend examines several of Whistler's palettes that were given to the University of Glasgow's Hunterian Art Gallery as part of the bequest from the artist's sister-in-law.
43. Joyce Hill Stoner, "Whistler's Views on the Restoration and Display of His Paintings," *Studies in Conservation* 42, no. 2 (1997): 107. As Stoner explains, his early biographers claimed that it consisted of copal, mastic, and turpentine.
44. "The Palace of Art (New Version)," *Punch*, July 7, 1877, 305, in Linda Merrill, *A Pot of Paint: Whistler V. Ruskin* (Washington, DC: Smithsonian Institution Press, 1992).
45. Roger de Piles, *Dialogue upon Colouring. Translated from the original French of Monsieur du Piles by Mr. John Ozell* (United Kingdom: n.p., 1711), 9.
46. See Tessa Solomon, "Art Supply Companies Contend with Racism as 'Flesh Tones' Come Under Scrutiny," *ARTnews*, August 27, 2020, https://www.artnews.com/art-news/news/art-supplies-racism-flesh-tones-1202697759/.
47. Lorna Roth, "Home on the Range: Kids, Visual Culture, and Cognitive Equity," *Cultural Studies, Critical Methodologies* 9, no. 2 (2009): 145.
48. Gareth Harris, "Paint Names like 'Flesh Tint' are Racially Biased says UK Fine Art supplier," *The Art Newspaper*, August 14, 2020.
49. See Margaret F. MacDonald, *James McNeill Whistler: Drawings, Pastels, and Watercolours; A Catalogue Raisonné* (London: Paul Mellon Centre for Studies in British Art, 1995). The entirety of MacDonald's catalogue raisonné of Whistler's paintings is searchable at https://www.whistlerpaintings.gla.ac.uk/. Whistler even once exhibited *The Princess from the Land of Porcelain* as *The Princess—Variations in Flesh Colour and Blue* in 1872.
50. For more on race and Whistler's work in Chile, see Alexis Clark, "Impressionism as Erasure: Whistler and the Chincha Islands War," in *Mapping Impressionist Painting in Transnational Contexts*, ed. Emily Burns and Alice Price (London: Routledge, 2022), 33–48.
51. In 2015, the Museum of Fine Arts, Boston came under fire for a public program known as Kimono Wednesdays, where visitors were encouraged to try on a kimono provided by the museum and pose with the painting—a continuation of a program held in Japan during the exhibition's earlier run there. The protests and counterprotests that ensued have been the subject of several articles, including Yuko Matsukawa, "Cross-Dressing as Whitewashing: The Kimono Wednesdays Protests and the Erasure

of Asian/American Bodies," *Inter-Asia Cultural Studies* 20, no. 4 (2019): 582-95; and Michelle Liu Carriger, "No 'Thing to Wear': A Brief History of Kimono and Inappropriation from Japonisme to Kimono Protests," *Theatre Research International* 43, no. 2 (2018): 165-84.

52. Suzanne Singletary, *James McNeill Whistler and France: A Dialogue in Paint, Poetry, and Music* (New York: Routledge, 2016), 153.
53. Byron Kim, oral history interview by Ann Shi on April 8, 2021, Houston Asian American Archives, Rice University Digital Scholarship Archive, https://scholarship.rice.edu/handle/1911/110655.
54. Julia Bryan-Wilson and Glenn Adamson, *Art in the Making: Artists and Their Materials from the Studio to Crowdsourcing* (London: Thames & Hudson, 2016), 43.
55. See Patricia Anne Cunningham, *Reforming Women's Fashion, 1850-1920: Politics, Health, and Art* (Kent, OH: Kent State University Press, 2003); and Stella Mary Newton, *Health, Art and Reason: Dress Reformers of the 19th Century* (London: J. Murray, 1974).
56. Kimberly Wahl, *Dressed as in a Painting: Women and British Aestheticism in an Age of Reform* (Lebanon: University of New Hampshire Press, 2013), 3.
57. See Elizabeth Emery, *Reframing Japonisme: Women and the Asian Art Market in Nineteenth-Century France, 1853-1914* (London: Bloomsbury Publishing, 2020) for a discussion of how the terms *Japonisme* and *Chinoiserie* were usually gender-based divisions used to describe modes of collecting and domestic display that were perceived as "male" and "female," respectively, rather than more objective terms describing the country of origin of the objects under discussion.
58. Whistler would eventually paint the entire dining room with an eye toward harmonizing the wall decorations with his painting. He called the result *Harmony in Blue and Gold—The Peacock Room.* The room brought him widespread notoriety and ended his relationship with the room's owner, his long-term patron (see **figure**).
59. There is some uncertainty as to whether Whistler owned this Kiyonaga print at the time he painted *The Balcony.* He may have come to possess it after he married Beatrice Godwin. See Ayako Ono, *Whistler and Artistic Exchange Between Japan and the West: After Japonisme in Britain* (London: Taylor & Francis, 2023), 66n8.
60. Adam Geczy, *Fashion and Orientalism: Dress, Textiles and Culture from the 17th to the 21st Century* (London: Bloomsbury Publishing, 2013), 116-23.
61. Cunningham, *Reforming Women's Fashion,* 137.
62. Terry wrote of Whistler in her memoir: "He sent my little girl a tiny Japanese kimono when Liberty was hardly a name." See Anna Marie Kirk, "Japonisme and Femininity: A Study of Japanese Dress in British and French Art and Society, c. 1860-c. 1899," *Costume* 42, no. 1 (2008): 122.
63. E. W. Godwin, *Dress and Its Relation to Health and Climate* (London: W. Clowes, 1884).
64. Richard W. Hayes, "The Aesthetic Interior as Incubator of Health and Well-Being," *Architectural History* 60 (2017): 296.
65. Advertisement reproduced in Kirk, "Japonisme and Femininity," 115.
66. Sutherland, *Whistler: A Life for Art's Sake*, 34-35.
67. Whistler's precise turn of phrase was "I wish you to have a fine collection of Whistlers!! — perhaps The collection." J. M. Whistler to Charles Lang Freer, July 29, 1899, Charles Lang Freer Papers, Freer Gallery Archives.
68. Lee Glazer and Amelia Meyer, *Charles Lang Freer: A Cosmopolitan Life* (Washington, DC: Freer Gallery of Art and Arthur M. Sackler Gallery, Smithsonian, 2017), 6.
69. Helen Tomlinson, *West Meets East: Charles L. Freer, Trailblazing Asian Art Collector* (Herndon, VA: Mascot Books, 2019).
70. Glazer and Meyer, *Charles Lang Freer*, 14.
71. Royal Cortissoz, "Freer Museum Soon to Be Built in Washington," *New York Tribune*, December 15, 1915.
72. This was one of thirty prints from the *Thirty-Six Views* series that were purchased from Yamanaka at this time. Charles Lang Freer Papers. FSA.A.01. Freer Gallery of Art and Arthur M. Sackler Gallery Archives. Gift of the estate of Charles Lang Freer, "List of Prints owned by Charles L. Freer," Y44, 30.
73. Linda Merrill, *With Kindest Regards: The Correspondence of Charles Lang Freer and James McNeill Whistler, 1890-1903* (Washington, DC: Smithsonian, 1995), 37.
74. Katharine Graham, *Personal History* (New York: Alfred A. Knopf, 1997), 1. On the first page of her biography, Graham—the daughter of Agnes and Eugene Meyer—notes that her parents first met at a Japanese print exhibition on 23rd Street. This was undoubtedly the Colonna Collection on view at the American Art Gallery on Broadway and 23rd. See "JAPANESE ART EXHIBIT; Rare Paintings, Pottery, Fine Prints, and Bronzes Shown," *The New York Times,* March 10, 1908, 6.
75. Agnes E. Meyer, *Chinese Painting: As Reflected in the Thought and Art of Li Lung-Mein* (New York: Duffield & Company, 1923).
76. Agnes E. Meyer, *Out of These Roots: The Autobiography of An American Woman* (Boston: Little, Brown and Company, 1953).

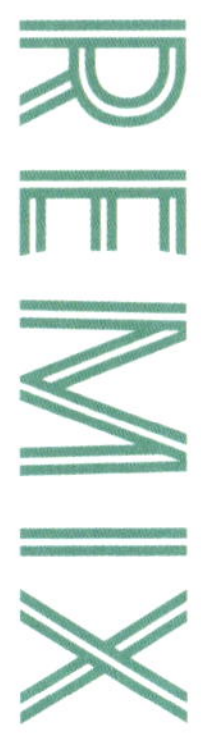

Do you remember the view from your childhood bedroom?

Drawing can be a powerful tool for unlocking memory. Once you start drawing, you may remember more things than you would have recalled using words alone.

You may want to start with the window frame. Was it plastic, or wood? Did the window have one pane of glass, or several? Add a detail that you remember from the view. As you build the picture, try to remember textures and sensations, and incorporate them as much as possible.

 draw in here

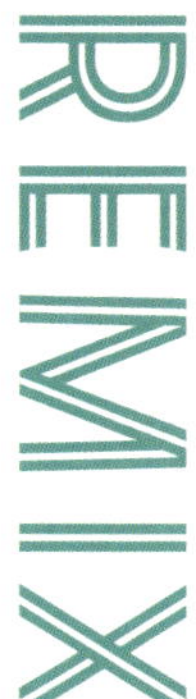

What is your ideal view from a balcony?

Start assembling materials for a collage, which can be gathered from magazines, printed from the internet, or even cut from the pages of this book. What kind of view are you trying to create? One that relaxes, or inspires? Creating a harmonious color palette may strengthen your intention, especially if you use colors that are symbolic or have a meaning that is special to you. Your view might be a fantasy location or perhaps a real place you have not yet visited. Are there any people in your view?

collage in here

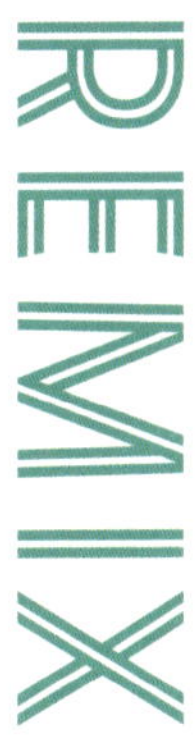

Can you picture yourself in the artist's place?

What colors would you use in this scene? How would you populate this balcony? What would you include in the landscape, and what would you exclude?

*You may want to photocopy the line drawing before you begin so that you can try this activity more than once.

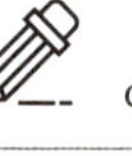
draw and color in here

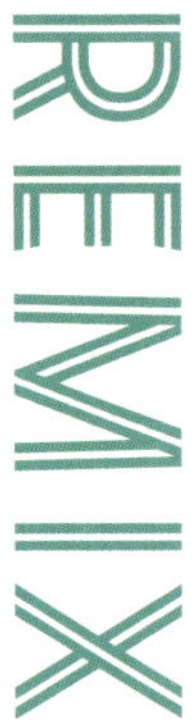

Can you build your own theater?
Whistler pop-out (toy theater)

Victorian toy theaters were commonly available as a concession at theatrical productions in nineteenth-century London. Theater-goers would purchase these as souvenirs, putting them together at home to recreate the experience in miniature. Reddington's theatrical print company manufactured this scene, which includes the red curtain and the proscenium arch with theater boxes, which serve as interior balconies for the viewing audience. You can pop out and fold these elements to create your own paper theater. How will you fill the stage? What does your audience see?

Remove the pop-out elements along the perforations and fold as instructed on the reverse.

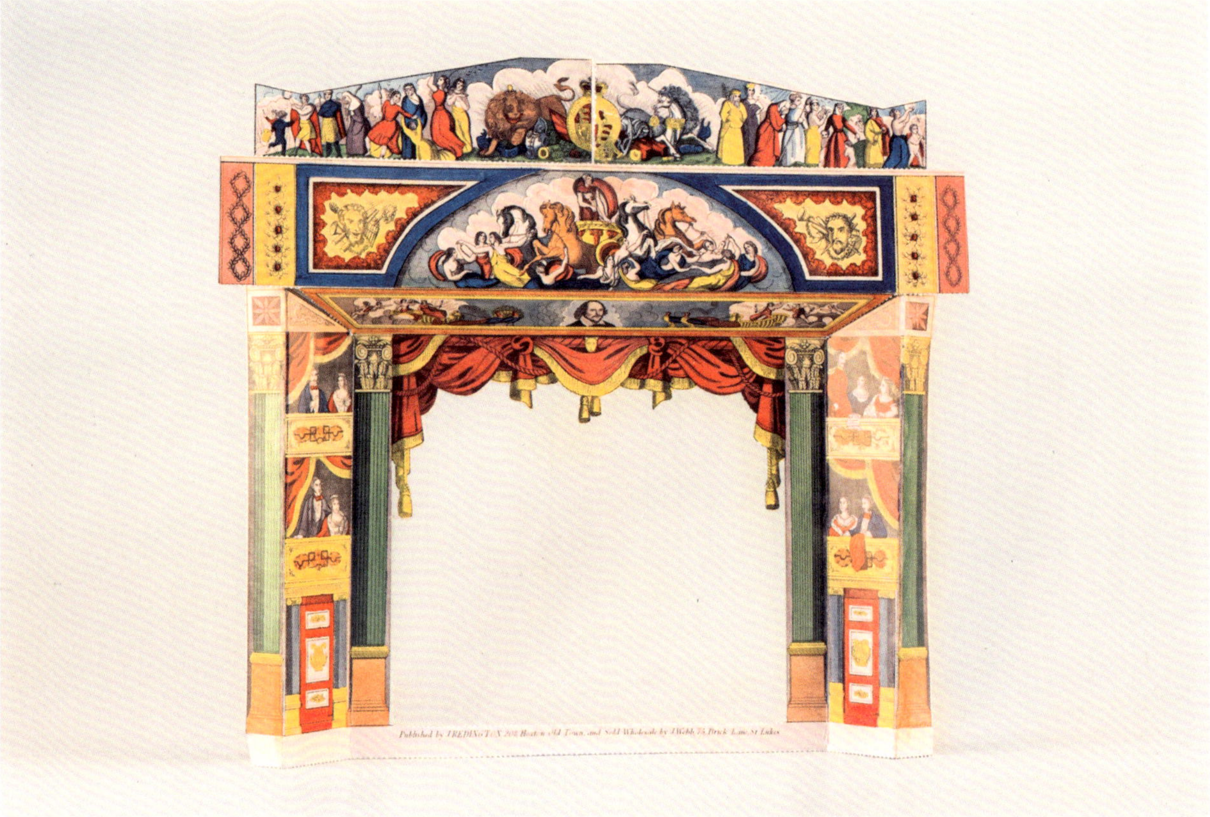

Redington's new and improved stage front. England, 1800–1899. Hand-colored etching and engraving on paper; 52 × 65 cm.

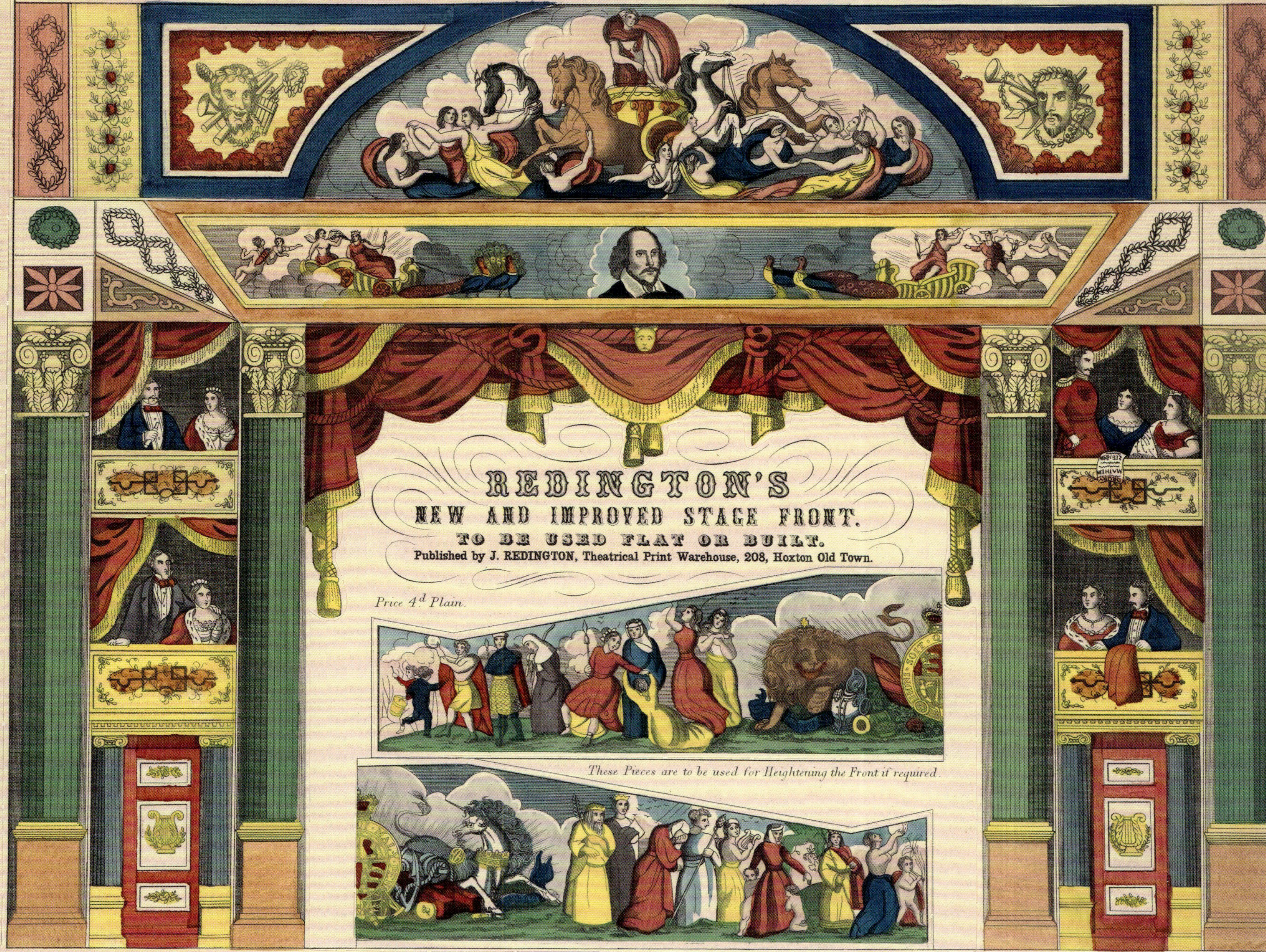
REDINGTON'S
NEW AND IMPROVED STAGE FRONT.
TO BE USED FLAT OR BUILT.
Published by J. REDINGTON, Theatrical Print Warehouse, 208, Hoxton Old Town.
Price 4d Plain.
These Pieces are to be used for Heightening the Front if required.
Published by J.REDINGTON, 208, Hoxton Old Town, and Sold Wholesale by J.Webb, 75, Brick Lane, St. Lukes.